SUICIDE PREVENTION

Series in Death, Dying, and Bereavement
Consulting Editor
Robert A. Neimeyer

FORMERLY THE **SERIES IN DEATH EDUCATION, AGING, AND HEALTH CARE**
HANNELORE WASS, CONSULTING EDITOR

Selected Titles

SUICIDE PREVENTION

Resources for the Millennium

Edited by
David Lester

BRUNNER-ROUTLEDGE
ALERE FLAMMAM
Taylor & Francis Group

USA	Publishing Office:	BRUNNER-ROUTLEDGE *A member of the Taylor & Francis Group* 325 Chestnut Street Philadelphia, PA 19106 Tel: (215) 625-8900 Fax: (215) 625-2940
	Distribution Center:	BRUNNER-ROUTLEDGE *A member of the Taylor & Francis Group* 47 Runway Road, Suite G Levittown, PA 19057-4700 Tel: (215) 269-0400 Fax: (215) 269-0363
UK		BRUNNER-ROUTLEDGE *A member of the Taylor & Francis Group* 27 Church Road Hove E. Sussex, BN3 2FA Tel: +44 (0) 1273 207411 Fax: +44 (0) 1283 205612

Suicide Prevention: Resources for the Millennium

1 2 3 4 5 6 7 8 9 0

Printed by Sheridan Books, Ann Arbor, MI, 2000.
Cover design by Ellen Seguin.
Edited by Hilary Ward and Dina Direnzo.

A CIP catalog record for this book is available from the British Library.
∞ The paper in this publication meets the requirements of the ANSI Standard Z39.48-1984 (Permanence of Paper).

Library of Congress Cataloging-in-Publication Data
Suicide prevention : resources for the millennium / edited by David Lester.
    p. cm. — (Series in death, dying, and bereavement, ISSN 1091-5427)
  Includes bibiliographical references and index.
  ISBN 0-87630-987-2 (alk. paper)
  1. Suicide—Prevention. 2. Suicidal behavior—Treatment. I. Lester, David, 1942– II. Series.

HV6545.S84228 2000
362.28'7—dc21

00-040341

ISSN 1091-5427
ISBN 0-87630-987-2 (case)

CONTENTS

I. UNDERSTANDING SUICIDE

II. APPROACHES TO PREVENTING SUICIDE

III. THE ORGANIZATIONS

CONTRIBUTORS

Alan Berman, Ph.D.
Executive Director
American Association of Suicidology
Washington, DC, USA

Eliane Bezençon
IFOTES
Switzerland

Rev. Michael Bonacci, M.F.A.
Executive Director
Compassion in Dying of Washington
Seattle, WA, USA

Ronald Bonner, Ph.D.
Chief Psychologist
Federal Correctional Institution
Allenwood, PA, USA

Marc Daigle, Ph.D.
Professor of Psychology
Université du Québec, Trois-Rivières
Canada

Rev. Dr. Clyde Dominish
Formerly, General Secretary
Lifeline International
Croydon, Australia

Diego De Leo, M.D., Ph.D.
Director, WHO Collaborating Centre for
    Suicide Research and Training in
    Suicide Prevention
Griffith University
Australia

Thomas, E. Ellis, Psy.D., ABPP
Professor of Psychology
West Virginia University School of
    Medicine
Charleston, WV, USA

Norman L. Farberow, Ph.D.
Professor Emeritus of Psychology
Department of Psychiatry
University of Southern California
Los Angeles, CA, USA

Faye Girsh, Ed.D.
Licensed Psychologist (CA)
Executive Director
The Hemlock Society USA
Denver, CO, USA

Robert D. Goldney, M.D.
Professor of Psychiatry, University of
    Adelaide
Medical Director, The Adelaide Clinic
South Australia
Australia

Antoon A. Leenaars, Ph.D.
University of Leiden
Netherlands

David Lester, Ph.D.
Professor of Psychology
The Richard Stockton College of New
    Jersey
Pomona, NJ, USA *and*
Executive Director
Center for the Study of Suicide
Blackwood, NJ, USA

Virginia Lindahl
Doctoral Candidate
Catholic University
Washington, DC, USA

Brian L. Mishara, Ph.D.
Professor, Psychology Department
Director, Centre for Research &
    Internvention on Suicide &
    Euthanasia
Université du Québec, Montrèal
Canada

Lloyd, Potter, Ph.D., M.P.H.
National Center for Injury Control and
    Prevention
Atlanta, GA, USA

Nils Retterstol, M.D.
Professor Emeritus of Psychiatry
University of Oslo
Norway

James R. Rogers, Ph.D.
Assistant Professor
Department of Counseling and Special
    Education
The University of Akron
Akron, OH, USA

Alec Roy, M.D.
Department of Veterans Affairs
New Jersey Health Care System
East Orange, NJ, USA

Wolfgang Rutz, M.D., Ph.D.
Regional Advisor for Mental Health
WHO Europe
Denmark

Armin Schmidtke, Ph.D.
Professor of Medical Psychology
University of Wûrzburg
Germany

Vanda Scott, M.Sc. (Econ)
Formerly Director General
Befrienders International
London, UK

Steven Stack, Ph.D.
Professor of Criminal Justice
Wayne State University
Detroit, MI, USA

H. M. van Praag, M.D., Ph.D.
Professor of Psychiatry
Maastricht University
The Netherlands

M. David Wallace
Doctoral Candidate
University of Windsor
Canada

SERIES FOREWORD

Readers of the suicidology literature—and especially compilations of edited chapters—are accustomed to encountering publications that are, in approximately equal parts, a blend of conjecture and recitation. The conjecture is often the work of bold pioneers in the field who have offered compelling descriptions of (some of) the dynamics of suicide, typically winnowed from years or decades of clinical engagement with suicide prevention, assessment, management, and (less often) treatment. The recitation consists of various admixtures of these initially audacious formulations, repeated with minor variation as the accepted clinical lore that guides intervention by both professional and paraprofessional helpers. When this clinical wisdom is given an empirical foundation, it is often of an epidemiological nature, providing a research warrant for the identification of various "risk groups" for suicidal and other forms of self-injurious behavior.

To this sometimes imaginative, often predictable literature, the present volume makes a unique contribution. In collecting together "resources for the next millennium" for suicidology, David Lester has compiled a handbook of surprising range and depth. Readers will find between these covers remarkably comprehensive and current discussions of theory, research, and practice relevant to suicide intervention arising from such core fields as psychiatry, psychotherapy, and crisis intervention. Telephonic emergency services are covered in all of their considerable variety, presenting international trends in sufficient detail that service providers in various parts of the world are able to learn from the successes—and sometimes the mistakes—of one another. Key organizations, from the American Association of Suicidology to Lifeline International, are described in lucid detail, conveying in one place essential features of their organizational development, goals, and structure in a way that is clarifying for newcomers as well as "old hands" in suicidology. In each case, Lester's editorial mandate that authors address historical, contemporary, and future dimensions of the area or organization has encouraged a style of writing that is both engaging and forward-looking, in effect addressing the classical questions: Who are we? Where have we come from? Where are we going? The answers tell the story of suicidology, and help readers position themselves and their own clinical, scholarly, and research efforts within it.

One other thing struck me forcibly as I read these pages, and that was the courage required to assemble contributions not only from those who have spent the whole of their careers combating self-induced death, but also from those who have defended its legitimacy when life appears unlivable. Thus, the reader will encounter authoritative histories of those organizations like the International Association for Suicide Prevention, alongside equally impassioned and informed descriptions of the Hemlock Society and other groups promoting a patient's right to hasten death when debilitating and terminal illness robs life of its meaning. Lester wisely avoids editorializing and offering easy resolutions of the complex moral issues that ensue from the occasional friction between these perspectives, but the reader cannot help being moved to deeper levels of personal questioning as a result of respectful presentation of competing perspectives.

In summary, Lester has accomplished precisely what he set out to do, and better than nearly anyone else could have done. He has provided a readable and multifaceted account of the "story" of suicidology, written by some of the persons most influential in its development at the end of the twentieth century. Bristling with new research findings, integrative models, practical advice, and insightful forecasts, *Suicide Prevention: Resources for the Millennium* leaves us poised on the horizon of what the field will become in the century to follow.

Robert A. Neimeyer, Ph.D.
Series Editor

PREFACE

Every decade for the past 40 years, I have reviewed the research on suicidal behavior. Sometimes I have been impressed, and sometimes I have been disappointed, by the progress of the previous 10 years (e.g., Lester, 1992). When I first reviewed the literature, I quoted Merton Kahne (1966) who was very negative about the research into suicidal behavior, but since then there have been some remarkable advances in our understanding of suicide and in our efforts to prevent suicide.

I am in the midst of my review of the suicide research of the 1990s, which will be my final effort, and it coincides with the end of the century. I solicited my colleagues for their thoughts on the "state of the art" in the field of suicidology. This book presents their views.

When I invited the participants to contribute to this volume, I asked them to focus not only on the past and the present but also the future. It is useful to know where we have been in the field and where we are now. But what makes the present volume useful is that it looks toward the future—where is the field going? What needs to be accomplished? Readers should, therefore, find direction for the future and ideas for projects. This is one of the features of the book that makes it suitable as a resource.

In addition, I made an effort to recruit colleagues who would write on prevention efforts and advances in counseling techniques as well as basic research. My aim was to provide readers with not just academic knowledge, but also ideas for preventing suicide, again to make this volume a resource.

Finally, there are many organizations in the field of suicidology, and we often belong to one or more of them. But these organizations rarely are provided with an opportunity to describe their goals and plans for the future. In the final section of this book, an officer or an administrator of each major organization in the field of suicidology and suicide prevention describes their organization—what has it done and what does it plan to do in the future? Again, these organizations are important for the field, and these essays provide a third resource for the reader.

We know well the old distinction between looking at a glass of milk, partially full, and seeing it as half-empty or as half-full—a pessimistic versus an optimistic outlook. It is my wish that the orientation of the present book shows a half-full outlook and will arouse hope in the readers and enthusiasm for the next century of efforts to understand and prevent suicide.

☐ References

Kahne, M. (1966). Suicide research. *International Journal of Social Psychiatry, 12,* 177–186.

Lester, D. (1992). *Why people kill themselves.* Springfield, IL: Charles C. Thomas.

UNDERSTANDING SUICIDE

CHAPTER 1   David Lester

The Epidemiology of Suicide

Epidemiology is concerned with the study of the occurrence of diseases in human populations, that is, in groups rather than separate individuals. Epidemiologists look for disease patterns in populations—communities, regions, or nations (Friedman, 1987).

Epidemiology is a quantitative science, and there are several standard terms employed. *Prevalence* refers to how many people in the group have the disease at a particular point in time and is determined by the following formula:

$$\text{prevalence rate} = \frac{\text{number of persons with the disease}}{\text{total number in group}}$$

Prevalence rates for fatal (completed) suicide are rarely used, though occasionally an author calculates how many people kill themselves in one day in the nation or the world. A screening of people in a community for current suicidal ideation would give a point-of-time prevalence for suicidal ideation.

Incidences describe the rate of development of a disease in a group over a time period and is computed as follows:

$$\text{incidence rate} = \frac{\text{number of persons developing the disease*per unit of time}}{\text{total number at risk}}$$

This is the most common measure used for fatal suicide. For example, the completed suicide rate in the United States in 1990 was 12.4 per 100,000 per year.

Under-reporting of suicide may occur for several reasons. In estimating the incidence of nonfatal suicidal behavior, people may decline to report self-involvement for fear of ridicule or stigma. In the reporting of fatal suicidal behavior, professionals may be reluctant to certify the death accurately for a variety of reasons including wanting to spare the family from being stigmatized or a fear of legal problems if the family disagrees with the assigned cause. In a study in the United States, Farberow, MacKinnon, and Nelson (1977) found that counties where lawyers (acting as coroners) certified death had lower suicide rates than counties where pathologists (acting as medical examiners) certified death. In some nations, such as Great Britain, many suicidal deaths are classified as undetermined whereas in other nations they would be classified as suicides. The recent increase in suicide rates in Roman Catholic countries such as Ireland is probably due in part to more valid classification of deaths.

☐ Basic Methods of Study

The two major approaches in epidemiological research are observational studies and experimental studies. In *observational studies*, the researcher merely observes the phenomena as they occur. For example, a description of the rates of suicide in a nation, the methods used, and the variation over time is an observational study. Observational studies are correlational in nature, and correlational studies do not provide strong evidence for cause-and-effect relationships.

In *experimental studies*, the researcher actively intervenes to change one of the variables in the research. Experimental studies have the advantage of providing evidence for cause-and-effect, that is, whether the variable that the research manipulated actually caused any changes observed.

Observational studies can be improved. First, *natural experiments* sometimes occur. For example, a nation may detoxify domestic gas slowly over a period of years (as it switches from very toxic coal gas to less toxic natural gas), and the effect of this change on the suicide rate can be monitored. Second, *statistical controls* for other possible causal factors can be incorporated into the research design and data analysis, permitting a multivariate analysis of the data (that is, using many variables). This can strengthen our certainty that a particular variable causes suicidal behavior.

Observational studies can be *descriptive* or *analytic*. Descriptive studies simply describe the phenomenon whereas analytic studies seek to explain the phenomenon.

Descriptive Studies

Descriptive studies describe the patterns of disease in the population. They study the association of the disease by variables such as age, gender, marital status, race, occupation, social class, geographic location, and time. This information identifies groups at high risk for a disease, assists the planning of services to respond to those with the disease, and provides clues to the etiology of the disease which may stimulate future analytical studies.

Age variations in the prevalence or incidence of a disease can be presented in two ways. A current or *cross-sectional presentation* shows the suicide rate in each age group in one year—different people are involved in each age group. A *cohort presentation* shows the suicide rate of a cohort over time as it ages. These two presentations can give quite different results. For example, the suicide rate by age in Canada in 1980 was:

10–14	1.5
15–19	18.9
20–24	29.1
25–29	30.8
30–34	25.0
35–39	24.2
40–44	23.5
45–49	30.7
50–54	29.2
55–59	28.1
60–64	27.9
65–69	28.2

with a peak for those aged 25–29. In contrast, the suicide rate of the Canadian male cohort born in 1911–1915 was:

0.7 per 100,000 per year when they were aged 10–14,
3.2 when they were aged 15–19,
7.6 when they were aged 20–24,
12.0 when they were aged 25–29,
8.9 when they were aged 30–34,
14.9 when they were aged 35–39,
19.2 when they were aged 40–44,
22.6 when they were aged 45–49,
27.9 when they were aged 50–54,
32.5 when they were aged 55–59,
29.8 when they were aged 60–64 and
26.0 when they were aged 65–69 in 1976–1980.

Thus the suicide rate for this cohort peaked when they were 55-59 years old (Lester, 1988a).

Variation by place is of interest because it may provide clues to etiology. For example, suicide rates have typically been high in Hungary. Hungarians have been quite concerned with their high national suicide rates, and see themselves as a highly depressed people in general. Several explanations are possible, including physiological differences between Hungarians and other national groups, differences in child rearing practices, or differences in social expectations (that is, Hungarians are aware of their high suicide rate and, therefore, suicide becomes more of an option to Hungarians when they are in crisis).

Robinson (1950) warned of the dangers of assuming that associations between variables over geographic regions can be generalized to individuals. For example, if suicide rates and church attendance are found to be correlated over the United

States of America, we cannot assume without further research that these two variables are associated over individuals. Robinson called this inappropriate generalization the *ecological fallacy*.

Variations over time can be *short-term* or *long-term*. Among the short-term effects, *epidemics* (or outbreaks) are of special interest. An epidemic is an occurrence of the behavior in a population in excess of the number of cases expected. The disease in an epidemic may affect only those who are susceptible—others may be immune or resistant as a result of inherent factors. An epidemic typically shows an increasing incidence over time to a maximum, followed by a steady diminution until it disappears almost completely as the supply of susceptible individuals is exhausted.

For example, Taiminen, Salmenperä, and Lehtinen (1992) reported on eight inpatient suicides during a three month period in their clinic in Finland. Six of the patients had close relationships with one another, and Taiminen et al. were able to document the influence of suggestion and identification on the occurrence of and the methods chosen by these suicides.

There may also be *recurrent* or *periodic* time trends—variations by time of day, day of week, and month of the year. For example, D. P. Phillips and Wills (1987) examined fatal suicides in the United States from 1973–1979 and found that suicide rates were above average on New Year's Day, July 4th, and Labor Day and for the five following days, but below average on the five days prior to the national holidays. In contrast, suicide rates were below average before, during, and after Memorial Day, Thanksgiving, and Christmas.

Long-term trends are also called secular trends and extend over years or decades. For example, Araki and Murata (1987) reported on secular trends for suicide in Japan for the 32 years following World War II (1950–1982). The suicide rate peaked for both men and women in the mid-1950s, dropped to lows in late 1960s, and diverged in the 1970s, increasing steadily for men while decreasing for women. Looking at these changes, Araki and Murata suggested that suicide rates decreased during times of economic prosperity and increased in the years prior to economic depressions. However, they did not test this hypothesis, leaving later investigators to do so.

Analytic Studies

Analytic studies, on the other hand, start with an hypothesis about the causes of suicide, and the data test this hypothesis. For example, Clarke and Lester (1989) hypothesized that the availability of methods for suicide would affect the suicide rate. They found that, as domestic gas was detoxified in England, the use of domestic gas for suicide declined dramatically, and the overall English suicide rate dropped by almost a third. Although this study was observational (the researchers themselves did not manipulate any of the variables), the results supported a particular hypothesis about the causes of suicidal behavior.

Cross-sectional or prevalence studies examine the relationship between suicide and other variables of interest in a defined population at one point in time. For example, Lester (1994) studied the regional variation of suicide rates over America in 1980 and found that a cluster of social variables including, divorce rates, alcohol consumption, church attendance, and interstate migration were strongly associated with one another and strongly associated as a group with the states' suicide rates. Lester concluded that his data supported Durkheim's (1897) classic theory of suicide which relates suicide rates to the levels of social integration and social regulation in the society.

Cohort Studies

Cohort studies explore the development of a behavior. A population free of the disease is identified, the so-called cohort, and followed for a period of time. Those with some attribute are compared to those without the attribute for the later development of the disease. Cohort studies are the best approach for answering the question of whether some attribute predisposes people to a disease. For example, Lester (1991b) studied 1528 gifted children identified in 1921 by Lewis Terman in California and their subsequent suicidal behavior. These children had intelligence test scores of 130 or higher, and were about 10 years old when the study was initiated. As of 1960, the researchers had lost contact with only 1.7% of the sample, an amazing achievement. Fifteen of the sample had killed themselves by 1987.[1]

Cohort studies provide the best evidence about the risk of disease development but they are expensive and time-consuming. The Terman study of gifted adolescents mentioned above started in the 1920s and has had to employ staff to follow-up the 1528 individuals ever since.

☐ The Epidemiology of Suicide: The Past and the Present

One of the most interesting phenomenon in suicidology is the international variation in suicide rates. Suicide rates vary tremendously, from a high in Hungary and Sri Lanka to a low in Egypt and Kuwait in 1990 (see Table 1). The differences in national suicides are large and stable. For example, Lester (1987b) found a correlation of 0.42 between the suicide rates of 14 European nations in 1875 and in 1975—one hundred years. Although there have been many doubts expressed about the validity of official suicide rates (e.g., Douglas, 1967), Sainsbury and Barraclough (1968) and Lester (1972) have found that the suicide rates of immigrant groups to the United States and Australia are strongly associated with the suicide rates in the home nations from which they came. Thus, for example, the Irish have a relatively low suicide rate and Irish immigrants to the United States and Australia, where they encounter the same medical examiners as other immigrant groups, also have relatively low suicide rates. Thus, national suicide rates appear to have

---

[1]One of the few prospective studies currently in progress is by Caroline Thomas (e.g., Graves and Thomas, 1991) in which 1046 entering medical students at Johns Hopkins University Medical School were tested on a variety of measures and followed up for the development of diseases and behaviors, including suicide.

TABLE 1. Suicide Rates Around the World in 1990 (from the World Health Organization unless otherwise noted) (WHO, annual)

Country	Suicide rate	Country	Suicide rate
Hungary	39.9	Puerto Rico	10.5
Sri Lanka	33.2[d]	Scotland	10.5
Finland	30.3	Uruguay	10.3
China	28.7	Northern Ireland	9.9
(Phillips & Liu, 1996)[g]		Netherlands	9.7
Slovenia	27.6	Ireland	9.5
Estonia	27.1	Romania	9.0
Russian Federation	26.5	Portugal	8.8
Lithuania	26.1	United Kingdom	8.1
Latvia	26.0	Korea, South	8.0[c]
Germany, East	24.4	England & Wales	7.8
Denmark	24.1	Italy	7.6
Austria	23.6	Spain	7.5
Belarus	23.6[f]	Zimbabwe	7.4
Switzerland	21.9	(Mugadza, 1996)	
Ukraine	20.7	Liechtenstein	6.7
USSR	21.1	Uzbekistan	6.8[e]
France	20.1	Argentina	6.7
Belgium	19.3[a]	Taiwan	6.7
Czech Republic	19.3	(Andrew Cheng, 1973)	
Kazakhstan	19.1	Israel	6.5
Czechoslovakia	17.9	IChile	5.6[a]
Luxembourg	17.8	Costa Rica	5.2
Germany, West	17.5	Venezuela	4.8[a]
Germany	17.5[e]	Barbados	4.7[b]
Sweden	17.2	Ecuador	4.6[b]
Japan	16.4	Macao	4.4[c]
Iceland	15.7	Panama	3.8[c]
Norway	15.5	Tadjikistan	3.8[e]
Yugoslavia	15.3	Greece	3.5
Bulgaria	14.7	Bahrain	3.1[b]
Mauritius	14.2	Columbia	3.1[e]
Trinidad & Tobago	13.7	Armenia	2.8
New Zealand	13.5	Malta	2.3
Singapore	13.1	Mexico	2.3
Poland	13.0	St Lucia	2.3[c]
Australia	12.9	Albania	2.1a
Canada	12.7	Maldives	2.0[c]
Krygyzstan	12.5	Bahamas	1.2[c]
USA	12.4	Kuwait	0.8[c]
Hong Kong	11.7	Egypt	0.04[c]

[a] 1990 rates not available—1989 data
[b] 1990 rates not available—1988 data
[c] 1990 rates not available—1987 data
[d] 1990 rates not available—1986 data
[e] 1990 data not available—1991 data
[f] 1990 data not available—1992 data
[g] 1990–1994

some degree of validity.

What is noteworthy about the suicide rates of nations around the world circa 1990 (Table 1) is the number of nations that do not report their mortality statistics to the World Health Organization, especially nations in Africa, the Middle East, and Central and South America. As a result, our knowledge of worldwide trends in suicide are limited to the nations that do report their mortality rates.

In all but one of the nations in Table 1, the male suicide rate is higher than the female suicide rate, though the difference is lower in Asian nations than elsewhere. The lone exception is China where women have a higher suicide rate than men (33.5 versus 24.2, respectively, per 100,000 per year for 1990–1994 [M. R. Phillips & Liu, 1996]). Lester (1990) found that 21 of 23 nations experienced an increase in the male suicide rate from 1970–1984, whereas only 14 of the 23 nations had increases in the female suicide rate. Thus, while male suicide rates seem to be rising worldwide, female rates are not.

Lester (1982) found that the male suicide rate rose with age in most nations of the world. For females, the distribution of suicide rates by age varied with the level of economic development of the nation. For the wealthiest nations, female suicide rates tended to peak in middle age. For poorer nations, the peak shifted to elderly women, while for the poorest nations, the peak shifted to young adult women. More recently, Girard (1993) confirmed that the distribution of suicide rates by age depended upon the level of economic development of the nation.

In the 1970s, there was concern over both rising elderly suicide rates (Lester, 1993) and rising youth suicide rates (Lester, 1988b). Data for the 1980s are shown in Table 2, where it can be seen that nations were equally likely to experience an increase or a decrease in overall male suicide rates, in male youth and male elderly suicide rates, and in female elderly suicide rates. The majority of nations experienced a decrease in overall female suicide rates and in female youth suicide rates.

Using time-series multiple regression analyses, Lester and Yang (1998) found that suicide rates in nations of the world from 1950–1985 were significantly associated with higher divorce rates and lower birth and marriage rates in the majority of the 21 nations studied, as predicted by Durkheim's (1897) classic theory of suicide.

☐ Predicting National Suicide Rates

A number of studies have appeared in recent years examining social correlates of national suicide rates. It is of interest to inquire, therefore, whether the results of this research could be used to identify a set of social variables which can predict national suicide rates.

Physiological Theories

One possible explanation, of course, for differences in the suicide rates of nations is that different nationalities differ in some relevant manner in their physiology.

TABLE 2. Percentage Change in Youth and Elderly Suicide Rates from 1980 to 1990

| | Percentage Change | | | | | |
| | Males | | | Females | | |
	Total	Youth	Elderly	Total	Youth	Elderly
Australia	+26	+51	−2	−7	+4	−13
Austria	−8	−13	+26	−10	−18	+5
Bulgaria	+8	+25	−11	+7	−43	+22
Canada	−4	−1	−15	−24	−7	−29
Costa Rica	−45	−6	+14	+14	−65	+infinity
Czechoslovakia	−10	−38	−5	−10	−4	−10[a]
Denmark	−12	−13	−6	−27	−87	+2
England/Wales	+10	+83	−10	−45	−33	−44
Finland	+19	+36	+50	+16	+21	+5
France	+6	−10	+6	0	−19	+5
Greece	+17	+73	+5	−21	+83	−61
Hong Kong	−12	−10	+6	−14	−12	−29
Hungary	−7	−36	−3	−19	+2	−17
Ireland	+73	+154	+289	+9	+21	−47
Israel	+17	−38	−1	−5	+175	−47
Italy	+13	+11	+34	−11	−17	−8
Japan	−8	−45	−14	−5	−43	−19
Netherlands	−4	−1	−17	−3	−3	+24
New Zealand	+51	+95	+8	−24	−17	−65
N Ireland	+107	+87	+20	+56	+213	+61
Norway	+27	+8	+29	+21	+91	+68
Portugal	+21	+42	+8	+15	−24	+45
Puerto Rico	+24	−19	+39	−25	−24	−100
Scotland	+30	+72	−7	−37	−42	−60
Singapore	+19	+48	−26	+15	−34	+14
Spain	+67	+65	+81	+86	+55	+102
Sweden	−13	−13	+13	−8	−9	+31
Switzerland	−14	−27	+8	−16	−49	+1
USA	+10	+9	+33	−11	−9	+11
USSR	−24	−24	+6	−16	+5	+6
West Germany	−21	−21	−1	−32	−20	−8
Yugoslavia	+4	−5	+22	+6	−36	+28

[a] The data for Czechoslovakia are for 1981 to 1990 since 1980 data were not published by the World Health Organization (WHO)
Calculated by David Lester based on WHO data.

Perhaps, for example, there are differences in inherited psychiatric disorders, particularly affective disorders, or in brain concentrations of serotonin, the neurotransmitter believed to be responsible for depression. As yet, there are no data to test these possibilities for a large sample of nations. However, Lester (1991a) found that estimated Bmax levels of 3H-imipramine platelet binding sites (a possible biochemical indicator of endogenous depressive disorder) in members of eight nations were significantly associated with the suicide rates of those nations. Thus, future research may identify physiological correlates of national suicide rates in a large sample of nations.

Lester (1987a) studied the associations between the proportions of people in 17 industrialized nations with the different types of blood (O, A, B, and AB) and the nations' suicide rates. He found that, the lower the proportion of Type O people and the higher the proportion of Type AB people, the higher the suicide rate.

Psychological Theories

The major psychological factors found to be associated with and predictive of suicidal behavior are depression (specifically hopelessness) and psychological disturbance, labeled variously as neuroticism, anxiety, or emotional instability (Lester, 1992b). Psychiatric disorder of any kind appears to increase the risk of suicide, with affective disorders and substance abuse leading the list.

Alcohol abuse and drug abuse are strongly linked with suicidal behavior. Not only are these behaviors seen as self-destructive in themselves (Menninger [1938] called them chronic suicide), but both attempted and completed suicide occur at high rates in substance abusers (Lester, 1992a).

Composition Theories

Moksony (1990) has noted that one simple explanation of differences in suicide rates between nations is that the national populations differ in the proportion of those at risk for suicide. For example, typically in developed nations, suicide rates are highest in the elderly. Therefore, nations with a higher proportion of elderly persons will have a higher suicide rate.

Social Theories

The most popular explanations of social suicide rates focus on social variables. These social variables may be viewed in two ways: as direct causal agents of the suicidal behavior, or as indices of broader, more abstract, social characteristics which differ between nations.

The most important theory for choosing relevant variables is that of Durkheim (1897). Durkheim hypothesized that the societal suicide rate was determined by a society's level of social integration (that is, the degree to which the people are bound together in social networks) and the level of social regulation (that is, the degree to which individual's desires and emotions are regulated by societal norms and customs). Durkheim thought that this association was curvilinear, but later sociologists have suggested that the association is linear in modern societies (Johnson, 1965), with suicide increasing as social integration and regulation decrease. Studies of samples of nations have found that suicide rates are associated with such variables as the birth rate, female participation in the labor force, immigration, and the divorce rate (Stack, 1980, 1981). Some investigators see these associations as suggesting a direct link between, say, divorce or immigration and suicidal behavior. For example, divorce may be associated with suicide at the aggregate level because divorced people have a higher suicide rate than those with other marital statuses. Other investigators see the associations as suggesting that divorce and immigration are measures of a broader and more basic social characteristic, perhaps social integration, that plays a causal role in suicide. In this latter case, nations with a higher rate of divorce may have a higher rate of suicide for those in all marital statuses.

In a cross-sectional (ecological) study of 25 nations in 1970, Lester (1994a) found that suicide rates were positively associated with the percentage of the elderly, the divorce rate, and the gross domestic product, and negatively with the percentage of people under the age of 15, the unemployment rate, and the birth rate. The association of suicide with birth and divorce rates is consistent with predictions from Durkheim's theory, the association with the percentage of elderly and young is consistent with a composition explanation of the suicide rate, and the association with unemployment and gross domestic product is consistent with previous research findings (Platt, 1984; Stack, 1981).

Predicting National Suicide Rates

This brief review of physiological, psychological, sociological, and compositional theories of suicide rates has identified a number of variables that theoretically should be associated with suicide rates or that have been found empirically to correlate with suicide rates. As a test of the utility of these variables, a set of these variables was tested for their ability to predict the suicide rates of a sample of developed nations with available data.

The variables chosen, together with their theoretical source, were: blood type (physiological), alcohol consumption (psychological), percentage of the elderly (compositional), and divorce and birth rates (sociological). The sample consisted of 18 industrialized nations first used by Lynn (1982) in a study of national character. Data on blood types were available for 17 of these nations, and the multiple linear regression equation was derived from these 17 nations. The results of the multiple regression analysis are shown in Table 3, where the five predictor variables can be seen to have provided a multiple R of 0.69.

Multivariate Analyses

Although there have been studies that have examined the associations among suicide rates and a small number of social variables, only two studies have examined the associations among a large set of social variables and national suicides, both using factor analysis.

Simpson and Conklin (1989) identified two clusters of variables which were

TABLE 3. Results of the Multiple Regression Analysis Predicting the Suicide Rate in 17 Industrialized Nations

Variable	Beta coefficient
birth rate	−0.07
divorce rate	0.12
alcohol consumption	0.26
% elderly	0.17
blood type	−0.48
R	0.69

associated with national suicide rates. One cluster had the highest loading from the Islam religion and the second cluster seemed to assess economic development. Suicide rates were lower in nations with less economic development and where Islam was a more important religion. Two other clusters (Christianity and the Eastern bloc) were not associated with suicide rates.

Lester (1996) in a similar study of the social correlates of national suicide rates identified 13 orthogonal (independent) factors for the social variables. Only one was associated with suicide rates: a factor that seemed to measure economic development (with high loadings from such social variables as low population growth and high gross domestic product per capita). Thus, these two studies agreed in finding that economic development is associated with higher suicide rates.

☐ The Future

There are several issues that must be addressed in the future of the epidemiological study of suicide.

Representation

It is noteworthy that many nations do not presently report mortality rates in general, and suicide rates in particular, to the World Health Organization. Data from Central and South America, Africa, and the Middle East were conspicuously absent. Thus, our knowledge of worldwide trends in suicide is biased. It is hoped that the reporting and investigation of suicide will become more widespread in the world in the 21st Century.

Generalizability

Individual nations are concerned with recent secular trends in their suicide rates. A rise or fall in the suicide rate of a nation is often the subject of published papers on suicide, but these changes have little application to the study of suicide unless the changes can be shown to occur in other nations as well. For example, the rise in youth suicide rates in the 1970s mentioned above was found in 23 nations and not found in six. Thus, this particular trend had widespread generality and became a phenomenon worthy of study.

Seeking Explanations

Once the generality of a trend has been documented, it is important to discover why some nations show the trend while other nations do not. Many recent studies of suicide, while examining suicide in more than one nation, have not attempted to search for explanations of observed differences.

Finding such explanations is not easy. For example, in his study of changing youth suicide rates in the 1970s, Lester (1988b) found no social correlates of the changes and, therefore, no clues as to the causes of the changes. While adult suicide rates were associated with the quality of life of nations, youth suicide rates were not; while changes in adult suicide rates of the nations were greater in nations with higher suicide rates, changes in youth suicide rates were not.

Such efforts are not, however, doomed to failure. Sainsbury, Jenkins, and Levey (1980) found that the proportion of young people in a nation and the divorce rate were positively associated with changes in the suicide rates of European nations. Such findings may be examined to see if they are in accord with predictions from sociological theories of suicide and, if not, may generate new theories.

Nonfatal Suicidal Behavior

The best research and theories have appeared for fatal (completed) suicide. Deaths are more important for government agencies to record, count, and publish. Thus, nonfatal suicidal behavior has been virtually ignored. It is important that better epidemiological studies of attempted suicide and suicidal ideation be conducted so that we begin to develop theories of these behaviors.

Recently, Platt et al. (1992) have begun a comparative epidemiological study of attempted suicide in 15 sites. Unfortunately, the sites are limited to cities in European nations and do not encompass the nations as a whole. But the study is innovative and may lay the groundwork for more comprehensive epidemiological studies in the future. Along the same lines, Linsky, Bachman, and Straus (1995) obtained estimates of the incidence in the previous year of suicidal ideation in America and sought social correlates of this. Thus, epidemiological research into nonfatal suicidal behavior is possible, and it is hoped that more such studies are carried out in the 21st Century.

☐ References

Araki, S., & Murata, K. (1987). Suicide in Japan. *Suicide and Life-Threatening Behavior, 17,* 64–71.

Clarke, R. V., & Lester, D. (1989). *Suicide: Closing the exits.* New York: Springer-Verlag.

Douglas, J. D. (1967). *The social meanings of suicide*. Princeton: Princeton University.

Durkheim, E. (1897). *Le suicide* [Suicide]. Paris: Felix Alcan.

Farberow, N. L., MacKinnon, D., & Nelson, F. (1977). Suicide. *Public Health Reports, 92*, 223–232.

Friedman, G. D. (1987). *Primer of epidemiology*. New York: McGraw-Hill.

Girard, C. (1993). Age, gender, and suicide. *American Sociological Review, 58*, 553–574.

Graves, P. L., & Thomas, C. B. (1991). Habits of nervous tension and suicide. *Suicide and Life-Threatening Behavior, 21*, 91–105.

Johnson, B. D. (1965). Durkheim's one cause of suicide. *American Sociological Review, 30*, 875–886.

Lester, D. (1972). Migration and suicide. *Medical Journal of Australia, i*, 941–942.

Lester, D. (1982). The distribution of sex and age among completed suicides. *International Journal of Social Psychiatry, 28*, 256–260.

Lester, D. (1987a). National distribution of blood groups, personal violence (suicide and homicide), and national character. *Personality & Individual Differences, 8*, 575–576.

Lester, D. (1987b). The stability of national suicide rates in Europe. *Sociology & Social Research, 71*, 208.

Lester, D. (1988a). An analysis of the suicide rates of birth cohorts in Canada. *Suicide and Life-Threatening Behavior, 18*, 372–378.

Lester, D. (1988b). Youth suicide. *Adolescence, 23*, 955–958.

Lester, D. (1990). Changes to suicide rates unique to Canada? *Canadian Journal of Public Health, 81*, 240–241.

Lester, D. (1991a). The association between platelet imipramine binding sites and suicide. *Pharmacopsychiatry, 24*, 232.

Lester, D. (1991b). Completed suicide in the gifted. *Journal of Abnormal Psychology, 100*, 604–606.

Lester, D. (1992a). Alcoholism and drug abuse. In R. W. Maris, A. L. Berman, J. T. Maltsberger, & R. I. Yufit (Eds.), *Assessment and prediction of suicide* (pp. 321–336). New York: Guilford.

Lester, D. (1992b). *Why people kill themselves*. Springfield, IL: Charles C. Thomas.

Lester, D. (1993). Attempts to explain changing elderly suicide rates. *International Journal of Geriatric Psychiatry, 8*, 435–437.

Lester, D. (1994a). *Patterns of suicide and homicide in America*. Commack, NY: Nova Science.

Lester, D. (1996). *Patterns of suicide and homicide in the world*. Commack, NY: Nova Science.

Lester, D., & Yang, B. (1998). *Suicide and homicide in the 20th Century*. Commack, NY: Nova Science.

Linsky, A. S., Bachman, R., & Straus, M. A. (1995). *Stress, culture, and aggression*. New Haven, CT: Yale University Press.

Lynn, R. (1982). National differences in anxiety and extraversion. *Progress in Experimental Personality Research, 11*, 213–258.

Menninger, K. (1938). *Man against himself*. New York: Harcourt, Brace & World.

Moksony, F. (1990). Ecological analysis of suicide. In D. Lester (Ed.), *Current concepts of suicide* (pp. 121-138). Philadelphia: Charles Press.

Mugadza, W. (July, 1996). Suicide attempts among young callers in Zimbabwe. Paper presented at the Befrienders Conference, Kuala Lumpur, Malaysia.

Phillips, D. P., & Wills, J. S. (1987). A drop in suicides around national holidays. *Suicide and Life-Threatening Behavior, 17*, 1–12.

Phillips, M. R., & Liu, H. Q. (July, 1996). Suicide in China. Paper presented at the Befrienders Conference, Kuala Lumpur, Malaysia.

Platt, S. (1984). Unemployment and suicidal behavior. *Social Science & Medicine, 19*, 93–115.

Platt, S., Bille-Brahe, U., Kerkhof, A., Schmidtke, A., Bjerke, T., Crepet, P., De Leo, D., Haring, C., Lonnqvist, J., Michel, K., Philippe, A., Pommereaux, X., Querejeta, I., Salander-Renberg, E., Temesvary, B., Wasserman, D., & Faria, J. (1992). Parasuicide in Europe. *Acta Psychiatrica Scandinavica, 85*, 97–104.

Robinson, W. S. (1950). Ecological correlations and the behavior of individuals. *American Sociological Review, 15,* 351–357.

Sainsbury, P., & Barraclough, B. M. (1968). Differences between suicide rates. *Nature, 220,* 1252.

Sainsbury, P., Jenkins, J., & Levey, A. (1980). The social correlates of suicide in Europe. In R. Farmer & S. Hirsch (Eds.), *The suicide syndrome* (pp. 38–43). London, UK: Croom Helm.

Simpson, M. E., & Conklin, G. H. (1989). Socioeconomic development, suicide and religion. *Social Forces, 67,* 945–964.

Stack, S. (1980). Domestic integration and the rate of suicide. *Journal of Comparative Family Studies, 11,* 249–260.

Stack, S. (1981). The effect of immigration on suicide. *Basic & Applied Social Psychology, 2,* 205–218.

Taiminen, T., Salmenperä, T., & Lehtinen, K. (1992). A suicide epidemic in a psychiatric hospital. *Suicide and Life-Threatening Behavior, 22,* 350–363.

WHO. (Annual). *Statistics annual.* Geneva: World Health Organization.

CHAPTER

Steven Stack

Sociological Research into Suicide

The sociological perspective on suicide focuses primarily on suicide at the aggregate or group level. This is in contrast to a psychological perspective that may attempt to locate the source of suicide in the personality structure (such as hopelessness and depression) of isolated individuals. Sociological research examines forces external to the individual (Stack, 1982).

The present chapter focuses on five sets of well-researched social forces. These are 1) demographic and temporal factors, 2) the intensity of economic strain, 3) the vitality of marriage and family life, 4) religion, and 5) copy cat effects that may be generated by media coverage of suicides. Each section looks at one of these factors and deals with work from the past and present, and makes suggestions for work for the future. Other sociological risk factors not covered here include the modernization processes of industrialization, urbanization, and secularization. Other omitted factors include opportunity considerations (such as firearm availability), alcohol consumption, occupation, work mobility, cohort analysis, migration, political factors (such as war and presidential elections), and musical subcultures.

The psychological and sociological perspectives on suicide are not mutually exclusive. Social forces may result in or be correlated with psychological states (depression, for example) that increase suicide potential. For example, divorce and unemployment can result in higher levels of depression which, in turn, increase suicide risk (Stack, in press-b).

☐ Significance of Suicide

Suicide currently constitutes the ninth leading cause of death for the general population. It is the third most common cause of death for persons aged 15–24 and the fifth leading cause of death for those aged 25–44 (National Center for Health Statistics, 1998). Unlike most causes of death, suicide can be prevented.

In 1996 30,903 people (or 85 per day) committed suicide in the United States. There have been approximately 30,000 suicides a year for more than a decade. This regularity in suicidal deaths may indicate that suicide is rooted in the social structure. It is not a random or chance event and may not be resolvable through psychologically-based prevention programs such as suicide prevention centers and hot lines.

The significance of suicide spreads beyond the 30,000 completed suicides each year. For each suicide victim there are, on average, six significant others of the suicide, or "survivors." Further, there are an estimated 250,000–600,000 unsuccessful suicide attempts each year. Approximately five million living Americans have attempted suicide. While there is more fear of being murdered than dying by suicide, it is more likely to die by one's own hand (11.6 persons per 100,000 per year) than by the hand of another (7.9 persons per 100,000 per year) (McIntosh, 1991; National Center for Health Statistics, 1998).

☐ Demographic and Temporal Correlates of Suicide

Basic data on demographic characteristics of suicide in the United States in 1988 and 1996 are provided in Table 1.

TABLE 1. Suicide By Gender, Race, and Age, 1988 And 1996, United States

	Number of suicides		Rate per 100,000 people in group	
	1988	1996	1988	1996
Total	30,407	30,903	12.4	11.6
Gender:				
Males	24,078	24,998	20.1	19.3
Females	6,329	5,905	5.0	4.4
Race:				
Whites	27,790	27.856	13.4	12.7
Blacks	2,022	2,164	6.7	6.5
Age:				
15–24	4,929	4,358	13.2	12.0
25–34	6,710	5,861	15.4	14.5
35–44	5,205	6,741	14.8	15.5
45–54	3,532	4,837	14.6	14.9
55–64	3,406	2,925	15.6	13.7
65–74	3,296	2,806	18.4	15.0
75–84	2,462	2,290	25.9	20.0
85+	605	759	20.5	20.2

Sources: U.S. Public Health Service, (1990); National Center for Health Statistics, (Nov. 1998).

Gender

Of the basic demographic factors, gender is the best predictor of suicide. Males are 4.4 times more likely than females to commit suicide (up from 4.0 times in 1988). Men have a rate of alcoholism (a risk factor in suicide) five times higher than women. Women have more negative attitudes towards suicide, and are more apt to seek professional help when they are suicidal, thus in some instances preventing suicide from occurring. Social gender roles may drive males to be "sturdy oaks," competitive, "success objects," and to be less in touch with their realm of feelings than females. As a consequence, males have not learned to deal as effectively with emotional problems as have females. Men are more apt than females to see no alternative to suicide in times of serious crises such as divorce, death of a spouse, or unemployment. For the future, a key issue is to weight the relative importance of these and other risk factors in the generation of the gender differential in suicide (Canetto, 1992; Lester, 1988; Stack, 1982, in press-a).

Race

In 1996, blacks continued to have a suicide rate half that of whites (6.5 for blacks versus 12.7 for whites). Given racial inequalities and discrimination, blacks tend to externalize aggression, that is, they are more apt than whites to blame society and others for their various frustrations. For example, black homicide, an extreme form of other-directed aggression, is currently 6.3 times higher than white homicide (29.8 versus 4.7). Black suicide may be low in spite of their high exposure to suicide risk factors (e.g., high unemployment and high divorce rates) since they have learned to vent frustration against others in the form of homicide rather than against themselves. The latter is possibly more of a white reaction. If we sum the suicide and homicide rate into a lethal aggression rate, blacks are twice as likely to commit acts of lethal aggression than whites (36.3 versus 17.4) (Lester, 1992; National Center for Health Statistics, 1998; Stack, 1982, in press-a). Future work on black suicide needs to take into account the variation in black homicide; the latter may be a key predictor of the variation in black suicide.

Age

From age 15 through age 74 there is currently little variation in suicide rates by age. These age groups have suicide rates between 12.0 and 15.5. Rates increase to 20 for groups 75 and over. While the teenage suicide problem has received substantial publicity, their rate is, in fact, the lowest of any group other than the 0–14 year old group. The suicide rate of the elderly has always been the highest of any age group. The loss of a spouse and friends through death, physical illness, financial difficulties upon retirement from a job, and so on, are factors often associated with suicide among the elderly (Lester, 1992; Stack, 1990a).

However, American females follow a different pattern. Their suicide rate increases up to age 50 and then declines with age, even after retirement. However, this inverted U-shaped age pattern for American females is markedly different than that of females in most other nations (Girard, 1993). For industrial nations the typical pattern for females is the same as that for men: Suicide rates increase with age even into retirement (Stack, in press-b). American females have one of the world's highest labor force participation rates. Perhaps the gains of such work-related connectedness offset the other causes of suicide in the aging process. Future work needs to address why American females follow an unusual pattern of suicide by age.

Temporal Patterns

With respect to temporal patterns, suicide is highest in the spring, during the first week of the month, and on Mondays. Additionally more people commit suicide on New Year's day more than on any other day of the year (U.S. Public Health Service, 1990). The stress of new beginnings (another year, another week at the job, and so on) may be too much for suicidal people to face (Gabennesch, 1988; Stack, 1995b).

Holiday periods, the five days before and after major public holidays, decrease suicide on the average by 102.5 suicides (Phillips & Wills, 1987). Holidays are said to reduce suicide by increasing social interaction and a feeling of belonging to others. However, the decrease in suicide is principally in the five days *before* the holiday. There is a rise in suicide during the five days after a holiday. This may be due to broken promises. Holidays increase expectations for social fulfillment. When these expectations are not fulfilled, suicide risk may increase (Gabennesch, 1988; Stack, 1995b). There is some racial variation in this effect, and future work needs to unravel the reasons for it (Stack, 1995b).

☐ Economic Strain and Suicide

Poverty

Durkheim (1897/1966) viewed poverty as a school of self-restraint. He believed that poverty toughened up the poor to the adversities of life and made them stronger. Hence their suicide rate would be relatively low. He also contended that the affluent have a higher suicide rate than the poor. The affluent being more educated than the poor, are more apt to question moral traditions that prevent suicide. They are also less bound to religion, and have much further to fall than the poor when they experience unemployment.

Modern researchers have often stressed the negative correlates of poverty that are related to suicide risk. The poor are most affected by many problems: street crime, divorce, severe mental troubles, dull jobs, alcoholism, and so on. It is often anticipated that this extra burden of stress factors would increase, not decrease, suicide risk for the poor and result in a high suicide rate (Stack, 1982, in press-a).

Modern research has largely failed to confirm Durkheim's speculations. A review of the literature for the last 30 years on socioeconomic status and suicide concluded that the lower the socioeconomic status, the higher the suicide risk (Boxer, Burnett, & Swanson, 1995). For example, laborers in Detroit have a suicide rate (87.5) five times that of white collar workers (17.8) (Stack, in press-a).

Future work is needed to unravel exactly which stressors trigger suicide among the poor. In particular, we need to know the relative weights of family, financial, substance abuse, and other risk factors in the generation of suicide among the poor.

Unemployment

Unemployment generally results in sudden deprivation. Suicide risk increases due to loss of work-related meanings such as income, friendships, and status. Long-term, involuntary unemployment is associated with psychological states that increase suicide risk such as depression, pessimism, and low self-esteem (Stack, 1982).

The ripple effect of unemployment can affect still other groups: 1) family members of the unemployed, 2) persons who fear that they may be laid off, 3) new entrants and reentrants to the labor force who experience difficulty finding work in a tight labor market, 4) formerly unemployed persons who are now working at jobs less desirable than their old ones (such as a college professor now driving a taxicab), and 5) many households as wages and salaries do not increase, and may even decrease, in recessions. Hence, times of unemployment can promote anxiety and depression for both the unemployed and the employed.

Literature reviews of over 90 studies on unemployment and suicide have documented a strong association between unemployment and suicide (Lester & Yang, 1997a; Platt, 1984). First, the unemployed themselves have a suicide rate substantially higher than that of the general population. Male suicides in London, for example, were three times as likely to be unemployed than males in general. In Austria, the unemployed have a suicide rate (98.3) four times greater than that of the general population (25.0) (Schony & Grausgruber, 1987). An American-based study reports that the unemployed have a suicide rate 30 times the national average (Stack, 1982).

Research results using national population aggregates studied over time tend to find an association between unemployment rates and suicide rates. For 10 of 14 nations studied, the greater the upward swing in unemployment, the greater the suicide rate (Lester & Yang, 1997b). For example, in Denmark a 1% rise in unemployment is associated with a 0.1% rise in suicide (Stack, 1990c).

Future work is needed to determine if it is unemployment that drives unemployed people to suicide or something associated with unemployment. For example, Platt (1984) cautions that psychiatric morbidity may be the cause of both unemployment and suicide.

☐ Marriage And Family Factors

Having a happy marriage and family life is generally rated first or second in the annual Gallop polls on values. Divorced persons have lost access to this key value. For divorced persons, the loss of supportive companionship, financial difficulties, and a deep sense of disorientation contribute to suicide potential (Lester, 1992; Stack, 1990c).

There are two major explanations that tie marriage and family factors to suicide risk: Durkheim's (1897/1966) theory of domestic integration and the status integration theory of Gibbs and Martin (1964). Durkheim argued that marriage protects against suicide by bonding the individual to group life; the individual subordinates him or herself to the goals and interests of the larger group. This gives life greater meaning. Second, the individual thinks less about individual problems and more about the problems of the group. As a consequence, he or she becomes less preoccupied with personal woes and is less suicidal as a consequence. Third, marriage reduces sexual anomie or unlimited sexual appetites. This provides stability to one's sexual life. In contrast, the single, divorced, and widowed, should have higher suicide rates since they are without these advantages of the married.

In status integration theory, Gibbs and Martin (1964) argued that statistically infrequent role sets (e.g., divorced males) are inherently stressful. It is argued that this is because people tend to avoid such role sets. For example, men tend to avoid the role set of father/spouse/seaman since it is difficult to perform well at being a father and spouse while away at sea for months. Such statistically uncommon role sets are expected to be marked by relatively high suicide rates. In addition, as role sets become more common, the associated suicide rates should decrease. As divorce gets more common, for example, it becomes easier for divorced people to find new mates, and their suicide risk should decline.

Research has supported both of these perspectives. Indeed, that divorced persons are low in domestic integration and have high suicide rates has been supported in most research papers for the United States (e.g., Stack, 1990f; Stafford, Martin, & Gibbs, 1990). Further, many research papers have supported a broad association between the rate of divorce and the rate of suicide, both for the United States (e.g., Breault, 1986; Wasserman, 1990) as well as other nations including Canada, Norway, and Denmark (Stack, 1989; Trovato, 1987). However, in a sweeping analysis for each of 21 nations during 1950–1985, Lester (1994) found only 10 nations that had a significant, positive relationship between divorce and suicide trends. Stack's (1995a) exhaustive review of 132 studies containing 789 findings from 1880–1995, found that 77.9% of the findings demonstrated a positive link between divorce and suicide.

Stack (1990f) tested both the Durkheimian and the status integration theory. For the period of the study (1960–1980), the status of being divorced became more statistically frequent. The number of divorced males aged 30–44 per 1,000 married males 30–44, for example, increased from 25 to 104. This is a four-fold increase. From this, Gibbs and Martin's theory would anticipate a decline in the incidence of suicide among the divorced. The status of being divorced is becoming less stressful for additional reasons. These include less stigma and a proliferation of support groups, dating services, and so on for the divorced person (e.g., Kowalski, 1990).

Data on selected suicide rates by marital status are provided in Table 2. In order to test status integration theory, Stack (1990f) computed coefficients of aggravation (COA) where COA = suicide rate of the divorced/suicide rate of the married. As divorce becomes more common, the COA should decrease. In the case of white males the COA declined from 1960–1980 for 11 of the 15 age groups. For white females it declined for 12 of the 15 age groups. Hence, Gibbs and Martin's theory is correct. As divorce became more common, the propensity for divorced people to suicide relative to that of married people decreased.

Stack's (1990f) investigation also supported Durkheim. While the COAs declined, divorced people still have a substantially higher suicide rate than married people. For example, for males aged 30–34, the COA fell from 6.47 to 4.34. Males in that group were still 4.34 times more likely to complete suicide than their married counterparts. Divorce certainly remains a very stressful condition, although, at the same time, divorce may be less stressful today than in 1960 (Stack, 1990f).

Finally, additional family-related variables may contribute to Durkheim's notion of integration or family bonding. Durkheim argued that having children would increase subordination of the potentially egoistic individual to family life and reduce suicide (1897/1966). The birth rate and the presence of children have been generally found to reduce suicide by intensifying such subordination and bonds (Stack, 1982). Dodge and Austin (1990) found that three generation households (where grandparents, children, and grandchildren live under one roof) reduce social isolation and elderly suicide. Finally, the proportion of persons living alone, an index of isolation from family life, was found to be the strongest predictor of suicide for large American cities (Gove & Hughes, 1980). Gundlach (1990), however, found that rates of divorce and living alone in urban areas predict suicide only when a key facilitator of suicide, firearms, is highly available.

The most critical issue for future research involves what it is about divorce that makes divorced people at risk for suicide. In particular, does divorce per se ac-

TABLE 2. Selected White Male Suicide Rates by Marital Status, Age, and Year, 1960 and 1980

	1960			1980		
	Married Suicide Rate	Divorced Suicide Rate	COA	Married Suicide Rate	Divorced Suicide Rate	COA
AGE						
30–34	12.0	77.6	6.47	14.4	62.6	4.34
35–39	15.6	87.9	5.63	15.3	67.0	4.37
40–44	20.3	104.4	5.14	15.9	72.9	4.58

COA = coefficient of aggravation

count for this or something associated with divorce? A thorny question is to what extent does psychiatric morbidity cause divorce which in turn causes suicide?

☐ Religion

Religion has been thought to influence suicide through three mechanisms: 1) religious integration or the sheer number of shared religious beliefs and practices, 2) religious commitment or adherence to a few specific beliefs such as belief in an afterlife, and 3) religious networks or the social support derived from interaction with coreligionists. The second two perspectives developed in the late 20th Century as the first one increasingly failed to explain differences in suicide.

Religious integration involves the subordination of the individual to religious beliefs and practices. For Catholics in Durkheim's day, these would include meatless Fridays and confession. This subordination is assumed to provide order and meaning to life and to protect against excessive egoistic preoccupation with one's own problems. It therefore lowers the risk of suicide. Suicide risk is reduced in proportion to the sheer number of such beliefs and practices, the essence of integration.

Catholicism was used as an index of religious integration by Durkheim since, at that time, Catholics followed many more rules and had more shared religious practices than Protestants. Over the last century, however, the differences between Catholics and Protestants have narrowed. Even rates of church attendance are now essentially equal between groups. Increasingly, studies reported no significant differences in suicide rates between Catholic and Protestant populations (Stack, 1982, in press-b).[1]

Stack (1983) and Stark, Doylen, and Rushing (1983) independently formulated a second perspective on religion and suicide—the religious commitment theory. They contend that only a few central religious beliefs and practices are needed to lower suicide risk. For example, belief in an afterlife can assuage all manner of suffering as opposed to committing suicide. Divorce, unemployment, and other adversities are more apt to be tolerated if eternal salvation is promised as a reward for perseverance. In contrast, many theological doctrines such as the belief that Jesus walked on water or beliefs in miracles, probably don't have the same impact on suicide prevention.

The religious commitment perspective has received strong support. Indicators of exposure to basic religious teachings, such as church membership and church attendance rates, for example, have generally been associated with lower suicide rates (Breault, 1988; Stack, 1983, 1985; Stark, Doyle, & Rushing, 1983; Trovato & Vos, 1990, 1992). For 261 Canadian census divisions, a 10% change in the proportion of the population with no religious affiliation, an index of low religious commitment, was associated with a 3.2% increase in the suicide rate (Hasselback, Lee, Yang, Nichol, & Wigle, 1991).[2]

---

[1] For an exception see Burr, McCall, and Powell-Griner (1994).
[2] For an exception see Bainbridge (1989).

A third perspective on religion and suicide is provided by Pescosolido and Georgianna (1989). According to religious networks theory, religion will lower suicide risk in proportion to the extent to which it facilitates friendship networks among coreligionists. The social support derived from such networks will provide a buffer against life's crises.

Such networks are more likely to have been developed and maintained in the "historical hub" of a religion, the area where the religion first developed. The historical hub of a religion is the area most apt to have a well developed religious infrastructure. This includes religious schools, hospitals, and social clubs. These institutions are expected to provide social support and lower suicide risk.

The available research tends to support network theory. For example, Evangelical Protestantism was found to lower suicide in the South, its stronghold, but aggravated suicide in the Northeast, where it is weakest. In contrast, religion reduces suicide in the Northeast for Jews. This is their historical hub. In the southern states, however, the percentage of Jewish people is unrelated to suicide, probably due to the fact that Jews are spread out and have little of a supportive infrastructure to increase social networking and support. Further analysis of suicide rates in 404 county groups found that the greater the proportion of religious denominations that promote networking, the lower the suicide. For example, the greater the percent of Evangelical Baptists in a county, the lower the overall suicide rate (Pescosolido, 1990; Pescosolido & Georgianna, 1989).

Thus, Durkheim's (1897/1966) original formulation of a link between Catholicism and low suicide risk may have been appropriate in his century. Since that time, new formulations of the link between religion and suicide have developed. While religious commitment and religious network theories show promise, they too have their limitations. The evidence in support of these two new perspectives is often less extensive and compelling than the evidence for arguments based on marital status and economic strain factors such as unemployment. Possibly in an increasingly secular society, religious correlates of suicide may not be as strong as secular correlates.

Unlike many other areas such as divorce or unemployment, all of the major sociological works on religion and suicide have used ecological data. Future work is needed based on individual-level data to see exactly what religious mechanisms account for suicide versus the lack of suicide in an appropriate control group.

☐ Copycat Effects

Durkheim argued that publicized stories about suicide would not have any appreciable impact on the national suicide rate (Durkheim 1897/1966). While his data were lean by modern standards, his remarks on possible media effects apparently stymied research in this area. For over 75 years there was no significant work on possible media impacts on suicide (Stack 1982).

A pioneering study of front page *New York Times* suicide stories was the first significant work on the subject (Phillips, 1974). Phillips determined that the average story increased the suicide rate by 3%. Phillips argued that such suicide stories increased suicide through fostering three perceptual mechanisms: 1) the glamorization of suicide, 2) suggesting suicide as a problem solving technique (e.g., suicide as an alternative to a slow death through cancer), and 3) the sheer appearance of a story in the press legitimated the act of suicide.

The imitation or copycat response may not be automatic. It may depend on additional characteristics of the story, the victim, and other matters such as the mood of the audience. More recent research on copycat effects finds that the imitation response depends on at least two things: 1) the type of suicide story and 2) the age of the target audience (see the review in Stack [1990e]).

A key distinction under type of story is between victims who are well known celebrities and ones who are not. Stack (1987) hypothesized that stories about celebrities would be the most likely to cause imitative suicides. This follows from Tarde's (1903) "law of imitation"—the inferior tend to copy the behavior of the superior.

A secondary distinction made by Stack (1987) was that the public might be more apt to identify with certain subtypes of celebrities than others. Americans would be expected to identify more with American celebrities than foreign ones, and with heroes rather than villains. Stack determined that in months with stories about the suicides of entertainment celebrities that happened during that month (e.g., Marilyn Monroe) there were 217 more suicides. In months with stories about the suicides of political heroes such as United States Senators, there were 50 additional suicides. However, other categories of celebrities such as artists, foreign celebrities, and the super rich had no impact at all on American suicide.

The nature of the life circumstances or problems faced by the suicide victim may prove to be critical to the extent that the audience identifies with the suicide victim. Stack (1990b) determined that stories about persons who were experiencing marital difficulties triggered a significant increase in imitative suicides.

The mood of the audience and its receptivity to suicide stories vary with age. The youth cohort is marked by a high incidence of suicidogenic conditions including high unemployment, high marital instability, and low religiosity. The mood of the elderly would also be receptive to copycat or imitative suicide given their high incidence of physical illness, social isolation as a result of the deaths of friends and spouse, and economic hardships. In contrast, middle-aged persons might not be as receptive given a lower incidence of physical illness, lower divorce, and a favorable financial status. Research has demonstrated the high incidence of copycat effects for the young (Stack, 1990e). Stories about suicide increase elderly suicide by 10 a month. Stories focusing specifically on elderly suicide victims increase it even more, by 19 a month (Stack, 1990a). Finally, as anticipated, the suicide rate of the middle aged is impervious to copycat effects (Stack, 1991).

Another key issue in copycat suicide is whether or not stories have to be about real suicides, that is, would make-believe suicides in fictional films result in copycat effects as well? A review of the work on both American and British soap operas found, however, no effect of fictional suicides on suicide in the real world (Stack, 1990e). The other major research evidence is from studies on the impact of the four made-for-television films on teenage suicide. These aired during 1984–1985.

A review of this work (Stack, 1990e) found only one study, based in New York City, where the showing of the films was associated with an increase in the teen-age suicide rate. There was no increase in suicide in Pennsylvania, California, and a sample of 19 cities (Stack, 1990e).

Stack (1990d) extended the analysis to the United States as a whole and also found no impact. A reassessment of the case of New York found that real life stories on a New York suicide epidemic aired at the same time as the fictional films. Stack contended that fictional stories may have to be backed up, simulta-neously, with real stories to have any impact.

As in the case of work on religion and suicide, future work is needed to study the copycat effect at the individual level. Through the use of psychological autopsy techniques, future work can assess what percentage of suicides involved copycat effects.

☐ Conclusions

From a sociological perspective, the roots of suicide are buried deep within the structure of society—its economic, familial, and religious fabric, and its cultural beliefs. In this view, suicide will remain a social problem in our society for many decades, and perhaps forever. It is unlikely that suicide will be remedied to any significant degree unless the social structure that helps to produce it also changes to a significant degree. Given that the social structure regulating economics, mari-tal states, religion, and other aspects of life has not changed substantially in the last 50 years, we would expect no appreciable change in the American suicide rate overall. The American suicide rate has indeed stabilized in the 11–13 per 100,000 range for the last several decades.

While the rates of some subgroups have increased or decreased in this period, the larger picture illustrates a stable rate. Often the structural gains for one group can be offset by the structural losses of another. For example, the suicide rate for women has dropped appreciably in the last two decades, but the suicide rate for men has increased. Increased female labor force participation is one of the fore-most structural changes in the last 50 years. Perhaps the benefits of this change are reaped principally by women (e.g., increased employment opportunities) and the costs are carried disproportionately by men (e.g., decreased employment op-portunities) (Stack, in press-b). The net effect on the total suicide rate therefore may be negligible.

Relationships between suicide on the one hand and economic, marital, reli-gious, and media based factors on the other have been established with ecological data or crude individual-level data. More micro-oriented analysis is needed to see exactly what individual-level processes account for these relationships. Work of this kind, however, is labor intensive and generally requires substantial funding. Granting agencies may remain as unreceptive to supporting grant applications on the social etiology of suicide as they have been in the past two decades. If so, this work may never be accomplished in any systematic form.

☐ References

Bainbridge, W. S. (1989). The religious ecology of deviance. *American Sociological Review, 54,* 288–295.

Boxer, P., Burnett, C., & Swanson, N. (1995). Suicide and occupation. *Journal of Occupational and Environmental Medicine, 37,* 442–452.

Breault, K. (1986). Suicide in America. *American Journal of Sociology, 92,* 628–656.

Breault, K. (1988). Beyond the quick and dirty. *American Journal of Sociology, 93,* 1479–1486.

Burr, J., McCall, P., & Powell-Griner, E. (1994). Catholic religion and suicide. *Social Science Quarterly, 75,* 300–318.

Canetto, S. (1992). Gender and suicide in the elderly. *Suicide and Life Threatening Behavior, 22,* 80–97.

Dodge, H., & Austin, R. (1990). Household structure and elderly Japanese female suicide. *Family Perspective, 24,* 83–97.

Durkheim, E. (1966). *Suicide.* New York: Free Press. (Original work published 1897) (translated by John A. Spaulding and George Simpson).

Gabennesch, H. (1988). When promises fail. *Social Forces, 67,* 129–145.

Gibbs, J., & Martin, W. (1964). *Status integration and suicide.* Eugene, OR: University of Oregon Press.

Girard, C. (1993). Age, gender, and suicide. *American Sociological Review, 58,* 553–574.

Gove, W., & Hughes, M. (1980). Re-examining the ecological fallacy. *Social Forces, 58,* 1157–1177.

Gundlach, J. H. (1990). Absence of family support, opportunity, and suicide. *Family Perspective, 24,* 7–14.

Hasselback, P., Lee, K. I., Yang, M., Nichol, R., & Wigle, D. (1991). The relationship of suicide rates to sociodemographic factors in Canadian census divisions. *Canadian Journal of Psychiatry, 36,* 655–659.

Kowalski, G. (1990). Marital dissolution and suicide in the U.S. for the 1980's. *Family Perspective, 24,* 33–40.

Lester, D. (1988). *Why women kill themselves.* Springfield, IL: Charles C. Thomas.

Lester, D. (1992). *Why people kill themselves.* Springfield, IL.: Charles C. Thomas.

Lester, D. (1994). Domestic integration and suicide in 21 nations, 1950–1985. *International Journal of Comparative Sociology, 35,* 131–137.

Lester, D., & Yang, B. (1997a). *The economy and suicide.* Commack, NY: Nova Science.

Lester, D., & Yang, B. (1997b). Unemployment and suicide. Paper presented at the annual meeting of the American Association of Suicidology, Memphis, Tennessee, April, 23–27.

McIntosh, J. (1991). U.S. Suicide. *Newsletter: Michigan Association of Suicidology,* Winter, 10–11.

National Center for Health Statistics. (November, 1998). Deaths: Final data for 1996. *National Vital Statistics Reports, 47*(9) 1–98.

Pescosolido, B. (1990). The social context of religious integration and suicide. *Sociological Quarterly, 31,* 337–357.

Pescosolido, B., & Georgianna, S. (1989). Durkheim, suicide and religion. *American Sociological Review, 54,* 33–48.

Phillips, D. (1974). The influence of suggestion on suicide. American Sociological Review, 39, 340-354.

Phillips, D., & Wills, J. S. (1987). A drop in suicides around major holidays. *Suicide and Life Threatening Behavior, 17,* 1–12.

Platt, S. (1984). Unemployment and suicidal behavior: A review of the literature. *Social Science and Medicine, 19,* 93–115.

Schony, W., & Grausgruber, A. (1987). Epidemiological data on suicide in upper Austria. *Crisis, 8,* 49–52.

Stack, S. (1982). Suicide: A decade review of the sociological literature. *Deviant Behavior, 4,* 41–66.

Stack, S. (1983). The effect of religious commitment on suicide. *Journal of Health and Social Behavior, 24,* 362–374.

Stack, S. (1985). The effect of domestic/religious individualism on suicide. *Journal of Marriage and the Family, 47,* 431–447.

Stack, S. (1987). Celebrities and suicide: A taxonomy and analysis. *American Sociological Review, 52,* 401–412.

Stack, S. (1989). The effect of divorce on suicide in Norway. *Journal of Marriage and the Family, 51,* 229–238.

Stack, S. (1990a). Audience receptiveness, the media, and aged suicide. *Journal of Aging Studies, 4,* 195–209.

Stack, S. (1990b). Divorce, suicide, and the mass media. *Journal of Marriage and the Family, 52,* 553–560.

Stack, S. (1990c). The effect of divorce on suicide in Denmark, 1951–1980. *Sociological Quarterly, 31,* 359–370.

Stack, S. (1990d). The effect of fictional television films on teenage suicide. *Social Science Quarterly, 71,* 391–399.

Stack, S. (1990e). Media impacts on suicide. In D. Lester (Ed.), *Current concepts of suicide* (pp. 107–120). Philadelphia: Charles Press.

Stack, S. (1990f). New micro-level data on the impact of divorce on suicide, 1959–1980. *Journal of Marriage and the Family, 52,* 119–127.

Stack, S. (1991). Social correlates of suicide by age: Media impacts. In A. Leenaars (Ed.), *Life span perspectives of suicide* (pp. 187–213). New York: Plenum Press.

Stack, S. (1995a). Divorce and suicide: A review of 132 studies, 1880–1995. Paper presented at the annual meeting of the Michigan Association of Suicidology, Holland, Michigan.

Stack, S. (1995b). The effect of holidays on race specific suicide and homicide. *Sociological Focus, 28,* 313–328.

Stack, S. (in press-a). Suicide: A 15-year review of the sociological literature, Part I: Cultural and economic factors. *Suicide and Life Threatening Behavior, 30*(2).

Stack, S. (in press-b). Suicide: A 15-year review of the sociological literature, Part II: Modernization and social integration perspectives. *Suicide and Life Threatening Behavior, 30*(2).

Stafford, M., Martin, W., & Gibbs, J. (1990). Marital status and suicide. *Family Perspective, 24,* 15–32.

Stark, R., Doyle, D. P., & Rushing, L. (1983). Beyond Durkheim: Religion and suicide. *Journal for the Scientific Study of Religion, 22,* 120–131.

Tarde, G. (1903). *The laws of imitation.* New York: Holt.

Trovato, F. (1987). A longitudinal analysis of divorce and suicide in Canada. *Journal of Marriage and the Family, 49,* 193–203.

Trovato, F., & Vos, R. (1990). Domestic/religious individualism and youth suicide in Canada. *Family Perspective, 24,* 69–82.

Trovato, F., & Vos, R. (1992). Married female labor force participation and suicide in Canada. *Sociological Forum, 7,* 661–677.

U.S. Public Health Service. (November, 1990). Advance report of final mortality statistics. *Monthly Vital Statistics Report, 39*(7, Suppl.), 1–52.

Wasserman, I. (1990). The impact of divorce on suicide in the U.S. *Family Perspective, 24,* 61–67.

CHAPTER 3

James R. Rogers

Psychological Research into Suicide: Past, Present, and Future

Defining Psychological Research In Suicidology

Currently in the Western world, suicide is a conscious act of self-induced annihilation, best understood as a multidimensional malaise in a needful individual who defines an issue for which suicide is perceived as the best solution. (Shneidman, 1987; p. 157)

Due to the nature of psychology, it is often difficult to distinguish between research that is "psychological" and research that is not "psychological." As suggested in the quote by Shneidman, this difficulty is heightened in the field of suicidology as a function of its multidimensional and, consequently, multidisciplinary nature. If we define psychology broadly as the study of mind and behavior, it is difficult to construct inclusion and exclusion criteria for deciding which research in suicidal behavior can be appropriately identified as psychological. According to Patton (1990), the fundamental disciplinary questions that differentiate psychology from other social science disciplines are "Why do individuals behave as they do?" and "How do human beings behave, think, feel, and know?" (p. 153). Although applying these questions to help differentiate between psychological, sociological, and anthropological research can be helpful, they are not particularly useful in distinguishing psychological research from research in the related human science disciplines of counseling, medicine, nursing, and psychiatry.

The distinction between the psychological and the nonpsychological in suicidology is especially problematic when one considers the historical roots of psychological thought, that is, psychology's early grounding in philosophy. For example, how does one draw a clear line between the philosophical writings related to suicide of individuals such as Hume (1783/1929), Kierkegaard (1848/1954), Nietzsche (1886/1966), Heidegger (1927/1962), Sartre (1947/1957), and Camus (1942/1955) and pure psychological research perspectives? Similarly, in consider-

31

ing psychological research, how would one rationalize the exclusion of a consideration of the major theoretical writings as they relate to the study of suicide in light of an expectation that theory and research are or should to be linked in a reciprocal relationship (Pedhazur & Schmelkin, 1991)?

Given the areas of overlap between psychological research in suicidology and research based in other disciplines and narrow versus broad definitions of research in general, reasonable individuals could differ in their categorizations of psychological research in this area. Rather than focus on the specific outcomes of psychological research into suicide, which would require the establishment of somewhat artificial boundaries around what is and is not psychological research, this chapter attempts to overview the past, present, and future of psychological research in suicidology in the Western world in terms of general methodological focus. That is, the first section of the chapter presents a brief overview of the major philosophical and theoretical traditions related to the understanding of suicide. The second section provides a brief analysis of the pragmatic focus of research in suicidology in the United States prompted by the 1966 creation of the Center for the Studies of Suicide Prevention by the National Institute of Mental Health (Resnik & Hathorne, 1972). Finally, section three presents a discussion of trends and directions for future psychological research in the area of suicidology with a specific focus on macro and complexity theories.

As a final caveat, while certainly not intended as a comprehensive review of the psychological study of suicide and suicidal behavior, this chapter will reference some of the extant literature in the field in support of the methodological overview. Consequently, omissions in terms of referenced work are reflective of this focus as opposed to any commentary on the quality, importance, or impact of specific works in the field.

☐ Psychological Study of Suicide in the Past: The Philosophical and Theoretical Traditions

This section briefly outlines the major philosophical and theoretical perspectives related to suicide and provides a backdrop for the subsequent presentation of four of the major theoretical models in psychology. The importance of theory in advancing understanding and guiding research has been argued in both the general philosophy of science literature (e.g., Lykken, 1991; Lynd, 1939) and in the psychological literature as it relates to suicidology (e.g., Lester, 1988). Thus, this section is intended to provide a basis for the interpretation of the current status of psychological research in suicidology as it relates to philosophical and psychological theory.

Philosophical Perspectives

According to Stillion and McDowell (1996), suicides or self-murders in some form or another have probably occurred almost as long as human beings have been in existence. Early suicide in the form of self-sacrifice has evolved over the millennia to encompass many other dimensions including self-punishment (e.g., the death of Judas Iscariot in 33 A.D.) and rational control over death (e.g., the death of Socrates in 399 B.C.). In the early Christian tradition, suicide was additionally viewed as a means of self-martyrdom; it was not until around 400 A.D. that suicide began to be defined as a crime against God and the state (Stillion & McDowell, 1996). This process of redefinition culminated in 1256–1272 A.D. with Thomas Aquinas's conceptualization of suicide as a clear sin against God (1265–1272/1975).

With the publication of *Biathanatos* (Donne, 1644/1982) and continuing with Hume's (1783/1929) *Essay on Suicide*, the strict definition of suicide as a sin began to be challenged from a philosophical perspective. During the time period of these two publications, the development of secular laws prohibiting suicide and attempts to define it as an illness (Esquirol, 1838; Merian, 1763) were under way. According to Stillion and McDowell (1996), the writings of Freud (1917/1961) established the foundation for the interpretation of suicide as a sign of mental illness. In contrast to defining suicide as a crime, sin, or illness, the existential writings of Hume (1783/1929), Kierkegaard (1954), Nietzsche (1886/1966), Heidegger (1962), Sartre (1957), and Camus (1955) argued that suicide can be an expression of freedom and responsibility and, as such, may represent an existential choice. In fact, much of the contemporary discussion related to rational suicide (e.g., Rogers & Britton, 1994; Werth, 1992, 1996) and physician assisted suicide (e.g., Battin, 1998; Hendin, 1998) is linked to existential thought in this area.

Psychological Perspectives

In his review of the issue of suicide from the perspective of classical psychological theories, Lester (1988) suggested that, in contrast to the attention given the subject of suicide in the sociological literature, none of the major contributing theorists in psychology have focused specifically on suicide. Despite this lack of specific attention to the topic, however, Lester (1988) and Leenaars (1990) have discussed a number of psychological theories and highlighted their interface with the field of suicidology.

For example, according to Leenaars (1990), the psychological study of suicide can be traced to the early theoretical work of Sigmund Freud. As indicated previously, Freud's (1917/1961) writings have been used to benchmark the interpretation of suicide as a sign of mental illness. Although Freud's conceptualization of suicide from the psychodynamic perspective was not extensively articulated, his recognition of many of the associated clinical features such as guilt, loss, revenge, humiliation, depression, and the view of suicidal behavior as a form of communication clearly predated and influenced the directions of subsequent empirical research (Lester, 1988). Additionally, Freud's early conceptualization of the dynamics of eros and thanatos as the life and death instincts has, in many ways, presaged the current literature in suicidology investigating the genetic and neurobiological correlates of suicide (e.g., Mann & Arango, 1999).

Social learning theory (Bandura, 1977) has also been suggested as a useful theoretical model for the study of suicidal behavior (Leenaars, 1990; Lester, 1988). In fact, Lester (1988) concluded that the research evidence for a learning component in suicidal behavior was "overwhelming" (p. 61). Imbedded in the stimulus/response/reinforcement paradigm of general learning theory, social learning theory includes attention to the transmission of suicidal attitudes and behaviors through social and family-based learning experiences. Bandura's (1977) extension of the basic learning model to include observational learning has found particular attention in suicidology as an heuristic for understanding the occurrence of suicidal behavior in families (e.g., Platt, 1993; Rogers & Carney, 1994), suicide clusters, pacts, and mass suicides (Lester, 1988).

Similarly, the cognitive behavioral perspective on suicide with its general focus on depression, hopelessness, and the role of cognition has been identified by Leenaars (1990) as having important implications for the study of suicide. According to Leenaars, the link between cognitive perspectives and suicide is most clearly articulated in the writings of Beck and his colleagues (e.g., Beck, Shaw, Rush, & Emery, 1979). Within this model, negative and often unrealistic views and expectations of one's self, the future, and the world lead to feelings of helplessness and hopelessness. These feelings can become overwhelming and lead one to suicide as a means of escaping the associated negative affect. Intervention in the cognitive model focuses on identifying the automatic and involuntary cognitions and testing those for empirical validity (e.g., Ellis & Newman, 1996).

While the above psychological theories address the issue of suicide in limited ways and as extensions of their larger theoretical perspectives, Shneidman (1987) developed a theory specific to suicide. Shneidman's cubic model of suicide is based on Murray's (1938) conceptualization of personality and consists of the three characteristics of press, perturbation, and pain. According to the model, press refers to "events done to the individual to which he or she reacts" (p. 174). While the press can be both positive and negative, threatening presses are those most relevant to suicide. Perturbation refers to the state of being upset, and pain is interpreted as psychological pain related to unrealized or blocked need fulfillment. Individuals experiencing high levels of press, perturbation, and pain, and who are motivated to escape that pain are those who commit suicide.

Although these four theories have been identified by Lester (1988) and Leenaars (1990) as having much to offer the area of suicidology in terms of theoretical understanding and guidance for empirical research, this promise has not been realized (Lester, 1988). What has occurred, instead, is a piecemeal investigation of empirically identified variables associated with suicidal behavior with little or no translation into broader theoretical perspectives.

☐ Psychological Research into Suicide in the Present: Pragmatics in Action

The contemporary study of suicidal behavior in the United States can be traced back to the work of Shneidman, Farberow, and Litman in the late 1950s and the subsequent creation of the Center for the Studies of Suicide Prevention by the National Institute of Mental Health (NIMH) in 1966 (Resnik & Hathorne, 1972). In combination, the investigations of Shneidman and his colleagues and the national initiative were instrumental in prompting the scientific community to begin to systematically investigate suicidal behavior as an important area of inquiry. The major methodological result of the NIMH policy and funding initiative was that research in suicide took on a predominantly pragmatic character. That is, the predominant focus in contemporary suicidology in the United States became the identification of risk and protective factors that influence suicidal behavior as opposed to understanding and theory development. This pragmatic focus resulted in the identification of a variety of biological, psychological, and sociological correlates of suicide and suicidal behavior (e.g., Blumenthal & Kupfer, 1990). Although the ultimate goal of this approach was to provide a basis for predicting and preventing suicide (e.g., Blumenthal & Kupfer, 1990; Maris, Berman, Maltsberger, & Yufit, 1992; Rogers, Alexander & Subich, 1994), there is little evidence to suggest that it has resulted in any reduction in the overall suicide rate (Lester, 1998) or increased the ability to predict suicide (Maris, Berman, Maltsberger, & Yufit, 1992).

As a secondary effect, the pragmatic approach to the problem of suicide prompted by the NIMH has contributed to the general lack of attention to theoretical grounding in the extant research. That is, much of the current psychological literature in suicidology is written from an atheoretical or microtheoretical perspective as opposed to proceeding from well articulated theoretical positions and retrospectively informing those theories. Additionally, much of the existing theory-linked research is a result of post hoc theorizing (Pedhazur & Schmelkin, 1991). This lack of prospective and broad theoretical grounding has had at least two effects on the knowledge base in suicidology. First, rather than developing of a coherent body of knowledge, the atheoretical, microtheoretical, and post hoc approaches have resulted in identifying a wide array of correlates to suicidal behavior with little understanding regarding how they are interrelated and may coalesce at the individual level to lead one to a decision to commit suicide. Second, as indicated earlier, without clearly identified theoretical specifications, it is difficult to unambiguously differentiate between psychological research and research emanating from other closely related fields.

As an example of atheoretical research in the psychological study of suicide, Mireault and de Man (1996) investigated predictors of suicidal ideation among elderly individuals. Although these authors identified their research as being based on a multifactor theory of suicide, it was not grounded in any clear psychological theory and was, in fact, atheoretical in nature. In their design, the authors identified a set of correlates of suicidal behavior from prior empirical investigations and cast them in a regression model to identify significant predictors of elder suicide. The authors made no attempt to place their findings within a theoretical framework.

Rogers (1992) is an example of theorizing at the micro level. Here, he suggested that the well-documented relationship between alcohol consumption and suicidal behavior could be understood based on the work of Steele and Josephs (1990). He suggested that the link might best be conceptualized as a function of the construct of "alcohol induced myopia" introduced by Steele and Josephs as part of their cognitive-social model for understanding alcohol's cognitive and behavioral effects. Rogers highlighted the overlap between the concept of alcohol induced myopia and the concept of tunnel vision or cognitive constriction which has often been identified as being associated with suicide (e.g., Shneidman, 1987). While making this link to cognitive-social theory may result in some degree of practical and heuristic value, it occurs in isolation from other empirically observed relationships to suicidal behavior and does not necessarily advance the field toward better understanding at a macro theoretical level.

In a similar fashion, Platt (1993) provides an example of the post hoc approach. In this research, Platt was interested in investigating the relationship of previous suicide attempts and exposure to suicidal behavior with current suicidal behavior. Although his research questions were not originally derived from social learning theory (Bandura, 1977), he interprets his results as a test of the observational learning model. Based on his analyses, he concluded that there was little evidence to support an observational learning component for suicidal behavior. Critiquing Platt (1993), Rogers and Carney (1994) highlighted the post hoc nature of both his analyses and theoretical conclusions. These authors suggested that, in order to appropriately test the observational learning paradigm, one would need to specify the theory a priori, derive testable hypotheses from the theory, and develop a methodology that would allow interpretation back to the theory. As suggested by Pedhazur and Schmelkin (1991), "Post hoc theorizing should not be confused with the meaningful and necessary process of theory refinement, revision, reformulation, or whatever the case may be, in light of research findings" (p. 185).

Finally, psychological research in suicidology has generally adhered to the deficit model embedded in the mental illness tradition. Based on this model, researchers have focused on discovering the deficiencies of suicidal as compared with nonsuicidal individuals. These deficiencies have then been interpreted as risk factors and, very often, their absence has been interpreted as protective factors. Two notable exceptions to this deficit model have been in the areas of an individual's reasons for living and rational suicide.

In the first exception to the deficit model, Linehan, Goodstein, Nielson, and Chiles (1983) constructed the Reasons for Living Inventory in an attempt to assess the "adaptive, life-maintaining characteristics of non-suicidal people" (p. 276). This effort at exploring the issue of suicide from a nondeficit perspective was mirrored by Westefeld and his colleagues with the construction and psychometric development of the College Student Reasons for Living Inventory (Westefeld, Cardin, & Deaton, 1992). While this approach can potentially be useful in understanding suicidal individuals through the study of nonsuicidal people, it continues to be overshadowed by research from the deficit perspective.

Rational suicide represents the other major area of departure in the contemporary psychological literature from the deficit model of suicide. Prompted in part by the emergence of the AIDS pandemic and the issue of physician assisted suicide, but with clear historical ties into the philosophical work of Hume (1783/1929),

Kierkegaard (1954), Nietzsche (1886/1966), Heidegger (1962), Sartre (1957), and Camus (1955), rational suicide has become a recent focus in the psychological literature (e.g., Werth, 1996). In contrast to the reasons for living research, the rational suicide issue has gained momentum through its connection with other right to die policy issues (e.g., Rogers, 1996) and can be expected to continue to impact the psychological study of suicide into the next century.

In summation, the current pragmatic approach to the psychological study of suicidal behavior has resulted in the development of a clearer picture of relevant correlates of suicide. This approach has clearly been important in the developmental process of the relatively young field of suicidology. These efforts, however, have not resulted in the expected reduction in suicidal behaviors nor have they increased predictive efficacy. In general, the psychological research in the area of suicidal behavior evidences a clear lack of theoretical cohesiveness. Psychological research in suicidology in the future should focus on the development of macro theories in order to provide organizing structures for what is currently known about suicide and human behavior in general. Future efforts directed at organization and cohesiveness have the potential to move the field well beyond the current stage of risk and protective factor identification that has been the hallmark of contemporary psychological investigations into suicide and may provide a reasonable link to the reemerging issue of rational suicide. This process should lead to a greater understanding of suicidal people and, perhaps, to the development of more effective strategies and interventions for working with suicidal individuals.

☐ The Future of Psychological Research in Suicidology: Macro Theories, Chaos, and Complexity

The final section provides some examples of areas for future psychological research in suicidology for the millennium. The first example is an outline of the early stages of development of a macro theory that may serve to organize the current body of knowledge in suicidology and link it with a broader theory of human behavior based in existential (e.g., Yalom, 1980) and constructivist (e.g., Mahoney, 1991) theories. This is followed by a brief presentation of chaos and complexity theoretical perspectives that have been applied in the realm of the physical sciences and seem to have promising applications in psychology (e.g., Masterpasqua & Perna, 1997).

An Existential-Constructivist Model

Following his review of the issue of suicide from the perspective of psychological theories, Lester (1988) suggested that advancements in the psychological study of suicidology might accrue through attempts to integrate the current body of knowledge with "classic psychological theories of human behavior" (p. 122). The existential-constructivist model for understanding suicide represents such an attempt at integration (Rogers, in press). This conceptualization attempts to combine classical existential theory derived from the work of Yalom (1980) and rooted in the philosophical literature (e.g., Kierkegaard, 1954; Nietzsche, 1886/1966) with critical constructivism as discussed by Mahoney (1991) and Neimeyer and Mahoney (1995).

This model posits that the existential issues of death, meaninglessness, isolation, freedom, and responsibility provide the underlying motivational dynamics for the development of individual and shared constructions of meaning. These constructions, according to Neimeyer (1995), are the result of the "basic human quest to seek relatedness, connection, and mutuality of meaning in spite of our uniqueness, using the common grounding provided by our language and our embodiment to form an intersubjective bridge between our phenomenal worlds" (p. 2). These constructions also include our world views and perceptions of reality, as well as our interpretations of ourselves, others, and relationships.

With its focus on the adaptive viability of constructions (Mahoney, 1991) and attention to human cognitive processes, this model can reasonably incorporate and explain many of the correlates of suicide and suicidal behavior identified through pragmatic research endeavors. Furthermore, the existential-constructivist model potentially allows for an integrative consideration of the various risk and protective factors in a human motivational context, thereby, enhancing our overall understanding of suicide. Additionally, with its grounding in existentialism, the existential-constructivist framework may provide a reasonable basis for conceptualizing the emerging issue of rational suicide and help guide research around this important topic in the future.

The existential-constructivist theory presented here is just one example of a number of possibilities for developing macro theories of suicide that may serve to link the current empirical knowledge base with classical psychological theories of human behavior. As suggested by Lester (1988) and supported by Pedhazur and Schmelkin's (1991) general philosophy of science discussion, what is needed in future psychological research in suicidology is the development of multiple macro theories of this type that can be empirically tested and validated. Efforts in this process should result in advances in the psychological understanding of suicide well beyond the current level.

Chaos and Complexity Theories

Given the lack of the current pragmatic focus of psychological research in suicidology to result in increased predictive efficacy and a reduction in the suicide rates (Lester, 1994, 1998), a number of authors have suggested that psychology in general, and the psychological study of suicidology specifically, may benefit from a consideration of the various nonlinear dynamic systems perspectives including chaos and complexity theories (e.g. Lester, 1994; Mishara, 1996; Masterpasqua & Perna, 1997; Rogers, 1995; Rogers & McGuirk, 1998). According to Eidelson (1997), chaos and complexity theories have evolved from investigations into the behavior of complex, dynamic, and interactive systems and have revealed that determinism and randomness often coexist, the whole is often more than the sum of its parts, instability is common, and behavioral change is frequently abrupt and discontinuous. Related to human behavior, Masterpasqua and Perna (1997) suggested that:

> We can no longer rely on models based on insulated, linear, and closed systems to explain a self in context and in continuous construction. We see the sciences of chaos and complexity as offering these new models and metaphors. They offer a basis from the physical and natural sciences from which to understand a postmodern self in continuous construction and reconstruction. (p. 7)

Chaos and complexity theories have already begun to appear in the psychological literature as models and metaphors for advancing the understanding of such psychological issues such as dissociative disorder (Derrickson-Kossman & Drinkard, 1997), psychological trauma (Lasser & Bethory, 1997), and the psychotherapeutic process (Mahoney & Moes, 1997). Thus, investigating their application to the study of suicide seems an appropriate direction for psychological research in the next millennium.

Nonlinear dynamic systems perspectives include chaos theory (e.g., Gleick, 1987) and the complexity theories of self-organized criticality (Bak & Chen, 1991) and catastrophe modeling (Stewart & Peregoy, 1983). These three general models and their possible impact on the psychological study of suicidology are briefly described below.

Chaos Theory

In his discussion of the difficulties inherent in the prediction of suicide, Lester (1994) suggested that the nonlinear theory of chaos may have significant implications for suicidologists. Based on the work of Lorenz (1979) and Gleick (1987), Lester introduced the concept of sensitive dependence on initial conditions into the psychological literature in suicidology. According to Lester (1994), "In suicidology, we expect and therefore search for major events which might lead to suicide subsequently, whereas perhaps the causes of suicide are more subtle" (p. 187). Similarly, Rogers (1995) suggested that this concept may have far-reaching implications for the field of suicidology in that "events in peoples' lives that have been viewed as having little or minor significance in terms of a causal relationship to suicidal behavior, may actually play a substantially greater role" (p. 139).

At the basis of chaos is the paradox that unpredictable behavior (i.e., suicide) can occur within predictable systems. According to Masterpasqua and Perna (1997), "Another way to understand this apparent paradox is that systems in chaos are determined, but not by linear methods. Chaos represents nonlinear deterministic behavior" (pp. 9–10). Translated into the psychological study of suicidology, chaos theory may provide a useful metaphor for understanding the inability of research to result in useful predictive models at the individual level. By giving up the unobtainable goal of individual prediction and incorporating the concepts of sensitive dependence on initial conditions and nonlinear modeling, the application of chaos theory to suicidology has the potential to move the field to a greater level of understanding of suicide and suicidal individuals.

Self-Organized Criticality

Self-organized criticality is a theory developed by Bak and Chen (1991) in order to explain how large interactive systems can evolve or self-organize toward a critical state in which a minor incident can lead to a catastrophic event. This state of precarious equilibrium has been referred to by Eidelson (1997) as the edge of chaos and a critical state between order and disorder. According to Eidelson, the classical example of self-organized criticality is the behavior of a pile of sand:

> As sand is slowly added from above, the pile's height increases until the slope reaches a critical state. At that point, any additional grains of sand will cause an avalanche of unpredictable magnitude. In fact, the distribution of landslides is best described by a power law, with a small slide far more likely than a large one. But perhaps most intriguing is the premise that the same conditions can produce different outcomes on different occasions. What remains relatively constant, however, is the critical state that the pile must return to before the next avalanche will occur. (Eidelson, 1997, pp. 54–55)

Rogers and McGuirk (1998) have suggested that the use of self-organized criticality as a metaphor for suicidal phenomena may have heuristic value. According to these authors, when applied to suicidal behavior, the self-organized criticality model may aid psychologists "in understanding the relative unpredictability of suicidal behavior and help explain why seemingly minor events can lead to suicidal and non-suicidal behaviors within the same individual at different points in time" (p. 139).

In their discussion of psychological systems and the self-organizing process, Rogers and McGuirk (1998) suggested that at a basic level, one could consider the human cognitive, affective, and symbolic systems as three of the possible psychological components of the complex system for modeling purposes. Each of these systems have their own self-organizing processes that interpret and assimilate new relevant information. Additionally, these systems interact in reciprocal ways and self-organize at a meta-system level. The meta-system, or individual, constantly self-organizes to what appears to be a state of equilibrium representing stability and some degree of behavioral predictability. This state of equilibrium, however, is only one of many possible equilibrium states and is actually the result of many "self-organized, far from equilibrium dynamical systems" (Eidelson, 1997, p. 43). Consequently, the equilibrium state represents a stable picture of the system or individual constantly at the edge of chaos.

In terms of suicide, Rogers and McGuirk (1998) suggested that self-organized criticality and the concept of multiple possible equilibrium states might be useful in explaining some current observations regarding suicidal behavior. For example, they suggested that the concept of multiple possible equilibrium states could be applied to the understanding of both resilience to negative life events and to suicidal crises, that is, a threatened equilibrium state may lead to a shift or reorganization to a different equilibrium state or, alternatively, to a catastrophic event such as suicide.

The application of self-organized criticality to the psychological study of suicide seems to have promise when considering the implications of the theory at the superficial level as presented here. Certainly, the theory appears to provide an appropriate metaphor for thinking about suicide and suicidal behavior and for organizing some of the empirical literature in suicidology. The challenge for the psychological study of suicidology in the future will be, as suggested by Eidelson (1997), to move from metaphor to modeling if complexity theories in general are going to advance the knowledge base in the behavioral sciences.

Catastrophe Modeling

Catastrophe theory provides a method for conceptualizing how smooth changes in the independent variable can lead to sudden changes in the dependent variable (Stewart & Peregory, 1983). Thus, related to human behavior, it attempts to explain "sudden changes or discontinuities in behavior that occur even though the underlying causative factors are continuous" (Rogers, 1995, p. 140).

Of a variety of catastrophe models, Rogers (1995) suggested that the cusp catastrophe model may be most appropriate for considering suicidal phenomena. Accordingly, in his brief discussion of catastrophe modeling, Rogers (1995) suggested that:

> The cusp catastrophe model, one of a number of general catastrophe models, seems particularly suited to considerations of suicidal behavior. In general, the cusp catastrophe model suggests that smooth changes in independent variables (e.g., press and perturbation) are sometimes associated with sudden discontinuous or abrupt changes in the independent [dependent] variables (e.g., nonsuicidal coping responses lead to suicide). Additionally, in some circumstances the same event history of the independent variables (e.g., identical levels of press and perturbation) can result in very different final values on the dependent variables (e.g., nonsuicidal coping responses at one time and a suicidal response at another time). This characteristic of divergence may have explanatory implications for suicidal behavior in the absence of an objectively identified triggering event. (p. 140)

As with chaos and self-organized criticality, catastrophe theory and specifically the cusp catastrophe model appear to provide useful metaphors for the psychological study of suicide for the next millennium. The translation of the nonlinear dynamic systems models into the behavioral sciences is at a very early stage. However, based on the use of these models in other areas of psychology and the brief discussion of their possible impact on the psychological study of suicide, efforts directed at interpreting these models in suicidology seem warranted.

☐ Conclusion

Despite its connection to the philosophical writings of the 18th Century and the more recent translations of classical psychological theory to address suicide and suicidal behavior, psychological research in suicidology barely goes back 40 years. Psychological research since the 1950s in this area has been focused on the pragmatic issues of prediction and intervention but has yet resulted in any reduction in the suicide rate or improved the ability to predict suicide at the individual level.

As suggested in this chapter, psychological research in suicidology in the next millennium may benefit from a focus on the development of macro theories that integrate the extant knowledge of suicide correlates with classical psychological theories of human behavior. Additionally, the field may benefit from efforts aimed at developing theoretical models based on the nonlinear dynamic systems perspectives of chaos, self-organized criticality, and catastrophe modeling, as well as other complexity theories, for understanding suicide and suicidal individuals.

Finally, perhaps it is time for suicidologists to let go of the hope of prediction that has driven much of the psychological research to date and increase the focus of gaining a clearer understanding of suicide at the individual level. As suggested by Lykken (1991)

> A natural scientist is not embarrassed because he cannot look at a tree and predict which leaves will fall first in the autumn or the exact path of the fall or where the leaf will land. Maybe individual lives are a lot like leaves; perhaps there is a very limited amount one can say about the individual case, based on a knowledge of leaves in general or people in general, without detailed, idiographic study of that particular case and even then it is hard to know how the winds will blow from one day to the next. (pp. 18–19)

☐ References

Aquinas, T. (1975). *Summa theologica (Vol. 38)*. London: Blackfriars. (Original work written 1265–1272)

Bak, P., & Chen, K. (January, 1991). Self-organized criticality. *Scientific American, 264,* 46–53.

Bandura, A. (1977). *Social learning theory.* Englewood Cliffs, NJ: Prentice Hall.

Battin, M. P. (1998). Ethical issues in physician assisted suicide. In M. Uhlmann (Ed.), *Last rights? Assisted suicide and euthanasia debate* (pp. 111–145). Grand Rapids, MI: Eerdmans.

Beck, A. T., Shaw, A. J., Rush, B. F., & Emery, G. (1979) *Cognitive theory of depression.* New York: Guilford Press.

Blumenthal, S. J., & Kupfer, D. J. (Eds.). (1990). *Suicide over the life cycle: Risk factors, assessment, and treatment of suicidal patients.* Washington, DC: American Psychiatric Press.

Camus, A. (1955). *The myth of Sisyphus, and other essays.* (J. O'Brien, Trans.). New York: Knopf. (Original work published 1942)

Derrickson-Kossmann, D. & Drinkard, L. (1997). Dissociative disorders in chaos and complexity. In F. Masterpasqua & P. A. Perna (Eds.), *The psychological meaning of chaos: Translating theory into practice* (pp. 117–145). Washington, DC: American Psychological Association.

Donne, J. (1982). *Biathanatos.* (M. Rudick & M. P. Battin, Trans.). New York: Garland. (Original work published 1644)

Eidelson, R. J. (1997). Complex adaptive systems in the behavioral and social sciences. *Review of General Psychology, 1,* 42–71.

Ellis, T. E., & Newman, C. F. (1996). *Choosing to live: How to defeat suicide through cognitive therapy.* Oakland, CA: New Harbinger Publications.

Esquirol, E. (1965). *Mental maladies: A treatise on insanity.* (Introduction by Raymond de Saussure). New York: Hafner.

Freud, S. (1961). Mourning and melancholia. In J. Strachey (Ed. and Trans.), *The standard edition of the complete psychological works of Sigmund Freud* (Vol. 14, pp. 243–258). London: Hograth Press. (Original work published 1917)

Gleick, J. (1987). *Chaos: Making a new science.* New York: Viking.

Heidegger, M. (1962). *Being and time.* (J. Macquarrie & E. Robinson, Trans.). New York: Harper & Row. (Original work published 1927)

Hendin, H. (1998). Assisted suicide and euthanasia: The Dutch experience. In M. Uhlmann (Ed.), *Last rights? Assisted suicide and euthanasia debate* (pp. 367–386). Grand Rapids, MI: Eerdmans.

Hume, D. (1929). *An essay on suicide.* Yellow Springs, OH: Kahoe. (Original work published 1783)

Kierkegaard, S. (1954). *Fear and trembling/The sickness unto death.* (W. Lowrie, Trans.). Garden City, NY: Doubleday. (Original work published 1848)

Lasser, C. J., & Bathory, D. S. (1997). Reciprocal causality and childhood trauma: An application of chaos theory. In F. Masterpasqua & P. A. Perna (Eds.), *The psychological meaning of chaos: Translating theory into practice* (pp. 147–176). Washington, DC: American Psychological Association.

Leenaars, A. A. (1990). Psychological perspectives on suicide. In D. Lester (Ed.), *Current concepts of suicide* (pp. 159-167). Philadelphia: Charles Press.

Lester, D. (1988). *Suicide from a psychological perspective.* Springfield, IL: Charles C. Thomas.

Lester, D. (1994). Reflections on the statistical rarity of suicide. *Crisis, 15,* 187–188.

Lester, D. (1998). Preventing suicide by restricting access to methods for suicide. *Archives of Suicide Research, 4,* 7–24.

Linehan, M. M., Goodstein, J. L., Nielson, S. L., & Chiles, J. A. (1983). Reasons for staying alive when you are thinking of killing yourself: The reasons for living inventory. *Journal of Consulting and Clinical Psychology, 51,* 276–286.

Lorenz, E. (1979, February). *Predictability: Does the flap of a butterfly's wings in Brazil set off a tornado in Texas?* Paper presented at the American Association for the Advancement of Science, Washington, DC.

Lykken, D. T. (1991). What's wrong with psychology anyway? In D. Cicchetti & W. M. Grove (Eds.), *Thinking clearly about psychology. Vol. 1: Matters of public interest* (pp. 3–39). Minneapolis, MN: University of Minnesota Press.

Lynd, R. S. (1939). *Knowledge for what?: The place of social science in American culture.* Princeton, NJ: Princeton University Press.

Mahoney, M. J. (1991). *Human change processes: The scientific foundations of psychotherapy.* New York: Basic Books.

Mahoney, M. J., & Moes, A. J. (1997). Complexity and psychotherapy: Promising dialogues and practical issues. In F. Masterpasqua & P. A. Perna (Eds.), *The psychological meaning of chaos: Translating theory into practice* (pp. 199–224). Washington, DC: American Psychological Association.

Mann, J. J., & Arango, V. (1999). The neurobiology of suicidal behavior. In D. G. Jacobs (Ed.), *The Harvard Medical School guide to suicide assessment & intervention.* San Francisco: Jossey-Bass.

Maris, R., Berman, A., Maltsberger, J., & Yufit, R. (Eds.). (1992). *Assessment and prediction of suicide.* New York: Guilford.

Masterpasqua, F. & Perna, P. A. (1997). *The psychological meaning of chaos: Translating theory into practice.* Washington, DC: American Psychological Association.

Merian, J. (1763). Sur la crainte de la mort, sur le mepris de la mort, sur le suicide, memorie [About the fear of death, about contempt for death, about suicide, recollection]. In Historie de l'Academie Royales des Sciences et Belles-Lettres de Berlin (Vol. 19).

Mireault, M., & deMan, A. F. (1996). Suicidal ideation among the elderly: Personal variables, stress and social support. *Social Behavior and Personality, 24,* 385–392.

Mishara, B. L. (1996). A dynamic developmental model of suicide. *Human Development, 39,* 181–194.

Murray, H. A. (1938). *Explorations in personality.* New York: Oxford University Press.

Neimeyer, R. A. (1995). An invitation to constructivist psychotherapies. In R. A. Neimeyer & M. J. Mahoney (Eds.), *Constructivism in psychotherapy* (pp. 1–8). Washington, DC: American Psychological Association.

Neimeyer, R. A., & Mahoney, M. J. (Eds.). (1995). *Constructivism in psychotherapy.* Washington, DC: American Psychological Association.

Nietzsche, F. (1966). *Beyond good and evil* (W. Kaufmann, Trans.). New York: Vintage. (Original work published 1886)

Patton, M. Q. (1990). *Qualitative evaluation and research methods* (2nd ed.). Newbury Park, CA: Sage.

Pedhazur, E. J., & Schmelkin, L. P. (1991). *Measurement, design, and analysis: An integrated approach.* Hillsdale, NJ: Lawrence Erlbaum Associates.

Platt, S. (1993). The social transmission of parasuicide: Is there a modeling effect? *Crisis, 14,* 23–31.

Resnik, H. L. P., & Hathorne, B. C. (Eds.), (1973). *Suicide prevention in the 70's.* DHEW Publication No. HSM 72-9054). Report of the results of a conference held in Phoenix in January, 1970. Washington, DC: U.S. Government Printing Office.

Rogers, J. R. (in press). Theoretical grounding: The "missing link" in suicide research. *Journal of Counseling and Development.*

Rogers, J. R. (1992). Suicide and alcohol: Conceptualizing the relationship from a cognitive-social paradigm. *Journal of Counseling and Development, 70,* 540–543.

Rogers, J. R. (1995). Chaos and suicide: The myth of linear causality. In D. Lester (Ed.), *Suicide '95: Proceedings of the 28th Annual Conference of the American Association of Suicidology* (pp. 139–140). Washington, DC: American Association of Suicidology.

Rogers, J. R. (1996). Assessing right to die attitudes: A conceptually guided measurement model. *Journal of Social Issues, 52,* 63–84.

Rogers, J. R., Alexander, R. A., & Subich, L. M. (1994). Development and psychometric analysis of the suicide assessment checklist. *Journal of Mental Health Counseling, 16,* 352–368.

Rogers, J. R., & Britton, P. J. (1994). AIDS and rational suicide: A counseling psychology perspective or a slide on the slippery slope. *The Counseling Psychologist, 22,* 171–178.

Rogers, J. R., & Carney, J. V. (1994). Theoretical and methodological considerations in assessing the "modeling effect" in parasuicidal behavior: A Comment on Platt (1993). *Crisis, 15,* 83–89.

Rogers, J. R., & McGuirk, H. A. (1998). Self-organized criticality and suicidal behavior. In J. McIntosh (Ed.), *Suicide 97: Proceedings of the 30th Annual Conference of the American Association of Suicidology* (pp 139–140). Washington, DC: American Association of Suicidology.

Sartre, J. P. (1957). *Existentialism and human emotions.* (B. Frechtman, Trans.). New York: Philosophical Library. (Original work published 1947)

Shneidman, E. S. (1987). A psychological approach to suicide. In G. R. Van den Bos & B. K. Bryant (Eds.), *Cataclysms, crises, and catastrophes: Psychology in action* (pp. 151–183). Washington, DC: American Psychological Association.

Steele, C. M., & Josephs, R. A. (1990). Alcohol myopia: Its prized and dangerous effects. *The American Psychologist, 45,* 921–933.

Stewart, I. N., & Peregoy, P. L. (1983). Catastrophe theory modeling in psychology. *Psychological Bulletin, 94,* 336–362.

Stillion, J. M., & McDowell, E. E. (1996). *Suicide across the life span: Premature exists.* Washington, DC: Taylor & Francis.

Werth, J. L. (1992). Rational suicide and AIDS. *The Counseling Psychologist, 20,* 645–659.

Werth, J. L. (1996). *Rational suicide?: Implications for mental health professionals.* Washington, DC: Taylor & Francis.

Westefeld, J., Cardin, D., & Deaton, W. (1992). Development of the College Student Reasons for Living Infentory. *Suicide and Life-Threatening Behavior, 22,* 442–452.

Yalom, I. D. (1980). *Existential psychotherapy.* New York: Basic Books.

CHAPTER 4

H. M. van Praag

Suicide and Aggression: Are They Biologically Two Sides of the Same Coin

Suicide and aggression are interrelated. Approximately 30% of violent individuals have a history of self-destructive behavior and 10–20% of suicidal persons have a history of violence (Plutchik & van Praag, 1990). Murder followed by suicide is no rarity, though the published figures vary widely in different countries and regions. Conversely, it has been repeatedly demonstrated that individuals who have attempted or completed suicide have been previously engaged in antisocial (violent) behaviors more frequently than control groups.

Plutchik and van Praag (1990) have proposed a theoretical model to explain the connection between suicide and violence. In this model a distinction is made between aggressive impulses and aggressive behavior. Aggressive impulses can be triggered by emotions such as anxiety, anguish, and anger; by events that are interpreted as threats or challenges; by losses of various kinds (e.g., loved ones, property, prestige, and territory); and by the urge to expand one's territory or sphere of influence.

Whether the aggressive impulse will be expressed as overt behavior is dependent on the presence of a large number of forces that may augment or weaken the strength of the aggressive impulse. A number of those so-called amplifiers and attenuators were ascertained, and are presented in Figure 1. They are called collectively Stage I Countervailing Forces, and together they determine whether the aggressive impulse will generate overt aggressive behavior.

A second set of variables determines the direction of the aggressive behavior once it is kindled—whether it will be directed towards oneself or towards others. Those variables are called Stage II Countervailing Forces, and those we identified are also presented in Figure 1.

As already mentioned, aggressive impulses can be triggered by a large variety

45

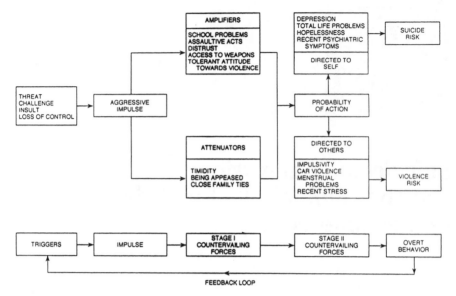

FIGURE 1. Two-stage model of suicide and violence (Plutchik and Van Praag, 1995)

of events and conditions. The impulse itself, however, is generated by particular neuronal alterations in the brain. If the aggression-regulating circuitry is basically unstable, even weak triggers might generate robust aggressive impulses.

In this model the underlying impulses leading to violent and suicidal behavior and their biological generators are postulated to be the same. The data so far are in accordance with this assumption and justify the decision to discuss the topic of the biological determinants of suicidal and aggressive behavior in one chapter.

We know of several (although still too few) neuronal systems involved in aggression regulation. I will restrict myself to the serotonin (5-hydroxytryptamine or 5-HT) system, because this is the one best studied, and because the available data permit therapeutic hypotheses that have already stimulated psychopharmacological research.

☐ Serotonin Metabolism And Affective State

CSF 5-HIAA

In 1970 we reported evidence suggesting reduced metabolism of 5-HT in a subgroup of depressed patients, namely lowered baseline and postprobenecid concentrations of the main metabolite of 5-HT, i.e., 5-hydroxyindoleacetic acid (5-HIAA) in cerebrospinal fluid (CSF) (van Praag, Korf, & Puite, 1970). CSF 5-HIAA and intracerebral 5-HIAA concentration are highly intercorrelated, both in experimental animals and in humans (Mignot et al., 1985; Stanley, Traskman, & Dorovine, 1985). Thus CSF 5-HIAA is a (crude) indicator of 5-HT breakdown in the brain.

Low CSF 5-HIAA appeared not to be correlated with a particular subtype of depression, e.g., bipolar or unipolar depression, nor with a particular depressive syndrome, e.g., the syndrome of vital (endogenous, melancholic) depression. Low CSF 5-HIAA was demonstrated to be, what we have called functionally specific—this variable was shown to be linked with components of the depressive syndrome that may or may not be prominently present in a particular depressive state. These 5-HT linked features were: Disturbances in anxiety regulation and in aggression regulation (Asberg, Traskman, & Thoren, 1976, 1984; van Praag, 1982, 1998; van Praag et al., 1987, 1990). Anxiety level and CSF 5-HIAA concentration were negatively correlated. Moreover, in the subgroup of depressives with low CSF 5-HIAA, suicide attempts were significantly more likely to occur than in depressives with normal or high CSF 5-HIAA levels. Low CSF 5-HIAA depressives, in addition, showed more hostility towards others than their counterparts without such 5-HT deviations.

Interestingly these correlations were not restricted to depression but demonstrated to be independent of psychiatric diagnosis. Anxiety correlated negatively with CSF 5-HIAA in several anxiety disorders. Low CSF 5-HIAA was found in suicidal subjects with schizophrenia (van Praag, 1983) as well as in a variety of personality disorders with heightened aggressivity such as antisocial personality disorder and borderline personality disorder (Traskman, Asberg, & Bertilsson, & Sjostrand, 1981) and in individuals with a life history of assaultive behavior (Brown, Goodwin, Ballenger, Goyer, & Major, 1979; Cocarro, 1992; Cocarro, et al., 1992). The latter correlations were particularly strong in impulsive aggression, i.e., aggression that is not premeditated but explodes impulsively (Linnoila et al., 1983).

Low CSF 5-HIAA, moreover, holds predictive information. First, Nordstrom et al. (1994) reported that suicidal patients with low CSF 5-HIAA on admission show an increased risk of repeat suicides in the year to follow. Second, newborns with a family history of antisocial behavior showed lower CSF 5-HIAA levels than newborns without such background (Constantino, Morris, & Murphy, 1997). Low CSF 5-HIAA newborns, moreover, had higher externalizing behavior scores at 30 months (Clarke, Murphy, & Constantino, 1991). The externalizing behavior score incorporates elements of aggressive preschool behavior and predicts aggressive behavior later in life.

These findings were mirrored in several monkey species (Highley et al., 1992; Mehlmann et al., 1994). Animals with lowered CSF 5-HIAA concentration show several signs of inflammable temper and increased risk-taking. They express more severe aggression and less affiliation behavior than animals with normal CSF 5-HIAA. They die prematurely, often as a result of wounds sustained in fights, and they are more involved in high-risk behaviors, such as long leaps in the forest and early emigration from natal groups. Pharmacological interventions, moreover, revealed that a global decrease in serotonergic functioning increases aggressive responding, while increasing serotonergic activity attenuates those responses.

In monkeys, CSF 5-HIAA is a quite stable variable with an inherited component (Highley et al., 1993). In depressed individuals, it was also shown to be a trait-related factor. Levels stay low after remission of the depression (van Praag, Plutchik, & Conte, 1986). For that reason, we have hypothesized that low CSF 5-HIAA is a vulnerability factor, increasing the risk of suicidal or aggressive behavior in situations unbearable or aversive to the individual.

Tryptophan Depletion

The findings discussed above suggest a connection between decreased 5-HT metabolism and disinhibition of (auto)aggressive impulses. The outcome of tryptophan depletion studies are in accordance with this hypothesis. 5-HT is a product of the essential aminoacid tryptophan. If a potion devoid of tryptophan and containing high concentrations of aminoacids competing with tryptophan for the same transport mechanism into the brain (the so-called competing aminoacids) is administered to normal test persons, the plasma tryptophan concentration is reduced by approximately 80% or more (Delgado et al., 1991; Klaassen et al., 1999a, Riedel, Klassen, Deutz, Van Someren, & van Praag, 1999; Young, Smith, Pihl, & Ervin, 1985). As a consequence tryptophan availability in the brain subsides, and 5-HT synthesis follows suit.

Tryptophan depletion leads to various disturbances in affective regulation in normal individuals. Mood lowering sets in, particularly in those with a family history of depression (Benkelfat, Ellenbogen, Dean, Palmour, & Young, 1994; Klaassen, et al., 1999a, 1999b). Anxiety and tension increase, and the triggering level for aggression drops, with increased irritability and hostility as a consequence. Aggression disturbances occur, particularly in those individuals in whom aggression levels were high to begin with (Cleare & Bond, 1995; Moeller et al., 1996; Smith, Pihl, Young, & Ervin, 1986).

Animals fed a tryptophan-free diet became increasingly aggressive (Gibbons, Barr, Bridger, & Liebowitz, 1979). Blocking 5-HT synthesis with a inhibitor of tryptophan hydroxylase, the enzyme involved in the first step of 5-HT synthesis, leads to increased aggressiveness and, additionally, to disturbances in controlling impulses other than aggression. Rodents for instance, increase, the frequency of performing a (rewarding) response despite the threat of punishment for responding.

In summary, disturbances in 5-HT metabolism, originally discovered in a subgroup of depressed patients appear to be diagnostically nonspecific and correlated with anxiety, suicidality, and violence across diagnoses.

The clustering of 5-HT disturbances in states of increased aggression, suicidality, and anxiety is not surprising if one takes into account that 1) in humans those affective states are highly intercorrelated across diagnoses (Apter et al., 1990) and 2) both in animals and humans serotonergic circuits play an important role in the regulation of both anxiety and aggression (Cologer-Clifford, Simon, Lu, & Smoluk, 1997; Saudou et al., 1994).

☐ Serotonin Receptor Function And Affective State

In a subgroup of depressed patients, not only was 5-HT metabolism shown to be disturbed, but also 5-HT receptor function was disturbed. The receptor disturbances were demonstrated with challenge tests. Initially, indirect 5-HT agonists were used, acting presynaptically and thus activating the 5-HT system as a whole. Fenfluramine, a 5-HT releaser and reuptake inhibitor, is a good example. Hormonal responses to this substance were repeatedly shown to be blunted in a subgroup of depressives, indicating downregulation of (perhaps only parts of) the 5-HT receptor system (Cowen & Wood, 1991; Deakin, Pennell, Upadhyaya, & Lofthouse, 1990).

The 5-HT system operates through at least 15 different, probably function-specific, receptors. Which of the 5-HT receptor subtypes are downregulated? The 5-HT_{1a} and 5-HT_{1d} receptors are probably among them. This was concluded from blunted hormonal responses to challenges with 5-HT_{1a} receptor agonists such as ipsapirone (Lesch et al., 1990) and the 5-HT_{1d} agonist sumatriptan (Murray, Sherwood, & O'Keane, 1998). The response to m-chlorophenylpiperazine (MCPP)—a relatively selective 5-HT_{2c} receptor agonist—in depression was not different from that in a control group (Kahn, Wetzler, Asnis, Papolos, & Van Praag, 1990). Other 5-HT receptor subtypes have not yet been studied in humans because of a lack of suitable challengers.

Are the 5-HT receptor dysfunctions depression-linked or, like the disturbances in 5-HT metabolism, associated with disturbed anxiety and aggression regulation, irrespective of psychiatric diagnosis? Although the jury is still out on this issue, the available evidence suggests the latter. A blunted prolactine response after a fenfluramine challenge has been recorded in antisocial personality disorders, other personality disorders with increased aggression ratings, and in subjects with a lifetime history of aggression, assaultiveness and impulsivity (particularly in men) (Moss, Yaon, & Panzak, 1990; O'Keane et al., 1992). Remarkably, even in normal individuals, Manuck et al. (1998) found a negative correlation between the prolactine/ fenfluramine response and degree of aggressiveness. Challenge tests with 5-HT_{1a} agonists revealed hyporesponsivity of this receptor subtype in personality disordered subjects with high aggression ratings (Cocarro, Gabriel, & Siever, 1990; Moeller et al., 1998).

The results with the 5-HT_{2c} agonist are less clear cut. Hormonal responses are positively correlated with anxiety, across diagnoses (Kahn, Westenberg, & Moore, 1995). The responsivity of that receptor in states of increased aggression, however, is uncertain. Some investigators have found a blunted response (Moss, Yaon, & Panzak, 1990), while others have been unable to confirm these data (Wetzler, Kahn, Asnis, Korn, & van Praag, 1991). The relation of 5-HT receptor responsivity and suicide has not been studied.

Like lowered CSF 5-HIAA, the receptor changes are probably trait-related. This conclusion is derived from studies in depressives in whom it was shown that a blunted prolactine/fenfluramine response, recorded in the depressive episode, persisted after remission (Florey, Mann, Manuck, & Muldood, 1998).

Correlations between 5-HT receptor responsivity and aggression were also found in monkeys. Animals with blunted prolactine response to fenfluramine showed a high frequency of overt aggression and less affiliative behavior as compared with animals with normal responses (Botchin, Kaplan, Manuck, & Mann, 1993). Direct evidence for the involvement of specific 5-HT receptors in aggression regulation is the observation that transgenic mice lacking the 5-HT_{1b} receptor are more aggressive than wild-type mice (Saudou et al., 1994).

In summary, associations have been found between aggressivity and diminished sensitivity of 5-HT receptors, especially the 5-HT_{1a} and the 5-HT_{1d} receptors. This correlation is found across diagnoses. 5-HT receptor function was found to be subnormal in depression, but the relation of this variable to suicidal behavior per se has not been studied.

☐ What Could Be the Origin of the 5-HT Disturbances Associated with Anxiety and (Auto)Aggressive Behavior?

The 5-HT disturbances discussed above could be mainly genetically determined or acquired during life.

Examples of environmental factors are conditions of rearing and social stress. Maternal offspring of macaque monkeys, for instance, reared by unrelated mothers, demonstrated lowered 5-HT concentration in the prefrontal cortex, lowered CSF 5-HIAA concentration and an increased risk of engaging in agonistic behavior (Fontenot et al., 1995; Kraemer, Ebert, Schmidt, & McKinney, 1989). Peters et al. (1986) reported that the offspring of mothers that had been subjected to low-level stressors during pregnancy showed decreased 5-HT synthesis and decreased number of 5-HT receptors in the hippocampus.

In humans several prenatal and perinatal complications show a relationship with antisocial behavior in later life (Kandel, Brennan, Mednick, Michelson, 1989). The first group includes exposure to maternal smoking, a factor which has been associated with later crime in male offspring (Brennan, Grekin, & Mednick, 1999). Emotionally depriving and damaging conditions early in life increase the risk of maladaptive behaviors in adulthood, including antisocial behavior. The impact of these harmful influences on the development of the 5-HT system, however, is not known.

Genetic factors, probably, have a share in the ultimate condition of the central serotonergic system. Pointing in that direction is the interesting finding of Constantino, Morris, and Murphy (1997) that infants of parents with antisocial personality disorder had lower CSF 5-HIAA than infants with negative family histories of antisocial personality disorder. Furthermore, impulsive personality traits were found to be more prevalent in the first-degree relatives of patients with blunted prolactine response to fenfluramine than among relatives of patients with normal responses (Cocarro, Silverman, Klar, Horvath, & Siever, 1994).

Polymorphisms in the gene coding for the 5-HT transporter were associated with self-report measures of anxiety-related traits (Lesch et al., 1996; Loesch & Mossner, 1998), and polymorphism of the tryptophan hydroxylase gene with suicidal behavior in depressed patients (Nielsen et al., 1998). Finally, Brunner et al. (1993) reported a large family in which several males showed borderline mental retardation and outbursts of impulsive aggression. This syndrome was associated with a selective deficiency of the monoamine oxidase-A (MAO-A) enzyme. In the affected males, a point mutation was identified in the 8th exon of the MAO-A gene on the X-chromosome. Samochowiec et al. (1999) found evidence that a 30-bp repeat polymorphism in the promotor region of the x-chromosomal gene confers increased susceptibility to antisocial behavior. Furthermore, transgenic (male) mice lacking the MAO-A gene are more aggressive than wild-type mice (Cases et al., 1995). The specific link between aggressive behavior and the MAO-A gene, however, has been questioned by Tuinier, Verhoeven, Scherders, Fekkes, and Pepplinkhuizen (1995).

☐ Stress/Serotonergic Dysfunction/ (Auto)Aggressive Behavior

While reviewing the data so far, I reach the conclusion that an association seems to exist between on the one hand, 5-HT dysfunctions generated by genetic and/or acquired factors, and on the other hand, disturbances in anxiety and aggression regulation.

In this connection I furthermore call attention to the following facts. First, suicidal behavior as well as acts of violence are closely connected with stressful life events and the presence of stressful events in the weeks and months preceding the deed (Roy, 1986; Paykel, Prusoff, & Meyers, 1975). Second, suicidal behavior, aggression and anxiety are strongly intertwined (Apter, Plutchik, & van Praag, 1993). We found, moreover, that in the one to three months before a suicide attempt is committed, anxiety is prominent, often assuming panic proportions (Apter, Plutchik, & van Praag, 1993; Apter et al., 1991; van Praag, Plutchik, & Conte, 1986). Third, suicide is closely linked to depression, a mood state that is a major precursor of suicide (Silver, Bohnert, Beck, & Marcus, 1971).

The question can now been raised whether one can conceive of a biological link between 5-HT related disturbances in anxiety and aggression regulation and stress-induced furtherance of anxiety and (self-) destructiveness. One indeed can, and I submit, hypothetically, that disinhibition of the hypothalamic-pituitary-adreno-cortical axis (HPA axis) can be considered to be such a bridge.

☐ Disinhibition of the HPA Axis as a Bridge Between Serotonergic Malfunctions and Increased Propensity to Act Out (Auto-)Aggressively

HPA Axis, Depression, and Stress

The HPA axis is activated in a subgroup of depressed patients (Johnson, Kamilaris, Chrousos, & Gold, 1992). This is evident from a number of observations such as: increased concentration of corticotropin releasing hormone (CRH) in cerebrospinal fluid and the nucleus paraventricularis; a blunted response of adrenocorticotropin (ACTH) after a CRH challenge, possibly as a consequence of downregulated CRH receptors on the pituitary gland, following increased concentrations of circulating cortisol; decreased suppression of ACTH and cortisol after dexamethasone administration and, finally, an increased cortisol secretion at all time-points during the 24-hour cycle and disappearance of the circadian rhythm (Sachar, et al., 1973).

Stress is likewise a activator of the HPA axis. Depression is often preceded by stressful life events and can occur concurrently with personality disorders that increase stressor sensitivity (Honig & van Praag, 1997). We do not know for sure whether disinhibition of the HPA axis in a subgroup of depressed patients is a phenomenon linked to this subgroup per se, or is a phenomenon caused primarily by stress preceding the depression and sustained by the presence of depression. Both viewpoints are viable.

In depression, an acquired or genetically determined defect of corticosteroid-receptor gene expression is conceivable (Barden, Reul, & Holsboer, 1995; Berrettini et al., 1994; Dinan, 1994; Murphy, Dhar, Missagh Ghadirian, Chouinard, & Keller, 1991). It could lead to marginal glucocorticoid feedback inhibition in normal conditions and early failure of this mechanism under stressful conditions. Affected individuals would be particularly vulnerable to the stress syndrome and possibly to depression.

In support of this hypothesis, Barden, Reul, and Holsboer (1995) found that several types of antidepressants increase corticosteroid receptor gene expression; increase the capacity of brain tissue to bind corticosteroids; and, finally, increase steroid receptor immunoreactivity in the brain. In this way feedback inhibition of HPA axis activity by cortisol will be increased. The time course of the action of antidepressants on corticosteroid receptor concentration follows that of clinical improvement (Reul, Stec, Soder, & Holsboer, 1993; Reul et al., 1994). On these grounds it has been suggested that the therapeutic effect of antidepressants is related to normalization of HPA-axis activity (Barden, Reul, & Holsboer, 1995).

On the other hand one has to acknowledge that activation of the HPA axis is the core endocrine response to stress, irrespective of the development of depression. Correlations have been found between cortisol plasma levels and anxious anticipation (Ceulemans, Westerberg, & van Praag, 1985) and negative affect (Buchanan, al'Absi, & Lovallo, 1999). Dexamethasone nonsuppression has been found in psychiatric diagnoses, apart from depression (Coppen et al., 1983) and the reduced ACTH response to CRH is likewise diagnostically nonspecific—it has been reported in panic disorder and anorexia nervosa as well (Checkley, 1992). Moreover, in anxious depressives the blunting of the CRH/ACTH response is more pronounced than in nonanxious depressives (Meller et al., 1995).

In conclusion, in a subgroup of depression the HPA axis is activated, leading to an overproduction of cortisol. It is unknown whether this phenomenon is specific for a particular depression type or part of the stress syndrome preceding the depression and subsequently sustained by the depression.

Serotonin/HPA Axis Interaction

Increased plasma concentrations of cortisol have a pronounced effect on the central serotonergic system, perhaps via at least two mechanisms.

First, sustained stress or sustained hypercortisolaemia reduces 5-HT metabolism (Weiss et al., 1981), possibly via activation of the enzyme tryptophan pyrrolase and the shunting of large amounts of tryptophan to the kinurenine pathway, leaving insufficient amounts of tryptophan for the synthesis of 5-HT (Maes et al., 1990).

A second mechanism is the reduced expression of 5-HT1a receptors, caused by excess cortisol (Meijer & De Kloet, 1994). Reduced numbers or reduced responsivity of the $5-HT_{1a}$ receptor system, will lead secondarily to hyperactivity of the $5-HT_{2c}$ system, since the two systems are reciprocally related (Krebs-Thomson & Geyer, 1998; Sanchez, 1996). In accordance with the animal data, in humans pretreatment with hydrocortisone leads to blunting of the hormonal responses to intravenous infusion of l-tryptophan (Porter, Hamisch, Allister-Williams, Lunn, & Young, 1998), an intervention that leads to increased production and release of 5-HT in the brain.

Diminished activity in $5-HT_{1a}$ circuits and increased activity in the $5-HT_{2c}$ system will cause destabilization of anxiety and aggression regulation (van Praag, 1996) and thus lead to increased risk of (auto) aggressive behavior.

☐ Biological Vulnerability for (Auto-)Aggressive Behavior

Human existence is a journey along events, some pleasurable, some traumatic. Most individuals are capable of coping with the latter; some however decompensate, manifesting symptoms of depression, and anxiety, or suicidal behavior or acting out in a violent way.

Obviously not everyone resorts to (auto-)aggressive acts if pressures mount. Hence, one has to postulate a vulnerability factor. Generally, increased propensity to resort to (auto-)aggression is linked to personality make-up, to traits that hamper adequate mobilization of defense mechanisms and to inadequate self-restraint (Nordstrom, Schalling, & Asberg, 1995). Such vulnerabilities, however, can also be conceived of in biological terms. To provide the biological vulnerability hypothesis with a kernel of credibility one has thus to argue plausibly that the biological factors suggested to be involved, i.e., 5-HT disturbances and hyperresponsivity of the HPA axis, are chronically present and can be regarded as trait factors.

This now has indeed been demonstrated. First of all, low CSF 5-HIAA persists after remission of the depression (van Praag, 1988). Animal experiments have revealed that CSF 5-HIAA is a strongly genetically determined and stable variable (Higly et al., 1993; Oxenstierna et al., 1986). Likewise the prolactine response to fenfluramine does not normalize after remission in patients that showed a blunted response while depressed (Florey, Mann, Manuck, & Muldoon, 1998). Thus, both the disturbances in 5-HF metabolism and those in 5-HT receptor function can be characterized as trait-factors.

Initially it was thought that signs of HPA axis overactivity in a subgroup of depressives receded after remission of the depression. Thus it was concluded that HPA axis disinhibition is a state-related factor. Recent studies however have shed a different light on this subject. First of all, it was demonstrated that HPA axis overactivity does not disappear completely. This was demonstrated with the Dexamethasone/CRH test, a refined variant of the dexamethasone suppression test (Holsboer-Trachsler, Stohler, & Hatzinger, 1991; Von Bardeleben & Holsboer, 1991). Moreover Modell et al. (1998) found, in healthy people with a high genetic load for affective disorders, an abnormal Dexamethasone/CRH test. The cortisol response fell between that of a control group and a group of depressed patients. The outcome of the Dexamethasone/CRH test remained moreover remarkably stable over time. This suggests that (mild) HPA axis hyperactivity is a trait-related factor.

☐ Biological Susceptibility to (Auto-)Aggression And Its Therapeutic Consequences

Based on the data discussed above, I hypothesize that in a subgroup of the normal population the HPA axis is habitually slightly over-responsive, and/or certain components of the 5-HT system, particularly those communicating via $5-HT_{1a}$, $5-HT_{1d}$ and $5-HT_2$ receptors, are marginally hyporesponsive. A combination of these two hypotheses is possible. The defects in the 5-HT system might be caused by chronic subclinical cortisol overproduction (Figure 2).

In times of stress, the HPA system is activated, ultimately leading to excessive release of cortisol. The cortisol oversupply causes decline of 5-HT synthesis, downregulation of the $5-HT_{1a}$, and upregulation of the $5-HT_{2c}$ receptor system. Its

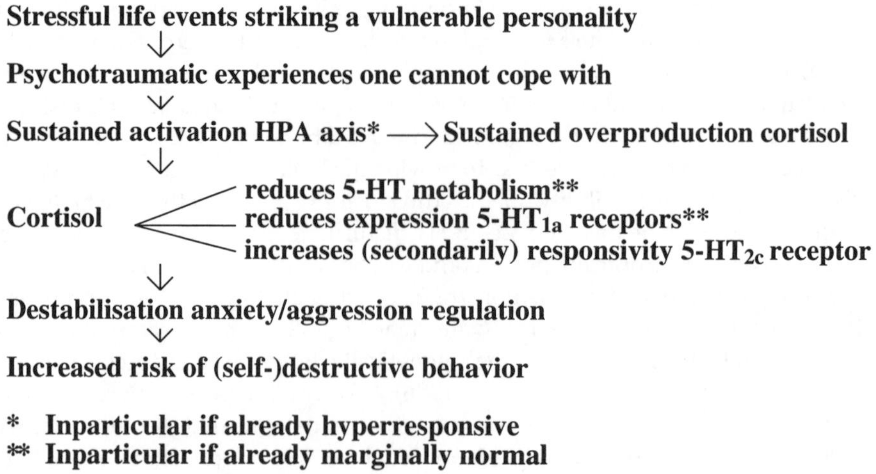

Stressful life events striking a vulnerable personality
↓
Psychotraumatic experiences one cannot cope with
∨
Sustained activation HPA axis* ⟶ Sustained overproduction cortisol
↓
Cortisol ⟨ reduces 5-HT metabolism**
        reduces expression $5-HT_{1a}$ receptors**
        increases (secondarily) responsivity $5-HT_{2c}$ receptor
↓
Destabilisation anxiety/aggression regulation
∨
Increased risk of (self-)destructive behavior

*   Inparticular if already hyperresponsive
** Inparticular if already marginally normal

FIGURE 2. Stressful life events / Biological interface / Affective pathology.

impact on the 5-HT_{1d} receptor is not known. Those in whom the 5-HT system already functions marginally are particularly prone to this effect.

Due to the disturbances in 5-HT_{1a} and 5-HT_2 receptor-regulated circuits, the anxiety level increases and aggressive impulses are fanned. Both factors increase the likelihood of aggressive behavior. As discussed above, the chance that aggressive impulses will give rise to overt aggressive behavior, and whether the aggressive behaviors will be self-directed or directed towards others is dependent on a number of adventitious factors (Figure 1).

Therapeutically this hypothesis implies that rational biological suicide and aggression prevention is a conceivable concept. One can predict such a result from compounds that antagonize the actions of CRH or cortisol, or both, and from 5-HT agonists, particularly those that activate the postsynaptic 5-HT_{1a} receptor system.

CRH and cortisol antagonists are being studied for their antidepressant potential, and the first reports seem promising (Arana et al., 1995; O'Dwyer, Ligtman, Masks, & Checkley, 1995; Missagh Ghadirian et al., 1995; Thakore & Dinan, 1995; Wolkowitiz et al., 1993). However, studies of their impact on (auto-)aggressive behavior per se are not yet available.

There is some emerging evidence that 5-HT agonists decrease the strength of suicidal impulses. Montgomery, Dunner, & Dunbar (1995) found that the selective serotonin reuptake inhibitor (SSRI) paroxetine reduces suicidal thoughts more strongly than the reference antidepressants (TCAs) and placebo, while Verkes et al. (1998) reported that paroxetine showed significant efficacy in patients with recurrent suicidal behavior but no major depression. In any case, the report that fluoxetine increases the risk of suicide (Teicher, Glod, & Cole, 1990) has not been confirmed (Leon et al., 1999).

Several studies in humans reported an ameliorating effect of SSRIs on aggressive behavior in borderline and other personality disorders (histrionic, antisocial, and narcissistic) (Coccaro & Kavoussi, 1997; Salzman, et al., 1995) while Knutson et al. (1998) found that paroxetine reduced hostility and negative affect and improved affiliative behavior in normal volunteers.

In animals abundant evidence exists that activating 5-HT_{1a} and 5-HT_{1b} (comparable to the 5-HT_{1d} receptor in humans) receptors leads to reduction of certain forms of aggressive behavior (Cologer-Clifford, Simon, Lu, Smoluk, 1997; Miczek, Hussain, & Faccidomo, 1998).

Until recently no selective, full postsynaptically acting 5-HT_{1a} agonist was available. The buspirone group of compounds act as partial 5-HT_{1a} receptor agonists in the hippocampus, but as 5-HT_{1a} receptor antagonists in the frontal cortex. Borsini et al. (1998) recently developed a compound, flibanserin, that does act as a full agonist of 5-HT_{1a} receptors, both in the hypothalamus and the frontal cortex. Based on the propounded hypothesis, I predict this substance may exert a pronounced anti (auto-)aggressive effect.

A caveat is warranted here. Increased biological specificity of a psychopharmacological compound will probably lead to increased psychopathological specificity. In other words, to study the psychopathological effects of a biologically highly specific compound in, for instance, a group of depressives without further phenomenological or biological specification, is bound to weaken possible therapeutic signals. The study of drugs with high biological specificity requires precise syndromal definition of the study group, dissection of the syndrome into its component parts, i.e., the psychological dysfunctions (van Praag, 1992, 1997) and the introduction of biological diagnostic criteria if available (van Praag, 1995, 1992, 1997). In this case I predict that flibanserin will exert an antisuicidal/anti-aggressive effect in depressed or personality disordered individuals with high anxiety and aggression ratings and with signs of disturbed serotonergic functioning, i.e., lowering of CSF 5-HIAA and blunted hormonal responses to flibanserin and, in addition, signs of HPA axis overactivity (on the Dexamethasone/CRH test).

☐ Other Biological Variables Supposedly Involved in Aggression Regulation and Linked to the 5-HT System

Vasopressin

While 5-HT inhibits aggressive impulses, other substances act as aggression facilitators. Examples are catecholamines, androgens, and arginine vasopressin (AVP). AVP and 5-HT probably have strong associations (Ferris, 1996).

AVP injected in the hypothalamus induces aggressive displays (Delville, Mansour, & Ferris, 1996), while AVP antagonists block such behaviors (Ferris & Potegal, 1988). AVP and 5-HT have overlapping receptor fields in the hypothalamus (Koolhaas, Van den Brink, Roozendaal, & Boorsma, 1990) and increasing 5-HT in that structure yields a pronounced fall in AVP levels (Delville, Mansour, & Ferris, 1996; Ferris et al., 1996). CSF AVP correlates positively with aggressive behavior in personality disordered individuals (Coccaro, Kavoussi, Hauger, Cooper, & Ferris, 1998). The prolactine response to fenfluramine shows a negative correlation with CSF AVP levels (Cocarro, Kavoussi, Hauger, Cooper, & Ferris, 1998) and finally SSRIs reduce CSF AVP levels (De Bellis, Gold, Geracioti, Listwak, & Kling, 1993).

There are enough reasons, therefore, to study AVP antagonists in states with increased (auto-)aggression.

Cholesterol

Low serum cholesterol is probably related to aggressive behavior. A number of reports have been published that established an increased mortality due to violent encounters in subjects with low cholesterol (Frick et al., 1987; Golomb, 1998). Low cholesterol was shown by some authors to be also associated with increased risk of suicide, both in the general population (Lindberg, Rastam, Gullberg, & Eklund, 1992; Muldoon, Manuck, & Matthews, 1990;) and in psychiatric inpatients (Gollier, Marzuk, Leon, Weiner, & Tardiff, 1996). Low cholesterol moreover has been found in antisocial and intermittent explosive personality disorder

(Virkkunen, 1979, 1983) as well as in borderline personality disorder (New et al., 1999). Pharmacological lowering of serum cholesterol, too, is supposedly related to nonillness-related mortality, i.e., mortality due to suicide or violent encounters (Frick et al., 1987). In animal studies, a correlation has likewise been found among low cholesterol diet and more aggressive and less affiliative behaviors (Kaplan et al., 1994). The animals, moreover, showed lowering of CSF 5-HIAA levels.

It has been suggested that cholesterol influences membrane fluidity and decreases the accessibility of 5-HT to 5-HT receptors, thus the serotonergic "tone" (Engelberg, 1992). Terao et al. (1997) found in healthy volunteers a positive correlation between serum cholesterol and hormonal responses to mCPP, suggesting a positive effect of cholesterol on 5-HT_2 receptor function. Conceivably, this is an effect adaptational to the lowered accessibility of 5-HT receptors.

A different mechanism was suggested by Hawthon, Cowen, Owens, Bond, and Elliott (1993). When cholesterol is increased there is a substantial rise in number of 5-HT receptors in synaptosome membrane preparations from mouse-brain, and vice versa: if membrane cholesterol decreases, then the number of 5-HT receptors drops. Since there is free exchange between cholesterol in membranes and cholesterol in the surrounding medium, low cholesterol may lead to diminution of serotonergic function.

☐ Summary

Disturbances in 5-HT metabolism and in the functioning of the 5-HT_{1a}, 5-HT_{1d}, and 5-HT_{2c} receptor systems have been found in depression. They are not universally present in this disorder, neither are they linked to one of the known subtypes of depression. Rather they are associated with disturbed functioning of particular psychological domains, not only in depression but across diagnoses. The domains in question are most notably anxiety and aggression regulation.

A second biological system that might be disturbed in depression is the HPA axis. Hyperactivity of this system is likewise not restricted to depression, but probably associated with anxious anticipation and negative affect, irrespective of diagnosis. Sustained hyperactivity of the HPA axis, leading to sustained overproduction of cortisol, causes diminution of 5-HT metabolism, downregulation of the 5-HT_{1a} receptor, and upregulation of the 5-HT_{2c} receptor system.

Both the HPA axis hyperresponsivity and the 5-HT disturbances are trait-related phenomena. I hypothesize that, under normal circumstances, these systems manage to function within normal limits, though marginally. Under conditions of stress, however, the HPA axis will be activated more readily than normal, and the 5-HT system will be prone to irregularities. Consequently aggression and anxiety regulating systems get unsettled and the risk of (auto-)aggressive behavior increases.

Thus, subclinical hyperresponsivity of the HPA axis and borderline functioning of the 5-HT system (5-HT metabolism; 5-HT_{1a}, 5-HT_{1d}, and 5-HT_{2c} receptor functioning) can be considered as biological risk factors for suicide and violence.

In individuals with chronic HPA axis or serotonergic disturbances as discussed in this chapter, I predict 1) ACTH and/or cortisol antagonists, and 2) selective, postsynaptic, full 5-HT$_{1a}$ and 5-HT$_{1d}$ agonists, and 3) 5-HT$_{2c}$ receptor antagonists will decrease the risk of (auto-)aggressive behavior under stressful conditions.

Since compounds of this nature are already available or will most probably become available in the near future, this hypothesis can soon be put to the test.

☐ References

Apter, A., van Praag, H. M., Plutchik, R., Sevy, S., Korn, M., & Brown, S. L. (1990). Interrelationships among anxiety, aggression, impulsivity, and mood. *Psychiatry Research, 32,* 191–199.

Apter, A., Plutchik, R., & van Praag, H. M. (1993). Anxiety, impulsivity and depressed mood in relation to suicidal and violent behavior. *Acta Psychiatrica Scandinavica, 87,* 1–5.

Apter, A., Kotler, M., Sevy, S., Plutchik, R., Brown, S. L., Foster, H., Hillbrand, M., Korn, M. L., & van Praag, H. M. (1991). Correlates of risk of suicide in violent and nonviolent psychiatric patients. *American Journal of Psychiatry, 148,* 883–887.

Arana, G. W., Santos, A. B., Laraia, M. T., McLeod-Bryant, S., Beale, M. D., Rarnes, L. J., Roberts, J. M., Dias, J. K., & Molloy, M. (1995). Dexamethasone for the treatment of depression. *American Journal of Psychiatry, 152,* 265–267.

Asberg, M., Traskman, L., & Thoren, P. (1976). 5-HIAA in the cerebrospinal fluid. *Archives of General Psychiatry, 33,* 1193–1197.

Barden, N., Reul, J. M. H. M., & Holsboer, F. (1995). Do antidepressants stabilize mood though actions on the hypothalamic-pituitary-adrenocortical system? *Trends in Neuroscience, 18,* 6–11.

Benkelfat, C., Ellenbogen, M. A., Dean, P., Palmour, R. M., & Young, S. N. (1994). Mood-lowering effect of tryptophan depletion. *Archives of General Psychiatry, 51,* 687–697.

Berrettini, W. H., Ferraro, T. N., Goldin, L. R., Weeks, D. E., Detera-Wadleigh, S., Nurnberger, J. I., & Gershon, E. S. (1994). Chromosome 18 DNA markers and manic-depressive illness. *Proceedings of the National Academy of Sciences, 91,* 5918–5921.

Borsini, F., Brambilla, A., Ceci, A., Cesana, R., Giraldo, E., Ladinsky, H., Monferini, E., & Turconi, M. (1998). Flibanserin. *Drugs of the Future, 23,* 916.

Botchin, M. B., Kaplan, J. R., Manuck, S. B., & Mann, J. J. (1993). Low versus high prolactin responders to fenfluramine challenge. *Neuropsychopharmacology, 9,* 93–99.

Brennan, P. A., Grekin, E. R., & Mednick, S. A. (1999a). Maternal smoking during pregnancy and adult male criminal behavior. (1999). *Archives of General Psychiatry, 56,* 215–219.

Brown, G. L., Goodwin, F. K., Ballenger, J. C., Goyer, P. F., & Major, L. F. (1979). Aggression in humans correlates with cerebrospinal amine metabolites. *Psychiatry Research, 1,* 131–139.

Brunner, H. G., Nelen, M., Breakefield, X. O., Ropers, H. H., & Van Oost, B. A. (1993). Abnormal behavior associated with a point mutation in the structural gene for monoamine oxidase A. *Science, 262,* 578–580.

Buchanan, T. W., al'Absi, M., & Lovallo, W. R. (1999). Cortisol fluctuates with increases and decreases in negative affect. *Psychoneuroendocrinology, 24,* 227–241.

Cases, O., Seif, I., Grimsby, J., Gaspar, P., Chen, K., Poumin, S., Muller, U., Aguet, M., Babinet, C., & Shih, J. C. (1995). Aggressive behavior and altered amounts of brain serotonin and norepinephrine in mice lacking MAOA. *Science, 268,* 1763–1766.

Ceulemans, D. L. S., Westenberg, H. G. M., & van Praag, H. M. (1985). The effect of stress on dexamethasone suppression test. *Psychiatry Research, 14,* 189–195.

Checkley, S. (1992). Neuroendocrine mechanisms and the precipitation of depression by life events. *British Journal of Psychiatry, 160,* 7–17.

Clarke, R. A., Murphy, D. L., & Constantino, J. N. (1999). Serotonin and externalizing behavior in young children. *Psychiatry Research, 86,* 29–40.

Cleare, A. J., & Bond, A. J. (1995). The effect of tryptophan depletion and enhancement on subjective and behavioural aggression in normal male subjects. *Psychopharmacology, 118,* 72–81.

Coccaro, E. F. (1992). Impulsive aggression and central serotonergic system function in humans. *International Clinical Psychopharmacology, 7,* 3–12.

Coccaro, E. F., Gabriel, S., & Siever, L. J. (1990). Buspirone challenge. *Psychopharmacological Bulletin, 26,* 393–405.

Coccaro, E. F., & Kavoussi, R. J. (1997). Fluoxetine and impulsive aggressive behavior in personality-disordered subjects. *Archives of General Psychiatry, 54,* 1081–1088.

Coccaro, E. F., Kavoussi, R. J., Hauger, R. L., Cooper, T. B., & Ferris, C. F. (1998). Cerebrospinal fluid vasopressin levels. *Archives of General Psychiatry, 55,* 708–714.

Coccaro, E. F., Silverman, J. M., Klar, H. M., Horvath, T. B., & Siever, L. J. (1994). Familial correlates of reduced central serotonergic system function in patients with personality disorders. *Archives of General Psychiatry, 51,* 318–324.

Cologer-Clifford, A., Simon, N. G., Lu, S. F., & Smoluk, S. A. (1997). Serotonin agonist-induced decreases in inter-male aggression are dependent on brain region and receptor subtype. *Pharmacology, Biochemistry & Behavior, 58,* 425–430.

Constantino, J. N., Morris, J. A., & Murphy, D. L. (1997). CSF 5-HIAA and family history of antisocial personality disorder in newborns. *American Journal of Psychiatry, 154,* 1771–1773.

Coppen, A., Abou-Saleh, M., Milln, P., Metcalfe, M., Harwood, J., & Bailey. J. (1983). Dexamethasone suppression test in depression and other psychiatric illness. *British Journal of Psychiatry, 142,* 498–504.

Cowen, P. J., & Wood, D. J. (1991). Biological markers of depression. *Psychological Medicine, 21,* 831–836.

Deakin, J. F., Pennell, I., Upadhyaya, A. J., & Lofthouse, R. (1990). A neuroendocrine study of 5-HT function in depression. *Journal of Psychopharmacology, 101,* 85–92.

De Bellis, M. D., Gold, P. W., Geracioti, T. D., Listwak, S. J., & Kling, M. A. (1993). Association of fluoxetine treatment with reductions in CSF concentrations of corticotropin-releasing hormone and arginine vasopressin in patients with major depression. *American Journal of Psychiatry, 150,* 656–657.

Delgado, P. L., Price, L. H., Miller, H. L., Salomon, R. M., Licinio, J., Krystal, J. H., Heninger, G. R., & Charney, D. S. (1991). Rapid serotonin depletion as a provocative challenge test for patients with major depression. *Psychopharmacological Bulletin, 27,* 321–330.

Delville, Y., Mansour, K. M., & Ferris, C. F. (1966). Serotonin blocks vasopressin-facilitated offensive aggression. *Physiology & Behavior, 59,* 813–816.

Dinan, T. G. (1994). Glucocorticoids and the genesis of depressive illness. *British Journal of Psychiatry, 164,* 365–371.

Engelberg, H. (1992). Low serum cholesterol and suicide. *Lancet, 339,* 727–729.

Ferris, C. F. (1996). Serotonin diminishes aggression by suppressing the activity of the vasopressin system. *Annals of the New York Academy of Sciences, 794,* 98–103.

Ferris, C. F., & Potegal, M. (1988). Vasopressin receptor blockade in the anterior hypothalamus suppresses aggression in hamsters. *Physiology & Behavior, 44,* 235–239.

Florey, J. D., Mann, J. J., Manuck, S. B., & Muldoon, M. F. (1998). Recovery from major depression is not associated with normalization of serotonergic function. *Biological Psychiatry, 43,* 320–326.

Fontenot, M. B., Kaplan, J. R., Manuck, S. B., Arango, V., & Mann, J. J. (1995). Long-term effects of chronic social stress on serotonergic indices in the prefrontal cortex of adult male cynomolgus macaques. *Brain Research, 705,* 105–108.

Frick, M. H., Elo, O., Haapa, K., Heinonen, O. P., Heinsalami, P., Helo, P., Huttunen, J. K., Kaitaniemi, P., Koskinen, P., & Manninen, V. (1987). Helsinki heart study. *New England Journal of Medicine, 317,* 1237–1245.

Gibbons, J. H., Barr, G. A., Bridger, W. H., & Liebowitz, S. F. (1979). Manipulation of dietary tryptophan. *Brain Research, 169,* 139–153.

Gollier, J. A., Marzuk, P. M., Leon, A. C., Weiner, C., & Tardiff, K. (1996). Low serum cholesterol and attempted suicide. *American Journal of Psychiatry, 152,* 419–423.

Golomb, B. A. (1998). Cholesterol and violence. *Annals of Internal Medicine, 128,* 478–487.

Hawthon, K., Cowen, P., Owens, D., Bond, A., & Elliott, M. (1993). Low serum cholesterol and suicide. *British Journal of Psychiatry, 162,* 818–825.

Highley, J. D., Mehlmann, P., Taub, D., Higley, S. B., Vickers, J. H., Suomi, S. J., & Linnoila, M. (1992). Cerebrospinal fluid monoamine and adrenal correlates of aggression in free-ranging rhesus monkeys. *Archives of General Psychiatry, 49,* 436–441.

Highley, J. D., Thompson, W. T., Champoux, M., Goldman, D., Hasert, M. F., Kraemer, G. W., Suomi, S. J., & Linnoila, M. (1993). Paternal and maternal genetic and environmental contributions to CSF monoamine metabolite concentrations in rhesus monkeys (Macaca mulatta). *Archives of General Psychiatry, 50,* 615–623.

Holsboer-Trachsler, E., Stohler, R., & Hatzinger, M. (1991). Repeated administration of the combined dexamethasone/CRH stimulation test during treatment of depression. *Psychiatry, 38,* 163–171.

Honig, A., & van Praag, H. M. (Eds.). (1997). *Depression: Neurobiological, psychopathological and therapeutic advances.* Chichester, UK: John Wiley.

Johnson, E. O., Kamilaris, T. C., Chrousos, G. P., & Gold, P. W. (1992). Mechanisms of stress. *Neuroscience Behavioral Reviews, 16,* 115–130.

Kahn, R. S., Westenberg, H. G. M., & Moore, C. (1995). Increased serotonin function and panic disorder. In G. M. Asnis, & H. M. van Praag (Eds.), *Panic disorder.* New York: John Wiley.

Kahn, R. S., Wetzler, S., Asnis, G. M., Papolos, D., & van Praag, H. M. (1990). Serotonin receptor sensitivity in major depression. *Biological Psychiatry, 28,* 358–362.

Kandel, E., Brennan, P. A., Mednick, S. A., & Michelson, N. M. (1989). Minor physical anomalies and recidivistic adult violent offending. *Acta Psychiatrica Scandinavica, 79,* 103–107.

Kaplan, J. R., Shively, C. A., Fontenot, M. B., Morgan, T. M., Howell, S. M., Manuck, S. B., Muldoon, M. F., & Mann, J. J. (1994). Demonstration of an association among dietary cholesterol, central serotonergic activity, and social behavior in monkeys. *Psychosomatic Medicine, 56,* 479–484.

Klaassen, T., Riedel, W. J., Honig, A., Van Someren, A., Deutz, N. E. P., & van Praag, H. M. (1999a). Mood effects of 24-hour tryptophan depletion in healthy first-degree relatives of patients with affective disorders. *Biological Psychiatry, 46,* 489–497.

Klaassen, T., Riedel, W. J., Deutz, N. E. P., Van Someren, A., & van Praag, H. M. Specificity of the tryptophan depletion method. (1999b). *Psychopharmacology, 141,* 279–286.

Knutson, B., Wolkowitz, O. M., Cole, S. W., Chan, T., Moore, E. A., Johnson, R. C., Terpstra, J., Turner, R. A., & Reus, V. I. (1998). Selective alteration of personality and social behavior by serotonergic intervention. *American Journal of Psychiatry, 155,* 373–379.

Koolhaas, J. M., Van den Brink, T. H. C., Roozendaal, B., & Boorsma, F. (1990). Medial amygdala and aggressive behavior. *Aggressive Behavior, 16,* 223–229.

Kraemer, G. W., Ebert, M. H., Schmidt, D. E., & McKinney, W. T. (1989). A longitudinal study of the effect of different social rearing conditions on cerebrospinal fluid norepinephrine and biogenic amine metabolites in rhesus monkeys. *Neuropsychopharmacology, 2,* 175–189.

Krebs-Thomson, K., & Geyer, M. A. (1998). Evidence for a functional interaction between 5-HT_{1a} and 5-HT_2 receptors in rats. *Psychopharmacology, 140,* 69–74.

Leon, A. C., Keller, M. B., Warshaw, M. G., Mueller, T. I., Solomon, D. A., Coryell, W., & Endicott, J. (1999). Prospective study of fluoxetine treatment and suicidal behavior in affectively ill subjects. *American Journal of Psychiatry, 156,* 195–201.

Lesch, K. P., Bengel, D., Heils, A., Sabol, S. Z., Greenberg, B. D., Petri, S., Benjamin, J., Muller, C. R., Hamer, D. H., & Murphy, D. L. (1996). Association of anxiety traits with a polymorphism in the serotonin transporter gene regulatory region. *Science, 274,* 1527–1531.

Lesch, K. P., Mayer, S., Disselkamp-Tietze, J., Hoh, A., Wiesmann, M., Osterheider, M., & Schulte, H. M. (1990). 5-HT_{1a} receptor responsivity in unipolar depression evaluation of ipsapirone-induced ACTH and cortisol secretion in patients and controls. *Biological Psychiatry, 28,* 620–628.

Lesch, K. P., & Mossner, R. (1998). Genetically driven variation in serotonin uptake. *Biological Psychiatry, 44,* 179–192.

Lindberg, G., Rastam, L., Gullberg, B., & Eklund, G. A. (1992). Low serum cholesterol concentration and short term mortality from injuries in men and women. *British Medical Journal, 305,* 277–279.

Linnoila, M., Virkkunen, M., Scheinin, M., Nuutila, A., Rimon, R., & Goodwin, F. K. (1983). Low cerebrospinal fluid 5-hydroxyindoleacetic acid concentration differentiates impulsive from nonimpulsive violent behavior. *Life Sciences, 33,* 2609–2614.

Maes, M., Jacobs, M. P., Suy, E., Minner, B., Leclercq, C., Christiaens, F., & Raus, J. (1990). Suppressant effects of dexamethasone on the availability of plasma l-tryptophan and tyrosine in healthy controls and in depressed patients. *Acta Psychiatrica Scandinavica, 81,* 19–23.

Manuck, S. B., Flory, J. D., McCaffery, J. M., Matthews, K. A., Mann, J. J., & Muldoon, M. F. (1998). Aggression, impulsivity, and central nervous system serotonergic responsivity in a nonpatient sample. *Neuropsychopharmacology, 19,* 287–299.

Mehlmann, P. T., Higley, J. D., Faucher, I., Lilly, A. A., Taub, D. M., Vickers, J., Suomi, S. J., & Linnoila, M. (1994). Low CSF 5-HIAA concentrations and severe aggression and impaired impulse control in nonhuman primates. *American Journal of Psychiatry, 151,* 1485–1491.

Meijer, O. C., & de Kloet, E. R. (1994). Corticosterone suppresses the expression of 5-HT$_{1a}$ receptor mRNA in rat dentate gyrus. *European Journal of Pharmacology: Molecular Pharmacology Section, 266,* 255–261.

Meller, W. H., Kathol, R. G., Samuelson, S. D., Gehris, T. L., Carroll, B. T., Pitts, A. F., & Clayton, P. J. (1995). CRH challenge test in anxious depression. *Biological Psychiatry, 37,* 376–382.

Miczek, K. A., Hussain, S., & Faccidomo, X. (1998). Alcohol-heightened aggression in mice. *Psychopharmacology, 139,* 160–168.

Mignot, E., Seffano, A., Laude, D., Elghozi, J. L., Dedek, J., & Scatton, B. (1985). Measurement of 5-HIAA levels in ventricular CSF (by LCEC) and in striatum (by in vivio voltammetry) during pharmacological modifications of serotonin metabolism in the rat. *Journal of Neural Transmission, 62,* 117–124.

Missagh Ghadirian, A., Engelsmann, F., Dhar, V., Filipini, D., Keller, R., Chouinard, G., & Pearson Murphy, B. E. (1995). The psychotropic effects of inhibitors of steroid biosynthesis in depressed patients refractory to treatment. *Biological Psychiatry, 37,* 369–375.

Modell, S., Laner, C. J., Schreiber, W., Huber, J., Krieg, J. C., & Holsboer, F. (1998). Hormonal response pattern in the combined DEX-CRH test is stable over time in subjects at high familial risk for affective disorders. *Neuropsychopharmacology, 18,* 253–262.

Moeller, F. G., Allen, T., Cherek, D. R., Dougherty, D. M., Lane, S., & Swann, A. C. (1998). Ipsapirone neuroendocrine challenge. *Psychiatry Research, 81,* 31–38.

Moeller, F. G., Dougherty, D. M., Swann, A. C., Collins, D., Davis, C., & Cherek, D. R. (1996). Tryptophan depletion and aggressive responding in healthy males. *Psychopharmacology, 126,* 97–103.

Montgomery, S. A., Dunner, D. L., & Dunbar, G. C. (1995). Reduction of suicidal thoughts with paroxetine in comparison with reference antidepressants and placebo. *European Neuropsychopharmacology, 5,* 5–13.

Moss, H. B., Yao, J. K., & Panzak, G. L. (1990). Serotonergic responsivity and behavioral dimensions in antisocial personality disorder with substance abuse. *Biological Psychiatry, 28,* 325–338.

Muldoon, M. F., Manuck, S. B., & Matthews, K. A. (1990). Lowering cholesterol concentration and mortality. *British Medical Journal, 301,* 309–314.

Murphy, B. E. P., Dhar, V., Missagh Ghadirian, A., Chouinard, G., & Keller, R. (1991). Response to steroid suppression in major depression resistant to antidepressant therapy. *Journal of Clinical Psychopharmacology, 11,* 121–126.

Murray, C. A. J., Sherwood, R., & O'Keane, V. (1998). Abnormal 5-HT$_{1d}$ receptor function in major depression. *Psychological Medicine, 28,* 295–300.

New, A. S., Sevin, E. M., Mitropoulou, V., Reynolds, D., Novotny, S. L., Callahan, A., Trestman, R. L., & Siever, L. J. (1999). Serum cholesterol and impulsivity in personality disorders. *Psychiatry Research, 85,* 145–150.

Nielsen, D. A., Virkkunen, M., Lappalainen, J., Eggert, M., Brown, G. L., Long, J. C., Goldmann, D., & Linnoila, M. (1998). A Tryptophan hydroxylase gene marker for suicidality and alcoholism. *Archives of General Psychiatry, 55,* 593–602.

Nordstrom, P., Samuelsson, M., Asberg, M., Traskman-Bendz, L., Asberg-Wistedt, A., Nordin, C., & Bertilsson, L. (1994). CSF 5-HIAA predicts suicide risk after attempted suicide. *Suicide and Life-Threatening Behavior, 24,* 1–9.

Nordstrom, P., Schalling, D., & Asberg, M. (1995). Temperamental vulnerability in attempted suicide. *Acta Psychiatrica Scandinavica, 92,* 155–160.

O'Dwyer, A. M., Ligtman, S. L., Masks, M. N., & Checkley, S. A. (1995). Treatment of a major depression with metyrapone and hydrocortisone. *Journal of Affective Disorders, 33,* 123–128.

O'Keane, V., Moloney, E., O'Neill, H., O'Connor, A., Smith, C., & Dinan, T. G. (1992). Blunted prolactin responses to d-Fenfluramine in sociopathy. *British Journal of Psychiatry, 160,* 643–646.

Oxenstierna, G., Edman, G., Isehus, L., Oreland, L., Ross, S. B., & Sedvall, G. (1986). Concentrations of monoamine metabolites in the cerebrospinal fluid of twins and unrelated individuals. *Journal of Psychiatric Research, 20,* 19–29.

Paykel, E. S., Prusoff, B. A., & Meyers, J. K. (1975). Suicide attempt and recent life events. *Archives of General Psychiatry, 32,* 327–333.

Peters, D. A. V. (1986). Prenatal stress. *Pharmacology, Biochemistry and Behavior, 24,* 1377–1382.

Plutchik, R., & van Praag, H. M. (1990). Psychosocial correlates of suicide and violence risk. In H. M. van Praag, R. Plutchik, & A. Apter (Eds.), *Violence and suicidality: Perspectives in clinical and psychobiological research.* New York: Brunner/Mazel.

Porter, R. J., Hamisch, R. H., Allister-Williams, M., Lunn, B. S., & Young, A. H. (1998). 5-Hydroxytryptamine receptor function in humans is reduced by acute administration of hydrocortisone. *Psychopharmacology, 139,* 243–250.

Reul, J. M., Labeur, M. S., Grigoriadis, D. E., De Souza, E. B., & Holsboer, F. (1994). Hypothalamic-pituitary-adrenocortical axis changes in the rat after long-term treatment with the reversible monoamine oxidase-A inhibitor moclobemide. *Neuroendocrinology, 60,* 509–519.

Reul, J. M., Stec, I., Soder, M., & Holsboer, F. (1993). Chronic treatment of rats with the antidepressant amitriptyline attenuates the activity of the hypothalamic-pituitary-adrenocortical system. *Endocrinology, 133,* 312–320.

Riedel, W. J., Klaassen, T., Deutz, N. E. P., Van Someren, A., & van Praag, H. M. (1999). Tryptophan depletion in normal volunteers produces selective impairment in memory consolidation. *Psychopharmacology, 141,* 362–369.

Roy, A. (Ed.). (1986). *Suicide.* Baltimore: Williams and Wilkins.

Sachar, E. J., Hellman, L., Roffwarg, H. P., Halpern, F. S., Fukushima, D. K., & Gallagher, T. F. (1973). Disrupted 24-hour patterns of cortisol secretion in psychotic depression. *Archives of General Psychiatry, 28,* 19–24.

Salzman, C., Wolfson, A. N., Schatzberg, A., Looper, J., Henke, R., Albanese, M., Schwartz, J., & Miyawaki, E. (1995). Effect of fluoxetine on anger in symptomatic volunteers with borderline personality disorder. *Journal of Clinical Psychopharmacology, 15,* 23–29.

Samochowiec, J., Lesch, K. P., Rottinann, M., Smolka, M., Syagailo, Y. V., Okladnova, O., Rommelspacher, H., Winterer, G., Schmidt, L. G., & Sander, T. (1999). Association of a regulatory polymorphism in the promoter region of the monoamine oxidase a gene with antisocial alcoholism. *Psychiatry Research, 86,* 67–72.

Sanchez, C. (1996). 5-HTia receptors play an important role in modulation of behavior of rats in a two-compartment black and white box. *Behavioral Pharmacology, 7,* 788–797.

Saudou, F., Amara, D. A., Dierich, A., LeMeur, M., Ramboz, S., Segu, L., & Buhot, M. C. (1994). Enhanced aggressive behavior in mice lacking 5-HT$_{1b}$ receptor. *Science, 265,* 1875–1878.

Silver, M. A., Bohnert, M., Beck, A. T., & Marcus, D. (1971). Relation of depression to attempted suicide and seriousness of intent. *Archives of General Psychiatry, 25,* 573–576.

Smith, S. E., Pihl, R. O., Young, S. N., & Ervin, F. R. (1986). Elevation and reduction of plasma tryptophan and their effects on aggression and perceptual sensitivity in normal males. *Aggressive Behavior, 12,* 393–407.

Stanley, M., Traskman, L., & Dorovine, K. (1985). Correlations between aminergic metabolites simultaneously obtained from human CSF and brain. *Life Sciences, 37,* 1279–1286.

Teicher, M. H., Glod, C., & Cole, J. O. (1990). Emergence of intense suicidal preoccupation during fluoxetine treatment. *American Journal of Psychiatry, 147,* 207–210.

Terao, T., Yoshimura, R., Ohmori, O., Takano, T., Takahashi, N., Iwata, N., Susuki, T., & Abe, K. (1997). Effect of serum cholesterol levels on metachlorophenylpiperazine-evoked neuroendocrine responses in healthy subjects. *Biological Psychiatry, 41,* 974–978.

Thakore, J. H., & Dinan, T. G. (1995). Cortisol synthesis inhibition. *Biological Psychiatry, 37,* 364–368.

Traskman, L., Asberg, M., Bertilsson, L., & Sjostrand, L. (1981). Monoamine metabolites in CSF and suicidal behavior. *Archives of General Psychiatry, 38,* 631–636.

Tuinier, S., Verhoeven, W. M. A., Scherders, M. J. W. T., Fekkes, D., & Pepplinkhuizen, L. (1995). Neuropsychiatric and biological characteristics of X-linked MAO-A deficiency syndrome. *New Trends in Experimental and Clinical Psychiatry, 11,* 99–107.

van Praag, H. M. (1982). Depression, suicide, and the metabolism of zerotonin in the brain. *Journal of Affective Disorders, 4,* 275–290.

van Praag, H. M. (1983). CSF 5-HIAA and suicide in non-depressed schizophrenics. *Lancet, ii,* 977–978.

van Praag, H. M. (1988). Serotonergic mechanisms and suicidal behavior. *Psychiatry and Psychobiology, 3,* 335–346.

van Praag, H. M. (1992). *Make Believes in Psychiatry or the Perils of Progress.* New York: Brunner/Mazel.

van Praag, H. M. (1995). Concerns about depression. *European Psychiatry, 10,* 269–275.

van Praag, H. M. (1996). Serotonin-related, anxiety/aggression-driven, stressor-precipitated depression. *European Psychiatry, 11,* 57–67.

van Praag, H. M. (1997). Over the mainstream. *Psychiatry Research, 72,* 201–212.

van Praag, H. M. (1998). Anxiety and increased aggression as pacemakers of depression. *Acta Psychiatrica Scandinavica, 98,* 81–88.

van Praag, H. M., Asnis, G. M., Kahn, R. S., Brown, S. L., Korn, M., Harkavy-Friedman, J. M., & Wetzler, S. (1990). Monoamines and abnormal behavior. *British Journal of Psychiatry, 157,* 723–734.

van Praag, H. M., Kahn, R., Asnis, G. M., Wetzler, S., Brown, S., Bleich, A., & Korn, M. (1987). Denosologization of biological psychiatry or the specificity of 5-HT disturbances in panic disorders. *Journal of Affective Disorders, 13,* 1–8.

van Praag, H. M., Korf, J., & Puite, J. (1970). 5-Hydroxindoleacetic acid levels in the cerebrospinal fluid of depressive patients treated with probenecid. *Nature, 225,* 1259–1260.

van Praag, H. M., Plutchik, R., & Conte, H. (1986). The serotonin-hypothesis of (auto)aggression. *Annals of the New York Academy of Sciences, 487,* 150–167.

Verkes, R. J., Van der Mast, R. C., Hengeveld, M. W., Tuyl, J. P., Zwinderman, A. H., & Van Kempen, G. M. J. (1998). Reduction by Paroxetine of suicidal behavior in patients with repeated suicide attempts but not major depression. *American Journal of Psychiatry, 155,* 543–547.

Virkkunen, M. (1979). Serum cholesterol in antisocial personality disorder. *Neuropsychobiology, 5,* 27–32.

Virkkunen, M. (1983). Serum cholesterol in levels in homicidal offenders. *Neuropsychobiology, 10,* 65–69.

Von Bardeleben, U., & Holsboer, F. (1991). Cortisol response to a combined dexamethasone-human corticotropin-releasing hormone challenge in patients with depression. *Journal of Neuroendocrinology 1,* 485–488.

Weiss, J. M., Goodman, P. A., Losito, B. G., Corrigan, S., Charry, J. M., & Bailey, W. B. (1981). Behavioral depression produced by an uncontrollable stressor. *Brain Reviews, 3,* 167–205.

Wetzler, S., Kahn, R. S., Asnis, G. M., Korn, M., & van Praag, H. M. (1991). Serotonin receptor sensitivity and aggression. *Psychiatry Research, 37,* 271–279.

Wolkowitz, O. M., Reus, V. I., Manfredi, F., Ingbar, J., Brizendine, L., & Weingartner, H. (1993). Ketoconazole administration in hypercortisolemic depression. *American Journal of Psychiatry, 150,* 810–812.

Young, S. N., Smith, S. E., Pihl, R. O., & Ervin, F. R. (1985). Tryptophan depletion causes a rapid lowering of mood in normal males. *Psychopharmacology, 87,* 173–177.

APPROACHES TO PREVENTING SUICIDE

CHAPTER

Lloyd B. Potter

Public Health and Suicide Prevention

☐ Suicide in the United States

In 1997, suicide was the eighth leading cause of death in the United States (Ventura, Anderson, Martin, & Smith, 1998). Each year there are more than 29,000 suicide deaths. About 80% of these suicide deaths are males. Across age, suicide rates are almost nonexistent among children under 10 years, then rates begin to increase among adolescents and continue to increase through 25 years of age (Figure 1). After 25 years of age the suicide rates are fairly level until about age 65 where the rate begins an increase through the oldest ages. However, we see a slightly different pattern of suicide when we examine numbers of deaths. Though suicide rates are slightly lower among youth compared to older Americans, application of a lower rate to larger numbers results in a larger number of deaths among younger Americans (Figure 2). Thus, the burden of suicide death in terms of numbers falls heavily on young people. In terms of trends in rates by age, we have seen increasing rates among the young, level or slightly declining rates among middle-aged, and stable or declining rates among the elderly.

☐ The Public Health Approach to Preventing Suicide

To effectively prevent the public health problem of suicide we must use science. The public health approach (Figure 3) provides a multi-disciplinary, scientific method of identifying effective strategies for prevention. This approach starts with defining the problem and progresses to identifying associated risk factors and causes, developing and evaluating interventions, and implementing interventions in programs. Although Figure 3 suggests a linear progression from the first step to the last, in reality many of these steps occur simultaneously, and the steps are

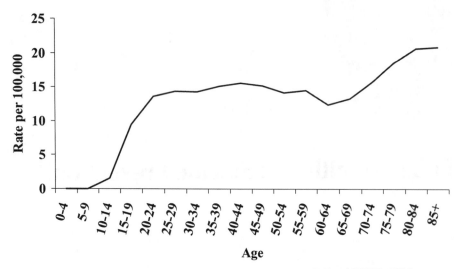

FIGURE 1. Suicide death rates by age, U.S., 1997. Source: NCHS & NCIPC, 1999.

often interdependent. For example, information systems used to define the problem may also be useful in evaluating programs. Similarly, information gained in program evaluation and implementation may lead to new and promising interventions.

Public health has traditionally responded to epidemics of infectious disease with a focus on environmental modification and vaccination. During the past few decades, public health has incorporated efforts to modify high-risk behavior, with the goal of preventing chronic disease and injury. Increasing rates of suicide among adolescents and young adults in the United States led the Centers for Disease Control and Prevention (CDC) to initiate efforts to prevent injuries from suicidal

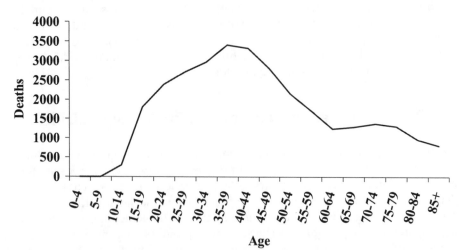

FIGURE 2. Suicide deaths by age, U.S., 1997. Source: NCHS & NCIPC 1999

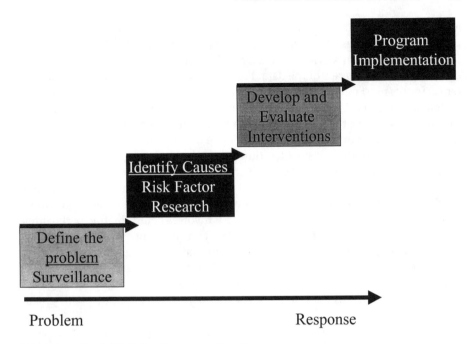

FIGURE 3. The Publich Health Approach to Prevention

behavior by using a public health approach (Potter, Powell, & Kacher, 1995; Potter, Rosenberg, & Hammond, 1998; Rosenberg, O'Carroll, & Powell, 1992; Rosenberg, Smith, Davidson, & Conn, 1987).

Defining The Problem

The first step involves delineating incidents of suicidal behavior and related mortality and morbidity. This step includes obtaining information on the demographic characteristics of the persons involved, the temporal and geographic characteristics of the incidents, and the severity and cost of the injury. The information collected should be useful for answering questions such as these: How often does suicidal behavior occur? When and under what circumstances does it occur? Who has been involved or witnessed the event? Were drugs or alcohol involved? These additional variables may be important in defining discrete subsets of suicidal behavior for which various interventions may be appropriate. Every community is unique, and we must collect information that will give an accurate picture of suicidal behavior and the related problems in specific communities.

For completed suicide, information about the problem comes from vital statistics. The foundation of the vital statistics system is death certificates that are usually completed by medical examiners or coroners. Most state and county offices of vital statistics have computerized vital statistics mortality files that are abstracted from death certificates. These records usually contain data on place, cause of death, age, sex, race, marital status, residence, and sometimes occupation and education. Data from states and territories are compiled by the CDC's National Center for Health Statistics (NCHS). NCHS provides additional editing to improve the consistency and accuracy of the data. For mortality, the passive vital statistics system captures most deaths attributed to and recorded as suicide. The vital statistics system in the United States is one of the more advanced and efficient systems in the world. However there are several limitations that impede our ability to take full advantage of mortality information. Some of the more important limitations include under-reporting of suicides, time lag, and sociodemographic information.

The under-reporting of suicide as a cause of death is a problem for the vital statistics system in the U.S. and probably for all efforts to count suicides (Kleck, 1988; Males, 1991; O'Carroll, 1989). The accuracy of suicide identification is lower than for most other causes of death because it involves determination of the intention of the deceased (Rosenberg et al., 1988). Thus mortality statistics for suicide tend to underestimate the magnitude of the problem, especially for specific types of injuries that lend themselves to varying interpretations of intention such as single car and plane crashes (Peck, & Warner, 1995; Ungs, 1994). This suggests a need to develop means for systematically identifying suicide deaths with greater sensitivity.

Prompt response to trends or epidemics are thwarted by the time between event occurrence and data availability. At the national level, United States mortality detail files are released two to three years after the event year. While NCHS does produce the Current Mortality Sample, which is available about four months after the main month of occurrence, the number of suicides captured in the 10% sample is insufficient to identify local epidemics. This time-lag in accessing complete data at the national level suggests that intervention-motivated surveillance of suicide would be more effective if reviewed at the state or local department of health, where vital statistics are compiled before being sent to NCHS.

In addition to under-reporting and time-lag, the vital statistics system captures little etiologically useful information on death certificates. Essentially data on place, cause of death, age, sex, race, marital status, residence, and sometimes occupation and education (since 1990) are collected. This precludes our ability to identify causal associations between other more modifiable individual characteristics and suicide. In one effort to overcome this deficiency, NCHS has initiated a periodic National Mortality Followback Survey. This survey samples death certificates, contacts proxies (next-of-kin, close friends) and attempts to obtain etiologically useful information on the decedent's behavior and risk characteristics.

In spite of these limitations, CDC produces periodic surveillance reports on suicide patterns and changes. These reports provide information about trends in the numbers and rates of suicide by age, sex, race and method of suicide, and may be used to target groups for more intensive study and intervention.

Morbidity Surveillance

Data collection systems for suicide morbidity are much less complete and less systematic compared to suicide mortality data collected by the United States Vital

Statistics system (Thacker & Berkelman, 1988). While the United States has no formal system for conducting surveillance of suicide-related morbidity, there are several data collection efforts that allow for some assessment of suicide-related morbidity. The National Hospital Ambulatory Medical Care Survey (NHAMCS) is a national probability survey of visits to hospital emergency and outpatient departments of non-Federal, short-stay, and general hospitals in the United States. In 1996, 489,000 emergency department visits were for injuries from suicidal behavior (Advance Data from Vital and Health Statistics, 1997).

The National Electronic Injury Surveillance System collects data a sample of hospitals in the United States in an effort to monitor product (nonfood) related hazards and is operated by the Consumer Product Safety Commission. This is a sample-based system that relies on a network of emergency room physicians. Because the focus is on consumer products, firearms-related injury information is also collected. In 1992, it was estimated that there were approximately 5197 nonfatal firearm-related suicide attempts (Annest, Mercy, Gibson, & Ryan, 1995). Furthermore, it is estimated that for every one nonfatal firearm-related suicide attempt, there were 7.1 completed firearm-related suicides. NEISS is being expanded to collect information on a broader range of injuries and may provide national estimates of attempted suicide (firearm and nonfirearm).

To monitor priority health-risk behaviors, including suicidal behavior among youth and young adults, the CDC developed the Youth Risk Behavior Surveillance System (YRBSS) (Kann, Kolbe, & Collins, 1993). The YRBSS includes national, state, territorial, and local school-based surveys of high school students. National surveys were conducted in 1990, 1991, 1993, 1995, and 1997. In 1997, 20.5% of students had seriously considered attempting suicide during the 12 months preceding the survey (Kann, Kolbe, & Collins, 1998). Overall, female students (27.1%) were significantly more likely than male students (15.1%) to have considered attempting suicide; Hispanic students (23.1%) were significantly more likely than black students (16.4%) to have considered attempting suicide. Approximately 7.7% of students reported they had attempted suicide one or more times during the 12 months preceding the survey. Overall, female students (11.6%) were significantly more likely than male students (4.5%) to have attempted suicide; Hispanic students (10.7%) were significantly more likely than white students (6.3%) to have attempted suicide. Nationwide, 2.6% of students reported having made a suicide attempt during the 12 months preceding the survey that resulted in an injury, poisoning, or overdose that had been treated by a doctor or nurse.

Efforts to conduct surveillance of suicide morbidity and mortality would be enhanced by enacting several specific activities. For mortality, efforts to publicize and encourage appropriate coding of suicide deaths may be effective in reducing the mortality undercount. Also, local review of suicide mortality statistics would reduce the time-lag between data collection and national release. In states and localities with suicide intervention programs, this may enhance efforts to provide effective services. Finally, surveillance data could augment etiological research if more information were collected on the deceased. For suicide, more specific identification of the means of suicide and perhaps on the location of death could enhance development of research questions that could be pursued in special studies.

While several potential sources of morbidity surveillance data exist, a consolidated effort to analyze these data is needed. Specifically, there is a need to estimate the burden of suicide-related morbidity in terms of social and economic costs. This information is an essential component of building public awareness and support for development of research and intervention.

Surveillance of suicide morbidity and mortality is an essential component in the public health approach to suicide prevention. Surveillance provides us with an understanding of the magnitude and trends of suicidal behavior. More importantly, because the components of the public health approach are interdependent, surveillance efforts provide information that is used to guide etiologic research.

Identifying Causes

Whereas the first step looks at the who, when, where, what, and how of suicide, the second step looks at why. This step may also be used to define populations at high risk and to suggest specific interventions. Risk and protective factors can be identified by a variety of scientific research methodologies, including rate calculations and ethnographic, cohort, and case-control studies. Whereas risk factors such as alcohol and drug use and misuse, media exposure to suicidal behavior, and social and economic influences have been explored, many questions remain regarding the role that these and numerous other possible causes play in producing suicidal behavior and, more importantly, how these and other risk factors may be modified to prevent suicidal behavior.

Ecological view of suicide

It is impossible to understand the causes of suicide without considering the interplay between the biology and the behavior of individuals, the immediate environments in which they act and are socialized, and social and economic institutions that define norms for behavior and influence processes that define environments. The ecological perspective has been developed theoretically and employed empirically in a number of forms in a variety scientific disciplines (e.g., Bronfenbrenner, 1977; Hawley, 1950, 1986). Ecological analysis allows for assessment of relations within systems. In the case of humans and suicidal behavior, the focus is on the relationship between the individual and the immediate setting, as well as with the larger social contexts, both formal and informal. The concept of the ecological environment is topological and involves a nested arrangement of systems, each contained within the next.

An ecological systems model of human development provides a useful framework for understanding the etiology of suicidal behavior as well as potentially identifying opportunities for intervention. A simplified version of this model has the individual existing and developing within the context of close interpersonal relationships (family and peers). Individuals, family, and peers exist and develop in the context of their community, and all of these exist within a broader social, cultural, economic, macrosystem. Each level influences and is influenced by other levels.

There are several implications of this ecological model for understanding suicidal behavior. First it allows for the direct influence of environmental factors (familial, societal, and physical) on behavior. The model also explicitly acknowledges the multilevel determinants of behavior. Fitting the model to suicidal behavior, it is not just family or community or societal factors but all of these that contribute to the development of suicidal behavior. Moreover these factors interact with one another to influence whether or not individuals engage in suicidal behavior.

Most etiologic research into suicidal behavior occurs at one level of analysis. Studies that are limited to one level of analysis are easier to conduct although, at higher levels of aggregation, they suffer from potential interpretation problems when attempting across-level interpretation (Glick & Roberts, 1994; Iversen, 1991; Richards, Gottfredson, & Gottfredson, 1990). A classic example is an ecological analysis is that of Emile Durkheim's (1951) study of suicide. He explored ecological associations between suicide rates and population characteristics (e.g., religion and marital status). While Durkheim was able to say there was an association between suicide rates of a population and population characteristics, he was not able to make statements of causation at the individual level of analysis. The discussion that follows utilizes the basic framework of the ecological model (individual, family and peers, community, macrosystem) as the basis for discussing research at each level.

At the individual level, there are biological and behavioral characteristics that have been associated with suicide. A number of studies have implicated hereditary factors and biological factors influencing the propensity for suicidal behavior (Arana & Hyman, 1989; Mann, 1987; Rainer, 1984; Roy, 1993). Substantial evidence has suggested that deficiencies in the serotonergic system is associated with suicidal behavior (Baldwin, Bullock, Montgomery, & Montgomery, 1991; Lowther et al., 1997; Mann, Arango, & Underwood, 1990; Ohmori, Arora, & Meltzer, 1992; Van Praag, 1991). A feeling of hopelessness is one characteristics that has been generally associated with suicidal behavior (Beck, Brown, & Steer, 1997; Beck, Steer, Beck, & Nwan, 1993; Beck, Steer, Kovacs, & Garrson, 1985; Hill, Gallagher, Thompson & Ishida, 1988; Keller & Wolfersdorf, 1993; Nimeus, Traskman-Bendz, & Alsen, 1997; Rotheram-Borus & Trautman, 1988; Shaffer et al., 1996; Weishaar & Beck, 1992). A number of psychiatric disorders have been associated with suicidal behavior such as depression (Adolescent suicide, 1996; Beck, Steer, Kovacs, & Garrison, 1985; Berglund, 1984; Brent, 1995; Brent et al., 1988; Grent, Kolko, Allan, & Brown, 1990; Brent, Perper, Moritz, Allman et al. 1993a; Harrington et al., 1994; Lewinsohn, Rohed, & Seeley, 1994; Osgood, 1992; Porsteinsson et al., 1997; Roy, 1986; Wolk & Weissman, 1996; Young, Fogg, Scheftner, & Fawcett, 1994), bipolar affective disorder (Ahrens, Grof, Moller, Muller-Oerlinghausen, & Wolf, 1995; Krupinski et al., 1998; Mueller-Oerlinghausen, Mueser-Causemann, & Volk, 1992; Tondo, Jamison, & Baldessarini, 1997; Tondo et al., 1998), conduct disorder (Apter, Bleich, Plutchik, Mendolsohn, & Tyano, 1988; Brent, Perper, Moritz, Baugher et al., 1993; Shaffer et al., 1996; Shafii et al., 1988), and alcoholism and substance abuse (Bryant, Garrison, Valois, Rivard, & Hinkle, 1995; Burge, Felts, Chenier, & Parrillo, 1995; Garrison, McKeown, Valois, & Vincent, 1993; Marzuk et al., 1992; Rossow & Amundsen, 1995; Roy, DeJong, Lamparski, Adinoff et al., 1991; Roy, DeJong, Lamparski, George et al., 1991; Shaffer et al., 1996; Shafii et al., 1988; Stack & Wasserman, 1995; Vilhjalmsson, Kristjansdotti, & Sueibjarnardottir, 1998; Windle & Windle, 1997) among others.

Family/Close Relationships

Characteristics of and behavior within the family environment profoundly influence the development of individuals. A number of family environment characteristics have been associated with suicide and suicidal behavior including family conflict or discord (Brent, 1995; Brent et al., 1994; Campbell, Milling, Laughlin, & Bush, 1993; Wright, 1985), parental attachment (DeJong, 1992), poor family functioning (Adams, Overholser, & Lehnert, 1994), childhood separation from parents (Bagley & Ramsay, 1985), child abuse and neglect (Bergman & Brismar, 1991; Brent et al., 1994; Briere & Runtz, 1986; Bryant & Range, 1997; Deykin, Alpert, & McNamara, 1985; Grossman, Milligan, & Deyo, 1991; Molnar, Shade, Kral, Booth, & Watters, 1998; Straus & Kantor, 1994), being a victim of intimate partner abuse/ conflict (Deykin, Alpert, & McNamara, 1985) and loss of a peer (Brent, Perper, Moritz, Friend et al., 1993; Brent, Perper, Moritz, Liotus et al., 1993; Brent et al., 1995; Brent, Moritz, Bridge, Perper, & Canobbio, 1996).

Another factor that may operate at the level of family and peers, although it is clearly linked to community characteristics, is access to means. A number of studies have indicated with varying degrees of rigor that access to firearms increases risk of completed suicide (Beautrais, Joyce, & Mulder, 1996; Boor & Bair, 1990; Brent et al., 1991; Brent, Perper, Moritz, Baugher et al., 1993b; Cummings, Koepsell, Grossman, Savarino, & Thompson, 1997; Medoff & Magaddino, 1983; Sloan, Rivaran, Reay, Ferris, & Kellerman, 1990).

Macrosystem

Internationally, suicide rates vary substantially (Diekstra & Garnefski, 1995; Krug, Dahlberg, & Powell, 1997) suggesting cultural differences in suicidal behavior. These cultural differences appear to result in variation of method selected (Adityanjee, 1986; Burvill, 1995; Canetto & Lester, 1995; Ko & Kua, 1995). Various indicators of economic factors have been explored in relation to suicide rates (Adityanjee, 1986; Araki & Murata, 1987; Burvill, 1995; Canetto & Lester, 1995; Cormier & Klerman, 1985; Ko & Kua, 1995; Ragland & Berman, 1990–1991; Reinfurt, Stewart, & Weaver, 1991; Yang, 1995; Yang & Lester. 1990). Studies generally support an association between economic factors and suicide, although several have not found an association.

There are a number of key concepts at several levels of aggregation (individual, family/peer, community, and macrosystem) that appear to be central for understanding the causes suicide. Unfortunately, there are no research findings that have been able to simultaneously link all these levels together to provide an understanding of the causes of suicide that would allow us to develop and implement highly effective multi-systemic interventions for the prevention of suicidal behavior. This highlights the issue of taxonomy. In reviewing the literature on suicide, very few studies use the same definitions. Variables and constructs that we use as predictors occupy a vast range as do variables and constructs that actually measure some form of suicidal behavior. Thus while there have been limited efforts to articulate taxonomy of suicide (O'Caroll et al., 1996) we are left with a rapidly developing field of research that is struggling for both a more refined taxonomy and a more developed framework for understanding the causes of suicide.

Developing And Testing Interventions

The next step is to develop interventions based largely on information obtained from the previous steps and to test these interventions. This step includes evaluating the efficacy of programs, policies, or interventions already in place. Methods for testing include prospective randomized controlled trials, comparisons of health outcomes in intervention and comparison populations, time-series analyses of trends in multiple areas, and observational research studies, such as case-control studies.

Preventive interventions are usually efforts to break a causal chain between the potential for a negative outcome and achieving that outcome. Thus, the development of preventive interventions depends on the previous step in the public health model—identifying and understanding the causes of suicidal behavior. In practice, however, interventions are often implemented and occasionally evaluated with little or no specification of the causal chain or how the intervention will affect the chain.

The Institute of Medicine report on reducing risks for mental disorders (Mrazek & Haggerty, 1994; Silverman & Felner, 1995a) suggests a framework for describing different intervention approaches based on the target of the intervention: Indicative, selective, and universal (Gordon, 1983). Indicated interventions are highly targeted interventions that involve identification, treatment and skill building among individuals and families. Selective interventions are targeted at high-risk groups with a focus on screening and group prevention activities. Universal interventions are targeted at communities or larger aggregations and may include media or educational campaigns and other broad population-based prevention strategies. This model appears to have some level of congruence with an ecological model of human development. As we find characteristics of individuals that put them at high risk of suicidal behavior, we can attempt to develop and evaluate indicated interventions to reduce this risk. Similarly, as we identify characteristics of groups that are indicative of members' potential for suicidal behavior and as we understand the causal pathways that may lead this group to experience suicidal behavior, we can develop, test, and deliver selective interventions that may lead to reductions of suicide. Finally, as we understand more of societal influences on development and expression of forms of suicidal behavior we will be able to implement universal interventions (laws, education, media images, etc.).

There have been a number of efforts to describe prevention strategies in various settings (Kalafat & Elias, 1995; Lipschitz, 1995; O'Carroll & Silverman, 1994; Silverman & Felner, 1995b; Silverman & Maris, 1995; Tanney, 1995). CDC has identified a number of strategies intended to prevent suicidal behavior among youth (O'Carroll, Potter, & Mercy, 1994). Types of interventions identified include school gatekeeper training, community gatekeeper training, general suicide education, screening programs, peer support programs, crisis centers and hotlines, means restriction, and intervention after a suicide. Unfortunately very few interventions have been evaluated thoroughly for efficacy and safety. Lack of sound evaluation remains one of the most significant barriers to identification and implementation of effective intervention strategies.

Implementing Interventions And Measuring Prevention Effectiveness

The final step is to implement interventions that have demonstrated effectiveness in preventing suicidal behavior. Data collection to evaluate the program's implementation and effectiveness is essential, because an intervention that has been found effective in a clinical trial or an academic study may perform differently in different settings. Another important component of this fourth step is determining the cost-effectiveness of such programs. Balancing the costs of a program against the cases prevented by the intervention can be very helpful to policy makers in determining optimal public health practice.

At the implementation phase, public health professionals must develop guidelines and procedures for putting effective programs in place, and they must consider various factors: involving parents and students in programs designed to prevent suicidal behavior; building effective coalitions across traditionally separate sectors such as substance abuse prevention, education, and public health; and continually assessing and improving the programs that are put into place. Assessing implementation and developing of implementation guidelines are especially important because we have little information on the successful implementation of programs. We also have little information on how interventions can be adapted for particular community values, cultures, and standards and, at the same time, allow for and benefit from racially and culturally diverse participation from all segments of the community.

Applying the public health approach to preventing suicidal behavior and related injury is a new endeavor. We are just beginning to implement more extensive surveillance efforts to better understand the problem. Very little research has been completed that provides definitive answers regarding the causes of suicidal behavior. Many suicide prevention programs are being implemented, and some of the first comprehensive evaluations of such programs are now being completed. Essentially, suicide prevention, addressed from a scientific perspective, is a young science. However, we have made some significant progress in recent years in defining the magnitude of the problem and the trends of suicidal behavior. Additionally, significant progress has been made toward defining a national agenda in the United States for the prevention of suicide (Davidson, Potter, & Ross, 1999).

Conclusion

Suicide is a public health problem that calls for application of the public health approach. This approach involves surveillance, epidemiological research, and implementation and evaluation of prevention programs. This effort is facilitated by the CDC's traditional and long-standing partnership with state and local health departments and with community-based organizations. However, the public health approach to suicide prevention requires additional development and refinement.

The CDC's efforts to reduce suicide incidence using the public health approach are intended to supplement and strengthen current and ongoing efforts by other Federal, state and local agencies and those of community-based organizations. Previous suicide prevention efforts have emphasized mental health therapy based on the high-risk model of injury prevention. Greater emphasis on population-based suicide prevention efforts is needed. Resources and efforts must be expanded in a continued struggle to reduce the economic and the emotional impact of suicide on society. The broadly-based public health approach provides a strong framework and rationale for the development and implementation of an effective national suicide prevention plan.

References

Adams, D. M., Overholser, J. C., & Lehnert, K. L. (1994). Perceived family functioning and adolescent suicidal behavior. *Journal of the American Academy of Child & Adolescent Psychiatry, 33,* 498–507.

Adityanjee, D. (1986). Suicide attempts and suicides in India. *International Journal of Social Psychiatry, 32,* 64–73.

Adolescent suicide. (1996). *Group for the Advancement of Psychiatry, 140,* 1–184.

Advance Data From Vital and Health Statistics, #293. (1997). Hyattsville, MD: National Center for Health Statistics.

Ahrens, B., Grof, P., Moller, H. J., Muller-Oerlinghausen, B., & Wolf, T. (1995). Extended survival of patients on long-term lithium treatment. *Canadian Journal of Psychiatry, 40,* 241–246.

Annest, J., Mercy, J., Gibson, D., & Ryan, G. (1995). National estimates of nonfatal firearm-related injuries. *Journal of the American Medical Association, 273,* 1749–1754.

Apter, A., Bleich, A., Plutchik, R., Mendelsohn, S., & Tyano, S. (1988). Suicidal behavior, depression, and conduct disorder in hospitalized adolescents. *Journal of the American Academy of Child & Adolescent Psychiatry, 27,* 696–699.

Araki, S., & Murata, K. (1987). Suicide in Japan. *Suicide & Life-Threatening Behavior, 17,* 64–71.

Arana, G. W., & Hyman, S. (1989). Biological contributions to suicide. In D. Jacobs & H. N. Brown (Eds.), *Suicide: Understanding and responding* (pp. 73–86). Madison, CT: International Universities Press.

Bagley, C., & Ramsay, R. (1985). Psychosocial correlates of suicidal behaviors in an urban population. *Crisis, 6,* 63–77.

Baldwin, D., Bullock, T., Montgomery, D., & Montgomery, S. (1991). 5-HT reuptake inhibitors, tricyclic antidepressants and suicidal behaviour. *International Clinical Psychopharmacology, 6*(Suppl. 3), 49–56.

Beautrais, A. L., Joyce, P. R., & Mulder, R. T. (1996). Access to firearms and the risk of suicide. *Australian & New Zealand Journal of Psychiatry, 30,* 741–748.

Beck, A. T., Brown, G. K., & Steer, R. A. (1997). Psychometric characteristics of the Scale for Suicide Ideation with psychiatric outpatients. *Behaviour Research & Therapy, 35,* 1039–1046.

Beck, A. T., Steer, R. A., Beck, J. S., & Newman, C. F. (1993). Hopelessness, depression, suicidal ideation, and clinical diagnosis of depression. *Suicide & Life-Threatening Behavior, 23,* 139–145.

Beck, A. T., Steer, R. A., Kovacs, M., & Garrison, B. (1985). Hopelessness and eventual suicide. *American Journal of Psychiatry, 142,* 559–563.

Berglund, M. (1984). Suicide in alcoholism. *Archives of General Psychiatry, 41,* 888–891.

Bergman, B., & Brismar, B. (1991). Suicide attempts by battered wives. *Acta Psychiatrica Scandinavica, 83,* 380–384.

Boor, M., & Bair, J. H. (1990). Suicide rates, handgun control laws, and sociodemographic variables. *Psychological Reports, 66,* 923–930.

Brent, D. A. (1995). Risk factors for adolescent suicide and suicidal behavior. *Suicide & Life-Threatening Behavior, 25*(Suppl.), 52–63.

Brent, D. A., Kolko, D. J., Allan, M. J., & Brown, R. V. (1990). Suicidality in affectively disordered adolescent inpatients. *Journal of the American Academy of Child & Adolescent Psychiatry, 29,* 586–593.

Brent, D. A., Moritz, G., Bridge, J., Perper, J., & Canobbio, R. (1996). The impact of adolescent suicide on siblings and parents. *Suicide & Life-Threatening Behavior, 26,* 253–259.

Brent, D. A., Perper, J. A., Allman, C. J., Moritz, G. M., Wartella, M. E., & Zelenak, J. P. (1991). The presence and accessibility of firearms in the homes of adolescent suicides. *Journal of the American Medical Association, 266,* 2989–2995.

Brent, D. A., Perper, J. A., Goldstein, C. E., Kolko, D. J., Allan, M. J., Allman, C. J., & Zelenak, J. P. (1988). Risk factors for adolescent suicide. *Archives of General Psychiatry, 45,* 581–588.

Brent, D. A., Perper, J. A., Moritz, G., Allman, C., Friend, A., Roth, C., Schweers, J., Balach, L., & Baugher, M. (1993). Psychiatric risk factors for adolescent suicide. *Journal of the American Academy of Child & Adolescent Psychiatry, 32,* 521–529.

Brent, D. A., Perper, J. A., Moritz, G., Baugher, M., Schweers, J., & Roth, C. (1993). Firearms and adolescent suicide. *American Journal of Diseases of Children, 147,* 1066–1071.

Brent, D. A., Perper, J. A., Moritz, G., Friend, A., Schweers, J., Allman, C., McQuiston, L., Boylan, M., Roth, C., & Balach, L. (1993). Adolescent witnesses to a peer suicide. *Journal of the American Academy of Child & Adolescent Psychiatry, 32,* 1184–1188.

Brent, D. A., Perper, J. A., Moritz, G., Liotus, L., Richardson, D., Canobbio, R., Schweers, J., & Roth, C. (1995). Posttraumatic stress disorder in peers of adolescent suicide victims. *Journal of the American Academy of Child & Adolescent Psychiatry, 34,* 209–215.

Brent, D. A., Perper, J. A., Moritz, G., Liotus, L., Schweers, J., Balach, L., & Roth, C. (1994). Familial risk factors for adolescent suicide. *Acta Psychiatrica Scandinavica, 89,* 52–58.

Brent, D. A., Perper, J. A., Moritz, G., Liotus, L., Schweers, J., Roth, C., Balach, L., & Allman, C. (1993). Psychiatric impact of the loss of an adolescent sibling to suicide. *Journal of Affective Disorders, 28,* 249–256.

Briere, J., & Runtz, M. (1986). Suicidal thoughts and behaviours in former sexual abuse victims. *Canadian Journal of Behavioural Science, 18,* 413–423.

Bronfenbrenner, U. (1977). Toward an experimental ecology of human development. *American Psychologist, 32,* 513–531.

Bryant, E. S., Garrison, C. Z., Valois, R. F., Rivard, J. C., & Hinkle, K. T. (1995). Suicidal behavior among youth with severe emotional disturbance. *Journal of Child & Family Studies, 4,* 429–443.

Bryant, S. L., & Range, L. M. (1997). Type and severity of child abuse and college students' lifetime suicidality. *Child Abuse & Neglect, 21,* 1169–1176.

Burge, V., Felts, M., Chenier, T., & Parrillo, A. V. (1995). Drug use, sexual activity, and suicidal behavior in U.S. high school students. *Journal of School Health, 65,* 222–227.

Burvill, P. W. (1995). Suicide in the multiethnic elderly population of Australia, 1979–1990. *International Psychogeriatrics, 7,* 319–333.

Campbell, N. B., Milling, L., Laughlin, A., & Bush, E. (1993). The psychosocial climate of families with suicidal preadolescent children. *American Journal of Orthopsychiatry, 63,* 142–145.

Canetto, S. S., & Lester, D. (1995). Gender and the primary prevention of suicide mortality. *Suicide & Life-Threatening Behavior, 25,* 58–69.

Cormier, H. J., & Klerman, G. L. (1985). Unemployment and male-female labor force participation as determinants of changing suicide rates of males and females in Quebec. *Social Psychiatry, 20,* 109–114.

Cummings, P., Koepsell, T. D., Grossman, D. C., Savarino, J., & Thompson, R. S. (1997). The association between the purchase of a handgun and homicide or suicide. *American Journal of Public Health, 87,* 974–978.

Davidson, L., Potter, L., & Ross, V. (1999). *Surgeon General's Call to Action.* Washington, DC: Office of the Surgeon General, Department of Health and Human Services.

DeJong, M. L. (1992). Attachment, individuation, and risk of suicide in late adolescence. *Journal of Youth & Adolescence, 21,* 357–373.

Deykin, E. Y., Alpert, J. J., & McNamara, J. J. (1985). A pilot study of the effect of exposure to child abuse or neglect on adolescent suicidal behavior. *American Journal of Psychiatry, 142,* 1299–1303.

Diekstra, R. F., & Garnefski, N. (1995). On the nature, magnitude, and causality of suicidal behaviors. *Suicide & Life-Threatening Behavior, 25,* 36–57.

Durkheim, E. (1951). *Suicide: A Study in Sociology.* New York: The Free Press.

Garrison, C. Z., McKeown, R. E., Valois, R. F., & Vincent, M. L. (1993). Aggression, substance use, and suicidal behaviors in high school students. *American Journal of Public Health, 83,* 179–184.

Glick, W. H., & Roberts, K. H. (1994). Hypothesized interdependence, assumed independence. *Academy of Management Review, 9,* 722–735.

Gordon, R. (1983). An operational classification of disease prevention. *Public Health Reports, 98,* 107–109.

Grossman, D. C., Milligan, B. C., & Deyo, R. A. (1991). Risk factors for suicide attempts among Navajo adolescents. *American Journal of Public Health, 81,* 870–874.

Harrington, R., Bredenkamp, D., Groothues, C., Rutter, M., Fudge, H., & Pickles, A. (1994). Adult outcomes of childhood and adolescent depression. *Journal of Child Psychology & Psychiatry & Allied Disciplines, 35,* 1309–1319.

Hawley, A. (1950). *Human ecology.* New York: Ronald Press.

Hawley, A. (1986). *Human ecology.* Chicago: University of Chicago Press.

Hill, R. D., Gallagher, D., Thompson, L. W., & Ishida, T. (1988). Hopelessness as a measure of suicidal intent in the depressed elderly. *Psychology & Aging, 3,* 230–232.

Iversen, G. R. (1991). *Contextual analysis.* Newbury Park, CA: Sage.

Kalafat, J., & Elias, M. J. (1995). Suicide prevention in an educational context. In M. M. Silverman & R. W. Maris (Eds.), *Suicide prevention: Toward the year 2000* (pp. 123–133). New York: Guilford.

Kann, L., Kinchen, S., Williams, B., Ross, J., Lowry, R., Hill, C., Grunbaum, J., Blumson, P., Collins, J., & Kolbe, L. (1998). Youth Risk Behavior Surveillance—United States, 1997. *Morbidity & Mortality Weekly Report, 47*(SS-3), 1–89.

Kann, L., Kolbe, L. J., & Collins, J. L. (1993). Measuring the health behavior of adolescents. *Public Health Reports, 108*(Suppl. 1).

Keller, F., & Wolfersdorf, M. (1993). Hopelessness and the tendency to commit suicide in the course of depressive disorders. *Crisis, 14,* 173–177.

Kleck, G. (1988). Miscounting suicides. *Suicide & Life-Threatening Behavior, 18,* 219–236.

Ko, S. M., & Kua, E. H. (1995). Ethnicity and elderly suicide in Singapore. *International Psychogeriatrics, 7,* 309–317.

Krug, E. G., Dahlberg, L. L., & Powell, K. E. (1996). Childhood homicide, suicide, and firearm deaths. *World Health Statistics Quarterly, 49*(3–4), 230–235.

Krupinski, M., Fischer, A., Grohmann, R., Engel, R. R., Hollweg, M., & Moeller, H. J. (1998). Psychopharmacological therapy and suicide of inpatients with depressive psychoses. *Archives of Suicide Research, 4,* 143–155.

Lewinsohn, P. M., Rohde, P., & Seeley, J. R. (1994). Psychosocial risk factors for future adolescent suicide attempts. *Journal of Consulting & Clinical Psychology, 62,* 297–305.

Lipschitz, A. (1995). Suicide prevention in young adults (age 18–30). In M. M. Silverman & R. W. Maris (Eds.), *Suicide prevention: Toward the year 2000* (pp. 15–170). New York: Guilford.

Lowther, S., De Paermentier, F., Cheetham, S. C., Crompton, M. R., Katona, C. L., & Horton, R. W. (1997). 5-HT1A receptor binding sites in post-mortem brain samples from depressed suicides and controls. *Journal of Affective Disorders, 42,* 199–207.

Males, M. (1991). Teen suicide and changing cause-of-death certification, 1953–1987. *Suicide & Life-Threatening Behavior, 21,* 245–259.

Mann, J. J. (1987). Psychobiologic predictors of suicide. *Journal of Clinical Psychiatry, 48*(December Suppl.), 39–43.

Mann, J. J., Arango, V., & Underwood, M. D. (1990). Serotonin and suicidal behavior. *Annals of the New York Academy of Sciences, 600,* 476–485.

Marzuk, P. M., Tardiff, K., Leon, A. C., Stajic, M., Morgan, E. B., & Mann, J. J. (1992). Prevalence of cocaine use among residents of New York City who committed suicide during a one-year period. *American Journal of Psychiatry, 149,* 371–375.

Medoff, M. H., & Magaddino, J. P. (1983). Suicides and firearm control laws. *Evaluation Review, 7,* 357–372.

Molnar, B. E., Shade, S. B., Kral, A. H., Booth, R. E., & Watters, J. K. (1998). Suicidal behavior and sexual/physical abuse among street youth. *Child Abuse & Neglect, 22,* 213–222.

Mrazek, P. J., & Haggerty, R. J. (1994). *Reducing risks for mental disorders.* Washington, DC: National Academy Press.

Mueller-Oerlinghausen, B., Mueser-Causemann, B., & Volk, J. (1992). Suicides and parasuicides in a high-risk patient group on and off lithium long-term medication. *Journal of Affective Disorders, 25,* 261–269.

Nimeus, A., Traskman-Bendz, L., & Alsen, M. (1997). Hopelessness and suicidal behavior. *Journal of Affective Disorders, 42,* 137–144.

O'Carroll, P. W. (1989). A consideration of the validity and reliability of suicide mortality data. *Suicide & Life-Threatening Behavior, 19,* 1–16.

O'Carroll, P. W., Berman, A. L., Maris, R. W., Moscicki, E. K., Tanney, B. L., & Silverman, M. M. (1996). Beyond the Tower of Babel. *Suicide & Life-Threatening Behavior, 26,* 237–252.

O'Carroll, P. W., & Potter, L. B. (1994). Suicide contagion and the reporting of suicide. *Morbidity & Mortality Weekly Report, 43*(RR–6), 9–17.

O'Carroll, P. W., Potter, L. B., & Mercy, J. A. (1994). Programs for the prevention of suicide among adolescents and young adults. *Morbidity & Mortality Weekly Report, 43*(RR–6), 1–7.

O'Carroll, P. W., & Silverman, M. M. (1994). Community suicide prevention. *Suicide & Life-Threatening Behavior, 24,* 89–91.

Ohmori, T., Arora, R. C., & Meltzer, H. Y. (1992). Serotonergic measures in suicide brain. *Biological Psychiatry, 32,* 57–71 .

Osgood, N. J. (1992). Suicide in the elderly. *International Review of Psychiatry, 4,* 217–223.

Peck, D. L., & Warner, K. (1995). Accident or suicide? *Adolescence, 30,* 463–472.

Porsteinsson, A., Duberstein, P. R., Conwell, Y., Cox, C., Forbes, N., & Caine, E. D. (1997). Suicide and alcoholism. *American Journal on Addictions, 6,* 304–310.

Potter, L. B., Powell, K. E., & Kachur, S. P. (1995). Suicide prevention from a public health perspective. *Suicide & Life-Threatening Behavior, 25*, 82–91.

Potter, L. B., Rosenberg, M. L., & Hammond, W. R. (1998). Suicide in youth. *Journal of the American Academy of Child & Adolescent Psychiatry, 37*, 484–487.

Ragland, J. D., & Berman, A. L. (1990–1991). Farm crisis and suicide. *Omega, 22*, 173–185.

Rainer, J. D. (1984). Genetic factors in depression and suicide. *American Journal of Psychotherapy, 38*, 329–340.

Reinfurt, D. W., Stewart, J. R., & Weaver, N. L. (1991). The economy as a factor in motor vehicle fatalities, suicides, and homicides. *Accident Analysis & Prevention, 23*, 453–462.

Richards, J. M., Gottfredson, D. C., & Gottfredson, G. D. (1990). Units of analysis and item statistics for environmental assessment scales. *Current Psychology, 9*, 407–413.

Rosenberg, M. L., Davidson, L. E., Smith, J. C., Berman, A. L., Buzbee, H., Gantner, G., Gay, G., Moore-Lewis, B., Mills, D., Murray, D., O'Carroll, P. W., & Jobes, D. (1988). Operational criteria for the determination of suicide. *Journal of Forensic Sciences, 33*, 1445–1456.

Rosenberg, M. L., O'Carroll, P. W., & Powell, K. E. (1992). Let's be clear. Violence is a public health problem. *Journal of the American Medical Association, 267*, 3071–3072.

Rosenberg, M. L., Smith, J. C., Davidson, L. E., & Conn, J. M. (1987). The emergence of youth suicide. *Annual Review of Public Health, 8*, 417–440.

Rossow, I., & Amundsen, A. (1995). Alcohol abuse and suicide. *Addiction, 90*, 685–691.

Rotheram-Borus, M. J., & Trautman, P. D. (1988). Hopelessness, depression, and suicidal intent among adolescent suicide attempters. *Journal of the American Academy of Child & Adolescent Psychiatry, 27*, 700–704.

Roy, A. (1986). Depression, attempted suicide, and suicide in patients with chronic schizophrenia. *Psychiatric Clinics of North America, 9*(1), 193–206.

Roy, A. (1993). Genetic and biologic risk factors for suicide in depressive disorders. *Psychiatric Quarterly, 64*, 345–358.

Roy, A., DeJong, J., Lamparski, D., Adinoff, B., George, T., Moore, V., Garnett, D., Kerich, M., & Linnoila, M. (1991). Mental disorders among alcoholics. *Archives of General Psychiatry, 48*, 423–427.

Roy, A., DeJong, J., Lamparski, D., George, T., & Linnoila, M. (1991). Depression among alcoholics. *Archives of General Psychiatry, 48*, 428–432.

Shaffer, D., Gould, M. S., Fisher, P., Trautman, P., Moreau, D., Kleinman, M., & Flory, M. (1996). Psychiatric diagnosis in child and adolescent suicide. *Archives of General Psychiatry, 53*, 339–348.

Shafii, M., Steltz-Lenarsky, J., Derrick, A. M., Beckner, C., et al. (1988). Comorbidity of mental disorders in the postmortem diagnosis of completed suicide in children and adolescents. *Journal of Affective Disorders, 15*, 227–233.

Silverman, M. M., & Felner, R. D. (1995a). The place of suicide prevention in the spectrum of intervention. *Suicide & Life-Threatening Behavior, 25*, 70–81.

Silverman, M. M., & Felner, R. D. (1995b). Suicide prevention programs. *Suicide & Life-Threatening Behavior, 25*, 92–104.

Silverman, M. M., & Maris, R. W. (1995). The prevention of suicidal behaviors. *Suicide & Life-Threatening Behavior, 25*, 10–21.

Sloan, J. H., Rivara, F. P., Reay, D. T., Ferris, J. A., & Kellerman, A. L. (1990). Firearm regulations and rates of suicide. *New England Journal of Medicine, 322*, 369–373.

Stack, S., & Wasserman, I. M. (1995). Marital status, alcohol abuse and attempted suicide. *Journal of Addictive Diseases, 14*(2), 43–51.

Straus, M. A., & Kantor, G. K. (1994). Corporal punishment of adolescents by parents. *Adolescence, 29*, 543–561.

Tanney, B. (1995). Suicide prevention in Canada. In M. M. Silverman & R. W. Maris (Eds.), *Suicide prevention: Toward the year 2000* (pp. 105–122). New York: Guilford Press.

Thacker, S. B., & Berkelman, R. L. (1988). Public health surveillance in the United States. *Epidemiologic Reviews, 10,* 164–190.

Tondo, L., Baldessarini, R. J., Hennen, J., Floris, G., Silvetti, F., & Tohen, M. (1998). Lithium treatment and risk of suicidal behavior in bipolar disorder patients. *Journal of Clinical Psychiatry, 59,* 405–414.

Tondo, L., Jamison, K. R., & Baldessarini, R. J. (1997). Effect of lithium maintenance on suicidal behavior in major mood disorders. *Annals of the New York Academy of Sciences, 836,* 339–351.

Ungs, T. J. (1994). Suicide by use of aircraft in the United States, 1979–1989. *Aviation Space & Environmental Medicine, 65,* 953–956.

Van Praag, H. M. (1991). Serotonergic dysfunction and aggression control. *Psychological Medicine, 21,* 15–19.

Ventura, S. J., Anderson, R. N., Martin, J. A., & Smith, B. L. (1998). Births and deaths: Preliminary data for 1997. *National Vital Statistics Reports, 47*(4).

Vilhjalmsson, R., Kristjansdottir, G., & Sveinbjarnardottir, E. (1998). Factors associated with suicide ideation in adults. *Social Psychiatry & Psychiatric Epidemiology, 33,* 97–103.

Weishaar, M. E., & Beck, A. T. (1992). Hopelessness and suicide. *International Review of Psychiatry, 4,* 177–184.

Windle, R. C., & Windle, M. (1997). An investigation of adolescents' substance use behaviors, depressed affect, and suicidal behaviors. *Journal of Child Psychology & Psychiatry & Allied Disciplines, 38,* 921–929.

Wolk, S. I., & Weissman, M. M. (1996). Suicidal behavior in depressed children grown up. *Psychiatric Annals, 26,* 331–335.

Wright, L. S. (1985). Suicidal thoughts and their relationship to family stress and personal problems among high school seniors and college undergraduates. *Adolescence, 20,* 575–580.

Yang, B. (1995). The differential impact of the economy on suicide in the young and the elderly. *Archives of Suicide Research, 1,* 111–120.

Yang, B., & Lester. D. (1990). Time-series analyses of the American suicide rate. *Social Psychiatry & Psychiatric Epidemiology, 25,* 274–275.

Young, M. A., Fogg, L. F., Scheftner, W. A., & Fawcett, J. A. (1994). Interactions of risk factors in predicting suicide. *American Journal of Psychiatry, 151,* 434–435.

CHAPTER 6

Ronald L. Bonner[2]

Moving Suicide Risk Assessment into the Next Millennium: Lessons from our Past[1]

☐ Traditional Approaches

To understand the evolution of suicide risk assessment, it is important to understand the traditional theoretical models which have guided research and application. Braucht (1979), in this historical review of suicide risk assessment, described two models: 1) the environmental/sociological model, and 2) the personological/ psychological model. The environmental/sociological model conceptualized suicide as a static event that resulted from environmental, demographic, and social factors. Research based on this model attempted to differentiate populations of suiciders and nonsuiciders based on these factors. In the second model, personological/psychological, suicide was viewed as an outcome of abnormal personological or psychological factors. Research based on the second model attempted to differentiate suiciders from nonsuiciders based on various personological traits. Generally, risk assessment was guided by these two models, and suicide risk was determined by the presence of these population characteristics. From retrospective, correlational comparisons between suiciders and

---

[1] To Diane and Jason—my life's greatest blessings. So often, our paths of self-destruction involve the loss of perspective of the good, blessings, and significant others our lives have and can touch. As helpers along this path, we would do well in our future to better see and appreciate the good and strengths in our lives, others, and the human condition. Perhaps, our greatest resource in suicide prevention for the new millennium will be found in this perspective and how our relationships can make a difference to those who suffer and who have lost perspective of these possibilities.

[2] The views expressed in this chapter are solely those of the author and do not necessarily represent those of his institutional affiliations.

nonsuiciders, risk assessment attempted to predict suicide by identifying population membership.

Durkheim's (1897/1951) classic theory of anomie and low social integration guided sociological risk research. A variety of sociodemographic variables have been studied within this paradigm, including sex (Brown & Sheran, 1972), race (Dublin, 1963), religion (Beit-Hallahmi, 1975), socioeconomic status (Breed, 1963), age (Brown & Sheran, 1972), marital status (Shneidman & Farberow, 1961), place of residence (McCulloch & Phillip, 1967), season of the year (Dublin, 1963), time of the day (Tuckman & Youngman, 1968), and social contagion (Phillips, 1979). Generally, significant differences were found on many of these factors between suiciders and nonsuiciders.

Freud's (1920/1950, 1917/1957) classic psychoanalytic theory hypothesized suicide to be the outcome of a psychological drive, namely the death instinct. In this theory, suiciders were thought to turn hostility against others toward self. Results of research on such psychodynamic constructs have been mixed. Vinoda (1966) found more hostility expressed in psychiatric records of suiciders than nonsuiciders. Others (Beck, 1967, Eisenthal, 1967; Fisher, 1971) have not found any differences in hostility between suicidal and control groups.

Results of research on personality assessment and suicide risk have likewise been inconsistent. Early on, Exner and Wylie (1977) concluded no constellation of variables on the Rorschach Test has been able to differentiate suiciders from nonsuiciders. Clopton and Baucom (1979) reached similar conclusions regarding the MMPI and stated:

> There is no indication that standard MMPI scales, MMPI profile analysis, or specifically developed MMPI suicide scales can reliably predict at useful levels. MMPI profiles are unlikely to be accurate enough to justify using the MMPI in suicide risk assessment. (p. 294)

More recent work on personality assessment has also suggested limitations in determining suicide risk. Eyman and Eyman (1992) discussed the empirically derived Adult Suicide Constellation and a Children's Suicide Constellation, using Exner's Comprehensive System for scoring the Rorschach Test (Exner & Weiner, 1982). They noted this configuration of eight or more variables correctly identified over 70% of completed suicides and over 80% of controls. Inconsistent or nonsignificant differences were reported between attempters and completers, short-term and long-term risk, and suicidal and nonsuicidal children. MMPI research, including item, scale, or profile analysis, was also reported as being unable to differentiate suicidal from nonsuicidal subjects. These researchers summarized that traditional psychological and personality testing was not very useful for direct suicide risk assessment. However, Eyman and Eyman (1992) concluded this review by making the argument that personality assessment can still be very valuable in identifying important correlates of suicide risk. In addition, they noted personality assessment was particularly helpful in identifying critical personality characteristics and ego functions which many hinder or protect a person when responding to major life stress and emotional crises, which ultimately may determine suicide risk.

Mikawa (1973), in reviewing the environmental and personological literature, concluded suicide prediction is unattainable. He noted that traditional research models isolated suicide from the fluid and dynamic interactions of environment and person in the victim's life. He also expressed concerns with the traditional definition of suicide, namely the completion, with no attention to the events and processes which lead up to suicide. He also pointed out the statistical problems due to a low base rate of completed suicide (13 per 100,000 per year), arguing that assessment methodologies would never be able to improve suicide prediction beyond simply assuming the event's nonoccurrence. Mikawa called for a new, process-oriented definition of suicidal behavior, that took into consideration developmental stages and dynamic interactions of environmental and personological factors. From this new definition, suicide was conceptualized in terms of a continuum of behavior, including ideation, planning, threats, attempts, and completion (Beck, Kovacs, & Weissman, 1979). Suicidal intention was viewed as the common pathway which moves a person along the suicide continuum or process. Movement was said to be a result of maladaptive coping processes that occur over time due to the influx of environmental and personological events and dynamics.

With the shift from a static group membership paradigm to a process paradigm, the area of suicide prediction and risk assessment moved forward. Suicide prediction, within what was now viewed as a complex and fluid process, was no longer viewed as a reasonable goal (Hughes, 1995; Polcorny, 1993). Also, suicide prediction was replaced with such terms as risk assessment or detection and was considered at best as a short time endeavor of clinical estimation. Within a brief time frame, risk detection was considered a "snapshot" of a constellation of environmental and personological risk factors where clinical judgment would be used to estimate the level of risk within a particular situation, time frame, and biopsychosocial constellation. This process fundamentally captures the idea and intention of suicide and its relation to the interplay of environmental and personological variables involved in the movement toward and away from suicide coping. Finally, it was proposed that risk factors could be categorized on system levels (e.g., psychological, social/situational, and physiological), stage of process entry (distal and proximal), and the mind state of suicide intention. Risk assessment then would target these data sources with the relative order of importance as noted: mind state of suicide intention, proximal risk factors involved in the specific suicide coping, and distal factors associated with static population characteristics.

☐ Mind State Risk Factors

According to Kral (1994):

> . . . suicide is caused by the idea of suicide and nothing else. It is a conscious option to kill oneself made by the individual, almost always to escape from unbearable psychological pain, or as Shneidman (1993) has recently put it, from unbearable "psychache." (p. 245)

Risk assessment, then, fundamentally must capture the history, nature, content, and quality of the suicide idea and its experiential meaning for the individual. All other risk factors at the various system levels are viewed as secondary, which render a person more vulnerable to the idea of suicide as a coping response. As Shneidman (1998) paraphrased the Bard: "the mind's the site to catch each suicide in its flight." (p. 250)

Aaron Beck and Associates (Beck, 1986; Beck, Kovacs, & Weissman, 1979; Beck & Lester, 1976; Beck, Schuyler, & Herman, 1974; Beck & Steer, 1989; Minkoff, Bergman, Beck, & Beck, 1973; Weishaar & Beck, 1992) have spent decades studying and dissecting the critical elements of the suicide idea. Their research has overwhelmingly demonstrated idea correlates of suicide risk, including the presence and extent of suicide ideation, the degree of suicide planning, the level of suicide intention and the wish to die, the lethality and availability of the method chosen, the planned opportunity for rescue, and future perspectives of hope and the likelihood of problem resolution. Generally speaking, the more elaborated the suicide idea and its planning, the greater the wish to die, the higher the potential lethality of the contemplated plan, and the more hopeless a person is, the greater the risk for suicidal behavior. Further, the history of the suicide idea and its action (attempts) is considered the greatest risk factor for future suicidal thinking, action, and ultimate suicide (Roy, 1992).

Beck's research team has developed a number of risk assessment instruments that standardize and systematically assess these mind state components. The Scale for Suicide Ideation (Beck, Kovacs, & Weissman, 1979) assesses the degree to which a person is thinking about suicide; including the ability to control suicidal wishes, the purpose of a contemplated plan, the strength of the person's wish to die (versus wish to live), and the access and lethality potential of the contemplated plan of attempt. The Suicide Intent Scale (Beck, Schuyler, & Herman, 1974) was developed to measure the severity of the person's wish to die during an actual suicide attempt, including the purpose of the attempt, attitudes toward living and dying, lethality of the attempt, and the opportunities for rescue of the attempt. The Hopelessness Scale (Beck, Weissman, Lester, & Trexler, 1974) assesses the degree and presence of hopeless expectations regarding one's problems of living and psychache relief. Other researchers (e.g., Eyman & Eyman, 1990; Reynolds, 1987) have developed similar measures that attempt to systematically assess the mind state of the suicidal individual.

Generally, these instruments are a significant improvement over traditional psychological tests as these instruments specifically target and standardize the components of the suicide idea. Many studies have supported these instruments in differentiating suicide ideators, attempters, completers, and nonsuicidal populations (e.g., Beck, Morris, & Beck, 1974; Beck, Schuyler, & Herman, 1974; Beck, Weissman, Lester,& Trexler, 1974; Bedrosian & Beck, 1979). Longitudinal research (Beck, Brown, Berchick, Stewart, & Steer, 1990; Beck & Steer, 1989) has shown hopelessness to be a strong predictor of eventual suicide. Rothberg and Geer-Williams (1992), however, in reviewing these scales caution that psychometric studies are still lacking, and all suicide measures are plagued by a high overclassification of suicidal subjects. Finally, the time issue becomes a major challenge in the use of such measures, as the mind state is constantly in flux, with risk level dependent on mind state and each unique interplay of environmental and person risk factors. Their utility, as with other risk assessment procedures, is short, time-limited, and related to the particular situation, person, and environment factors involved in coping behavior.

☐ Primary Proximate Risk Factors

Psychological Risk Factors

The psychological domain refers to other mental and emotional states that might render a person vulnerable to the suicide idea and its previously discussed components. Most importantly, the affective state of the suicidal individual is intolerable, emotional pain. Shneidman (1985) describes this state as "perturbation" and "psychache," the experience of endless turmoil, the dark tunnel of despair, the overwhelming sense of being trapped with no way of escape.

Depression

Depression is the most common psychological syndrome associated with suicidality. Depression accounts for approximately 80% of suicides and presents a lifetime risk of suicide of 15% for depressed persons (Murphy, 1985; Sommers-Flanagan, & Sommers-Flanagan, 1995). Diagnoses of major depression and bipolar disorder are most common, with key affective features of severe psychic anxiety, panic attacks, insomnia, agitation, and distractibility (Clark & Fawcett, 1992).

Other Mental Disorders

Psychotic thinking, including suicide command hallucinations and depressive delusions associated with schizophrenia, is another high risk factor for suicide. Robins (1986) has reported up to a 19% lifetime risk of suicide for those individuals who suffer from schizophrenia. Other mental disorders at risk for suicide include borderline personality disorder, panic disorder, and substance abuse (Maris, Berman, & Maltsberger, 1992).

Tanney (1992), in reviewing the literature, has reached the following conclusions. First, a history of any diagnosed mental disorder is an important risk factor in increasing the likelihood of suicidal behavior. Second, specific mental disorders, such as mood disorders, increase the risk for suicide over other types of mental disorders. Third, comorbidity of mental disorders is a stronger risk factor for suicide than single syndromes. However, the fact remains that the majority of persons diagnosed with a mental disorder do not engage in suicidal behavior. Beck's work (e.g., Beck, Brown, Berchik, Stewart, & Steer, 1990; Beck & Steer, 1989; Weishaar and Beck, 1992) suggests it is the experience of hopelessness and despair among the affectively and mentally afflicted that determines who will move toward suicidal coping and action.

Physiological Risk Factors

Underlying such psychological states, physiological reactions are occurring that may make certain individuals vulnerable to the suicide idea and its progression.

Neurotransmitter Dysfunction

Lester (1995), in reviewing the literature, concluded that the role of serotonin dysfunction in suicidal behavior has been consistently supported. Postmortem studies of suicide completers have found low brainstem levels of serotonin (Moscicki, 1995). Clinical studies of suicide attempters have found decreased level of the serotonin metabolite 5-HIAA (Moscicki, 1995). Nordstrom, Samuelson, Asberg, Traskman-Bendz, Aberg-Wistedt, Nordin and Bertilsson (1994) demonstrated that deficient levels of a serotonin metabolite predicted short range suicide risk. The exact role of serotonin deficiency in suicide is still unclear. Low serotonin levels are associated with other correlates of suicide risk, namely the mood disorders, impulsivity, and violence. Its independent role in suicidality is in question.

Heredity

Suicidal behavior and its associated psychological illnesses tend to run in families. The role of genetics has been studied in this regard. It does appear clear that genetic factors play an important role in major psychotic and affective disorders associated with suicide risk (Moscicki, 1995). However, an independent, genetic influence for suicide risk per se has not yet been supported (Lester, 1997). The current perspective is that there is a genetic vulnerability to mental illness, from which a subgroup of individuals may contemplate suicide as an idea and progress to various actions as a coping response.

Drug/Alcohol Abuse

The use and abuse of alcohol or drugs produces physiological and psychological changes that can render an individual vulnerable to the suicide idea and its progressive manifestations. As Lester (1997) has stated:

> The use of alcohol and drugs may lower inhibitions and impair judgment of a person contemplating suicide and therefore make the act more likely, and alcohol and drug use aggravate other risk factors for suicide such as depression. (p. 135)

Moscicki (1995), in reviewing the literature, concluded that substance abuse is found in the majority of completed and attempted suicides. Roy and Linnoila (1986) have found approximately 20% of all suiciders are alcoholic and some 18% of alcoholics end their life by suicide. About half of all suiciders were intoxicated at the time of their death (Moscicki, 1995). Finally, suicide attempts have been shown to increase in frequency, lethality, and suicide intent as the use of intoxicants increase (Crumley, 1990).

☐ Primary Distal Risk Factors

Social/Situational Risk Factors

The relationship of various distal sociodemographic characteristics and suicide risk is the most researched area in the literature (Anderson, Townsend, Everly, & Lating, 1995). A number of population characteristics have been commonly associated with suiciders and attempters. Some of the more notable risk factors are reviewed here.

Demographics

Consistently, males suicide much more often than females, while females *attempt* suicide much more often than males (Lester, 1997). Older age is associated with suiciders, with the older white male having the highest suicide risk across the life span (Kral & Sakinofsky, 1994). The most dramatic suicide rate increase has been in adolescent males, which has tripled over the last 30 years (Lester, 1997). By ethnic group, Native Americans carry the highest suicide risk, followed by whites, and then blacks (Sederer, 1994). Suicide rates are higher among the single, widowed, and divorced than the married (Sederer, 1994). Chew and McCleary (1994) have presented a life course theory of suicide risk which explains how such static, demographic factors can impede motivation and activate opportunities for suicide action.

Life Stress/Problems In Living

The idea of suicide and its intention are usually precipitated in part because of negative life events and problems in living that are experienced as insurmountable, intolerable, and hopeless. Suicide completers and attempters have been found to experience significantly more negative life events in the six months preceding the suicide act than the general population or other clinical controls (Cochrane & Robertson, 1975; Hagnell & Rorsman, 1980; Paykel, Prusoff, & Myers, 1975).

Research has further delineated specific types of negative life stressors that increase the risk for suicide. Family trauma, poor parenting environments, and physical and sexual abuse all have been cited as risk factors for suicide (Lester, 1997). Interpersonal loss and conflict is a common trigger for younger suicides (Rich, Fowler, Fogerty, & Young, 1988). Work problems and unemployment are associated with suicides (Maris, 1981), as well as the availability and ownership of firearms (Brent, Perper, Allman, Moritz, Wartella, & Zelenak, 1991). Finally, exposure to suicide models in families, friends, and the media has been associated with an increased risk for suicide (Moscicki, 1995).

☐ Contemporary Approaches

Integrative Models In Suicidology

Suicidology and its applications are now in a position to point to various risk factors for the suicide idea and its action, such as the suicidal and hopeless state of mind, depression, psychache, mental illness, substance abuse, demographics, life stress and problems in living, and suicide models. Recent theoretical work has developed multifactorial models to integrate such risk factors into an organized framework. This framework helps explain how risk factors relate to each other and the suicide process. Such models have guided innovative risk assessment schemes and will ultimately lead to new applications as the future evolves. While a number of models have been proposed, this review will consider three of these models to illustrate the multifactorial and process-oriented direction to which the areas of suicide causation and risk assessment have moved.

Transaction, Developmental Model

Most recently, King (1998) has elaborated on a transactional model of suicide risk development. From this view, psychache is seen as the final common pathway to suicide risk which develops over time from the dynamic interplay of various risk vulnerabilities and significant life events. Individual differences in genetic and constitutional vulnerabilities, caregiving environments, life experiences, and social stressors are hypothesized to result in multiple pathways of coping. The further existence of other suicide risk factors such as mental illness, substance abuse, social isolation, and a host of psychological vulnerabilities can move a person in a variety of directions across the lifespan. Difficulties in one area can affect or exacerbate other areas, while strengths and coping resources can minimize or protect an individual from other risk factors (moving an individual away from suicide risk). Suicide risk within this model is viewed as an individual determinant that ultimately arises when a person's threshold for suffering of psychache is overloaded.

While the above description is simplified, several important implications of this model for risk assessment are apparent. First, there are many possible pathways to suicide risk. Risk assessment, therefore, may need to utilize multiple models for different developmental pathways for different subsets of at-risk individuals (e.g., youth at risk, elderly at risk, substance abusers, borderline personality, and self-mutilators). Second, risk assessment is an individualized and idiosyncratic clinical process, that seeks to capture the unique interplay of coping strengths and weaknesses, the threshold for psychache, and the suicide mental state. Third, and a related issue, risk assessment must be driven by developmental/life-course theory, as different risk factors mean different things and carry different influences at different stages of a person's life.

Stress And Coping Model

The stress and coping model of suicide risk has been most influential in recent literature in integrating risk factors (Braucht, 1979; Josepho & Plutchik, 1994; Rubenstein, 1986; Schotte & Clum, 1982, 1987). From this perspective, individuals at risk for suicide are hypothesized to have various biopsychosocial vulnerabilities which render them unprepared or ill equipped to handle environmental and social demands or problems. With continued life stress, ineffective coping, and growing frustrations, individuals are thought to develop increasing psychache, hopelessness, and ultimately suicide intention.

Yufit and Bongar (1992) have elaborated on this model by proposing that suicide risk is a loss of psychological equilibrium in coping with life cycle stressors and a decreased capacity for a positive future time perspective. In this model, a number of theoretical proposals regarding coping and psychological equilibrium are offered. First, psychological equilibrium, defined as a healthy adaptation to change, is a function of adequate coping skills predominating over one's vulnerability to stress. Second, negative time equilibrium is a function of the fear of the future, plus nostalgia for the past. Third, positive time equilibrium is a function of a planned future time orientation and an acceptance and integration of past events. Fourth, maintaining a vital balance during critical stressful life events is a function of resilient and buoyant coping and adaptation abilities, predominating over vulnerability and the loss of future time perspective.

The stress-coping model of suicide risk emphasizes that coping skills, vulnerabilities, stress level, and future perspective are essential data sources in determining psychache threshold and suicide intention. Psychache and loss of future time perspective (hopelessness) ultimately are viewed as developing from an individual's inability to cope with life stress and problems of living. Coping processes, self-efficacy, and future expectations all are important variables in estimating a person's risk for suicide.

State of Mind Model

Along similar lines, our work (e.g., Bonner & Rich, 1991, 1988a, 1988b; Rich & Bonner, 1990) has developed a state of mind model of suicide risk. In this perspective, suicide risk is viewed as a function of a hopeless state of mind, in which ideation, planning, intention, and lethality develop in relative proportion to the degree of a person's hopelessness. This suicide state of mind is thought to vary in intensity, frequency, and lethality depending upon the variable influence of a number of biopsychosical vulnerabilities. None of these risk factors are thought to be necessary or sufficient for suicide intention, but a combination of factors are thought to create psychache and suicide intention dependent on each person's unique threshold for emotional pain. Such risk factor combinations may vary in risk level as a function of sex, age, race, or cultural characteristics.

Risk assessment based on this state of mind model emphasizes the content and meaning of the person's state of mind with regard to suicide ideas, intention, and hopelessness. Once the mind state is captured, the particular configuration of vulnerabilities and strengths will be assessed to understand its relation to the variable mind state of the individual. History is viewed as essential to risk assessment as the more often and more elaborated a person's mental state for suicide has been, the more likely this repertoire will be repeated with similar stressful events and emotional triggers and frustrations.

In reviewing the direction of integrative models, several important implications for risk assessment technology should be noted. First, risk assessment needs to be dynamic, individualized, and multifactorial with suicidal mind state at the core of the assessment. Second, within the assessment of mind state, the level and threshold for psychache, coping ability, and future time perspective must be directly assessed. Third, risk factors or vulnerabilities that directly impact psychache and the suicide mind state must be evaluated, including mental illness, depression, substance abuse, and stress level. Fourth, at the tertiary or distal level, such factors as sex, neurotransmitter dysfunction, family history, and at risk child-rearing/family environments will need to be considered for persons who come from unique populations at risk. On all levels of risk assessment, the existence of coping strengths and psychosocial resources will need to be considered as potential negaters and protectors from suicide risk. Fifth, risk assessment is necessarily time, state, and situationally limited. We will be unable to predict long-term suicide risk. Based on these implications and current integrative models, a variety of assessment schemes and protocols have developed, several of which are reviewed next.

☐ Instruments to Estimate Suicide Risk

Motto's (1985) monumental work on the development of an empirically-derived, comprehensive instrument to estimate suicide risk began this new direction. In his words, the purpose and goal of suicide risk assessment is as follows:

> We know that suicide risk is a dynamic, ever changing phenomenon, influenced by numerous, uncontrollable factors, and that the probability of a suicidal outcome fluctuates in a way that calls for monitoring by repeated clinical assessments. The use of a scale has never been intended to predict suicide, but simply to supplement clinical judgment at the time an evaluation is done. (p. 139)

In Motto's scale, 15 areas across system domains are assessed by the clinician, including mental state of suicide ideation, intention, lethality of method, mental and mood status, personal and familial history of psychiatric illness, stress level, and at risk demographics. Risk factors are weighted with differential scoring based on the literature and empirically discriminatory value. A total overall score is then calculated to estimate the level of current suicide risk, ranging from very low, low, moderate, high, and very high.

Motto (1992) has continued this integrative model for risk estimation over the years with several key concepts. First, in line with Shneidman's (1998) concept of psychache, Motto speaks of risk estimation as primarily the clinician's judgment of how close a person's emotional pain is to his or her pain tolerance threshold at a given time. Moreover, secondary risk factors are considered important in lowering threshold, thereby increasing risk. Such secondary factors include sleep deprivation, intoxication, neurotransmitter dysfunction, and stress level. Second, Motto stresses the importance of both clinical and empirical approaches to risk estimation. The clinical approach attempts to understand the life experience of the individual, his or her level of psychache, coping resources, and future expectations (orientation). The empirical approach utilizes and integrates data from multiple system sources that represent risk for populations of suiciders. Ultimately, risk estimation is the clinician's integration of clinical and empirical methods and his or her intuition of how close a person seems to be to the threshold of psychache and suicide intention, given the particular array of present risk factors

Suicide Assessment Battery

Yufit's (1991) presidential address to the American Association of Suicidology called for a comprehensive suicide assessment battery that integrates clinical and empirical methods and multiple data sources. Yufit proposed a core battery to target suicide mental state, coping abilities, and future time perspective. This core battery included a Focused Interview, a Suicide Screening Checklist, a Coping Abilities Questionnaire, and a Time Questionnaire. A secondary battery was also proposed to address general personality structure, coping style, and psychosocial needs, that would define vulnerability or strength in the event of significant negative life events and life adversity.

In these proposed batteries, Yufit outlined three major components in the assessment of suicide potential with risk factors delineated. First, the following vulnerability variables are considered primary: hopelessness, internalized anger, depression, and substance abuse. The secondary factors are rigid cognitive style, primary orientation to the past, lack of belonging, psychiatric history, isolation, and loneliness. Finally, the third area of risk assessment pertains to coping abilities, or lack thereof, that may help negate or increase suicide intention. The factors for this third area are trust in self and others, resiliency in adapting to change or loss, capacity for intimacy and love, sense of belonging, a well-developed future time perspective, and continuity of self (identity). Yufit has proposed a differential weighting scoring scheme, to be empirically derived by future research, with various at risk populations.

SAD PERSONS Scale

Other less sophisticated multifactorial risk assessment schemes have been developed to help the clinician. The SAD PERSONS Scale (Patterson, Dohn, Bird, & Patterson, 1983) was devised as an acronym to guide the clinician in assessing ten empirically-validated risk factors. SAD PERSONS refers to the following suicide risk factors: **s**ex, **a**ge, **d**epression, **p**revious attempt, **e**thanol (alcohol) abuse, rational thinking loss, social supports lacking, organized plan for suicide, no spouse, and sickness. Patterson et al. (1983) recommended a scoring of one point for the presence of each risk factor for a total possible risk score of ten. In terms of intervention, these researchers have suggested treatment follow-up for persons with a score of 3–4, possible hospitalization and a contract for safety with persons with a score of 5–6, and definite hospitalization or commitment for persons with a score of 7–10. Juhnke (1994) has demonstrated the utility of this scale in training clinical students to conduct effective suicide risk assessments.

M.A.P. Guide

Along similar lines, our work has developed other multifactorial schemes to help guide the clinician in conducting suicide risk assessments. The acronym of M.A.P. was devised to target the key modalities of suicide risk assessment, namely the Mental State for Suicidality, the Affective State of Suicidality, and the Psychosocial Context of Suicidality (Bonner, 1992b, 1990). The Mental State domain refers to the thoughts and perceptions associated with suicidal intention. Such cognitions encompass suicide ideation, plans and motives for suicide, cognitive and reality controls, hopelessness, and reasons for living. The Affective State modality refers to the nature, level, and threshold of emotional pain or psychache, which contributes to hopelessness and suicide intention. Other related mood influences would also be considered in the assessment of this modality, such as mood illnesses, underlying physiology (e.g., serotonin disturbance), and the use of or addiction to mood altering drugs. The Psychosocial Context domain refers to the life and social situation of the person, including life stressors, problems of living, social supports, repertoire of coping skills, and larger sociodemographic stressors that may negatively impact coping. Such stressors are viewed as taxing an individual and, over time for some vulnerable individuals, will lead to continued frustration, emotional distress, psychological breakdown, and suicide intention.

Multimodal, B.A.S.I.C. I.D. Analysis

To expand this analysis, we (Bonner & Michalik-Bonner, 1996) applied the multimodal B.A.S.I.C. I.D. scheme of Arnold Lazarus (1995) to suicide risk assessment. From this perspective, suicidality and risk were viewed as a B.A.S.I.C. I.D. process that is defined, determined, and maintained by some transaction of Behavior, Affect, Sensations, Images, Cognitions, Interpersonal Systems, and Drugs (Physiology/Genetics). The culmination of these system transactions were hypothesized to lead to suicide risk by a process and progression of ineffective coping, varying levels of hopelessness, and ultimate suicide intention. Risk assessment from this analysis directed systematic and direct evaluation of each of these modalities, including current status as well as historical functioning.

The targets of assessment for each of these modalities are outlined below. The Behavioral Modality refers to past and current suicidal behavior, including motives, intention, lethality, associated life and death wishes, current ideas and plans, behavioral (dys)control, and family behavioral history of suicidality. The Affective Modality has targets of psychache and its threshold, depression, mania, anxiety, and panic. The component of Sensations refers to anxiety and psychomotor arousal, depression and psychomotor retardation, hallucinations or delusions with suicide or death themes, and withdrawal. Images are assessed by examining the presence of suicide or death fantasies or helpless or hopeless images of self and future outcome. The Cognitive component refers to suicidal ideation and contemplation, cognitive rigidity, hopeless expectancies, lack of adaptive, life-oriented beliefs, psychotic processing, and weak cognitive controls. The Interpersonal System is examined by looking closely at the life situation of the person, including the presence of negative life stressors and problems of living, social isolation, and larger sociodemographic and cultural stressors which may be taxing coping ability. Finally, the Drugs Component looks at the possible underlying pathological biochemistry of affective or thought disorders, genetic influences, and alcohol or drug abuse.

The methods of multimodal risk assessment likewise need to be multifactorial, in order to insure comprehensive and convergent information on the actual status of risk factors and vulnerabilities. Moreover, as noted previously, strengths, resources, or buffers in one area may compensate or protect an individual from another area of risk. Juhnke (1994) has recommended three critical methods for risk assessment: clinical interview, empirical evaluation, and consultation with significant others and previous treatment providers. Yufit's (1991) proposal for a comprehensive suicide assessment battery similarly emphasized multimethod risk assessment, including clinical interviews, empirical scales, and psychosocial history examination. Sommers-Flanagan and Sommers-Flanagan's (1995) work outlined a systematic approach to methods and risk factors in this process, with emphasis on consultation and acquiring a thorough sampling of historical information as it relates to the various risk factors. Likewise, these authors emphasized the importance of a systematic approach for documenting a clinically, ethically, and legally sound risk assessment with a corresponding plan for case management.

☐ Into The New Millennium

As we now approach the crossroads to the next millennium, our accomplishments and future goals may be best judged by Yufit's (1991) hopeful prophecy a decade earlier:

> It is hoped that, by the year 2000, research efforts will have produced an assessment profile sheet that encompasses all of the major dimensions—psychological, psychiatric, diagnostic, demographic, historical, self-destructive/self-harm lifestyle (e.g., drug abuse, workaholism), economic factors, and even biological parameters, such as the role of brain metabolites like serotonin. (p. 160–161)

On the one hand, the profile has been established with demonstrated risk factors across these system domains. We have rich theory to guide us in the understanding and application of suicide risk assessment. We now know what to look for and have some innovative assessment schemes and empirical scales to guide us systematically through this process. The goal of long-term prediction remains unattainable. Risk assessment and estimation, however, is a reasonable goal within a limited time frame, when the dynamic, multifactorial process of suicide risk with variable state and situational constraints are considered. The mind state of suicidal ideation (and its progression) and psychache threshold will continue to be the most potent risk factors of the profile. All other system factors, distal or proximate, static or fluid, contribute to vulnerability, poor coping, hopelessness, and suicide intention.

On the other hand, our challenge in the next century is to more systematically refine this profile, determine empirically the relative importance of factors, which factors can compensate (or cannot) for others, and by which methods we can more reliably and validly assess suicide risk. Ironically, Yufit's prophetic call a decade earlier has been recently answered by his announcement in *Suicide and Life-Threatening Behavior* (1998):

> As recently appointed Assessment Editor, I want to make periodic reports on the use of existing, published psychological measures that claim to evaluate suicidal potential. Such measures would include "suicide scales" within larger psychological measures, as well as tests specifically aimed at assessing suicide potential. New measures, in the process of being developed, can also be considered.
>
> Questions to be answered include the following: How useful have these assessment measures been? Are some better suited for screening, others to evaluating degree of lethality of the intention (or attempt)? Do any distinguish self-harm from self-destructive intent, or immediate risk versus long term risk? Does the use of more than one measure, or even a battery of measures improve accuracy, sensitivity, specificity of the assessment process? Are there useful measures existing, not yet published, which an author would be willing to share?
>
> At this stage, the format is open: a letter on your experiences, or a more formal report. I would very much like to develop some structure into the still very underdeveloped, nebulous area of assessment of suicidal potential. Respond directly to SLTB. (pp. v)

As we now approach these remaining goals, a few ever-pressing general themes in suicide risk assessment will need to be more seriously considered in our progress. Definition specificity in terms of suicide outcome, behaviors, and criteria targets is critical to improved risk estimation. Researchers and clinicians will need to specify exactly the suicidal behavior for which risk is being estimated for (e.g., ideation, types of attempts, types of completions), the stage of the suicidal process, and the degree of lethality involved. Estimation judgments should also include the internal and external conditions for the behavior being estimated, the time frame, and relative probabilities. Quick access to established base rates for different criteria behaviors (and populations) is vital as well as the research data on improvement of classification with risk factor subpopulations. This information obviously becomes increasingly complex with multifactorial and interactional models of risk estimation.

Along similar lines, the literature has now moved to a point where different multifactorial risk models are needed for different suicidal, psychosocial, and demographic populations. Moreover, risk factors may be more important, less important, or not at all important for different populations, individuals, and suicide stages. The areas of risk factor weighting and (non)compensatory interactions will be extremely important for future progress. These are all critical questions in need of empirical answers. The sobering case of jail suicides, for example, illustrates the limited usefulness of commonly-used risk models. Other than the use of drug or alcohol intoxicants, most jail suicide victims are without other established risk factors (Bonner, 1992a). The single, most important risk factor appears to be environmental, whereby detainees are placed in conditions of isolation and social deprivation, which quickly results in suicide (Bonner, 1992a).

With different models of suicide risk estimation, it also becomes important to know what methods of assessment are available, and what methods are better than others for different populations. A system needs to be established that lists methods available, advantages and disadvantages, and psychometric information on reliability and validity for different populations.

The ever increasing complexity of suicide risk assessment's future is apparent, in different multifactorial models, differential weighting, and multiple assessment methods. However, our advancement is timely as we are in the midst of the information processing age where computer systems can organize, summarize, and analyze such data quickly and direct the clinician to the most useful model and methods for risk estimation. It is conceivable that, within the next decade, a data base and analytical system could exist in which the clinician simply needs to enter key identifying information for an individual and the system will then generate a best fit model and method template to guide the clinician's assessment. Such systems will evolve and grow in direct relation to the advancement of our science, and specifically how successful we have been in responding to Yufit's questions and poignant call for structure and unity in the field.

Our scientific and technical advancements in the next millennium for suicide risk assessment will be ultimately judged by how helpful such procedures have been to the clinician in better seeing and understanding the world of the suicidal person. It is only this human understanding that, most of the time, will open the suicidal mind to possibilities of relief, hope, and recovery.

☐ References

Anderson, K., Townsend, S., Everly, G., & Lating, J. (1995). Suicide risk assessment in crisis situations: Clinical utility of an abbreviated self-report measure. *Crisis Intervention, 1,* 225–230.

Beck, A. T. (1967). *Depression: Clinical, experimental, and theoretical aspects.* New York: Harper and Row.

Beck, A. T. (1986). Hopelessness as a predictor of eventual suicide. *Annals of the New York Academy of Sciences, 487,* 90–96.

Beck, A. T., Brown, G., Berchick, R. J., Stewart, B. L., & Steer, R. A. (1990). Relationship between hopelessness and ultimate suicide: A replication with psychiatric outpatients. *American Journal of Psychiatry, 147,* 190–195.

Beck, A. T., Kovacs, M., & Weissman, A. (1979). Assessment of suicidal ideation: The scale of suicide ideation. *Journal of Consulting and Clinical Psychology, 47,* 343–352.

Beck, A. T., & Lester, D. (1976). Components of suicidal intent in completed and attempted suicides. *Journal of Psychology, 92,* 35–38.

Beck, R. W., Morris, J. B., & Beck, A. T. (1974). Cross-validation of the suicide intent scale. *Psychological Reports, 34,* 445–446.

Beck, A. T., Schuyler, D., & Herman, I. (1974). Development of the suicide intent scale. In A. T. Beck, H. L. P. Resnick, & D. J. Lettieri (Eds.), *The prediction of suicide* (pp. 45–56). Bowie, MD: Charles Press.

Beck, A. T., & Steer, R. A. (1989). Clinical predictors of eventual suicide: A 5 to 10 year prospective study of suicide attempters. *Journal of Affective Disorders, 17,* 203–209.

Beck, A. T., Weissman, A., Lester, D., & Trexler, L. (1974). The measurement of pessimism: The hopelessness scale. *Journal of Consulting and Clinical Psychology, 42,* 861–865.

Bedrosian, R. C., & Beck, A. T. (1979). Cognitive aspects of suicidal behavior. *Suicide and Life-Threatening Behavior, 9,* 87–96.

Beit-Hallahmi, B. (1975). Religion and suicidal behavior. *Psychological Reports, 37,* 1303–1306.

Bonner, R. L. (1990). A "M.A.P." to the clinical assessment of suicide risk. *Journal of Mental Health Counseling, 12,* 231–236.

Bonner, R. L. (1992b). Isolation, seclusion, and psychosocial vulnerability as risk factors for suicide behind bars. In R. Maris, A. Berman, J. Maltsberger, & R. Yufit (Eds.), *Assessment and prediction of suicide* (pp. 398–420). New York: Guilford.

Bonner, R. L. (1992a). Suicide prevention in correctional facilities. In L. Van de Creek, S. Knapp, & T. Jackson (Eds.), *Innovations in clinical practice: A source book* (Vol. 11, pp. 467–480). Sarasota, FL: Professional Resource Press.

Bonner, R. L., & Michalik-Bonner, D. (1996). The suicidal patient in private practice: A multimodal approach. *Psychotherapy in Private Practice, 14*(4), 1–15.

Bonner, R. L., & Rich, A. R. (1988a). A prospective investigation of suicidal ideation in college students: A test of a model. Suicide and Life-Threatening *Behavior, 18,* 245–258.

Bonner, R. L., & Rich, A. R. (1988b). Negative life stress, social problem-solving appraisal, and hopelessness: Implications for suicide research. *Cognitive Therapy and Research, 12,* 849–856.

Bonner, R. L., & Rich, A. R. (1991). Predicting vulnerability to hopelessness under conditions of negative life stress. *Journal of Nervous and Mental Disease, 179,* 29–32.

Braucht, G. (1979). Interactional analysis of suicidal behavior. *Journal of Consulting and Clinical Psychology, 47,* 653–669.

Breed, W. (1963). Occupational mobility and suicide among white males. *American Sociological Review, 28,* 179–188.

Brent, D. A., Perper, J. A., Allman, C. J., Moritz, G. M., Wartella, M. E., & Zelenak, J. P. (1991). The presence and accessibility of firearms in the homes of adolescent suicides: A case-control study. *Journal of the American Medical Association, 266,* 2989–2995.

Brown, T. R., & Sheran, J. J. (1972). Suicide prediction: A review. *Life-Threatening Behavior, 2,* 67–98.

Chew, K., & McCleary, R. (1994). A life course theory of suicide risk. *Suicide and Life-Threatening Behavior, 24,* 234–244.

Clark, D. C., & Fawcett, J. (1992). Review of empirical risk factors for evaluation of suicidal patients. In B. Bongar (Ed.), *Suicide: Guidelines for assessment, management, and treatment* (pp. 16–48). New York: Oxford University Press.

Clopton, J. R., & Baucom, D. H. (1979). MMPI suicide ratings of suicide risk. *Journal of Personality Assessment, 43,* 293–296.

Cochrane, R., & Robertson, A. (1975). Stress in the lives of parasuicides. *Social Psychiatry, 10,* 161–171.

Crumley, F. E. (1990). Substance abuse and adolescent suicidal behavior. *Journal of the American Medical Association, 263,* 3051–3056.

Dublin, L. I. (1963). *Suicide: A sociological and statistical study.* New York: Ronald Press.

Durkheim, E. (1951). *Suicide.* (J. A. Spalding, & G. Simpson, Trans.) Glencoe, IL: Free Press. (Original work published 1897)

Eisenthal, S. (1967). Suicide and aggression. *Psychological Reports, 21,* 745–751.

Eyman, J. R., & Eyman, S. K. (1990). Suicide risk and assessment instruments. In P. Cimbolic & D. Jobes (Eds.), *Youth suicide: issues, assessment, and intervention* (pp. 9–32). Springfield, IL: Charles C. Thomas.

Eyman, J. R., & Eyman, S. K. (1992). Personality assessment in suicide prediction. In R. Maris, A. Berman, J. Maltsberger, & R. Yufit (Eds.), *Assessment and prediction of suicide* (pp. 183–201). New York: Guilford.

Exner, J. E., & Weiner, I. (1982). *The Rorschach: A comprehensive system* (Vol. 3). New York: Wiley.

Exner, J. E., & Wylie, J. (1977). Some Rorschach data concerning suicide. *Journal of Personality Assessment, 41,* 339–348.

Fisher, S. (1971). The value of the Rorschach for detecting suicide trends. *Journal of Projective Techniques, 15,* 250–254.

Freud, S. (1950). *Beyond the pleasure principle.* New York: Liveright. (Original work published 1920)

Freud, S. (1957). Mourning and melancholia. *Standard edition of the complete psychological works.* London: Hogarth Press. (Original work published 1917)

Hagnell, O., & Rorsman, B. (1980). Suicide in the Lundby study: A controlled prospective investigation of stressful life events. *Neuropsychobiology, 6,* 319–332.

Hughes, D. H. (1995). Can the clinician predict suicide. *Psychiatric Services, 46,* 449–451.

Josepho, S. A., & Plutchik, R. (1994). Stress, coping, and suicide risk in psychiatric patients. *Suicide and Life-Threatening Behavior, 24,* 48–57.

Juhnke, G. A. (1994). Teaching suicidal risk assessment to counselor education students. *Counselor Education and Supervision, 34,* 52–57.

King, C. A. (1998). Suicide across the lifespan: Pathways to prevention. *Suicide and Life-Threatening Behavior, 28,* 328–337.

Kral, M. J. (1994). Suicide: A social logic. *Suicide and Life-Threatening Behavior, 24,* 245–255.

Kral, M., & Sakinofsky, I. (1994). A clinical model for suicide risk assessment. In A. Leenaars, J. Maltsberger, & R. Neimeyer (Eds.), *Treatment of suicidal people* (pp. 19–31). Washington, DC: Taylor and Francis.

Lazarus, A. A. (1995). Multimodal therapy. In R. J. Corsini & D. Wedding (Eds.), *Current psychotherapies* (5th ed., pp. 322–355). Itasca, IL: Peacock.

Lester, D. (1995). The concentration of neurotransmitter metabolites in the cerebrospinal fluid of suicide individuals: A meta-analysis. *Pharmacopsychiatry, 28,* 45–50.

Lester, D. (1997). *Making sense of suicide.* Philadelphia, PA: Charles Press.

Maris, R. W. (1981). *Pathways to suicide: A survey of self-destructive behaviors.* Baltimore: John Hopkins University Press.

Maris, R., Berman, A., & Maltsberger, J. (1992). Summary and conclusions: What we have learned about suicide assessment and prediction. In R. Maris, A. Berman, J. Maltsberger, & R. Yufit (Eds.), *Assessment and prediction of suicide* (pp. 640–672). New York: Guilford.

McCulloch, J. W., & Phillip, A. S. (1967). Social factors associated with attempted suicide: A review of the literature. *British Journal of Psychiatric Social Work, 9,* 30–36.

Mikawa, J. K. (1973). An alternative to current analysis of suicidal behavior. *Psychological Reports, 32,* 323–330.

Minkoff, K., Bergman, E., Beck, A. T., & Beck, R. W. (1973). Hopelessness, depression, and attempted suicide. *American Journal of Psychiatry, 130,* 455–459.

Moscicki, E. K. (1995). Epidemiology of suicidal behavior. *Suicide and Life-Threatening Behavior, 25,* 22–35.

Motto, J. A. (1985). Preliminary field testing of a risk estimator for suicide risk. *Suicide and Life-Threatening Behavior, 15,* 139–150.

Motto, J. A. (1992). An integrated approach to estimating suicide risk. In R. Maris, A. Berman, J. Maltsberger, & R. Yufit (Eds.), *Assessment and prediction of suicide* (pp. 525–539). New York: Guilford.

Murphy, G. E. (1985). Suicide and attempted suicide. In R. Michels (Ed.), *Psychiatry* (Vol. 1, pp. 1–17). Philadelphia, PA: Lippincott.

Nordstrom, P., Samuelson, M., Asberg, M., Traskman-Bendz, L., Aberg-Wistedt, A., Nordin, C., & Bertilsson, L. (1994). CSF 5-HIAA predicts suicide risk after attempted suicide. *Suicide and Life-Threatening Behavior, 24,* 1–9.

Patterson, W. M., Dohn, H. H., Bird, J., & Patterson, G. A. (1983). Evaluation of suicidal patients: The SAD PERSONS scale. *Psychosomatics, 24,* 343–349.

Paykel, E. S., Prusoff, B. A., & Myers, J. K. (1975). Suicide attempts and recent life events. *Archives of General Psychiatry, 32,* 327–333.

Phillips, D. P. (1979). Suicide, motor vehicle fatalities, and the mass media: Evidence toward a theory of suggestion. *American Journal of Sociology, 84,* 1150–1174.

Polcorny, A. D. (1993). Suicide prediction revisited. *Suicide and Life-Threatening Behavior, 23,* 1–10.

Reynolds, W. M. (1987). *The suicidal ideation questionnaire.* Odessa, FL: Psychological Assessment Resource.

Rich, A. R., & Bonner, R. L. (1990). *A process model of suicidal behavior.* Unpublished manuscript, Indiana University of Pennsylvania, Indiana, PA.

Rich, C. L., Fowler, R. C., Fogerty, L. A., & Young, D. (1988). San Diego suicide study: III. Relationship between diagnoses and stressors. *Archives of General Psychiatry, 45,* 589–592.

Robins, E. (1986). Psychosis and suicide. *Biological Psychiatry, 21,* 665–672.

Rothberg, J. M., & Geer-Williams, C. (1992). A comparison and review of suicide prediction scales. In R. Maris, A. Berman, J. Maltsberger, & R. Yufit (Eds.), *Assessment and prediction of suicide* (pp. 202–217). New York: Guilford.

Roy, A. (1992). Genetics, biology, and suicide in the family. In R. Maris, A. Berman, J. Maltsberger, & R. Yufit (Eds.), *Assessment and prediction of suicide* (pp. 574–588). New York: Guilford.

Roy, A., & Linnoila, M. (1986). Alcoholism and suicide. *Suicide and Life-Threatening Behavior, 16,* 244–276.

Rubenstein, D. H. (1986). A stress-diathesis theory of suicide. *Suicide and Life-Threatening Behavior, 16,* 182–197.

Schotte, D. E., & Clum, G. A. (1982). Suicidal ideation in a college population: A test of a model. *Journal of Consulting and Clinical Psychology, 50,* 690–696.

Schotte, D. E., & Clum, G. A. (1987). Problem-solving skills in suicidal psychiatric patients. *Journal of Consulting and Clinical Psychology, 55,* 49–54.

Sederer, L. (1994). Managing suicidal inpatients. In A. Leenaars, J. Maltsberger, & R. Neimeyer (Eds.), *Treatment of suicidal people* (pp. 167–182). Washington, DC: Taylor and Francis.

Shneidman, E. (1985). *Definition of suicide.* New York: Wiley.

Shneidman, E. S. (1993). Suicide and psychache. *Journal of Nervous and Mental Disease, 181,* 147–149.

Shneidman, E. S. (1998). Further reflections on suicide and psychache. *Suicide and Life-Threatening Behavior, 28,* 245–250.

Shneidman, E. S., & Farberow, N. L. (1961). Statistical comparison between attempted and committed suicide. In N. L. Farberow & E. S. Shneidman (Eds.), *The cry for help* (pp. 19–47). New York: McGraw-Hill.

Sommers-Flanagan, J., & Sommers-Flanagan, R. (1995). Intake interviewing with suicidal patients: A systematic approach. *Professional Psychology: Research and Practice, 26,* 41–47.

Tanney, B. L. (1992). Mental disorders, psychiatric patients, and suicide. In R. Maris, A. Berman, J. Maltsberger, & R. Yufit (Eds.), *Assessment and prediction of suicide* (pp. 277–320). New York: Guilford.

Tuckman, J. & Youngman, W. F. (1968). A scale for assessing suicide risk of attempted suicides. *Journal of Clinical Psychology, 24,* 17–19.

Vinoda, K. S. (1966). Personality characteristics of attempted suicides. *British Journal of Psychiatry, 112,* 1143–1150.

Weishaar, M. E., & Beck, A. T. (1992). Clinical and cognitive predictors of suicide. In R. Maris, A. Berman, J. Maltsberger, & R. Yufit (Eds.), *Assessment and prediction of suicide* (pp. 467–483). New York: Guilford.

Yufit, R. I. (1991). Suicide assessment in the 1990s. *Suicide and Life-Threatening Behavior, 21,* 152–163.

Yufit, R. I. (1998). Announcement. *Suicide and Life-Threatening Behavior, 28,* v.

Yufit, R. I., & Bongar, B. (1992). Suicide, stress, and coping with life cycle events. In R. Maris, A. Berman, J. Maltsberger, & R. Yufit (Eds.), *Assessment and prediction of suicide* (pp. 553–573). New York: Guilford.

7

Alec Roy

Psychiatric Treatment in Suicide Prevention

Psychiatric patients are at increased risk of suicide. Using a meta-analysis approach, Harris and Barraclough (1997) searched the medical literature from 1966 to 1993 to find reports on the mortality of psychiatric disorders. They abstracted 249 reports with two years or more of follow-up and compared the observed numbers of suicide with those expected. A standardized mortality ratio (SMR) was calculated for each psychiatric disorder. They found that of 44 disorders considered, 36 had a significantly raised SMR for suicide. They concluded that virtually all psychiatric disorders have an increased risk of suicide except mental retardation and dementia.

This group went on to study the 79 follow-up reports in the meta-analysis that also reported the number of deaths from all causes as well as the number of suicides (Inskip, Harris, & Barraclough, 1998). Using statistical modeling techniques, they found that the lifetime suicide risks for the disorders most closely associated with suicide were lower than those generally quoted; they estimated 7% for alcohol dependence, 6% for affective disorder and 4% for schizophrenia. This chapter reviews the major psychiatric treatment trends in suicide prevention in the past, the present, and the future. Each psychiatric disorder will be reviewed separately.

☐ The Past

Depression

The Epidemiology Catchment Area (ECA) study reported a 2.3% one month prevalence rate for a major depression episode in the general population (Regier et al., 1990). Depression is one of the most important risk factors for suicide. For example, in the psychological autopsy of Robins, Murphy, Wilkinsson, Gassner, and Kayes (1959) study, 45% of suicide victims were diagnosed as having had primary depression, as were 30% in a second study, and 64% in a third study. Follow-up studies report that about one in six depressed patients (15%) die by committing suicide, though many of these studies were carried out from inpatient samples and before lithium prophylaxis was available (reviewed by Jamison, 1990).

The characteristics of unipolar depressives who commit suicide were examined by the Finnish Suicide Research Center in a psychological autopsy study (Isometsa et al., 1994). Males were over-represented as 45 of the 71 unipolar suicide victims were male (63%) and 26 female (37%). Thus, male sex is a risk factor for suicide among depressed subjects. The mean age was 50 years. The great majority (85%) of subjects were complicated cases of depression with comorbid diagnoses, and comorbidity varied with sex and age. For example, males were over-represented among the third of the depressed suicides with comorbid substance abuse. Older suicide victims had more comorbid physical illness and fewer personality disorders, which were found more among younger suicide victims.

In relation to treatment, 75% of the depressed suicides had a history of psychiatric treatment, and two thirds had had psychiatric treatment during the last year. However, only 45% were receiving psychiatric treatment at the time of suicide. The mean time from last contact with a health care provider was 39.0 ± 89.8 days. Eighteen percent had face-to-face contact with a health care professional the same day they committed suicide, 39% had visited a professional within the last week, and 66% within the 3 months before suicide. In 60% the reason for the visit was psychiatric and in 40% it was somatic.

Most depressed suicide victims had received no treatment for depression. The antidepressant treatment of depression before death was either absent or inadequate. Only 3% had received antidepressants in adequate doses, 7% weekly psychotherapy, and 3% electroconvulsive therapy (ECT) (Table 1). None of the 24 depressives with psychotic features had received adequate psychopharmacological treatment. Only 8% committed suicide using antidepressants. Men had received less treatment for depression than women and more often used violent suicide methods.

TABLE 1. Antidepressant Treatment Received by 66 Male and Female Suicide Victims with Major Depression

	Males (N = 42)		Females (N = 24)		Total (N = 66)	
	N	%	N	%	N	%
Antidepressant						
None	33	79	11	46	44	67
Tricycle equivalent dose (mg)						
0–74	3	7	6	25	9	14
75–149	5	12	6	25	11	17
150–300	1	3	1	4	2	3

$X^2 = 5.97$, df = 1, p = 0.02 (with Yates's correction)
Table from Isometsa et al. (1996), used with permission.

Thus, the Finnish workers found that although about half of the depressed suicide victims were receiving psychiatric care at the time of death, few were receiving adequate treatment for depression. They concluded that for suicide prevention in major depression, great improvements in treatment and follow-up are required, particularly for male depressives.

Bipolar Disorder

Bipolar patients have a raised suicide risk. There is, however, no difference in suicide rates between unipolar and bipolar patients. Some studies have shown that the suicide rate among bipolar II patients is higher than among bipolar I patients. Between 25–50% of bipolar patients attempt suicide at least once. Women are more likely than men to attempt suicide; there is no strong data showing a preponderance of males among bipolar suicides. Mixed and delusional manic states are associated with a greater risk of suicide. As in unipolar depression, substance abuse comorbidity and treatment noncompliance are associated with a raised suicide risk (reviewed in Jamison, 1990).

Alcoholism

It is estimated that there are 13.7 million alcoholics in the United States. Alcoholics have an increased risk of suicide with a lifetime suicide risk of 2.2–3.4% percent according to Murphy and Wetzel (1990). More men than women are found among alcoholic suicide victims. Alcoholics usually commit suicide after years of alcoholism. Comorbidity plays an important role, alcoholics with comorbid depressive disorders being at particularly high risk (Cornelius et al., 1995; Roy & Linnoila, 1986). Workers in St. Louis examined the relationship of suicide in alcoholics to specific life events (Murphy, Armstrong, Hermele, Fisher, & Clendenin, 1979). Among 31 alcoholic suicides, 48% had lost a loved one during the year before they committed suicide, and 32% had experienced such a loss during their last six weeks. The St. Louis group examined the lives of 50 other alcoholic suicides. Loss of a close relationship was the most frequently cited precipitating event. Other events included job trouble, financial difficulties, and trouble with the law. For only one of the 50 suicide victims could no precipitating event be identified. Thus, the heavy drinking appears to cause trouble in relationships and life which then precipitates the depression during which the alcoholic suicides (Murphy, 1986).

Other predictors of suicide were also searched for by comparing 67 alcoholic suicides with a community sample of 106 male alcoholics on six putative suicide risk factors (Murphy, Wetzel, Robins, & McEvoy, 1992). These included recent heavy drinking, presence of major depression, suicidal thoughts, poor social support, living alone, and unemployment. The alcoholic suicide victims differed significantly from the living alcoholics on all six of these risk factors (Table 2). Every one of the suicide victims had at least one of these risk factors. Three victims had one factor, three had two factors, and eight had all six factors. By comparison, only

TABLE 2. Comparison of Frequency of Risk Fctors in White Male Alcoholics who Committed Suicide and in Living Alcoholic Controls

Risk Factor	Number and Percentage of Subjects	
	Alcoholics Who Committed Suicide n = 67	Living Alcoholics n = 106
Recent heavy drinking	65 (97%)	44 (42%)
Talk/threat of suicide	53 (79%)	24 (23%)
Little social support	50 (75%)	28 (26%)
Major depressive disorder	39 (58%)	5 (5%)
Unemployed	36 (54%)	19 (18%)
Living alone	30 (45%)	18 (17%)

From Murphy et al. (1992), used with permission.

one living alcoholic had four factors and none had more than four factors (Table 3). Murphy, et al. concluded that the risk of suicide increases as the number of risk factors increases. The presence of as few as four of these factors may identify four fifths of alcoholics at highest risk for suicide (Murphy et al., 1992).

Schizophrenia

Schizophrenia afflicts approximately 1% of the population. The suicide risk is high among schizophrenic patients: It is generally considered that up to 10% die by committing suicide (reviewed in Caldwell & Gottesman, 1992). Most schizophrenics who commit suicide do so during the first few years of illness. Thus, schizophrenic

TABLE 3. Distribution of Risk Factors in White Male Alcoholics who Committed Suicide and in Living Alcoholics

Number of Risk Factors per Subject	Number of Alcoholics Who Committed Suicide n = 67	Number of Living Alcoholics n = 106
0	0	26
1	3	31
2	3	34
3	15	14
4	19	1
5	19	0
6	8	0

The risk factors are current heavy drinking, major depression, poor or no social support, unemployment, living alone, and suicidal thoughts or communication. From Murphy et al. (1992), used with permission.

TABLE 4. Schizophrenic Suicide Victims and Living Schizophrenic Controls Compared for History of Depression

	Schizophrenic suicides N = 30	Schizophrenic controls N = 30	Significance
Psychiatric history			
past depressive episode	17	5	p < .001
past treatment for depression	14	7	p < .05
Last episode			
depressed in last episode	16	4	p < .001
treated for depression	9	6	n.s.

From Roy (1982b), used with permission.

suicides tend to be relatively young and about 75% are unmarried males. Approximately 50% have made a previous suicide attempt. Depressive symptoms are closely associated with their suicide (Roy, 1982b, 1986) (Table 4). Studies have reported that depressive symptoms were present during the last period of contact in up to two thirds of schizophrenic patients who committed suicide; only a small percent commit suicide because of hallucinated instructions or to escape persecutory delusions (Roy, Mazonson, & Pickar, 1984). Up to a third of schizophrenic suicides occur during the first few weeks and months following discharge from a hospitalization; another third commit suicide while inpatients (reviewed in Rossau & Mortensen, 1997). Other life events, like ejection from the family, also precipitate suicide (Lipschitz, 1995). Schizophrenia is a frequent diagnosis in state hospital inpatient suicides (Roy & Draper, 1995).

Premorbid Functioning And Insight

Drake and Cotton (1986) noted that some of their schizophrenic suicide victims had shown high premorbid achievement, high self-expectations of performance, and high awareness of their pathology. They commented that in such patients "Given their inability to achieve major life goals, they felt inadequate, feared further deterioration of their mental abilities, and decided to end their lives rather than continue living with chronic mental illness" (p. 558). Drake and Cotton concluded that such patients "are likely to experience hopelessness defined as negative expectancies about the future and other psychological features of depression" (p. 558).

Positive and Negative Symptoms and Schizophrenic Suicide

Fenton, et al. (1997), in a follow up study, found that schizophrenic patients who committed suicide had significantly lower negative symptom severity at index admission than patients without suicidal behaviors. Two positive symptoms (suspiciousness and delusions), however, were more severe among suicides. The paranoid schizophrenic subtype was associated with an elevated suicide risk (12%) and the deficit subtype was associated with a reduced risk (1.5%) of suicide. They concluded that this suggests that prominent negative symptoms, such as diminished drive, blunted affect, and social and emotional withdrawal, counter the emergence of suicidality in patients with schizophrenia and that the deficit syndrome defines a group at relatively low risk for suicide. Prominent suspiciousness in the absence of negative symptoms defines a relatively high-risk group. Kaplan and Harrow (1996), in a two year follow-up, similarly found that psychotic symptoms predicted later suicidal activity in schizophrenics while deficit symptoms did not.

Personality Disorder

Suicide is the cause of death for up to 10% of patients with borderline personality disorder and for 5% with antisocial personality disorder (Paris, 1990; Stone, 1990). Recently the Finnish group reported that 67 of a random sample of 229 suicide victims had an Axis II personality disorder (Henrikson et al., 1993). About one fifth (n = 43, 19%) of all the 229 suicides had a Cluster B diagnosis (dramatic, emotional or erratic) compared to the estimated prevalence of 4–5% in the general population. Ten percent of the sample (n = 23) had a Cluster C diagnosis (anxious or fearful), and only one a Cluster A diagnosis (odd or eccentric). Ninety-five percent of the personality disordered suicides were associated with comorbid Axis I depressive syndromes, substance abuse disorders, or both.

The Finnish group next compared the personality disordered suicides with sex and age matched suicide victims without personality disorder. Suicides with Cluster B personality disorders were more likely than comparison subjects to have substance abuse disorders (79% vs. 40%) and previous nonfatal suicide attempts (70% vs. 37%) and were less likely to have Axis III physical disorders (29% vs. 50%). Suicide victims in Cluster B had almost always (98%) either comorbid depressive syndromes (74%), substance abuse disorders (79%), or both (55%). These workers found no evidence of impulsive suicides that would have occurred without Axis I disorders. In contrast subjects with Cluster C personality disorders did not differ from their controls on any variable.

Drug Dependence

The National Institute of Drug Abuse estimates that there are four million drug addicts in the United States, two to three million who are cocaine dependent and another 850,000 who are heroin dependent (Leshner, 1999). There is an increased suicide risk among drug abusers. For example, the suicide rate of heroin addicts is about 20 times greater than that of the general population. Marzuk et al. (1992) found that 29% of suicides in New York aged 21–30 tested positive for cocaine. The availability of lethal amount of drugs, intravenous use, associated antisocial personality disorder, chaotic life-style, comorbid depression, and impulsivity are some of the factors that predispose drug dependent persons to suicidal behavior, particularly when dysphoric and intoxicated.

Panic Disorder

Data from the ECA Study showed that 20% of individuals with panic disorder had made a suicide attempt at some time (Weissman, Klennan. Markowitz, Ovellette, & Phil, 1989). This high rate was similar to the rate for individuals with major depression. When panic disorder patients without comorbidity were examined the lifetime rate of suicide attempts remained raised at 7%. Similarly individuals with social phobia have increased rates of suicidal ideation and suicide attempts (Schneier, Johnson, Horning, Liebowitz, & Weissman, 1992). However, the Finnish group found that current panic disorder was rare among completed suicides, being found in only 1.2% of all suicides (Henriksson, Isometsa, Kuoppasalmi, Heikkinen, Marttunen, & Lonnquist, 1996). However, panic disorder suicide victims had superimposed major depression and substance abuse, and associated personality disorders.

Comorbidity In Suicide Victims

Comorbidity is common among suicide victims (Conwell et al., 1996). For example, the Finnish group reported that while 93% of a random sample of 229 suicide victims had an Axis I psychiatric disorder, two or more diagnoses on Axis I were present for 44% of the suicide victims (Henriksson et al., 1993). The most prevalent disorders were depressive disorders (59%) and alcohol dependence or abuse (43%). A personality disorder diagnosis on Axis II was made for 31% and at least one medical diagnosis on Axis III for 46% of the suicides. Only 12% of the suicide victims received only one Axis I diagnosis without any comorbidity.

Attempted Suicide

Individuals who attempt suicide are important consumers of mental health services. There are no national, population-based data on attempted suicide (Moscicki, 1995). Estimates of lifetime prevalence of attempts in adults range from 1.1–4.3 per 100; estimates of 12-month prevalence of attempts range from 0.3–0.8 per 100 (Moscicki, O'Carroll, Rae, Locken, Roy, & Regier, 1988). There is a preponderance of females, and 50% are under 30 years of age; there is an excess of divorced persons, and the lower social classes are over-represented. Females aged 15–19 years have the highest rate of suicide attempts (Moscicki, 1995).

Hospital studies show that about 40% of those who attempt suicide have a history of psychiatric treatment. Psychiatric assessments reveal that about 50% have personality disorder, and up to 40% have other psychiatric disorders. The most common diagnosis that is not a personality disorder is depression (up to 40% of women and 30% of men). However, among serious suicide attempters, Beautrais et al. (1996) found that 90% had a psychiatric disorder, with high rates of mood disorder, substance abuse and antisocial personality disorder. The incidence of comorbidity was high: 56% had two or more disorders. The risk of a serious suicide attempt increased with increasing psychiatric comorbidity. On the basis of multiple logistic regression, Beautrais et al. found that those making serious suicide attempts reported elevated rates of sociodemographic disadvantage, disadvantageous childhood experiences, personality disorder traits, psychiatry morbidity, and exposure to adverse life events. Of those making serious suicide attempts, two thirds (65.9%) had risk factors from four or more of these five risk factor domains, compared to only 4.6% of control subjects. Those who reported a total of five or more individual risk factors had odds of a serious suicide attempt which were 127 times greater than those with fewer than three risk factors.

About 40% of attempters have made a previous attempt. Follow-up studies show that between 13–35% will repeat during the next two years. During this time, up to 7% will make two or more attempts; 2.5%, three or more attempts; and 1% will make five or more attempts. It is recognized that those who attempt suicide and those who commit suicide represent different populations with some overlap. Approximately 1% of persons who *attempt* suicide will *commit* suicide during the following year. The risk of subsequent suicide varies with sex and age (Nordstrom, Asberg, Aberg-Wistedt, & Nordin, 1995.)

☐ The Present and the Future

As reviewed above, the literature shows that individuals with psychiatric disorders are at an increased risk of suicide. In general the suicide risk is state-dependent, that is, the risk is greatest when the individual is suffering from the psychiatric disorder (and its comorbidity). The risk is lowest when the psychiatric disorder is treated and the illness is in remission. Thus, adequate treatment of psychiatric disorders is also suicide prevention. Treatment interventions with individuals with psychiatric disorders appear to be the best currently available and feasible-to-implement ways to reduce suicide.

Different intervention treatments may have their impact by 1) reducing suicidal ideation or attempts; 2) reducing impulsivity, anger, and self-directed aggression; 3) improving compliance with treatment and medication-taking; 4) reducing clinical symptoms or course features associated with suicide risk (e.g., recurrence of illness); 5) treating comorbid disorders; 6) arranging community supports and continuity of care during the post-discharge period; and 7) educating physicians about the recognition and treatment of depression and how to assess suicide risk. The sparse literature on the effects of different psychosocial and pharmacological treatments on suicidality in the various psychiatric disorders is reviewed below along with suggestions for future research.

Suicide Prevention by Treating Psychiatric Disorders

Major Depression

The Present. It has been estimated that a randomized sample of at least 20,000 depressed patients would be needed to statistically demonstrate a significant difference in suicide rate over one year between those receiving antidepressant medication and those receiving placebo (Isacsson, Bergman, & Rich, 1996). Such a study is impractical and unethical. However, Isacsson et al. used pharmacoepidemiologic methods to calculate that in Sweden from 1988–1991, the risk for suicide among depressed patients treated with antidepressants was 141 per 100,000 person years and, among the untreated, 259 per 100,000 per years (i.e., higher among the untreated). Thus, they concluded that about 100 suicides per year were prevented among those treated with antidepressants and that several hundred might have been prevented among those who did not receive antidepressants. (Sweden has a population of 8.8 million.) Isacsson et al. observed that this number is consistent with the actual decrease in the number of Swedish suicides since 1970 and parallels the steady increase in the use of antidepressants in Sweden. In the years 1991–1994, the use of antidepressants in Sweden increased 50% and was paralleled by a 10% decrease in suicide rates (Isacsson, Holmgrenn, Druid, & Bergman, 1997). In Denmark, a similar decreasing suicide rate among those who seek treatment has been paralleled by an increased use of antidepressants. Such data support the notion that antidepressant medication use decreases the risk for suicide among depressed individuals.

Diminished serotonin in the brain is implicated in suicidal behavior; it has been suggested that antidepressants that have their main therapeutic action by improving brain serotonergic neurotransmission might be particularly useful in diminishing suicidal ideation in depressed patients. In support of this hypothesis some, but not all, studies with the selective serotonin reuptake inhibitor (SSRI) antidepressants (fluvoxamine, zimelidine and citalopram) reported significantly greater improvement in suicidal ideation in the first two weeks of treatment compared with treatment with the antidepressants amitriptyline, dothiepin, and mianserin which have their main therapeutic impact on the noradrenergic neurotransmitter system. However, after six weeks of treatment there were no significant differences (reviewed in Mann & Kapur, 1991). One study found that depressed patients with a history of suicide attempts had a better antidepressant response to an SSRI than to a noradrenergic antidepressant (Sacchetti, Vita, Guameria, & Comacchia, 1991). Another study reported that use of the noradrenergic antidepressant maprotiline was associated with higher suicide attempt and suicide rate than placebo (reviewed in Montgomery, 1997). There is no evidence that SSRIs trigger emergent suicidal ideas over and above rates that may be associated with depression and other antidepressants (reviewed in Mann & Kapur, 1991).

The Future. Suicide prevention strategies should involve intensive efforts to diagnose and treat more depressed patients. Effective psychopharmacologic and psychotherapeutic treatments for depression are available. Studies show that most depressed suicide victims are not receiving antidepressant treatment (Isacsson, Holmgren, Druid, & Bergman, 1997; Isometsa et al., 1994; Roy, 1982a; Schou & Weeke, 1988). Continuation therapy with antidepressants, after the acute six week treatment period, will prevent relapse into depression and the risk of suicide. Future research questions about preventing suicide in depression include:

1. Whether any acute antidepressant treatment or adjuvant medication, has an effect on acute suicidal ideation, intent, and planning separate from its effect on other depressive symptoms.
2. Whether antianxiety interventions in the acutely depressed will lower the acute suicide risk by reducing the acute suicide risk factors of anxiety/agitation (reviewed by Fawcett, Bush, Jacobs, Kravitz, & Fogg, 1997).
3. Whether increasing compliance with continuation treatment of antidepressant medication will prevent suicide behavior in depressed patients.
4. Whether treating substance abuse comorbidity will lessen the risk of suicidal behavior in depressed patients.
5. Whether increasing serotonergic neurotransmission in depressed patients who have low central serotonin will change their future risk of further suicidal behavior, that is, effect their threshold for suicide behavior.

Bipolar Disorder

The Present.   There is a large body of data suggesting that lithium treatment reduces suicidal behavior and mortality in patients with recurrent affective disorder. Tondo, Jamison, and Baldessarini (1997) reviewed the evidence of a possible antisuicide action of lithium maintenance treatment in 28 published studies involving over 17,000 patients with major affective disorder. They found that most studies showed supportive evidence of the antisuicide effects of lithium. They estimated that the risk of suicides and attempts averaged 3.2 versus 0.37 per 100 patient-years without lithium versus with lithium—an 8.6 fold difference ($p < 0.03$).

Tondo et al. (1997) also reported a new study of 284 bipolar I and II patients. Suicidal acts occurred at a rate of 2.2% of subjects per year in 8.3 years of illness prior to lithium treatment. During 6.3 years of lithium treatment the risk of suicidal acts was 0.4%, that is, 5–6 times less ($p < 0.0001$). Moreover, after 161 patients discontinued lithium, their risk for all suicidal acts rose 7.2 fold (16 fold in the first year), and fatalities increased by 8.6 fold.

It is also of interest that in a study comparing lithium with another mood stabilizer, carbamezipine, only lithium treated patients remained completely free of suicides (Greil et al., 1997). Furthermore, in patients with a history of suicide attempts, a reduction was found in both responders and nonresponders to lithium, suggesting that lithium's antisuicide benefit may occur in addition to its prophylactic effect.

The Future.   Lithium maintenance treatment is already strongly indicated in bipolar patients, and now in those who have exhibited suicidal behavior. In the future we need to know if further suicide prevention in recurrent affective disorder is facilitated by determining:

1. Whether lithium has an antisuicide action in unipolar and other disorders as well as in bipolar disorder.
2. Whether other mood stabilizing treatments used with bipolar patients, such as valproate, might also have antisuicide benefits.
3. Whether pharmacotherapy with mood stabilizers combined with specific psychotherapy may have greater impact on preventing bipolar suicides.
4. Whether lithium's effect on brain serotonergic neurotransmission is the basis of its antisuicide action.

Schizophrenia

The Present.   Many schizophrenics who commit suicide are noncompliant with neuroleptics (Heila, Isometsa, Henriksson, Heikkinen, Marttunen, & Lonnquist, 1997). Thus, increasing their compliance with neuroleptics will decrease their risk of suicidal behavior. Recently Meltzer and Okayli (1995) reported that the atypical neuroleptic clozapine reduced suicidal behavior in schizophrenia. Schizophrenic patients ($N = 88$) who were resistant to treatment with typical neuroleptics were treated with clozapine and prospectively evaluated for suicidality for periods of six months to seven years. Clozapine treatment during the follow-up period resulted in markedly less suicidality. The number of suicide attempts with a high probability of success decreased from five to zero. The decrease in suicidality was also associated with improvement in depression and hopelessness. In a comparison of two atypical neuroleptics, Tran et al. (1997) found that the rate of suicide attempts was significantly lower with olanzapine than with risperidone (0.6% vs.. 4.2%, $p = 0.03$).

In multiple family therapy (MFT) the patient and his family attend regular sessions along with three or four other patients and their families. MFT has been shown to lead to less frequent and shorter hospitalizations, reduced rates of relapse, and nearly 90% medication compliance (reviewed in Harkavy-Friedman & Nelson, 1997). Schizophrenic suicide victims have often had frequent hospitalization and are often noncompliant with medication.

The majority of schizophrenic patients who commit suicide have comorbid depression. Studies have shown that both tricyclic antidepressants and SSRIs treat depressive symptoms in schizophrenia. However, although depression is a major risk for suicidal behavior in schizophrenics, there have been no antidepressant treatment studies in schizophrenics selected because of high suicide risk. Interestingly, it has recently been shown that treatment with the atypical neuroleptic olanzapine led to a significantly greater reduction in depressive symptoms in schizophrenics than treatment with the typical neuroleptic haloperidol (Tollefson, Sanger, Lu, & Thieme, 1998). Another important comorbidity in suicidal schizophrenics is substance abuse, for which there are no treatment data (reviewed in Harkavy-Friedman & Nelson, 1997).

The Future.   Schizophrenic patients require long-term treatment with neurolep-tic medication and psychosocial therapies. Increasing compliance with treatment is an important way to diminish the risk of suicidal behavior, as is the vigorous treatment of comorbid depression. Currently the available data are probably not strong enough to allow firm recommendations about the use of atypical neuroleptics in suicidal schizophrenics. In the future we need to know whether preventing suicide in schizophrenia might be facilitated by answers to the following:

1. Does prophylactic continuation treatment with antidepressant medication in schizophrenic patients who have had major depression and exhibited suicidal behavior prevent the development of further depressive episodes and associ-ated suicidal behavior?
2. Are SSRIs better than tricyclic antidepressants in the acute and continued treat-ment of depressed suicidal schizophrenics?
3. Since suicide is most common in the first few years of illness, a trial of clozapine in such schizophrenics selected as they have exhibited suicidality or hopeless-ness, regardless of whether they are neuroleptic-resistant, would be informa-tive. The effect of other atypical neuroleptics in preventing suicidal behavior in schizophrenia needs further study in schizophrenic patients selected because they are at particularly increased suicide risk.
4. Does treatment of comorbid substance abuse or dependence lessen the risk of suicidal behavior in schizophrenics?
5. Does cognitive psychotherapy impact on suicidal ideation and behavior in young schizophrenics who develop hopelessness about their future?
6. Does family education about schizophrenia and how to cope with an afflicted family member, or multiple family therapy (to increase compliance and reduce relapse), reduce suicidal ideation or behavior in patients at high suicide risk?

Alcoholism

The Present.   In general, alcoholics who exhibit suicidal behavior are drinking and not abstinent. The suicide risk in abstinent alcoholics is very greatly reduced (Murphy, 1986) Thus, recent studies with naltrexone and acamprosate that pro-long abstinence from alcohol are important (Sass, Soykan, Mann, & Ziegldansberger, 1996). Naltrexone is an opiate antagonist. Both Volpicelli, Alterman, Hayashida, and O'Brien (1992) and O'Malley et al. (1992) demonstrated, in recently abstinent alcoholics, that naltrexone was superior to placebo in pre-venting relapse back into drinking (23% vs.. 54.3% in the Volpicelli et al. study). Such data are important because alcoholics who are currently drinking are rela-tively inaccessible to clinicians for purposes of suicide prevention. In contrast, alcoholics who become recently abstinent by virtue of a detoxification, alcohol rehabilitation, or other services are accessible to clinicians, and high suicide risk alcoholics can then be identified for suicide prevention.

Although depression is a major risk factor for suicidal behavior in alcoholics, there has been a paucity of studies examining the efficacy of antidepressant medication in depressed alcoholics. This is particularly relevant as Murphy (1986) concluded that the most important intervention to reduce the overall suicide rate among alcoholics is the vigorous treatment of major depression. However, recently McGrath et al. (1996) reported significant improvement in depressive symptoms in currently drinking, primary depressed alcoholics treated with the antidepressant imipramine. Mason, Kossis, Ritvo, and Cutler (1996) administered desipramine to recently withdrawn alcoholics and showed that, among the subsample with depressive symptoms, those receiving desipramine showed significant improvement compared with those receiving placebo.

Diminished central serotonin has been implicated in the etiology of both depression and alcoholism (Roy & Linnoila, 1993). Thus, treatment studies using selective serotonin reuptake inhibitors (SSRIs) are of particular interest. Recently, Cornelius et al. (1997) found that fluoxetine led to a significant reduction in both depressive symptoms and drinking in recently withdrawn alcoholics. Roy (1998) found that the SSRI sertraline led to significant attenuation of depression in recently abstinent alcoholics.

The Future.   Recently abstinent alcoholics require continuing Alcoholics Anonymous or other relapse prevention program attendance and psychosocial treatment to help maintain their sobriety which reduces their suicide risk greatly. Treatment of comorbid depression will also lessen the risk of suicide. Future research into suicide prevention in alcoholics include:

1. Although recent studies show that acute trials of antidepressant medication is efficacious in depressed alcoholics in general, continuation trials are needed in high suicide risk depressed alcoholics to examine the impact over time on further suicidal behavior.
2. As life events caused by drinking (e.g., fired for smelling of alcohol) are often associated with the precipitation of a depressive episode in alcoholics during which they suicide, it is particularly important to keep high suicide risk alcoholics abstinent (Roy, 1996). Thus, trials of naltrexone and acamprosate to prolong abstinence are needed in alcoholics selected because they are at high risk for depression and suicide behavior.
3. Do substance abuse educational programs influence the suicide rate by age group and gender?
4. Does alcohol tax policy influence the suicide rate by age group and gender?

Borderline Personality Disorder (BPD)

The Present.   These patients are difficult to treat. However, there have been two treatment strategies used with suicidal BPD patients that show promise. The first is cognitive-behavioral treatment of chronically parasuicidal female BPD patients (Linehan, Armstrong, Suarez, Allmon, & Heard, 1991). This behaviorally-oriented outpatient psychotherapy, called dialectical behavior behavior therapy (DBT), is a manualized treatment that includes concomitant weekly individual and group therapy. Individual DBT applies directive, problem-oriented techniques balanced with supportive techniques; group therapy follows a psychoeducational format. Behavioral skills in three main areas are taught: 1) interpersonal skills, 2) distress tolerance and reality acceptance skills, and 3) emotion regulation skills.

The Linehan et al. (1991) study treatment lasted one year. The control condition was treatment as usual in the community. There were three major results. First, there was a significant reduction in the frequency and medical risk of parasuicidal behavior among patients who received DBT ($n = 22$) compared with controls ($n = 22$) (median: 5 parasuicide acts vs. 9, $p < 0.005$). Second, DBT retained patients in treatment longer (attrition rate 16.7% vs. 50%, $p < 0.001$). Third, days of inpatient psychiatric hospitalization were fewer for DBT subjects (average 8.5 vs. 38.9 days, $p < 0.05$). During the initial six months of follow-up, DBT patients had significantly less parasuicidal behavior and less anger (Linehan, Heard, & Armstrong, 1993). At one year follow-up DBT patients had significantly higher Global Assessment Scale scores.

The second treatment strategy is the treatment of impulsive aggression, a key feature in BPD patients. Impulsive aggressive behavior is strongly associated with both attempts as suicide and completed suicide, particularly in those with personality disorder. Evidence for the presence of an inverse relationship between central serotonergic neurotransmission and impulsive aggressive behavior has been accumulating over the last 20 years (reviewed in Asberg, 1997; Pandey, 1997). Thus, it is of interest that a number of open studies have suggested that SSRIs reduce aspects of impulsive aggressive behavior (reviewed in Coccaro & Kavoussi, 1997). Recently Coccaro and Kavoussi (1997) reported a double-blind, placebo-controlled, 12-week study of the SSRI fluoxetine in 40 nondepressed personality disordered patients with histories of impulsive aggression. A third of the patients had BPD. Fluoxetine treatment led to sustained reductions in scores for irritability and aggression and significantly greater Clinical Global Impression ratings of improvement. Salzman et al. (1995) similarly reported that fluoxetine significantly reduced anger in BPD. Thus, enhanced serotonergic neurotransmission in the brain has antiaggressive and antianger effects in borderline and other personality disorders. Interestingly, divalproex sodium (depakote) which has a different neurochemical profile, has also been shown in open trials to reduce impulsivity and anger in BPD patients (Hollander, Grossman, Stein, & Kwon, 1996).

The Future.   The treatment of personality disorder patients currently involves various psychotherapeutic techniques. Treatment of comorbid depression and substance use will lessen the risk of suicide. Some future research issues about suicide prevention in these patients include:

1. If the most powerful therapeutic elements of one year DBT could be determined (e.g., individual or group?) less-time consuming, shorter, cheaper and more practical treatment might be designed that could have greater general clinical utility.
2. Do booster sessions at intervals after the end of DBT prolong its effect?

3. Are longer trials of SSRIs (e.g., one or two years) in BPD patients selected for suicidal behavior are needed?
4. Is there augmentation of beneficial effects, particularly on suicidal behavior, by combination treatment of DBT plus SSRIs?
5. Double-blind, placebo-controlled trials of depakote (with cognitive therapy) in suicidal BPD patients are needed.

Drug Dependence

The Present.   Comorbid depression is the most serious risk factor for suicidal behavior in drug-dependent patients. Recently, Nunes et al. (1998) showed, in a double-blind placebo controlled study, that imipramine was an effective antidepressant in depressed opiate-dependent patients receiving methadone. Among the 84 adequately treated patients, 57% receiving imipramine were rated as responders compared to 7% receiving placebo ($p < 0.001$).

The Future.   Treatment of drug dependence involves psychotherapy and psychosocial treatment and methadone maintenance in heroin addicts. Abstinence from illicit drug-taking diminishes the risk of suicidal behavior as does treating comorbid depression. Some future issues in relation to suicide prevention in this group might include:

1. Is acute antidepressant medication as effective in cocaine-dependent patients with comorbid depression and suicidal ideation or behavior?
2. Does continued antidepressant medication in comorbidly depressed drug-dependent patients prevent future depression and suicidal behavior?
3. Does combining acute and continuation antidepressants with psychotherapeutic and behavioral interventions reduce attrition, augment compliance, or augment the antidepressant in drug-dependent patients with comorbid depression and suicidal behavior?

Postdischarge Period

The Present.   The postdischarge period is a time of increased risk for suicide in psychiatric patients (Goldacre, Seagroatt, & Hawton, 1993; Motto, 1976; Temoche, Pugh, & MacMahon, 1964). For example, in one study, 26 of the 58 (44%) suicides of recently discharged patients occurred within three months of discharge from their last hospitalization (Roy, 1982a). There is only one study that tested an intervention in the postdischarge period. Among 3,006 psychiatric patients admitted because of a depressive or suicidal state, Motto (1976) randomized those who declined postdischarge treatment or dropped out in less than a month into two subgroups, designated "contact" and "noncontact." Contact patients received a regular communication from the researcher who had interviewed them as inpatients. This was usually a short letter or, at times, a telephone call. Such contacts were monthly for four months, then every two months for eight months, and finally every three months for four years (i.e., 24 contacts in 5 years). At four years post discharge 20 of 242 no-contact controls had committed suicide compared with 12 of 230 contact patients (8.3 % vs. 5.2%). Although not statistically significant, Motto concluded that this result showed that "a systematic approach to reducing [suicide risk] can be applied for a prolonged period" (p. 229).

The Future.   On discharge from hospitalization, patients at high risk for suicide need a planned aftercare with continuity of treatment. Although the postdischarge period is a period of greatly increased suicide risk for psychiatric patients, there have been no other preventive efforts studied in this period. Other postdischarge suicide preventive strategies need to be tested in psychiatric patients at increased risk for suicide. They might include more intensive aftercare, continuing outpatient or day patient care, and community supports where appropriate.

Prevention of a Re-attempt at Suicide

The Present.   Psychosocial interventions to prevent the repetition of a suicide attempt have, in general, been ineffective. Ten of 12 randomized controlled trials published since 1980 have failed to show a significant decrease in the suicide re-attempt rate (reviewed in Hawton et al., 1998; Linehan, 1997). Hospitalization, home visits, intensive follow-up, domiciliary care, immediate access to services, outpatient problem-solving, social skills training, interpersonal skills training, and intensive in-patient and community intervention have all failed to reduce the re-attempt rate.

Among the psychosocial interventions tested, only two cognitive-behavioral approaches showed a significant reduction in repeat rate. Salkovskis, Atha, and Storer (1990), in a small controlled study, found that patients at high risk of re-peated suicide attempts randomized to five one-hour sessions of cognitive-behavioral problem-solving (n = 12) improved significantly more than treatment as usual controls (n = 8) on depression, hopelessness, suicidal ideation, and target problems and significantly fewer re-attempted in the six months after the index attempt (O vs.. 3, $p < 0.05$). The second study, the one of DBT by Linehan, et al. (1991), has been reviewed above.

There have been four psychopharmacologic intervention studies, of which two are positive. Montgomery and Montgomery (1982) studied 37 suicide attempters who had made at least one previous suicide attempt and who were not depressed. Only 3 of 14 attempters randomized to an intramuscular monthly injection of 20 mg. of the neuroleptic flupenthixol decanoate for six months re-attempted suicide compared with 12 of 16 attempters receiving placebo (21% vs. 75%). Most recently a Dutch group (Verkes et al., 1998) reported a one year double-blind study comparing the SSRI paroxetine and placebo in 91 patients who were recruited from emergency rooms after attempting suicide for at least the second time. None of the patients had experienced a major depressive episode or had any other major Axis I diagnosis. The great majority had Cluster B personality disorders (impulsive, antisocial, and dramatic). Among the 30 patients who had attempted suicide fewer than five who received paroxetine only re-attempted suicide compared with 12 of the 33 such patients who received placebo (17% vs. 36%, p = 0.03). The paroxetine patients also showed a significant decrease in anger at week two of the trial (p = 0.02). There were no significant differences in depressed mood or hopelessness. Verkes et al. (1998) concluded that enhancing brain serotonergic function with an SSRI may reduce suicidal behavior among patients who have attempted suicide more than once but who do not suffer from major depression.

The Future. General hospital services for attempted suicides should be of high standard. They might include multidisciplinary staff, who are adequately trained and supervised, a complete assessment procedure including interviews with relatives and other important individuals, quiet offices where interviews can be conducted in privacy, and the arrangement of appropriate aftercare. Future research on prevention efforts include:

1. A shift from assessing broad interventions to examining specific treatments for homogeneous subgroups of attempters.
2. More studies of SSRIs, combined with cognitive behavioral therapy, are needed
3. The flupenthixol deconoate study requires replication.

Suicide Prevention In Psychiatric Patients By Screening

The Present. Screening for suicidality could be implemented among psychiatric patients as they are already in clinical settings. For example, Malone, Szanto, Corbell, & Mann (1995) found, among 50 depressed inpatients, that the clinicians failed to document past suicidal acts in 24% of the patients at admission and 28% at discharge. Asnis et al. (1993) reported that 55% of outpatients in a general psychiatric outpatient clinic had suicidal ideation, and 25% had made a previous attempt, with half of these having made multiple attempts. These data suggest an opportunity for suicide prevention high risk patients.

The Future. Litman (1995) has estimated that approximately three million people per year in the United States become seriously suicidal. He argues that a focus on screening and case finding would bring many more suicidal individuals into suicide prevention through treatment. He further notes that at any one time there are relatively few high suicide risk individuals but several million individuals who have a low to moderate risk for suicide. He suggests that it is in the identification and treatment of such individuals that there is potential for suicide prevention.

However, there may be practical barriers to screening that need to be overcome. For example, a great deal of work has been carried out in attempting to devise inventories and formal standardized questionnaires to assist the process of assessing suicide risk. Problems of specificity and sensitivity have led to the conclusion that scales of this kind can currently be no more than useful adjuncts to routine clinical assessment (Morgan, 1994). Litman (1995) suggests that the future use of computer technology in diagnosis might allow suicide assessment in all settings where consumers of mental health services are found. Interactive computer programs for history taking could for example, include questions about suicidal ideation and suicide attempts.

Biological Risk Factors

The Present.   Diminished function of the neurotransmitter serotonin in the brain is involved in suicidal behavior. The evidence for this comes from cerebrospinal fluid (CSF), neuroendocrine challenge, and blood platelet studies of serotonergic function in patients who have exhibited suicidal behavior (reviewed in Asberg, 1997; Pandey, 1997). Postmortem neurochemical studies of the brains of suicide victims have also shown changes in the serotonergic system, particularly in the ventrolateral prefrontal cortex (reviewed in Arango, Underwood, & Mann, 1997).

Low CSF concentrations of the serotonin metabolite 5-hydroxyindoleacetic acid (5-HIAA) is associated with suicidal behavior has been replicated many times and across various psychiatric diagnoses, suggesting a relationship with suicidal behavior rather than with a specific diagnosis (reviewed in Asberg, 1997). Similarly, postmortem neurochemical changes appear to be of equal magnitude across diagnostic groups, also suggesting a correlation with suicidal behavior rather than with a specific psychiatric diagnosis (reviewed in Arango, Underwood, & Mann, 1997). Furthermore, low CSF 5-HIAA and blunted neuroendocrine responses to serotonergic challenges have been shown to persist over time after episodes of illness. Thus, serotonergic abnormalities appear to represent trait abnormalities rather than illness-related state changes. Serotonergic trait abnormalities are thought to lead to a lowering of the threshold for suicidal behavior at times of stress or psychiatric illness. Impaired prefrontal cortex serotonergic function may underlie a reduced ability to resist impulses to act on suicidal thoughts (Arango, Underwood, & Mann, 1997).

Of interest for prevention studies is that low CSF 5-HIAA has been found to be associated with further suicidal behavior in depressed patients (Nordstrom et al., 1994; Roy, DeJong, & Linnolla, 1989; Traskman, Asberg, Bertilsson, & Sjustrand, 1981). For example, Traskman et al. found at follow-up that the one year mortality from suicide was 22% in those psychiatric inpatients who had made a suicide attempt and had a CSF 5-HIAA level below the mean of the attempter group. Nordstrom, et al. examined completed suicide in a sample of 92 depressed patients who had had a CSF 5-HIAA determination. They found that 8 of the 11 patients who committed suicide within one year belonged to the below-the-median CSF 5-HIAA subgroup. The one year suicide risk in that subgroup was 17% as compared with 7% among those with above-the-median CSF 5-HIAA. They concluded that low CSF 5-HIAA predicts short-range suicide risk in the high risk group of depressed patients who have attempted suicide.

The Future.   Although no biologic measure has current clinical feasibility, research in this areas should proceed. CSF 5-HIAA determination is impractical in most settings. However, brain imaging of central serotonin systems using ligands requires evaluation, especially as single photon emission tomography (SPECT) is available in most medical centers.

Genetic Risk Factors

The Present.   Data from clinical, twin, and adoption studies suggest that genetic factors play a role in suicidal behavior (reviewed in Roy, Rylander, & Sarchiapone, 1997). For example, a family history of suicide has been found to be associated with suicidal behavior in all psychiatric diagnoses (Roy, 1983). Twin studies have shown that monozygotic twins, who share 100% of their genes, have a significantly higher concordance for both suicide and attempted suicide than dizygotic twins who share 50% of their genes (Roy, Segal, Centerwall, & Robinette, 1991; Roy, Segal, & Sarchiapone, 1995). Adoption studies show that significantly more biological relatives of adoptees who committed suicide had themselves suicided in comparison with biological relatives of control adoptees (Schulsinger, Kety, Rosenthal, & Wender, 1979). As these suicides were largely independent of the presence of psychiatric disorder, Schulsinger et al. proposed that there is a genetic predisposition for suicide independent of, or additive to, the major psychiatric disorders associated with suicide.

Tryptophan hyroxylase (TPH) is the enzyme involved in the biosynthesis of serotonin. A polymorphism in the TPH gene with two variants, U and L, has been identified. A history of suicide attempts was significantly associated with TPH genotype among violent offenders ($p = 0.02$). In fact, 34 of the 36 subjects who attempted suicide had either the UL or LL genotype. Thus, it was concluded that the presence of the L allele was associated with an increased risk of a suicide attempts (Nielsen et al., 1994). Also a history of multiple suicide attempts was found most in subjects with the LL genotype and to a lesser extent among those with the UL genotype. This led to the suggestion that the L allele was associated with repetitive suicide behavior. The UL and LL genotypes also had lower CSF-HIAA than the UU genotype. Thus, the presence of one TPH L allele may indicate a reduced capacity to hydroxylate tryptophan to 5-hydroxytrytrophan in the syn-

TABLE 5. Population Association Between Tryptophan Hydroxylase Genotype and History of Severe Suicide Attempts in Impulsive Violent Offenders

Genotype	With severe suicide attempt $n = 98$	Without severe suicide attempt $n = 70$
UU	8	26
UL	63	26
LL	27	18

$p < 0.0001$, for all.
Adapted from Nielsen et al. (1998), used with permission.

thesis of serotonin, producing low central serotonin turnover, a reduced ability to contain suicidal impulses, and low CSF 5-HIAA. The TPH genotype data have been replicated and the most highly significant relationship with serious suicide attempts in the combined group is shown in Table 5 (Nielsen et al., 1998).

The Future.   Future genetic studies ultimately aimed at improving suicide prevention include:

1. Does screening for a family history of suicide in patients help in the clinical setting in identification of risk for suicide?
2. Does TPH genotyping of patients who have made previous serious suicide attempts aid in predicting future suicidal behavior?
3. Should other genetic variants associated with suicide should be researched?
4. Should specific mechanism(s) by which genetic variants influence suicide risk needs to be determined?

Future Suicide Prevention in Psychiatric Patients by Improved Prediction

A further barrier to the delivery of suicide prevention efforts is that it is not currently possible to identify the psychiatric patient at increased risk for suicide. This barrier is particularly important as prevention depends on prediction. Unfortunately, studies have shown that no sociodemographic factor or clinical feature, or combination, reliably identifies patients at high risk for suicide (Pokorny, 1983; Roy, Schreiber, Mazonson, & Pickar, 1986). Too many false positives (predict suicide, get nonsuicide) and false negatives (predict nonsuicide, get suicide) are identified. This is partly because suicide has a low base rate, and too few actual suicides and too many nonsuicides are identified (Murphy, 1983). However, it may also reflect the associated barrier to suicide prevention efforts of a lack of detailed knowledge about the genetic and biologic suicide threshold risk factors that are found in only some individuals within a particular psychiatric disorder, and which increase their suicide risk. Only approximately 4% of alcoholic, depressed, and schizophrenic patients commit suicide and 30–50% attempt suicide. We are, how-

---

TABLE 6. People at Highest Risk for Suicide

White Males
Aged 24–35 or over 50
Recently widowed, separated, or divorced
History of suicide attempts
History of psychiatric disorder, in particular depression, alcoholism, or schizophrenia
Low CSF 5-HIAA or serotonergic deficiency
Family history of suicidal behavior or affective disorders

From Blumenthal & Kupfer (1986), used with permission.

ever, not currently able to identify and predict which patient will exhibit suicidal behavior. It is highly likely that those that do so have genetic and biologic vulnerabilities lowering the threshold for suicidal behavior (Table 6). More knowledge might lead to the delineation of reliable genetic and biologic markers of increased risk and, thus, permit better prediction of suicidal behavior and the development of more specific psychopharmacologic and other prevention efforts for high risk subgroups. For example, carefully monitored longitudinal studies of medications that raise the threshold for suicidal acts could be carried out in patients determined by genetic or biologic markers to be at increased suicide risk.

☐ References

Arango, V., Underwood, M., & Mann, J. J. (1997). Biologic alterations in the brain stems of suicides. *Psychiatric Clinics of North America, 20,* 581–594.

Asberg, M. (1997). Neurotransmitters and suicidal behavior: The evidence from cerebrospinal fluid studies. *Annals of the New York Academy of Sciences, 836,* 158–181.

Asnis, G., Friedman, R., & Sanderson, W. (1993). Suicidal behaviors in adult psychiatric outpatients. *American Journal of Psychiatry, 150,* 108–112.

Beautrais, A., Joyce, R., Mulder, R., Fergusson, D., Deavoll, B., & Nightingdale, S. (1996). Prevalence and comorbidity of mental disorders in persons making serious suicide attempts. *American Journal of Psychiatry, 153,* 1009–1015.

Blumental, S. J., & Kupfer, D. J. (1986). Generalizable treatment strategies for suicidal behavior. *Annals of the New York Academy of Science, 487,* 327–340.

Caldwell, C., & Gottesman, I. (1992). Schizophrenia: A high risk factor for suicide. *Suicide and Life-Threatening Behavior, 42,* 479–493.

Coccaro, E., & Kavoussi, R. (1997). Fluoxetine and impulsive aggressive behavior in personality disordered subjects. *Archives of General Psychiatry, 54,* 1081–1088.

Conwell, Y., Duberstein, P., Cox, C., Herrman, J., Forbes, N., & Caine, E. (1996). Relationship of age and Axis I diagnoses in victims of completed suicide: A psychological autopsy study. *American Journal of Psychiatry, 153,* 1001–1008.

Cornelius, J., Salloum, I., Ehler, J., Jarrett, P., Cornelius, M., Perel, J., & Thase, M. A. (1997). Fluoxetine in depressed alcoholics: A double-blind, placebo-controlled trial. *Archives of General Psychiatry, 54,* 700–705.

Cornelius, J., Salloum, I., Mezzich, J., Cornelius, M. D., Fabrega, H., Ehler, J. G., Ulrich, R. F., Thase, M., & Mann, J. J. (1995). Disproportionate suicidality in patients with comorbid major depression and alcoholism. *American Journal of Psychiatry, 152,* 358–364.

Drake, R., & Cotton, P. (1986). Depression, hopelessness and suicide in chronic schizophrenia. *British Journal of Psychiatry, 148,* 554–559.

Fawcett, J., Bush, K., Jacobs, D., Kravitz, H., & Fogg, L. (1997). Suicide: A four-pathway clinical biochemical model. *Annals of the New York Academy of Sciences, 836,* 288–301.

Fenton, W., McGlashan, T., Victor, B., & Blyler, C. (1997). Symptoms, subtype and suicidality in patients with schizophrenia spectrum disorders. *American Journal of Psychiatry, 154,* 199–204.

Goldacre, M., Seagroatt, V., & Hawton, K. (1993). Suicide after discharge from psychiatric inpatient care. *Lancet, 342,* 283–286.

Greil, W., Ludwig-Mayerhofer, W., Erazo, N., Schochlin, C., Schmidt, S., Engel, R. R., Czernik, A., Giedke, H., Muller-Oerlinhausen, B., Osterheider, M., Rudolf, G. A., Sauer, H., Tegeler, J., & Wetterling, T. (1997). Lithium versus carbamazepine in the maintenance treatment of bipolar disorders. *Journal of Affective Disorders, 43,* 151–161.

Harkavy-Friedman, J. M., & Nelson, E. A. (1997). Assessment and intervention for the suicidal patient with schizophrenia. *Psychiatric Quarterly, 68*, 361–375.

Harris, E. C., & Barraclough, B. M. (1997). Suicide as an outcome for mental disorders. *British Journal of Psychiatry, 170*, 205–228.

Hawton, K., Arensman, E., Townsend, E., Bremner, S., Feldman, E., Goldney, R., Gunnell, D., Hazell, P., Van Heeringen, K., House, A., Owens, D., Sakinofsky, I., & Traskman-Bendz, L. (1998). Deliberate self-harm: Systematic review efficacy of psychosocial and pharmacological treatments in preventing repetition. *British Medical Journal, 317*, 441–447.

Heila, H., Isometsa, E. T., Henriksson, M. M., Heikkinen, M. E., Marttunen, M., & Lonnqvist, J. K. (1997). Suicide and schizophrenia. *American Journal of Psychiatry, 154*, 1235–1242.

Henriksson, M., Aro, H., Marttunen, M., Isometsa, E., Heikkinen, M., Kuoppasalmi, K., & Lonnqvist, J. (1993). Mental disorders and comorbidity in suicide. *American Journal of Psychiatry, 150*, 935–940.

Henriksson, M., Isometsa, E., Kuoppasalmi, K., Heikkinen, M., Marttunen, M., & Lonnqvist, J. (1996). Panic disorder in completed suicide. *Journal of Clinical Psychiatry, 57*, 275–281.

Hollander, E., Grossman, R., Stein, D., & Kwon, J. (1996). Borderline personality disorder and impulsive-aggression: The role for divalproex sodium treatment. *Psychiatric Annals, 26*, 5464–5469.

Inskip, H., Harris, C., & Barraclough, B. (1998). Lifetime risk of suicide for affective disorder, alcoholism and schizophrenia. *British Journal of Psychiatry, 172*, 35–37.

Isacsson, G., Bergman, U., & Rich, L. (1996). Epidemiological data suggest antidepressants reduce suicide risk among depressives. *Journal of Affective Disorders, 41*, 1–8.

Isacsson, G., Holmgren, P., Druid, H., & Bergman, U. (1997). The utilization of antidepressants: A key issue in the prevention of suicide. *Acta Psychiatrica Scandinavica, 96*, 94–100.

Isometsa, E., Henriksson, M., Aro, H., Heikkinen, M., Kuoppasalmi, K., & Lonnqvist, J. (1994). Suicide in major depression. *American Journal of Psychiatry, 151*, 530–536.

Isometsa, E., Henriksson, M., Heikkinen, M., Aro, H., Marttunen, M., Kuoppasalmi, K., & Lonnqvist, J. (1996). Suicide among subjects with personality disorder. *American Journal of Psychiatry, 153*, 667–673.

Jamison, K. (1990). Suicide. In F. Goodwin & K. Jamison (Eds.), *Manic depression* (pp. 227–244). Baltimore: Williams & Wilkins.

Kaplan, K., & Harrow, M. (1996). Positive and negative symptoms as risk factors for later suicidal activity in schizophrenics versus depressives. *Suicide and Life-Threatening Behavior, 26*, 105–121.

Leshner, A. (1999). NIDA Notes, National Institute on Drug Abuse, 14,4, 3–4.

Linehan, M. (1997). Behavioral treatments of suicidal behaviors. *Annals of the New York Academy of Sciences, 836*, 302–328.

Linehan, M., Armstrong, H., Suarez, A., Allmon, D., & Heard, H. (1991). Cognitive-behavioral treatment of chronically parasuicidal borderline patients. *Archives of General Psychiatry, 48*, 1060–1064.

Linehan, M., Heard, H., & Armstrong, H. (1993). Naturalistic follow-up of a behavioral treatment for chronically parasuicidal borderline patients. *Archives of General Psychiatry, 50*, 971–974.

Lipschitz, A. (1995). Suicide prevention in young adults (aged 18-30). *Suicide and Life-Threatening Behavior, 25*, 155–169.

Litman, R. (1995). Suicide prevention in a treatment setting. *Suicide and Life-Threatening Behavior, 25*, 134–142.

Malone, K. M., Szanto, K., Corbell, E. M., & Mann, J. J. (1995). Clinical assessment versus research methods in the assessment of suicidal behavior. *American Journal of Psychiatry, 152*, 1601–1607.

Mann, J. J., & Kapur, S. (1991). The emergence of suicidal ideation and behavior during antidepressant pharmacotherapy. *Archives of General Psychiatry, 48*, 1027–1033.

Mason, B., Kocsis, J., Ritvo, E., & Cutler, R. (1996). A double-blind placebo-controlled trial of desipramine for primary alcohol dependence stratifed on the presence or absence of major depression. *Journal of the American Medical Association, 275,* 761–767.

Marzuk, P., Tardiff, K., Leon, A., Stajic, M., Morgan, E., & Mann, J. J. (1992). Prevalence of cocaine use among residents of New York City who committed suicide during a one-year period. *American Journal of Psychiatry, 149,* 371–375.

McGrath, P., Nunes, E., Stewart, J., Goldman, D., Agosti, V., Oupek-Welikson, K., & Wuitkin, F. (1996). Imipramine treatment of alcoholics with primary depressions placebo-controlled clinical trial. *Archives of General Psychiatry, 53,* 232–240.

Meltzer, H., & Okayli, G. (1995). Reduction of suicidality during clozapine treatment of neuroleptic-resistant schizophrenia: Impact on risk-benefit assessment. *American Journal of Psychiatry, 152,* 183–190.

Montgomery, S. (1997). Suicide and antidepressants. *Annals of the New York Academy of Sciences, 836,* 329–338.

Montgomery, S., & Montgomery, D. (1982). Pharmacologic prevention of suicidal behavior. *Journal of Affective Disorders, 4,* 291–298.

Morgan, G. (1994). Assessment of risk. In R. Jenkins, S. Griffiths, I. Wylie, K. Hawton, G. Morran, & A. Tylee (Eds.), *The prevention of suicide* (pp. 46–51). London: HMSO.

Moscicki, E. (1995). Epidemiology of suicidal behavior. *Suicide and Life-Threatening Behavior, 25,* 22–35.

Moscicki, E., O'Carroll, P., Rae, D., Locke, B., Roy, A., & Regier, D. (1988). Suicide attempts in the Epidemiologic Catchment Area Study. *Yale Journal of Biology and Medicine, 61,* 259–268.

Motto, J. (1976). Suicide prevention for high-risk persons who refuse treatment. *Suicide and Life-Threatening Behavior, 6,* 223–230.

Murphy, G. (1983). On suicide prediction and prevention. *Archives of General Psychiatry, 40,* 343–344.

Murphy, G. (1986). Suicide in alcoholism. In A. Roy (Ed.), *Suicide* (pp. 89–96). Baltimore: Williams & Wilkins.

Murphy, G., Armstrong, J., Hermele, S., Fisher, J., & Clendenin, W. (1979). Suicide and alcoholism. *Archives of General Psychiatry, 36,* 65–69.

Murphy, G., & Wetzel, R. (1990). The lifetime risk of suicide in alcoholism. *Archives of General Psychiatry, 47,* 383–392.

Murphy, G., Wetzel, R., Robins, E., & McEvoy, L. (1992). Multiple risk factors predict suicide in alcoholism. *Archives of General Psychiatry, 49,* 459–463.

Nielsen, D., Goldman, D., Virkkunen, M., Tokola, R., Rawlings, R., & Linnoila, M., (1994). Suicidality and 5-hydroxyindoleacetic acid concentration associated with a tryptophan dydroxylase polymorphism. *Archives of General Psychiatry, 51,* 34–38.

Nielsen, D., Virkkunen, M., Lappalainen, J., Eggert, M., Brown, G., Long, J., Goldman, D., & Linnoila, M. (1998). A tryptophan hydroxylase marker for suicidality and alcoholism. *Archives of General Psychiatry, 55,* 593–602.

Nordstrom, P., Asberg, M., Aberg-Wistedt, A., & Nordin, C. (1995). Attempted suicide-predicts suicide risk in mood disorders. *Acta Psychiatrica Scandinavica, 92,* 345–350.

Nordstrom, P., Samuelsson, M., Asberg, M., Traskman-Bendz, L., Aberg-Wistedt, A., Nordin, C., & Bertilsson, L. (1994). CSF 5-HIAA predicts suicide risk after attempted suicide. *Suicide and Life Threatening Behavior, 24,* 1–9.

Nunes, E., Quitkin, F., Donavan, S., Deliyannides, D., Ocepek-Welikson, K., Konig, T., Brady, R., McGrath, P., & Woody, G. (1998). Imipramine treatment of opiate-dependent patients with depressive disorders: A placebo-controlled trial. *Archives of General Psychiatry, 55,* 153–160.

O'Malley, S., Jaffe, A., Chana, G., Schottenfeld, R., Myer, R., & Rounsaville, B. (1992). Naltrexone and coping skills therapy for alcohol dependence: A controlled study. *Archives of General Psychiatry, 46,* 881–887.

Pandey, G. (1997). Altered serotonin function in suicide: Evidence from platelet and neuroendocrine studies. *Annals of the New York Academy of Sciences, 836,* 182–200.

Paris, J. (1990). Completed suicide in borderline personality disorder. *Psychiatric Annals, 20*(1), 19–21.

Pokorny, A. (1983). Prediction of suicide in psychiatric patients: Report of a prospective study. *Archives of General Psychiatry, 40,* 249–257.

Regier, D. A., Farmer, M. E., Rae, D. S., Locke, B. Z., Keith, S. J., Judd, L. L., & Goodwin, F. K. (1990). Comorbidity of mental disorders with alcohol and other drug abuse: Results from the Epidemiologic Catchment Aread (ECA) study. *Journal of the American Medical Association, 264,* 2511–2518.

Robins, E., Murphy, G., Wilkinson, R., Gassner, S., & Kayes, J. (1959). Some clinical considerations in the prevention of suicide based on a study of 134 successful suicides. *American Journal of Public Health, 49,* 888–889.

Rossau, C., & Mortensen, P. (1997). Risk factors for suicide in patients with schizophrenia: Nested case-control study. *British Journal of Psychiatry, 171,* 355–359.

Roy, A. (1982a). Risk factors for suicide in psychiatric patients. *Archives of General Psychiatry, 39,* 1089–1095.

Roy, A. (1982b). Suicide in chronic schizophrenia. *British Journal of Psychiatry, 141,* 171–177.

Roy, A. (1983). Family history of suicide. *Archives of General Psychiatry, 40,* 971–974.

Roy, A. (1986). Depression, attempted suicide and suicide in patients with chronic schizophrenia. *Psychiatric Clinics of North America, 9,* 193–206.

Roy, A. (1996). Aetiology of secondary depression in male alcoholics. *British Journal of Psychiatry, 169,* 753–757.

Roy, A. (1998). Placebo-controlled study of sertraline in depressed recently-abstinent alcoholics. *Biological Psychiatry, 44,* 633–637.

Roy, A., DeJong, J., & Linnolla, M. (1989). Cerebrospinal fluid monoamine metabolites and suicidal behavior in depressed patients: A five-year follow-up study. *Archives of General Psychiatry, 46,* 609–612.

Roy, A., & Draper, R. (1995). Suicide among psychiatric hospital inpatients. *Psychological Medicine, 52,* 199–202.

Roy, A., & Linnoila, M. (1986). Alcoholism and suicide. *Suicide and Life-Threatening Behavior, 16,* 244–273.

Roy, A., & Linnoila, M. (1993). Depression in alcoholism. In J. J. Mann & D. J. Kupfer (Ed.), *The biology of depressive disorders* (pp. 109–125). New York: Plenum Press.

Roy, A., Mazonson, A., & Pickar, D. (1984). Attempted suicide in chronic schizophrenia. *British Journal of Psychiatry, 144,* 303–306.

Roy, A., Rylander, G., & Sarchiapone, M. (1997). Genetics of suicide: Family studies and molecular genetics. *Annals of the New York Academy of Sciences, 836,* 135–157.

Roy, A., Schreiber, J., Mazonson, A., & Pickar, D. (1986). Suicidal behavior in schizophrenic patients: A follow-up study. *Canadian Journal of Psychiatry, 31,* 737–740.

Roy, A., Segal, N., Centerwall, B., & Robinette, D. (1991). Suicide in twins. *Archives of General Psychiatry, 48,* 29–32.

Roy, A., Segal, N., & Sarchiapone, M. (1995). Attempted suicide among living cotwins of twin suicide victims. *American Journal of Psychiatry, 152,* 1075–1076.

Sachetti, E., Vita, A., Guameria, L., & Comacchia, M. (1991). The effectiveness of fluoxetine, nortiptyline and desipramine in major depressives with suicidal behavior: Preliminary findings. In G. Cassano & H. Akiskal (Eds.), Clinical and therapeutic links (pp. 47–53). London: Royal Society of Medicine Services Limited.

Salkovskis, P., Atha, C., & Storer, D. (1990). Cognitive-behavioral problem solving in the treatment of patients who repeatedly attempt suicide: A controlled trial. *British Journal of Psychiatry, 157,* 871–876.

Salzman, C., Wolfson, A., Schatzberg, A., Looper, J., Henke, R., Albanese, A., Schwartz, J., & Miyawaki, E. (1995). Effect of fluoxetine on anger in symptomatic volunteers with borderline personality disorder. *Journal of Clinical Psychopharmacology, 15,* 23–29.

Sass, H., Soyka, M., Mann, K., & Zieglgansberger, W. (1996). Relapse prevention by acamprosate. *Archives of General Psychiatry, 53,* 673–680.

Schneier, R., Johnson, J., Horning, C., Liebowitz, M., & Weissman, M. (1992). Social phobia: Comorbidity and morbidity in an epidemiologic sample. *Archives of General Psychiatry, 49,* 282–288.

Schou, M., & Weeke, A. (1988). Did manic-depressive patients who committed suicide receive prophylactic or continuation treatment at the time? *British Journal of Psychiatry, 153,* 324–327.

Schulsinger, R., Kety, S., Rosenthal, D., & Wender, P. (1979). A family study of suicide. In M. Schou & E. Stromgren (Eds.), *Origins, prevention and treatment of affective disorders* (pp. 277–287). New York: Academic Press.

Stone, M. (1990). *The fate of borderline patients.* New York: Guilford.

Temoche, A., Pugh, R., & MacMahon, B. (1964). Suicide rates among current and former mental institution patients. *Journal of Nervous and Mental Diseases, 138,* 124–130.

Tollefson, G., Sanger, T., Lu, Y., & Thieme, M. (1998). Depressive signs and symptoms in schizophrenia: A prospective blinded trial of olanzapine and haloperidol. *Archives of General Psychiatry, 55,* 250–258.

Tondo, L., Jamison, K., & Baldessarini, R. (1997). Effects of lithuim maintenance on suicidal behavior in major mood disorders. *Annals of the New York Academy of Sciences, 836,* 339–351.

Tran, P., Hamilton, S., Kuntz, A., Potvin, J., Andersen, S., Beasley, C., & Tollefson, G. (1997). Double-blind comparison of olanzapine versus risperidone in the treatment of schizophrenia and other psychotic disorders. *Journal of Clinical Psychopharmacology, 17,* 407–418.

Traskman, L., Asberg, M., Bertilsson, L., & Sjostrand, L. (1981). Monoamine metabolites in CSF and suicidal behavior. *Archives of General Psychiatry, 38,* 631–636.

Verkes, R., van der Mast, R.. Hengeveld. M., Tuyl, J., Zwindeman, A., & van Kempen, G. (1998). Reduction by paroxetine of suicidal behavior in patients with repeated suicide attempts but not major depression. *American Journal of Psychiatry, 155,* 543–547.

Volpicelli, J., Alterman, A., Hayashida, M., & O'Brien, C. (1992). Naltrexone in the treatment of alcohol dependence. *Archives of General Psychiatry, 49,* 876–880.

Weissman, M., Klennan, G., Markowitz, J., Ouellette, R., & Phil, M. (1989). Suicidal ideation and suicide attempts in panic disorder and attacks. *New England Journal of Medicine, 321,* 1209–1214.

8

CHAPTER

Thomas E. Ellis

Psychotherapy with Suicidal Patients

When one reviews the enormous literature on suicide assessment, one is first struck by the magnitude of the number of studies, scales, papers, and books. The second striking finding is the relative lack of writing about the practical aspects of "how to do the interview" (Shea, 1998, p. 471).

This statement regarding suicide assessment interviews can be said to apply equally well to psychotherapy with suicidal patients. The clinical approach to the conceptualization and treatment of suicidal behavior is a relatively new development. As such, the art and science of psychotherapy with suicidal individuals truly can be said to be in its infancy. The quantity and quality of literature on suicidal individuals, while substantial, pale in comparison to the research and clinical literature on various other clinical phenomena, such as anxiety or mood disorders. Moreover, writings about suicidal individuals have had much more to say about risk assessment and the psychodynamics of suicide than about specific and concrete therapeutic interventions that a clinician may use to lower the probability that a patient will commit suicide.

This chapter will examine psychotherapeutic approaches[1] to suicidal individuals from the perspectives of several theoretical orientations and time frames. We first examine what might be considered the "presuicidology" era, using the establishment of the Los Angeles Suicide Prevention Center in 1958 as a point of demarcation. We then explore developments in the recent past leading up to the current day. Finally, in light of recent developments, we consider issues for the future development of psychotherapeutic interventions for persons at risk of suicide.

---

[1] For purposes of discussion, the term psychotherapy will refer to verbal interventions, including behavior therapy, oriented toward achieving lasting symptomatic relief through learning and personal growth. This discussion will not address crisis intervention, inpatient care, or biological interventions.

129

☐ Early 20th Century: Transition from Moralistic Judgment to Psychological Explanation

In many respects, the view of suicide as a personal problem for which a person should receive help can be regarded as a novel development of the 20th Century, for there is remarkably little evidence for such a view prior to Sigmund Freud. It is true that some efforts to discourage suicide were evident centuries ago. For example, the stoic Roman philosopher Epictetus (50–120 AD) actively opposed suicide, admonishing his students against the then popular notion that suicide was an acceptable, even noble, alternative to difficult life circumstances (Farberow, 1988). However, throughout the next two millennia, suicide was variously seen as a moral, legal, philosophical, or spiritual, but not clinical, issue. English law provided for mutilation of the corpse of a suicide and the withholding of any inheritance from heirs until well into the 19th Century. Beginning during the time of St. Augustine, the Catholic church taught that suicide was a certain path to eternal suffering, a view still held in some religious quarters. Even William James, in his two-volume opus examining almost every imaginable aspect of human functioning (James, 1890/1950), mentioned suicide in only one brief passage, and this dealt with aspects of the self, not deliberate self-destruction. In a different work, he maintained that suicide was a "religious disease," to be addressed through lifestyle changes (James, 1947). Interestingly, in a foreshadowing of the modern cognitive therapy movement, he commented, "Believe that life is worth living, and your belief will help create the fact" (Colt, 1991, p. 197).

Although the transition is still incomplete, the view of suicide as a product of disordered functioning, and therefore an appropriate matter for caring concern and clinical objectivity, is very much a phenomenon of the 20th Century. One the first signs of this shift was the creation in 1905 of the National Save-a-Life League in New York City. Begun by a Baptist minister after he counseled a young woman as she lay dying from self-poisoning, this organization ran newspaper ads asking suicidal individuals to contact them rather than attempt suicide (Allen, 1984). This may have been the first example of a concerted attempt to offer help to suicidal individuals rather than terrorize them with threats of punishment (Colt, 1991).

Credit for the first efforts to develop psychological understanding of suicidal phenomena (as opposed to Durkheim's (1897/1951) sociological perspective) belongs to Sigmund Freud. Discussions of suicide appeared sporadically in his writings on other subjects, and his views changed markedly during his lifetime. However, his clinical approach to suicide, as well as to sex and aggression, helped substantially to move suicide out of the realm of moral imperatives and into the domain of science.

Litman (1967) divides the development of Freud's ideas on suicide into two stages. In his early writings, Freud showed how his theory of the unconscious motivation of behavior applied equally well to suicidality. In his analysis of several cases, he observed a variety of motivations to self-destruction, including self-punishment, revenge, the fantasy of joining a deceased loved one, seeking attention, and a cry for help. However, by the time of the 1910 meeting of the Vienna Psychoanalytical Society on suicide (probably the first "suicidology conference"), Freud was still hesitant to draw any definitive conclusions. His primary concern was the inability of psychoanalytic theory to reconcile the strength of instincts toward survival and reproductive viability (the life and sexual instincts) with the reality of self-annihilation. He concluded by suggesting to his colleagues, "Let us suspend our judgment until experience has solved this problem" (Litman, 1967, p. 332).

A possible resolution to the seeming contradiction between suicide and life instincts came with the introduction of the concepts of ego splitting and the death instinct. Freud believed that in the aftermath of the loss of a love object, part of the ego creates a "shadow" of the lost object through the process of identification. Because this object is not completely integrated into the personality, part of the ego "splits" and sits in judgment of the rest. Suicide, at least in the case of melancholia, was thought to originate in murderous rage against the lost object. Because the object is no longer available, "...he "kills" him by destroying the internalized image of him" (Colt, 1991, p. 196). A few years later, still struggling to explain masochism and suicide, Freud revised his views on the basic instincts and introduced the destructive, or death, instinct. Though generally kept in check by the ego defenses, the death instinct was thought to be unleashed in the presence of this punitive part of the ego, now referred to as the superego. In suicide, a sadistic superego essentially abandons the ego, recapitulating parental abandonment, and setting the stage for self-destruction (Litman, 1967).

Despite these substantial contributions, Freud never proposed a comprehensive theory of suicide. It remained for Karl Menninger and Gregory Zilboorg in the 1930s to focus specifically upon suicidal phenomena and to further develop psychodynamic formulations. In *Man Against Himself*, Menninger (1938) observed that unconscious motivations to suicide went beyond retroflected hostility against a love object. In his famous suicide triad, he proposed that necessary conditions for suicide included, not only the wish to kill, but also a wish to be killed and a wish to die. These motivations were thought to derive, respectively, from the ego, superego, and id (Menninger, 1933) and can be said to parallel the affective experiences of hostility, guilt, and despair. Menninger believed that, because the suicide fatality is by definition both killer and victim, the person who wished to die but had no wish to be killed, or who wished to be killed but did not wish to kill, and so forth, would not likely commit suicide. He also introduced the notion that suicidal phenomena might extend beyond self-inflicted death to forms of "chronic" or "partial" suicide, such as alcoholism and self-mutilation (Colt, 1991).

In a series of papers in the 1930s, Zilboorg took issue with what he viewed as oversimplified explanations of suicide and questioned whether the death instinct added anything to what was already known about suicide—that people do indeed kill themselves. Anticipating the development of disorder-specific therapies in the 1980s and 1990s, he showed that Freud's formulation of suicide in melancholics might not apply to suicidality in other diagnostic groups (Zilboorg, 1936). Notably, he addressed suicide in schizophrenia and in what might now be viewed as borderline personality disorder (Maltsberger & Goldblatt, 1996).

During the first half of the 20th Century, psychological theorizing about suicide was almost exclusively the province of psychoanalysis. Even early behaviorists, while criticizing the tendency of psychoanalytic writers to speculate freely and without empirical support about the inner workings of their patients' minds, were essentially silent on the subject of suicide. John B. Watson, B. F. Skinner, and others built behavioral theory with a focus on observable phenomena (behaviors and the environmental events that influence them) and the insistence that theories be empirically based and testable. Dollard and Miller (1950) attempted to translate psychoanalytic notions into behavioral terms. However, it was not until the development of cognitive-behavioral theory in the 1970s and 1980s that the empirical discoveries of behavior therapy were brought to bear in the area of suicide.

☐ Current Perspectives

The dawn of the 20th Century saw dramatic changes in ideas about suicide. As Durkheim (1897/1951) showed the influence of sociological factors and Freud (e.g., 1933) and his followers examined the effects of childhood events and unconscious factors, suicidal individuals began to be seen less as sinners and more as victims deserving help. Thus, the stage was set for concerted efforts to prevent suicides by environmental and psychological methods. The establishment of the Los Angeles Suicide Prevention Center (LASPC) in 1958 can be viewed as the beginning of the Modern Era of understanding and treating individuals at risk of suicide.

The LASPC had a profound impact on the way suicide and suicidal people were viewed by clinicians and the public. Equally important, suicidality for the first time came to be viewed as a legitimate area for scientific inquiry. The clinical innovations of the LASPC focused primarily upon crisis intervention, i.e., working with individuals who were in an acutely suicidal state, helping to restore them to equilibrium (survive the crisis), and providing services appropriate to their circumstances. These innovations had major effects upon clinicians. Moreover, a substantial portion of subsequent clinical writings focused on accurate risk assessment and management of patients in suicidal crisis.

However, the purpose of this chapter is not to discuss crisis intervention with suicidal individuals, but rather to address psychotherapeutic treatment, i.e., interventions aimed at addressing underlying psychological vulnerability factors that contributed to the suicidal crisis in the first place and that, if not remedied, place the person at risk for future suicidal crises. The section that follows reviews recent developments in the psychoanalytic model of suicide and describes several other approaches that have emerged in recent years.

Psychodynamic Theory

Contemporary writers define psychodynamic therapy as a form of psychotherapy that "deals with interpersonal relations, recurrent conflict patterns, and ultimately the *meaning* of actions and experience" (Hendin, 1991, p. 1150). Key mechanisms of change are the therapeutic relationship itself and development of insight into historical and unconscious origins of the problem. In the case of suicidality, the view of suicide as the result of aggression turned inward upon an ambivalently regarded, introjected love object remains prominent. As described by Bongar (1991), the therapist must "help patients to work through and understand their sense of murderous rage with a self-object that has disappointed them" (p. 126). However, contemporary developments also include greater appreciation of the interpersonal communication function of self-harm. Consequently, the therapeutic process includes examination of the messages that might be conveyed to significant others (including the therapist) through suicidal threats or behaviors.

In keeping with the development of object relations theory (e.g., Kernberg, 1983; Kohut, 1977) and the more prominent focus on interpersonal processes, the modern practice of psychodynamic psychotherapy addresses the importance of empathy in working with suicidal individuals. In discussing a case of suicide in the context of inadvertent behavior by care providers, Havens (1965) removes any doubt that the "blank slate" stance of the analyst is misplaced with suicidal patients. He reminds caregivers of their tendency to underestimate their importance to suicidal patients and urges that therapists must be willing to "stay with the battle and feel, not [run] from what must be borne" (p. 406).

Maltsberger (1986) has systematized psychodynamic principles into a "method of psychodynamic formulation" of suicidality. Emphasis is on the specific situational stressors that trigger suicidality and the resources (environmental and psychological) that might act as buffers against self-destruction (Lovett & Maltsberger, 1992). Special attention is paid to the extreme difficulty that suicidal individuals experience replacing losses. Remediation of this relative lack of "inner resources" is a major goal of therapy. During periods of crisis, the therapist is often in the position of supplying coping resources until the patient is able to use therapy to develop his or her own ability to cope. Development of new, soothing introjects also plays a prominent role.

A final contribution of psychodynamic theory, with special relevance to the treatment of suicidal patients, is the concept of countertransference hate. First articulated by Maltsberger and Buie (1973), countertransference hate can be regarded as a legitimate concern for any clinician working with suicidal patients, regardless of theoretical orientation. Because of the intense emotional reactions evoked by suicidal individuals—from rage to anxiety to despair—therapists working with these patients must be mindful of their own behavior toward patients lest these behaviors damage the therapeutic alliance or even trigger suicidal acts. This model suggests that therapist reactions ranging from becoming overinvolved with the patient to distancing from or even abandoning the patient may be manifestations of defenses against awareness of hatred for the patient. The suggested remedy, as is the case in transference in general, is awareness coupled with appropriate self-restraint against countertherapeutic acting-out.

Although relatively little research has been conducted testing psychodynamic theories of suicide, a recent contribution provides empirical support for some aspects of the theory. Kaslow and colleagues (1998) assessed 99 inpatients with recent suicidal histories to test four psychodynamic concepts proposed to explain suicide: 1) self-directed aggression, 2) object loss, 3) ego functioning disturbance, and 4) pathological object relations. When compared to a nonsuicidal group of patients, the suicidal patients differed mainly in their difficulties in interpersonal relationships and lower levels of separation-individuation in self and object representations. The authors concluded that there was strong support for the object relations viewpoint and limited support for the object loss and aggression hypotheses. In acknowledging limitations of the study, the authors recommended further research in the area.

Shneidman's Contribution

While clearly influenced by psychodynamic concepts (including transference, unconscious processes, and symbolism), Edwin Shneidman's approach to the suicidal individual cuts across theories of psychotherapy, as well as academic disciplines. His greatest contributions to psychotherapy are perhaps most appropriately regarded as generic strategies for working with suicidal individuals. Foremost among these is the concept of reducing "psychache" (Shneidman, 1993). It is Shneidman's view that the proximate cause of suicide is unbearable psychic pain, and that the chief focus of the therapist working with an acutely suicidal patient should be on decreasing upset. This means entering a relationship unlike any other, including conventional psychotherapy. The differences lie in the almost exclusive focus on keeping the patient alive by various means (such as involving significant others and removing firearms) and by handling transference differently. Specifically, "the transference . . . and countertransference . . . can legitimately be much more intense and more deep than would be seemly or appropriate (or even ethical) in ordinary psychotherapy . . . "(Shneidman, 1993, p. 141).

Shneidman's discussions of treatment strategies focus primarily upon severely and acutely suicidal individuals. Treatment targets two proposed components of suicide risk: constriction and perturbation. Constriction is addressed by showing the patient a range of alternatives and thereby guiding him or her away from the dichotomous life or death perspective. Perturbation is addressed "by doing anything and almost everything possible to cater to the infantile idiosyncrasies, the dependency needs, the sense of pressure and futility, the feelings of hopelessness and helplessness that the individual is experiencing" (Shneidman, 1993, p. 142). After the level of lethality is reduced, the therapist is advised to pursue treatment procedures similar to those used with other patients.

Cognitive And Behavioral Approaches

As research on learning theory and behavior modification fueled the rising popularity of behavior therapy in the late 1960s and early 1970s, behavior therapists began to turn their attention to the problem of suicidal behaviors. According to Linehan (1981), this first occurred when Frederick and Resnik (1971) drew from Dollard and Miller's work in conceptualizing suicidal behavior as a product of personality, past learning and reinforcement history, and environment. Diekstra

(1973) proposed that suicidal behavior be viewed as a learned method of coping with crises, with important instrumental value, that is, the suicidal person has certain outcome expectations (whether conscious or not), and suicidal behaviors are learned to the extent that the individual is reinforced or expects a desirable outcome. Such desired outcomes might range from effecting a change in a significant other's behavior (in the case of nonfatal suicidal acts) to the individual's concepts of a peaceful afterlife.

Publication of Beck and colleagues' *Cognitive Therapy of Depression* in 1979 helped usher in "the cognitive revolution" in psychotherapy. Beck had been traditionally trained in psychoanalytic psychotherapy, but his research efforts to explore the theorized relationship between hostility and depression had proven disappointing. He then began testing an hypothesis that the negative thinking observed in depressed people might be accessible and modifiable directly, i.e., without primary emphasis on unconscious or childhood sources of current depressed thoughts and feelings. By helping the patient to identify and correct various cognitive distortions, such as overgeneralization or black-and-white thinking, it was thought that much of the "fuel" for the depression would be eliminated. An impressive body of subsequent research has supported the accuracy of this prediction regarding depression and other psychological disorders (for a recent review, see DeRubeis & Crits-Cristoph, 1998).

After reviewing research on cognition and suicide, Ellis (1986) proposed that principles of cognitive therapy might be adapted to address specific cognitive characteristics of suicidal individuals, such as cognitive rigidity and impaired problem-solving. In a similar vein, Schotte and Clum (1987) presented a "diathesis-stress-hopelessness" model of suicide, with the diathesis being a cognitive deficit in problem-solving.

Research regarding cognition and suicide has been conducted on several fronts. Hopelessness has been shown to be a key mediator between depression and suicidality, with significant predictive validity (Beck, Brown, & Steer, 1989; Minkoff, Bergman, Beck, & Beck, 1973). Linehan and colleagues (1983) have shown that reasons for living can be measured reliably, predict suicidality, and can be utilized as a powerful therapeutic device (Linehan, 1993). The association between suicidality and problem-solving deficits is one of the most consistent findings in the research on cognition and suicide (Pollock & Williams, 1998; Schotte & Clum 1987). Williams and Broadbent (1986) point to research on impoverished autobiographical memory as a possible explanation for these problem-solving deficits, which might be attributable to a lack of a detailed information base upon which to draw. Ellis and Ratliff (1986) compared equally depressed suicidal and nonsuicidal psychiatric patients on measures of irrational beliefs and dysfunctional attitudes and found that the suicidal patients scored significantly higher on need for achievement and acceptance and showed a much greater tendency to believe that emotional problems were caused by external events rather than by their attitudes and interpretations of events. Finally, Hewitt and colleagues (1994) recently reported that " . . . perfectionism [is] involved in suicide ideation even when other psychological factors, such as depression and hopelessness, are considered" (p. 455).

Multifactorial Models

Considerable research reflects an association between suicidality and an assortment of variables relevant to the conduct of cognitive therapy. However, cognition constitutes only one component of any model of human behavior. The field of suicidology is now just beginning to complement theoretical work on the multifactorial nature of suicidal behavior with empirically-based multidimensional models. For example, Yang and Clum (1996) recently proposed a model based on a review of the research literature that showed evidence for both a direct connection between early life experience and later suicidal behavior and the mediational role of cognitive factors between these two variables. Taking a somewhat different approach, Lewinsohn, Rohde, and Seeley (1996) used structural equation modeling to show a significant role for cognition in mediating between psychopathology, physical illness, environmental stress, and interpersonal problems, on the one hand, and suicidal behavior on the other. It is reasonable to predict from this model that the effects of adverse life experiences can be ameliorated if cognitive factors can be modified.

Cognitive therapy with suicidal individuals requires a specific formulation of the cognitive processes in each individual that predisposes him or her to hopelessness and suicidal ideation. It then utilizes a variety of methods to modify these cognitions. For example, Weishaar and Beck (1990) suggest that patients with cognitive rigidity (one of the components of ineffective problem-solving) can be helped through visualization of alternate solutions to problem situations. Hopelessness, on the other hand, is approached through patient exploration of the individual's situation, while assessing for and correcting instances of overestimation of problems or underestimation of resources. Throughout, Weishaar and Beck emphasize the importance of "collaborative empiricism" to ensure that the clinician fully understands the patient's situation and that the patient feels understood and supported. Fremouw, de Perczel and Ellis (1990) also emphasize tailoring therapy to the individual and suggest distinguishing between the "depressed/hopeless" and "communication/control" patients. They recommend helping the former to modify such beliefs as "My family would be better off without me," while assisting the latter to reassess and replace suicidal threats and behaviors as a problem-solving strategy.

In perhaps the most thorough development of the problem-solving model to date, Chiles and Strosahl (1995) suggest to patients that suicide is a valid option, though ultimately a counterproductive means of dealing with emotional pain. In this manner, any shame associated with moral condemnation of suicidality is averted while setting the stage for examining alternate solutions. The authors also alert clinicians to reinforcement contingencies operating around suicidal behavior, such as when clinicians or family members inadvertently reward suicidality through increased attention or repeated hospitalizations.

Problem-solving training with suicidal individuals has been described by various other authors, including Salkovskis, Atha, and Storer (1990) and Linehan (1993). Further extending specific guidelines for effecting cognitive change, Freeman and Reinecke (1993) describe 20 cognitive and 10 behavioral techniques for use with suicidal patients.

Finally, Rudd and Joiner (in press) recently reviewed the now substantial body of research on cognition and suicide and proposed an integrative approach to treating suicidal individuals within a cognitive-behavioral framework. They attempt to articulate a "suicidal belief system" and a dynamic "suicidal mode" that describe common cognitive features of suicidality while also allowing for individual variability and individualized treatment planning.

Separation Theory and Voice Therapy

Developed by Robert Firestone (1997), separation theory and voice therapy integrates concepts from psychodynamic theory and existential psychology, with overtones of cognitive therapy. It is based on Firestone's concept of the fantasy bond, in which the young child develops an illusion of connection to its mother as a defense against the pain of separation. Because of parental ambivalence, the child is thought to incorporate both positive and negative attitudes towards the self. The greater the degree of parental rejection or hostility, the more significant the role of the anti-self system, represented by the concept of the "voice." Developed from observations of patients who expressed harshly self-critical thoughts as second-person accusations ("You're such a slob. You don't deserve to be happy."), the voice is defined as "an integrated system of negative thoughts and feelings, antithetical to the self and cynical toward others, that is at the core of maladaptive behavior" (p. 16). At its extreme, the voice encourages and triggers self-harm and suicidal behavior.

The voice serves as a central construct in the theory and as a main point of entry for therapy. The primary technique is to encourage patients to explore negative attitudes toward themselves by expressing them aloud in the form of self-critical statements in the second person. The purpose is to develop insight and objectivity through the strong emotional reactions that often result. Unlike cognitive therapy, voice therapy expressly discourages therapists from replacing self-critical thoughts with more realistic ones, focusing rather on the historic origins of the disturbance. Suicidal patients are helped to see that their self-destructive impulses stem from critical or hostile messages that were adopted from the parents and that the voice is in fact "alien" to their real self.

Family Therapy

In contrast to comprehensive theories of psychopathology and therapy, such as psychodynamics and cognitive therapy, family therapy is more of a strategic orientation that might be used to implement therapeutic interventions from various theoretical foundations. The common thread is the view that the family environment influences family members in important ways and that ameliorating family dysfunction can go a long way toward relieving perturbation in suicidal individuals.

This view was first expressed from a psychodynamic perspective by Joseph Richman (1986). In commenting on the relative lack of empirical evidence of aggression in suicidal individuals, Richman turns Freud's formulation of self-directed hostility around and asks who in the patient's family might harbor hostility towards the patient and covertly or overtly communicate death wishes to the patient. The therapist asks, not only "Whom does the patient want to kill?" but also "Who wants him to die?" Hostility is viewed as reciprocally influenced by actions of the patient and socially-influenced attitudes of family members toward the patient. Family therapy seeks to reduce hostility by facilitating communication, mutual respect, and individual autonomy.

Spirito (1997) reviews a variety of other approaches to family therapy with suicidal patients. Prominent among these is family cognitive-behavioral therapy. Consistent with the cognitive model, cognitive-behavioral family therapy (McLean & Taylor, 1994), seeks to alleviate hopelessness and to identify and restructure maladaptive cognitions. In addition, the therapist focuses on improving communication, increasing mutually rewarding behaviors, and decreasing punishing behaviors among family members. The family is shown how to be specific about expectations and feelings and how to solve problems in a systematic manner. Interventions have been tailored for both suicidal adolescents and a suicidal parent.

Family influences in the development of suicidality have been subjected to considerable empirical scrutiny (see Brent, 1995, for a review). However, in his recent critical review, Wagner (1998) questions the rigor of such studies, which often are correlational in nature.

Group Therapy

If it is accepted that suicidality is related to low self-esteem, social isolation, and dysfunctional problem-solving, then it stands to reason that treatment in a group setting might offer significant resources towards its remediation. However, group therapy continues to experience relatively low visibility in the suicide literature, despite its introduction more than 30 years ago. Clinicians often anticipate significant problems with treating depressed, suicidal individuals in groups, including the prospect of patients' fueling each other's despair. This is despite published opinions to the contrary. For example, Asimos and Rosen (1978) challenged the conventional wisdom in describing ten years' experience with such groups.

In one of the earliest published descriptions, Farberow (1968) described a relatively atheoretical formulation for group therapy with suicidal patients based on a crisis intervention model. The theoretical stance viewed the group as a ready source of nurturance, support, and renewed relations for individuals characterized by chronic feelings of loneliness and rejection. The program was designed as a brief, open-ended model, although it was found that patients often returned to the group as an ongoing source of support.

A recent adaptation of the group treatment model is described by Linehan (1993, see discussion below). As is often the case with group treatment approaches, Linehan's model combines group procedures with individual therapy. In addition, Rudd and colleagues (1996) report results of a large-scale study of an intensive, outpatient treatment program for suicidal young adults, in which the experimental intervention (which was group-based) showed superior results to the treatment as usual condition.

Specialized Procedures

Through the years, it has become increasingly evident that a homogeneous, one size fits all approach to treating suicidal patients is not desirable. Suicidal processes and treatment indications may differ appreciably from one person to another, depending upon individual and situational variables. Therapeutic procedures with suicidal patients have most commonly been developed along one of two lines of classification: age and diagnostic group.

Age groups generally are addressed within a developmental perspective. For example, Berman and Jobes (1994) comment that "Individual psychotherapy is the treatment of choice with the suicidal adolescent; however, family therapy is often the more appropriate treatment when family conflict or psychopathology is central to the adolescent's struggle toward autonomy" (p. 93). Similarly, Goldman and Beardslee (1999) emphasize the importance of both individual and family work, while assessing the ratio of risk and resource factors to determine the level of care and protection needed (p. 435). Cognitive techniques are commonly recommended for suicidal adolescents, usually including training in problem-solving skills (Spirito, 1997).

Approaches to the suicidal elderly patient also are patterned after developmental issues, but may be based on any number of therapeutic orientations. Issues include deterioration of physical abilities, economic decline, marginalization by society, and deaths of friends and loved ones. Osgood and Thielman (1990) present an overview of therapy strategies used with older suicidal individuals, including psychodynamic psychotherapy, cognitive therapy, reminiscence and life review therapy, and family therapy.

Richman (1986) observed that the specific therapeutic modality is probably less important than not only recognizing that elderly patients can benefit from therapy in the first place, but also communicating to the patient awareness and respect for his or her wisdom and experience. In addition, he expresses agreement with Maltsberger's (1991) emphasis on supplying support through family and outside resources, as well as the importance of warmth, encouragement, and availability.

Despite relative differences in focus (particularly regarding precipitating factors), descriptions of psychotherapeutic interventions for older adults are difficult to distinguish from therapies in general. Whether or not therapy should be different for the elderly is difficult to determine, since research for the most part has not definitively established that suicidal processes vary in this population in ways that have significant implications for treatment. Clark (1992) presented psychological autopsy data showing that, contrary to conventional wisdom, elderly persons who committed suicide typically were not socially isolated, under severe stress, or in worse physical health than their peers. He hypothesized the presence of "a lifelong character fault" (p. 24) which interferes with adaptation to the normal aging process. If research along these and similar lines confirms such deficit hypotheses, then therapy strategies specifically tailored to the psychological needs of suicidal elderly patients might reasonably be expected.

In addition to interventions focused on age groups, recent years have seen the development of interventions geared to suicidal individuals with specific psychiatric symptom pictures. Prominent among these have been borderline personality disorder (BPD) and chronic suicidality. Beginning in the 1980s, Marsha Linehan began writing about her research on the treatment of young, suicidal females with BPD and the therapeutic approach she developed, Dialectical Behavior Therapy (DBT; Linehan, 1987, 1999). Although DBT is restricted neither to BPD nor to suicidal individuals, it does specifically take into account the psychological characteristics and treatment needs of these overlapping populations. Key aspects include

> acknowledgment of the patient's sense of emotional desperation (validation strategies), a matter-of-fact attitude about current and previous parasuicidal and other dysfunctional behaviors . . . , an active attempt to 'reframe' suicidal and other dysfunctional behaviors as part of the patient's learned problem-solving repertoire, and continuing efforts to focus therapy on active problem solving . . . Therapists actively teach emotion regulation, interpersonal effectiveness, distress tolerance, and self-management skills . . . (p. 272).

Setting DBT apart from many other therapeutic approaches with suicidal individuals has a track record of rigorous, largely positive, outcome research (e.g., Linehan, 1993; Linehan, Heard, & Armstrong, 1993).

Distinct from patients who are acutely suicidal or who are not actively suicidal but have risk factors for suicide are patients who exhibit chronic suicidality or repetitive suicidal episodes. Chiles and Strosahl (1995) have developed an unorthodox approach to management and treatment, based upon principles of reinforcement and cognitive-behavior therapy. They point out that, in a person without a history of reinforcement for effective problem-solving strategies, suicidal talk and behavior often are remarkably effective ways of obtaining relief from emotional distress due to responses from family members, care providers, and others. They further caution clinicians against becoming involved in a showdown with a patient, as the therapist attempts to prevent the very behavior upon which the patient has relied for solace. Instead, they advise validating emotional pain and the patient's reality that suicidality is the only apparent response to the situation. The therapist then seeks to socially reinforce whatever healthy coping behaviors the patient might have employed and explore the pros and cons of adaptive problem-solving strategies for the future. Rather than spending extended periods of time on the telephone with suicidal patients, they recommend teaching patients to use coping cards with reminders for coping strategies developed collaboratively in-session. They also recommend random support calls in order to show that suicidal crises are not required to get the therapist's attention. They question the usefulness of routine hospitalization in response to suicidal crises and offer alternatives, such as arranging for periodic, brief admissions initiated by the patient as he or she learns to recognize the need for support before that need escalates into an emotional crisis that might trigger a suicidal response.

Efficacy Research

The voluminous literature on psychotherapy with suicidal patients is remarkable for the relative absence of scientific demonstrations of efficacy. Implicit in this literature is the notion that, by treating suicidal individuals according to certain prescribed guidelines, the risk of suicidal acts in the future can be reduced. Edited volumes of chapters on the treatment of various groups of suicidal individuals tend to be long on advice for treating these patients but short on objective evidence that the purpose of lowering suicidality is in fact being achieved.

To the contrary, what little controlled research has been conducted reveals modest desired effects, if that. For example, Hirsch, Walsh, and Draper (1982) concluded on the basis of their literature review that there was little evidence that individual psychotherapy prevented suicidal behavior. Allard, Marshall, and Plante (1992) randomly assigned suicidal patients to either usual care or an intensive, eclectic therapeutic intervention and found no difference between groups in the number of repeat suicide attempts following treatment.

Recent studies of therapeutic interventions with suicidal patients are almost exclusively from a cognitive-behavioral orientation and have produced modestly encouraging results. Patsiokas and Clum (1985) compared nondirective therapy, cognitive restructuring, and problem-solving training and found that the problem-solving group exhibited superior problem-solving abilities and lower hopelessness compared to the other two groups. The problem-solving group also showed a 60% drop in suicidal ideation posttreatment, compared to 40% in the cognitive restructuring group and zero in the nondirective group. A later randomized study testing interpersonal problem-solving skills found that in the year after conclusion of treatment, 25% of those in a treatment comparison group had repeat suicide attempts, compared to 10.5% of those in the problem-solving condition (McLeavey, Daly, Ludgate, & Murray, 1994).

Linehan and colleagues (1991) used a randomized design to compare DBT to treatment as usual in the community in a sample of chronically suicidal women with borderline personality disorder. Although they found no differences between groups after one year of treatment on depression, hopelessness, or suicidal ideation, the DBT group had significantly fewer and less lethal suicide attempts, a lower therapy dropout rate, and fewer days of psychiatric hospitalization. They reported continued superiority to conventional treatment for the DBT group at one-year posttreatment follow-up (Linehan, Heard, & Armstrong, 1993).

Rudd and colleagues (1996) tested a time-limited, outpatient group intervention based on a problem-solving and social competence paradigm in a large ($N = 264$), randomized clinical trial with young adults. They found both the experimental and treatment as usual interventions to be effective in reducing suicidal ideation and behavior, as well as associated symptomatology, with no significant differences between groups. However, the experimental treatment was more effective in keeping higher risk patients in treatment, a significant finding in light of recent evidence of a strong association between premature termination of therapy and eventual suicide (Dahlsgaard, Beck, & Brown, 1998).

A thorough analysis of the import of this body of research is beyond the scope of this chapter. However, some cause for optimism is contained in recent literature reviews. Van der Sande and colleagues (1997) conducted a meta-analysis of psychosocial interventions following suicide attempts, using further attempts as an outcome criterion. They identified 15 randomized controlled trials and divided them into four categories: 1) psychiatric management of poor compliance, 2) guaranteed inpatient shelter, 3) psychosocial crisis intervention, and 4) cognitive-behavioral therapy. They found that only the cognitive-behavioral treatment showed a significant preventive effect on repeated suicide attempts. However, they advised caution in interpreting the findings, since methodological issues in the cognitive-behavioral therapy studies left room for uncertainty regarding the magnitude of effect and generalizability of the results to populations other than those examined in the studies.

Hawton and associates (1998) recently published a systematic review of the efficacy of randomized controlled trials of various interventions in preventing future self-harm behavior. They found that various, specific interventions (from contact cards to problem-solving training) had been shown to be superior to comparison conditions in preventing deliberate self-harm. However, they added that "[t]here remains considerable uncertainty about which forms of psychosocial and physical treatments of patients who harm themselves are most effective" (p. 441) and express "urgent need for large trials of promising therapies for this substantial clinical population" (p. 446).

☐ Summary and Synthesis

Because the outcome research on psychotherapeutic interventions with suicidal individuals currently falls well short of definitive conclusions, clinicians also must be guided by the clinical wisdom of the field. Although theorists vary widely in their theoretical perspectives and rationales for their interventions, it is nevertheless possible to glean a number of characteristics of therapy with suicidal persons that cut across disparate theoretical orientations. Indeed, the similarities in language and technique are sometimes remarkable, given the paradigm conflicts that are evident in other contexts. The following are several common threads (summarized in Table 1) which run through the collective tapestry of psychotherapeutic interventions for suicidal individuals.

Communicating Empathy and Nonjudgment

Long recognized as axiomatic in psychotherapy in general, the key role of empathy and nonjudgment with suicidal individuals was first articulated by Havens (1965) and later developed by Jacobs (1989) and others. Similarly, this time from a behavioral perspective, Chiles and Strosahl (1995) recommend a combination of acceptance and validation:

TABLE 1. Common Factors in Psychotherapy with Suicidal Individuals

---

Communicating empathy and nonjudgment
Providing external support while building inner resources
Restoring hope
Addressing environmental influences
Fortifying reasons for living
Facilitating problem-solving
Developing understanding of instrumental functions of suicidality
Treating the underlying disorder

. . . emphasize that the pain is quite understandable given the circumstances but that the method of dealing with the circumstances is faulty. Remember, your patient is often doing the reverse. He or she is assuming that the pain is not legitimate but that the methods of dealing with it are (p. 212).

Many authors, particularly Maltsberger and Buie (1973), alert clinicians to the possible anti-empathic influences of (often unconscious) negative thoughts and feelings about suicide and towards the patient.

Providing External Support While Building Inner Resources

Psychodynamic writers speak of providing sustaining resources while helping the patient to develop good internal objects. Cognitive-behavior therapists help the patient to get problems solved while helping him or her to develop improved problem-solving skills. In either case, there is recognition that, while in suicidal crisis, the patient lacks the ability to cope adequately with the situation and requires assistance in doing so. In addition, what contributed to the development of the suicidal response to crisis in the first place is thought to have been an enduring trait-like deficiency which must be corrected, lest the patient remain at suicidal risk when the next loss or major stressor comes along.

Restoring Hope

Perhaps the best validated psychological risk factor for suicide, hopelessness, is universally recognized as a key target in both crisis intervention and psychotherapeutic treatment of suicidal individuals. Restoration of hope is variously viewed as a direct target in therapy or an expected outcome of interventions focused on other issues. In any event, there is wide agreement that it is an important index of concern to be kept in sharp focus at all times by the treating clinician.

Addressing Environmental Influences

The importance of environmental influences has long been emphasized by crisis interventionists. Those in the psychotherapy arena have steadily come to the realization over the past few decades that an exclusive focus "between the patient's ears" is inappropriate with suicidal patients. Of special significance is enlisting the support and possible therapy involvement of the patient's significant others, as well as utilizing community resources to ensure that the therapist is not heroically attempting to serve as the patient's sole lifeline.

Fortifying Reasons for Living

Linehan, Goodstein, Neilson, and Chiles (1983) were the first to operationalize and measure reasons for living as a formal theoretical construct in the study and treatment of suicidality. However, the general concept pervades the suicidology literature, finding expression as much as 100 years ago in William James' (1947/1950) essay, "Is Life Worth Living?" This construct has potential usefulness both for assessing suicide risk and for structuring the therapy intervention. The cognitive therapy concept of selective abstraction has been especially useful in this context in alerting clinicians to the fact that patients often fail to recognize extant reasons for living due the filtering effect of the depressive mood state (Beck, Rush, Shawn, & Emery, 1979).

Facilitating Problem-Solving

Considering the substantial empirical evidence of diminished problem-solving skills in suicidal patients (see above), it stands to reason that problem-solving facilitation would be a prominent aspect of therapy, regardless of theoretical orientation. At a minimum, this would be expressed by providing assistance to the patient to solve current problems (financial, legal, employment, relationship, etc.) that are contributing to a current crisis. Additionally, therapists should teach (whether didactically or through modeling) skills required to solve problems in a methodical, nonimpulsive manner (see Clum & Lerner, 1990; Linehan, 1993). Reduced hopelessness would be an expected result of such interventions.

Developing Understanding of Instrumental Functions of Suicidality

Whether viewed pejoratively as manipulation or compassionately as a cry for help, it is generally recognized that suicidal talk and self-harm behavior often function as something other than a pursuit of death. Psychodynamic theorists have spoken eloquently of the various motivations to suicidality and the importance of helping the patient to develop insight into conscious and unconscious motives. For example, Hendin (1991) states that "Suicidal patients are unique in their use of the possibility of ending their lives as a way of dealing with both internal conflict and relations with other people" (p. 1154). From a behavioral perspective, Chiles and Strosahl (1995) similarly remind the clinician that nonfatal suicidal behavior is often highly effective in reducing emotional distress and is thereby reinforced. They recommend showing the patient how suicidality is serving as a problem-solving strategy and helping them to develop alternate strategies that are less dangerous and more effective.

Treating the Underlying Disorder

The relationship between psychological disorders and suicide is undeniable. In his review of the area, Tanney (1992) states that "mental disorders can lay claim to a position in the first rank of the matrix of causation" (p. 310). While it is clear that exclusive focus on psychiatric diagnosis would be an incomplete approach to treatment, it is equally clear that treating such underlying conditions is a crucial component in a comprehensive approach to reducing suicide risk. Focused treatment of affective disorders (Clark & Goebel-Fabbri, 1999), schizophrenia (Reid, 1998), and substance abuse (Murphy, 1992) appears to be especially important.

☐ Future Directions

Trends

The waning years of the 20th Century have seen substantial changes, which, assuming they continue, will bring major changes to the treatment of suicidal individuals. Indeed, similar tunes seem to be emanating from a variety of different composers.

Shift from "management" to treatment

Until recently, the typical article or chapter on interventions with suicidal patients shied away from the term treatment in favor of management. Stemming from roots in the crisis intervention literature, such guidelines focused on such issues as availability in-between sessions and when to hospitalize. The operating assumption generally was that, "when the person is no longer highly suicidal-then the usual methods of psychotherapy . . . can be usefully employed" (Shneidman, 1981, p. 345).

Hendin (1995) disparagingly refers to some writings on the management of suicidal patients as " . . . guides designed to help the therapist outmaneuver the potentially suicidal person" (p. 185). There is clearly growing recognition that specialized treatments for suicidal patients (beyond crisis intervention) are within reach. Suicidal individuals differ psychologically in some trait-like ways from other patients, even within the same diagnostic group. Targeting these characteristics during the noncrisis phase of therapy might serve to reduce vulnerability to future suicidal episodes (Fremouw, de Perczel, & Ellis, 1990). This recognition has given rise to treatments more tailor-made for suicidal individuals, such as Linehan's (1993) Dialectical Behavior Therapy and Maltsberger's method of psychodynamic formulation (Lovett & Maltsberger, 1992).

From Control to Collaboration

Also true to its crisis intervention roots, psychotherapy with suicidal patients has traditionally dictated that the therapist's first and foremost responsibility was to "keep the patient alive." This has translated into a significant focus in therapy sessions on ongoing risk assessment and common use of involuntary hospitalization as the therapist felt obligated to ensure the patient's safety. However, recent years have seen challenges to these practices from various quarters, propelled by a combination of the failure of attempts to predict suicide (e.g., Pokorny, 1983) and growing recognition of the crucial role of the therapeutic alliance. Hendin (1995) cautions that preoccupation with preventing a patient from killing himself or herself might create

> . . . a state of mind and way of relating to suicidal patients that often make treatment unsuccessful. . . . All the precautions and all the management may result in encouraging one of the most lethal aspects of the suicidal individual, that is, his tendency to make someone else responsible for his staying alive. (p. 185)

Similarly, though from a very different theoretical perspective, Chiles and Strosahl (1995) recommend that the therapist acknowledge (to both patient and self) that suicide is clearly an available problem-solving option and that the job of the therapist is not to keep the patient alive so much as to assist with developing alternate problem-solving strategies aimed at making life the preferable alternative. Consistent with a trend toward a more collaborative model is the increasingly common questioning of the advisability of the traditional antisuicide contract (e.g., Miller, Jacobs, & Gutheil, 1998).

Building Tolerance for Frustration and Pain

Although the general thrust of treatment with suicidal individuals seeks to reduce psychological pain (Shneidman, 1993), it is becoming increasingly recognized in a variety of arenas that, because suicidal individuals exhibit difficulty tolerating loss, conflict, and frustration, they require assistance developing greater acceptance of both their own imperfections and the painful exigencies of life. Whether conceptualized as empathic "sitting with" the patient's pain (Jacobs, 1989, p. 334) or enhancement of "distress tolerance skills" (Linehan, 1993), the trend is away from the assumption (sometimes held by therapist and patient alike, to the detriment of both) that virtually all suffering is unnecessary and therefore must be eliminated. Ultimately, the choice to go on living might hinge on, not only reduction of suffering, but also on acceptance of the reality of suffering as part of the human condition (Hayes, 1998).

Research

Despite recent advances in clinical interventions with suicidal individuals, further advancement is hampered by gaps in two fundamental areas of research: randomized clinical trials and classification. In a 1998 keynote address to the American Association of Suicidology, Marsha Linehan contrasted the profusion of randomized studies of psychotherapeutic interventions for anxiety disorders and depression with the paucity of such studies of suicidal individuals. Observing that research protocols commonly screened out suicidal individuals, she reported that the literature currently contained only 13 randomized clinical trials of outpatient intervention strategies with suicidal individuals. She concluded that we currently do not know what, if any, interventions are effective in reducing suicidality and that we have no way of knowing until the number and quality of randomized clinical trials with severely suicidal individuals increases substantially.

However, high quality clinical trials will not be possible without prior progress in descriptive research. Development and testing of clinical interventions is seriously hampered by a lack of understanding of subtypes within what is commonly acknowledged to be a heterogeneous population. Ellis (1988) reviewed the literature on subtypes of suicidal patients and concluded, not only that there was no consensus in the field, but also that this area of investigation was seriously fragmented, in part because different investigators studied substantially different variable domains. On an even more basic level, definitions of such terms as suicide attempt vary considerably from one study to another, resulting in serious problems generalizing across studies. O'Carroll and associates (1996) took an important first step towards rectifying this problem, but much work remains to be done.

Industrialization of Mental Health Services

The field is just beginning to grapple with the complex issues involved in the treatment of suicidal patients in the new world of managed mental health care. Is there an inherent clash between limitations on mental health benefits and effective treatment of persons at risk of suicide? Are suicidal individuals truly in need of prolonged treatment, or should clinicians' protests viewed in the same light as previous protests that have been proven invalid by the advent of effective, brief treatments for disorders such as major depression and panic disorder? What is the clinician's responsibility when a patient's session allowance runs out and the patient is still viewed as at-risk? Should managed care companies share liability when a patient commits suicide in the wake of restricted access to care? These and many other complex questions await answers from clinical, scientific, business, and political arenas at the dawn of the 21st Century.

☐ References

Allard, R., Marshall, M., & Plante, M. C. (1992). Intensive follow-up does not reduce the risk of repeat suicide attempts. *Suicide and Life-Threatening Behavior, 22,* 303–314.

Allen, N. (1984). Suicide prevention. In C. Hatton & S. Valente (Eds.), *Suicide: Assessment and intervention* (pp. 11–13). Norwalk, CT: Appleton-Century-Crofts.

Asimos, C. T., & Rosen, D. H. (1978). Group treatment of suicidal and depressed persons: Indications for an open-ended group therapy program. *Bulletin of the Menninger Clinic, 42,* 515–518.

Beck, A. T., Brown, G., & Steer, R. (1989). Prediction of eventual suicide in psychiatric inpatients by clinical ratings of hopelessness. *Journal of Consulting and Clinical Psychology, 57,* 309–310.

Beck, A. T., Rush, A. J., Shaw, B. F., & Emery, G. (1979). *Cognitive therapy of depression.* New York: Guilford.

Berman, A. L., & Jobes, D. A. (1994). Treatment of the suicidal adolescent. In A. Leenaars, J. Maltsberger, & R. Neimeyer (Eds.), *Treatment of suicidal people* (pp. 89–100). Washington, DC: Taylor and Francis.

Bongar, B. (1991). *The suicidal patient: Clinical and legal standards of care.* Washington, DC: American Psychological Association.

Brent, D. A. (1995). Risk factors for adolescent suicide and suicidal behavior: Mental and substance abuse disorders, family environmental factors, and life stress. *Suicide and Life-Threatening Behavior, 25* (Suppl.), 52–63.

Chiles, J. A., & Strosahl, K. D. (1995). *The suicidal patient.* Washington, DC: American Psychiatric Press.

Clark, D. C. (1992). Narcissistic crises of aging. *Suicide and Life-Threatening Behavior, 23,* 21–26.

Clark, D. C., & Goebel-Fabbri, A. E. (1999). In D. G. Jacobs (Ed.), *Harvard Medical School guide to suicide assessment and intervention* (pp. 270–286). San Francisco: Jossey-Bass.

Clum, G. A., & Lerner, M. (1990). A problem solving approach to treating individuals at risk for suicide. In D. Lester (Ed.), *Current concepts of suicide* (pp. 194–202). Philadelphia: The Charles Press.

Colt, G. W. (1991). *The enigma of suicide.* New York: Touchstone.

Dahlsgaard, K. K., Beck, A. T., & Brown, G. K. (1998). Inadequate response to therapy as a predictor of suicide. *Suicide and Life-Threatening Behavior, 28,* 197–204.

DeRubeis, R. J., & Crits-Cristoph, P. (1998). Empirically supported individual and group psychological treatments for adult mental disorders. *Journal of Consulting and Clinical Psychology, 66,* 37–52.

Diekstra, R. (1973). A social learning theory approach to the prediction of suicidal behavior. Paper presented at the Seventh International Congress on Suicide Prevention, Amsterdam.

Dollard, J., & Miller, N. E. (1950). *Personality and psychotherapy: An analysis in terms of learning, thinking, and culture.* New York: McGraw-Hill.

Durkheim, E. (1951). *Suicide: A study in sociology.* Glencoe, IL: Free Press. (Original work published in 1897).

Ellis, T. E. (1986). Toward a cognitive therapy for suicidal individuals. *Professional Psychology, 17,* 125–130.

Ellis, T. E. (1988). Classification of self-destructive behavior: A review and step toward integration. *Suicide and Life-Threatening Behavior, 18,* 358–371.

Ellis, T. E., & Ratliff, K. (1986). Cognitive characteristics of suicidal and nonsuicidal psychiatric inpatients. *Cognitive Therapy and Research, 10,* 625–634.

Farberow, N. L. (1968). Group psychotherapy with suicidal persons. In H. Resnick (Ed.), *Suicidal behaviors: Diagnosis and management* (pp. 328–340). Boston: Little Brown.

Farberow, N. L. (1988). The history of suicide. In G. Evans, & N. L. Farberow (Eds.), *Encyclopedia of suicide* (pp. vii–xxvii). New York: Facts on File.

Firestone, R. W. (1997). *Suicide and the inner voice.* Thousand Oaks, CA: Sage.

Frederick, C., & Resnik, H. L. P. (1971). How suicidal behaviors are learned. *American Journal of Psychotherapy, 25,* 37–55.

Freeman, A., & Reinecke, M. A. (1993). Cognitive therapy of suicidal behavior: A manual for treatment. New York: Springer.

Fremouw, W., de Perczel, M., & Ellis, T. E. (1990). *Suicide risk: Assessment and response guidelines.* New York: Pergamon.

Freud, S. (1965). *New introductory lectures on psycho-analysis.* New York: Norton. (Originally published in 1933).

Goldman, S., & Beardslee, W. R. (1999). Suicide in children and adolescents. In D. G. Jacobs (Ed.), *Harvard Medical School guide to suicide assessment and intervention* (pp. 417–442). San Francisco: Jossey-Bass.

Havens, L. L. (1965). The anatomy of a suicide. *New England Journal of Medicine, 272,* 401–406.

Hawton, K., Arensman, E., Townsend, E., Bremner, S., Feldman, E., Goldney, R., Gunnell, D., Hazell, P., van Heeringen, K., House, A., Owens, D., Sakinofsky, I., & Traskman-Bendz, L. (1998). Deliberate self harm: Systematic review of efficacy of psychosocial and pharmacological treatments in preventing repetition. *British Medical Journal, 317,* 441–447.

Hayes, S. (1998). Human suffering. Presidential address to the Association for Advancement of Behavior Therapy. Washington, DC.

Hendin, H. (1991). Psychodynamics of suicide, with particular reference to the young. *American Journal of Psychiatry, 148,* 1150–1158.

Hendin, H. (1995). *Suicide in America.* New York: Norton.

Hewitt, P. L., Flett, G. L., & Weber, C. (1994). Dimensions of perfectionism and suicide ideation. *Cognitive Therapy and Research, 18,* 439–460.

Hirsch, S. R., Walsh, C., & Draper, R. (1982). Parasuicide: A review of treatment interventions. *Journal of Affective Disorders, 4,* 299–311.

Jacobs, D. (1989). Psychotherapy with suicidal patients: The empathic method. In D. Jacobs & H. Brown (Eds.), *Suicide: Understanding and responding* (pp. 329–342). Madison, CT: International Universities Press.

James, W. (1947). Is life worth living? *Essays on faith and morals.* New York: Longmans, Green, and Co., 1–31.

James, W. (1950). *The principles of psychology.* New York: Dover. (Original work published 1890)

Kaslow, N. M., Reviere, S. L., Chance, S. E., Rogers, J. H., Hatcher, C. A., Wasserman, F., Smith, L., Jessee, S., James, M. E., & Seelig, B. (1998). An empirical study of the psychodynamics of suicide. *Journal of the American Psychoanalytic Association, 3,* 777–796.

Kernberg, O. F. (1983). Object relations theory and character analysis. *Journal of the American Psychoanalytic Association, 31,* 247–272.

Kohut, H. (1977). *The restoration of the self.* New York: International Universities Press.

Lewinsohn, P. M., Rohde, P., & Seeley, J. R. (1996). Adolescent suicidal ideation and attempts: Prevalence, risk factors, and clinical implications. *Clinical Psychology: Science and Practice, 3,* 25–46.

Linehan, M. M. (1981). A social-behavioral analysis of suicide and parasuicide: Implications for clinical assessment and treatment. In J. F. Clarkin & H. J. Glazer (Eds.), *Depression: Behavioral and directive intervention strategies* (pp. 229–294). New York: Garland.

Linehan, M. M. (1987). Dialectical Behavior Therapy for borderline personality disorder. *Bulletin of the Menninger Clinic, 51,* 261–276.

Linehan, M. M. (1998). Is anything effective for reducing suicidal behavior? Paper presented at the 31st Annual Conference of the American Association of Suicidology, Bethesda, MD, April.

Linehan, M. M. (1993). *Cognitive-behavioral treatment of borderline personality disorder.* New York: Guilford.

Linehan, M. M. (1999). Standard protocol of assessing and treating suicidal behaviors for patients in treatment. In D. G. Jacobs (Ed.), *The Harvard Medical School guide to suicide assessment and intervention* (pp. 146–187). San Francisco: Jossey-Bass.

Linehan, M. M., Armstrong, H. E, Suarez, A., Allmon, D., & Heard, H. L. (1991). Cognitive-behavioral treatment of chronically parasuicidal borderline patients. *Archives of General Psychiatry, 48,* 1060–1064.

Linehan, M. M., Goodstein, J., Neilson, S., & Chiles, J. (1983). Reasons for staying alive when you are thinking of killing yourself: The Reasons for Living inventory. *Journal of Consulting and Clinical Psychology, 51,* 276–286.

Linehan, M. M., Heard, H. L., & Armstrong, H. E. (1993). Naturalistic follow-up of a behavioral treatment for chronically parasuicidal borderline patients. *Archives of General Psychiatry, 50,* 971–974.

Litman, R. E. (1967). Sigmund Freud on suicide. In E. S. Shneidman (Ed.), *Essays in self-destruction* (pp. 324–344). New York: Science House.

Lovett, C. G., & Maltsberger, J. T. (1992). Psychodynamic approaches to the assessment and management of suicide. In B. Bongar (Ed.), *Suicide: Guidelines for assessment, management, and treatment* (pp. 160–175). New York: Oxford University Press.

Maltsberger, J. T. (1986). *Suicide risk: The formulation of clinical judgment.* New York: New York University Press.

Maltsberger, J. T. (1991). Psychotherapy with older suicidal patients. *Journal of Geriatric Psychiatry, 24,* 217–234.

Maltsberger, J. T., & Buie, D. H. (1973). Countertransference hate in the treatment of suicidal patients. *Archives of General Psychiatry, 30,* 625–633.

Maltsberger, J. T., & Goldblatt, M. J. (1996). *Essential papers on suicide.* New York: New York University Press.

McLean, P., & Taylor, S. (1994). Family therapy for suicidal people. *Death Studies, 18,* 409–426.

McLeavey, B. C., Daly, R. J., Ludgate, J. W., & Murray, C. M. (1994). Interpersonal problem-solving skills training in the treatment of self-poisoning patients. *Suicide and Life-Threatening Behavior, 24,* 382–394.

Menninger, K. A. (1933). Psychoanalytic aspects of suicide. *International Journal of Psychoanalysis, 14,* 376–390.

Menninger, K. A. (1938). *Man against himself.* New York: Harcourt, Brace & World.

Miller, M. C., Jacobs, D. G., & Gutheil, T. G. (1998). Talisman or taboo: The controversy of the suicide-prevention contract. *Harvard Review of Psychiatry, 6,* 78–87.

Minkoff, K., Bergman, E., Beck, A., & Beck, R. (1973). Hopelessness, depression, and attempted suicide. *American Journal of Psychiatry, 130,* 455–459.

Murphy, G. E. (1992). *Suicide in alcoholism.* New York: Oxford University Press.

O'Carroll, P. W., Berman, A. L., Maris, R. W., Moscicki, E. K., Tanney, B. L., & Silverman, M. M. (1996). Beyond the Tower of Babel: A nomenclature for suicidology. *Suicide and Life-Threatening Behavior, 26,* 237-252.

Osgood, N. J., & Thielman, S. (1990). Geriatric suicidal behavior: Assessment and treatment. In S. J. Blumenthal & D. J. Kupfer (Eds.), *Suicide over the life cycle: Risk factors, assessment, and treatment of suicidal patients* (pp. 341–380). Washington, DC: American Psychiatric Press.

Patsiokas, A. T., & Clum, G. A. (1985). Effects of psychotherapeutic strategies in the treatment of suicide attempters. *Psychotherapy, 22,* 281–290.

Pokorny, A. D. (1983). Prediction of suicide in psychiatric patients: Report of a prospective study. *Archives of General Psychiatry, 40,* 249–257.

Pollock, L. R., & Williams, J. M. G. (1998). Problem solving and suicidal behavior. *Suicide and Life-Threatening Behavior, 28,* 375–387.

Reid, S. (1998). Suicide in schizophrenia: A review of the literature. *Journal of Mental Health, 7,* 345–353.

Richman, J. (1986). *Family therapy for suicidal people.* New York: Springer.

Rudd, M. D., & Joiner, T. (in press). *Treating suicidal behavior: A time-limited approach.* New York: Guilford.

Rudd, M. D., Rajab, M. H., Orman, D. T., Stulman, D. A., Joiner, T., & Dixon, W. (1996). Effectiveness of an outpatient intervention targeting suicidal young adults: Preliminary results. *Journal of Consulting and Clinical Psychology, 64,* 179–190.

Salkovskis, P. M., Atha, C., & Storer, D. (1990). Cognitive-behavioural problem-solving in the treatment of patients who repeatedly attempt suicide: A controlled trial. *British Journal of Psychiatry, 157,* 871–876.

Schotte, D. E., & Clum, G. A. (1987). Problem-solving skills in suicidal psychiatric patients. *Journal of Consulting and Clinical Psychology, 55,* 49–54.

Shea, S. (1998). *Psychiatric interviewing: The art of understanding* (2nd ed.). Philadelphia: Saunders.

Shneidman, E. (1981). Psychotherapy with suicidal patients. *Suicide and Life-Threatening Behavior, 11,* 341–346.

Shneidman, E. (1993). *Suicide as psychache: A clinical approach to self-destructive behavior.* Northvale, NJ: Aronson.

Spirito, A. (1997). Individual therapy techniques with adolescent suicide attempters. *Crisis, 18,* 62–64.

Tanney, B. L. (1992). Mental disorders, psychiatric patients, and suicide. In R. W. Maris, A. L. Berman, J. T. Maltsberger, & R. I. Yufit (Eds.), *Assessment and prediction of suicide* (pp. 277–320). New York: Guilford.

Van der Sande, R., Buskens, E., Allart, E., van der Graaf, Y., van Engeland, H. (1996). Psychosocial intervention following suicide attempt: A systematic review of treatment interventions. *Acta Psychiatrica Scandinavica, 96,* 43–50.

Wagner, B. M. (1998). Family risk factors for child and adolescent suicidal behavior. *Psychological Bulletin, 121,* 246–298.

Weishaar, M. E., & Beck, A. T. (1990). Cognitive approaches to understanding and treating suicidal behavior. In S. J. Blumenthal, & D. J. Kupfer (Eds.), *Suicide over the life cycle* (pp. 469–498). Washington, DC: American Psychiatric Press.

Williams, J. M. G., & Broadbent, K. (1986). Autobiographical memory in suicide attempters. *Journal of Abnormal Psychology, 95,* 144–149.

Yang, B., & Clum, G. A. (1996). Effects of early negative life experiences on cognitive functioning and risk for suicide: A review. *Clinical Psychology Review, 16,* 177–195.

Zilboorg, G. (1936). Differential diagnostic types of suicide. *Archives of General Psychiatry, 35,* 270–391.

9

CHAPTER

Brian L. Mishara
Marc Daigle

Helplines and Crisis Intervention Services: Challenges for the Future

☐ Diversity In Activities To Attain A Common Goal

This chapter looks at a wide range of services that are designed to help persons in a suicidal crisis and to prevent suicide by means of personal contact by telephone or face-to-face. Such intervention services operate under many names. Befrienders International, which operates in 41 countries, offers help to people in distress. In North America, there are numerous crisis centers, helplines, and suicide prevention centers which vary considerably in the services they provide. Some focus on helping suicidal individuals, their family, and friends, but others offer help for a wide variety of other problems. These organizations are often volunteer-based, but are not necessarily so. Sometimes professionals or trained paraprofessionals provide services to callers. Some services only provide help on the telephone, while others are involved in a wide range of activities including face-to-face counseling, school education programs, and support groups for the bereaved.

Despite these tremendous differences, there appears to be some common ground: All these services provide immediate telephone help to callers who are suicidal. The form of help which they provide varies from more interventionist approaches, that may be called crisis intervention to more passive approaches, such as active listening. Because callers may never phone back, all the intervention styles may be considered to be quite different from long-term interventions, such as psychotherapy. Although their activities may differ, North American organizations may apply to be certified by the American Association of Suicidology if they meet standards which this organization has judged to be necessary in order to provide effective suicide prevention activities. Similarly, organizations which adhere to the practices of the Samaritans may apply for membership in Befrienders

International, based in London, England. However, it is important to note that accreditation or membership neither provides information about the effectiveness of the services, nor guarantees any formal monitoring of the nature of the services provided.

Thus, we have a curious situation: Different centers around the world provide different types of telephone services to different client populations using either lay or professional helpers, yet they are often certified by or are members of the same national and international organizations. Furthermore, within their local region they are generally identified as key organizations devoted to suicide prevention. As we shall see later in this chapter, the situation appears even more unusual because of the limited amount of research and evaluative studies that support the usefulness of these activities in actually preventing suicides.

☐ Origins of Suicide Prevention Organizations

Probably the earliest organization devoted primarily to suicide prevention was the Lemberg Volunteer Rescue Society from 1893 to 1906. In 1906 the Salvation Army opened an Antisuicide Bureau in London and the same year a religious-based organization the National Save-A-Life League was founded in New York City.

In 1947, after World War II, a professionally staffed center focusing on the prevention of suicide was established at the neuropsychiatric clinic of the University of Vienna (Trowell, 1979). In 1953, the Anglican Minister, Reverend Chad Varah, began offering help to suicidal persons out of a central London church. The newspapers quickly gave national publicity to Reverend Varah and published his phone number throughout the country. When they referred to Varah as the Samaritan Priest, the name caught on and was used to identify telephone helplines following the model which Reverend Varah developed.

According to the story told by Varah (personal communication; also see Day, 1974), Varah originally offered traditional psychotherapy free of charge for suicidal persons in London. The publicity for his activities attracted numerous volunteers who wanted to help him, and volunteers were soon involved in taking appointments and seeing that callers were comfortable while waiting for their therapy sessions with the "expert." Varah soon discovered that many desperate people went away without keeping their appointments after the long wait to see him. Many left in much better spirits than when they arrived. He attributed this improvement in suicidal individuals to the discussions they had with the lay volunteers in the waiting room, who sympathetically listened to their troubles while they waited. Varah then created a voluntary-based organization where people without professional qualifications, but with some natural abilities as helpers, were trained to talk with and befriend suicidal individuals on the telephone and sometimes in person. The Samaritan movement has grown to such an extent that the parent organization, Befrienders International, has 350 centers in over 40 countries with 31,000 volunteers, of which the Samaritans of the United Kingdom has over 19,000 volunteers.

In the United States, suicide prevention activities developed in a somewhat different manner. The Los Angeles Suicide Prevention Center, established by Norman Farberow and Edwin Shneidman in 1958, was founded "for the evaluation, referral, treatment, follow-up and overall prevention of suicidal behavior" (Suicide Prevention Center of Los Angeles, 1966). This center was established by a professional staff of physicians, psychologists, social workers, and nurses. The center, which eventually developed a large voluntary component (including 24-hour telephone interventions) was originally focused on offering professional services, with complementary goals of training and education as well as conducting research on suicidal behavior. A few years later, in 1963, in Brooklyn (New York) a service was established at the Kings County Psychiatry Hospital in which resident physicians answered the phone lines and offered appointments for face-to-face interventions in the clinic.

Since those early days, there has been a proliferation of telephone helplines concerned with suicide prevention as well as specialized hotlines or helplines for youth, members of the gay community, persons with specific problems such as alcoholism or drug addictions, as well as a wide range of other problems, such as depression and compulsive gambling. Many North American centers were inspired by the Los Angeles Center model, whereas centers elsewhere in the world were often inspired by the Samaritan movement in England.

☐ Do Telephone Helplines and Crisis Intervention Services Prevent Suicide?

Despite the proliferation of crisis intervention services throughout the world, there is relatively little concrete data indicating whether these services are helpful and, more specifically, are effective in preventing suicide. At an individual clinical level, persons who work in these services consistently report that they have experienced success in helping desperate suicidal people and have sometimes even saved lives. Perhaps it is the clinical or gut feeling that continues to incite people to develop telephone suicide prevention services and encourages volunteers and professionals who work at these services to continue their involvement. Like many others, the authors of this chapter can easily recount personal experiences where they believe they saved the life of a desperate suicidal individual. However, persons in the scientific community demand empirical proof that these activities prevent suicide, rather than subjective personal impressions. Many cures for human anguish and mental health problems have numerous proponents, and these espoused treatments include many bizarre activities, including interventions from extra-terrestrial beings and praying to a magic crystal. Very often believers in these more unusual treatments recount the success of their activities with the same vehemence as the authors of this chapter recount their successes in suicide prevention. The fact that people like to use telephone suicide prevention services and do call in increasing numbers each year is not sufficient proof that the services attain their goal of preventing suicide. Popularity is good to have, but it is a poor indication of the effectiveness of the service in preventing suicide. Unfortunately, hard data proving the effectiveness of these suicide prevention activities are quite limited. The following section reviews what we know about the effectiveness of telephone suicide prevention services.

☐ Outcome Studies of the Effectiveness of Telephone Helplines

There are three types of effects of suicide prevention services that have been studied: 1) changes in suicide rates in target populations, 2) satisfaction with services, and 3) follow-up, repeated use of the services by client, and referral compliance.

Changes in Suicide Rates in Target Populations

To effectively study the effect of any prevention activity on suicide rates within a population, we must be able to isolate the effects of the specific suicide prevention activity from all the other significant influences upon rates of suicide in the target population. Unfortunately, this is both theoretically and empirically impossible to attain. Nevertheless, several ingenious methodologies have been used in order to help determine if suicide prevention activities have an effect in preventing suicides.

Bagley (1968) investigated volunteer telephone help by The Samaritans in England. He recognized, like Stengel (1964), that callers to the services may be more likely to attempt than complete suicide. Nevertheless, in a period when suicide rates in England and Wales were declining, he investigated variations in suicide rates in 30 towns, half of which had Samaritan activities for at least two years, compared to the other half, which did not have Samaritan helplines available. He found that suicide rates declined only in the Samaritan towns.

Bagley's study was criticized by Kreitman (1976) who asserted that the decline in suicide rates in the United Kingdom were best understood as being due to the reduced toxicity of domestic gas, a frequent means of suicide in those years. He found that only suicide by means of toxic gas was reduced, not suicide by other means. The Bagley study was also criticized by Barraclough, Jennings, and Moss (1977; Lester, 1990) for its simple statistical design. Barraclough, et al. used complex matching procedures to compare experimental and control towns and found no significant differences in suicide rates. The Barraclough et al. study can be criticized since, by the time this investigation was conducted, Samaritan services had developed to such an extent that a majority of the population in the United Kingdom had access to Samaritan services. Even if there were no services in a specific town, services were generally available in a neighboring town that suicidal individuals could call at little cost.

The outcome approach of looking for changes in population suicide rates did not fare well in North America in the 1960s and 1970s. For example, in Los Angeles county, where the first American telephone suicide prevention center was established, suicide rates increased while they stayed the same in three other California counties (Weiner, 1969). Lester (1974) and Bridge, Potkin, Zung, and Soldo (1977) found no effects of suicide prevention centers on suicide rates using matched comparisons.

The lack of effects in population studies is disappointing, but it can be easily understood when one considers the crude nature of comparisons between changes in the low frequency phenomenon of suicidal deaths in large populations that include persons who did and did not have contact with any specific organization. One would expect crisis centers to have an effect only upon those people who contact the centers for help. Since a small proportion of any population actually calls telephone helplines, one of the first questions to ask is whether these organizations attract the type of clients who actually need help.

Dew, Bromet, Brent, and Greenhouse (1987) conducted a meta-analysis that indicated prevention centers succeed in attracting the target population of people at risk to commit suicide. They found the proportion of suicides among clients to the centers was greater than the proportion of suicides in the general population. Several other researchers compared the profile of persons who complete suicides and suicide attempters in the general population with the profiles of callers at suicide prevention center (Greaves, 1973; Lester, 1972; Maris, 1969; Morissette, 1982; Roberge, 1982; Sawyer, Sudak, & Hall, 1972). These comparisons indicate that the profile of callers is more similar to attempters than completers. For example, young women, who are much more likely than men to attempt suicide rather than complete suicide, are more represented among callers (Miller, Coombs, Leeper, & Barton, 1984; Mishara & Daigle, 1992; Murphy, Wetzel, Swallow, & McClure, 1969). These studies would lead one to conclude that centers attract more attempters or parasuicides than completers.

Interpretation of effects on target populations are also complicated by the fact that helplines and crisis centers often do not limit their activities to suicidal callers. The percentage of callers at centers dedicated to suicide prevention who are actually considered "suicidal" has been reported to be between 5–20% (Eastwood, Brill, & Brown, 1976; France, 1982; Knickerbocker & McGee, 1973; Lester, 1972). The only example that is a striking exception is in the Province of Quebec where Mishara and Daigle (1992) reported almost all callers are suicidal or calling about persons they know who are suicidal. This may be due to the clear identification of Quebec suicide prevention centers as specializing in suicide and the availability in the province of a large number of other helplines for dozens of other types of problems.

If one assumes that the effects of telephone help should only be observed in persons that are characteristic of callers to the services in a region, one can take heart from the study by Miller, Coombs, Leeper, & Barton (1984). They found that there were significant decreases in suicide rates in counties which had suicide prevention centers, but only for white women 25 years old and younger. This is understandable because young women in this age range constituted the largest group contacting these centers.

Satisfaction With Services

If the goal is to prevent suicides, satisfaction rates do not constitute direct proof of the effectiveness of a service. Nevertheless, one may argue that satisfaction, or perceived helpfulness by the client, is a proximal result of the process of intervention—a proximal result that may be predictive of the more distal desired result of changes in suicide rates. There are a great many studies of client satisfaction, all of which have shown favorable results (e.g., Apsler & Hoople, 1976; King, 1977; McKenna, Nelson, Chatterson, Koperno, & Brown, 1975; Motto, 1971; Rogers & Rogers, 1978; Stein & Cotler, 1973; Stein & Lambert, 1984; Streiner & Adam, 1987; Tekavcic-Grad & Zavasnik, 1987; Wold, 1973). Generally, between 60–80% of clients report that they have been helped by the services they received. Because of the confidential nature of calls, response rates in satisfaction studies are generally poor (ranging from 40–80%). This leaves open the possibility of a positive bias: Those who are satisfied by services are more likely to be contacted in follow-ups than those who are unhappy with service or worse off after their contact with the agency. The fact that satisfaction studies have always shown highly positive results, no matter where or how they are conducted, may be interpreted as indicative of the fact that these services are generally appreciated by people who use them. However, the lack of important variations in results suggests that either clients always say that they are pleased with the help they receive regardless of the circumstances, or that it does not matter what or how services are provided in order to satisfy callers.

Follow-up, Repeated Use of Services, and Referral

The fact that clients often call back to a center has been interpreted as an indication that the services are appreciated or helpful. Speer (1971) found that 20% of callers called more than twice. Depending on the follow-up delay in the studies, estimates vary from 23–37% of callers (Apsler & Hoople, 1976; Murphy, Wetzel, Swallow, & McClure, 1969; Wold, 1973). Mishara and Daigle (1992) estimated that 25% of helpline callers to the Montreal and Sherbrooke (Quebec) suicide prevention centers are frequent repeating callers who account for 63% of all the calls theses centers receive.

Another objective measure of the efficacy of a center is the proportion of callers who show up at the services to which they have been referred. Murphy, Wetzel, Swallow, and McClure (1969) estimated a rate of 51% of helpline callers don't show up for their referral appointments. Lester (1970) estimated that the rate of no-show fluctuates between 44–71% for internal psychotherapy services. Paul and Turner (1976) reported that the rate of not showing up to appointments was a good measure of the evolving efficacy of a center. In their study the rate of those coming to appointments, increased from 64% to 81% as the center developed more experience in learning how to best help their clients.

Studies of the Process of Intervention

Several researchers have assumed that if intervention centers have good practices then they should have good results from their interventions. This led to investigations of the process of intervention in suicide prevention. Two types of process studies can be found in the research literature: *technical aspects* of accomplishing certain tasks during the process of intervention and *clinical aspects* of the clinical interaction that are considered to be helpful.

Technical Aspects

Looking at technical aspects of an intervention is based upon a program evaluation approach (Rossi & Freeman, 1986). This classical approach in program evaluation starts with the stated objectives of the service and proceeds to evaluate specific tasks performed during the telephone intervention that are specifically related to those objectives. Many studies of technical aspects of interventions have focused upon administrative aspects, such as verification of the quality of the collection and registration of information on the clients (Kolker & Katz, 1971; Whittemore, 1970). Others (Lester, 1970; McGee et al., 1972; McGee, 1973) investigated how long it took to actually reach the helper on the phone as an indication of how effectively services provide help to clients. Fowler and McGee (1973) proposed a global approach using a nine-point evaluation of what they felt were essential tasks in telephone interventions. They classified these tasks into three dimensions: securing the communication with the caller, assessing the caller's condition, and developing a plan of action. A more elaborate approach was developed by Walfish, Tulkin, Tapp, Slaikeu, and Russel (1976) with the Walfish Crisis Contract Scale. This scale focuses on four elements of evaluation: exploration of callers' internal and external resources, exploration of the callers' feelings about a contract or plan of action, assessment of the critical nature of the situation, and exploration of the practicalities of the plan of action.

Ross and Motto (1971) and later Motto, Brooks, Ross, and Allen (1974) felt that one must look beyond what happens on the telephone in order to develop standards for accreditation of centers. They developed norms under six administrative headings: organizational standards, staffing standards, service standards, consultation standards, program evaluation, and ethical standards that could be rated on a 33-item scale from 0 (nonacceptable) to 4 (excellent). McGee (1974) used an administrative approach in his evaluation of ten American centers but put more emphasis on community criteria: utilization of nonprofessionals, having professionals as consultants, emphasis on prevention, avoidance of the pathology concept, membership in a network of agencies, and commitment to evaluation research. He found that centers with the worst ratings in his evaluation were out of operation two years later. He then interpreted this as external validity to his evaluations. These evaluations of the technical aspects of the functioning of the intervention centers inspired the accreditation guidelines used by the American Association of Suicidology (1989). Since the technical aspects evaluated do not concern the actual nature of the intervention services provided, agencies with very different forms of clinical practices can be accredited using these guidelines.

Clinical Aspects

Studies of clinical aspects of telephone interventions were inspired by evaluations of psychotherapy by professionals (Garfield & Bergin, 1986; Goodman & Dooley, 1976; Greenberg & Pinsof, 1986; Hill & Corbett, 1993; Kiesler, 1973; Lambert, Christensen, & DeJulio, 1983). Thus, the clinical model was originally concerned with evaluating facilitative, therapeutic relationships, such as the conditions that Rogers felt were essential for effective outcomes according to his model of psychotherapy: empathy, warmth, and genuineness (Rogers, 1951; Truax & Carkhuff, 1967).

Lester (1970) rated a small sample of telephone interventions conducted by clinical associates and by new volunteers on the dimensions of empathy, respect, genuineness, concreteness, and self-disclosure. He found that clinicians were more "adequate," but both groups had ratings which were much lower than one would expect according to the theoretical model.

Knickerbocker and McGee (1973) used the same model of clinical effectiveness and similarly found that no group was performing at a sufficiently high level according to what is expected by the Rogerian theoretical model. However, they found higher levels of facilitative characteristics in the nonprofessional group of telephone helpers. Hirsch (1981) used a subjective methodology of listening to volunteers and professionals on the phone in an American and British center. He reported that volunteers were more patient, kind, and reassuring. On the other hand, professionals appeared to be more rigorous, challenging, and oriented to diagnosis. Genthner (1974) used a methodology which would probably not be acceptable according to many ethical guidelines today. He had a fictitious caller role play the same situation and called ten different community-based hotlines. He found that all centers were too low in facilitative characteristics according to the Truax and Carkhuff (1967) model. Genthner found that ratings on facilitative characteristics increased when the callers confronted the helpers concerning their abilities. The author interprets this finding as indicating that callers can sometimes control the type of help they receive on the telephone. Other researches (France & Kalafat, 1975; Kalafat, Boroto, & France, 1979) have shown that specific training can increase the facilitative response ratings of volunteers.

Several other more elaborate methods have been used to assess clinical aspects of telephone helplines. For example, D'Augelli et al. (1978) devised the Helping Scales Verbal Response System with three categories and eight subcategories concerning content and affect in responses, closed questions, open questions, influence, advice, self-involvement, and self-disclosure. They found that university helpline volunteers were too directive and did not use enough open questions. Crocker (1985) added several dimensions to traditional facilitative characteristics, including talking time, advice, and problem-solving. He found that what occurred on the telephone was not necessarily in accordance with what volunteers were trained to do.

Although most of the approaches included classic Rogerian models based upon characteristics of empathy, warmth, and genuineness, research in the 1980s tended to also include more directive characteristics such as assessment of risk and the nature of the crisis, and problem-solving behaviors (Echterling, Hartsough, & Zarle, 1980; Slaikeu, 1984). All of the evaluations of clinical characteristics were based upon a priori models of what qualities or tasks were best in all interventions with suicidal clients. However, studies often ignored whether or not callers were actually suicidal and used the same criteria for good interventions as for bad ones regardless of the nature and extent of the crisis situation. The evaluation of the validity and usefulness in these studies is based upon the acceptance of the theoretical model underlying the intervention. Since outcome measures were not related to evaluations of the intervention process, it is difficult to know to what extent intervention characteristics that are thought to be helpful were actually of use in preventing suicide.

Outcome as Related to Process

The studies summarized in the previous section have all assumed that certain practices are more desirable than others and that helping people on the telephone in certain ways will lead to successful outcomes. Most of the studies have borrowed their methodology from research on the process of professional psychotherapy (e.g., Garfield & Bergin, 1986; Goodman & Dooley, 1976; Greenberg & Pinsof, 1986; Hill & Corbett, 1993; Kiesler, 1973; Lambert, Christensen, & DeJulio, 1983). The theoretical model that is the basis for these evaluations was generally the Rogerian approach that specifies several well-defined techniques that are supposed to be conducive to positive therapeutic outcome (Rogers, 1951; Truax & Carkhuff, 1967). These techniques (but not necessarily the entire Rogerian therapeutic method) are relevant to telephone crisis interventions since they are often taught to volunteers in different centers. In order to explore to what extent these and other specific intervention styles are related to positive outcomes, Mishara and Daigle (1997) conducted a study in which they related process measures to assessments of outcome.

The Mishara and Daigle (1997) study involved listening to 617 telephone calls from suicidal callers at two primarily French-speaking Canadian suicide centers in Montreal and Sherbrooke, Québec. The centers provide telephone help and a variety of other services to suicidal clients, family, and friends of suicidal individuals, and persons bereaved by suicide. The volunteer helpers receive 32 hours of training on the nature of suicidal crisis and at least an equal amount of on-line supervision on how to help on the telephone, but they were not taught specific active listening skills according to a Rogerian model, as is the practice in many American centers.

In this study, almost all of the 145 volunteers gave their consent to have researchers listen confidentially to calls without their knowledge. The 617 calls that were observed were conducted by 110 different volunteers and they represented a structured random sample of calls received by different volunteers at different times of the day.

This investigation evaluated the process of telephone interventions by classifying each of the responses by volunteers according to a list of 20 categories which were developed to describe the nature of what occurs on the telephone during interventions (Daigle & Mishara, 1995). After testing and refinement of the measures and assessment of the reliability of the classification system, the 20-item Helper's Response List was used to classify a total of 66,953 responses during the calls in a reliable manner. Statistic analyses of these responses using cluster analytic techniques indicated that intervention styles could be classified in two broad categories: a Rogerian Style that consisted of more nondirective and empathic responses, and a Directive Style that included more investigation by direct questions as well as advice and suggestions.

In the study three outcome measures were used: 1) observers' ratings of depressive mood at the beginning and end of calls using a standardized rating scale, 2) changes in the suicidal urgency scores from the beginning to the end of the call as rated by the telephone helper, and 3) whether a specific contract was made by the end of the call, including verification if the contract was upheld as indicated in subsequent contacts with the suicidal caller.

It should be noted that the intervention style that could be classified as Rogerian always included directive components that were part of the center's practices, such as the assessment of suicidal urgency by direct questions, asking callers to make a contract to not attempt suicide, and asking about possible solutions for the individual's troubles. Within this context where all calls were somewhat directive, the results indicated that using a more Rogerian style was related to significantly more decreases in depression and were associated with more likelihood of making a contract with the caller before the end of the call. Subsequent analyses indicated that although there was no significant relationship between the use of Rogerian categories and changes in suicidal urgency among repeated (chronic) callers to the center, a higher level of use of Rogerian categories was significantly related to greater reductions in urgency among callers who were in acute crises and who had not been calling the center repeatedly. Similarly, nonchronic callers appeared to benefit more from the use of more Rogerian categories in that this was related to an increased likelihood of making a contract by the end of the call.

This study by Mishara and Daigle (1997)suggests that there may be advantages to certain types of telephone intervention techniques and that the relative advantages of different techniques may vary according to the nature of the suicidal caller. In this study, the suicide prevention centers did not teach specific intervention styles. The use of more Rogerian or Directive techniques could thus be interpreted as being characteristics to be sought out during recruitment and selection of potential volunteers. However, it is also possible that these skills can be taught by including practice in certain techniques in the training of helpers.

In the above study, the outcome measures were limited by the availability of easily identifiable data from the callers. These outcome measures were not sufficiently sophisticated to indicate whether the centers actually had an effect on diminishing the risk of a suicide attempt or completed suicides. These measures may be considered to be quite limited when compared to the more systematically sound methods that have been used in assessing psychotherapy outcomes. However, because of the confidential nature of calls, it is difficult to conduct the type of long-term follow-up which would be necessary to assess the eventual effects of telephone interventions on future suicidal behavior. We conclude that the development of better outcome measures is one of the most important challenges facing researchers interested in studying the overall effects of volunteer community telephone interventions as well as the relative effectiveness of different styles or characteristics of interventions.

☐ Challenges for the Future

Why Do We Do It If We Cannot Prove It Works?

There is very little proof that suicide prevention centers, helplines, crisis centers and Samaritan organizations actually prevent suicides. Although it is clear that people like to use these services and clients give high ratings in their evaluation of the quality of the services they receive, we have very little empirical evidence of how often lives are saved or if there are fewer nonlethal suicide attempts. Some research has shown that telephone interventions have immediate or proximal effects that may be theoretically linked to decreased suicidality (Mishara & Daigle, 1997). Nevertheless, it is prudent to ask if there is sufficient evidence to continue supporting these activities if we cannot offer substantial proof that there is a significant effect on suicidal behavior.

It may be of some consolation to telephone suicide prevention centers that they are not alone in lacking empirical support for the effectiveness of their activities. There is also little evidence (an exception is the study by Rutz, Von Knorring, & Walinder, 1989) that professional mental health services have been able to decrease suicide rates in any population, despite continued advances in psychopharmacology and therapy techniques.

Recent research on suicide indicates that persons who end their life by suicide (suicide completers) are different from suicide attempters or parasuicides as they are called in Europe. People who complete suicides are more likely to suffer from long-term mental health problems, including alcoholism and substance abuse. It is difficult to see how helplines and crisis centers would have a lasting impact on these long standing serious disorders. One might expect that they would be more likely to have a beneficial effect in helping attempters avoid repeated nonlethal suicidal behavior.

In a time when resources are scarce and there are many competing activities to attract volunteers, crisis intervention services and helplines may have to become increasingly concerned with evaluating the impact of their services. Perhaps certain methods of intervention or types of services are more effective than others. It is also possible that some services are not effective or are harmful in some instances. Perhaps volunteer services, which do not depend upon government or public financing, will continue to face little pressure to evaluate their activities.

Maybe their survival in the future only depends upon continued use of their service and the availability of a sufficient number of motivated volunteers. However, if suicide prevention organizations do not examine the effectiveness of their activities, some day there may be a phenomenon similar to what occurred in the children story "The Emperor's New Clothes." As the little boy proclaimed the obvious fact that the Emperor was wearing no clothes at all, it is possible that, unless research and program evaluations offer proof that these intervention services are effective, people may realize one day that their claims of preventing suicide are unfounded.

Changing Demographics and Changing Practices

In most of the industrialized world, birth rates have been decreasing and life expectancies increasing, which results in a shift of the demographic distribution by age group. The elderly make up greater proportion of the population, and there are fewer young people, but at the present time, there are a plethora of services focused upon youth. Middle age persons constitute the majority of callers to helplines and similar services, but there are important generational differences that affect patterns of use. The current generation of the elderly are often reluctant to pick up the phone and recount their problems to strangers. Seeing a therapist or counselor or getting help for mental problems are often negatively viewed by today's elders. However in the next 10–20 years, the elderly population will be replaced by a generation who are much more favorable to using helplines, counselors, and therapists. Baby boomers, who will become the elders of the near future, are more likely to pick up the phone to get help. Because of changing demographics and generational differences in attitudes and patterns of using services, one of the challenges in the future for telephone help organizations will be to meet the needs of an increasing elderly clientele.

Changing Technologies and Their Implications for Telephone Help

Telecommunications technologies are expanding rapidly. Many of the current and future improvements both challenge the anonymity and confidentiality of telephone help and create opportunities for new developments in practices. Several years ago tracing a call would be a long and costly procedure that could only be used in the most desperate of circumstances, providing the organization permitted call tracing at all. Now, identifying the origins of a call is increasingly simple and inexpensive. The mere fact that the technologies exist that permit the identification of callers may have already influenced the attitudes of callers and helpers in many areas of the world. Despite verbal assurances of anonymity or confidentiality, callers may be suspicious because of their knowledge that these technologies are widely available. Furthermore, organizations must determine if, under certain circumstances, for example when the life of a minor child is in danger, they will break their vow of confidentiality and try to identify callers. These technological developments will require adjustments in policy as well as adjustments in practices now that the anonymity of callers can be disregarded with simple call-display features.

Another increasing technological advance is the increased availability of the internet and other global technologies. Suicide chat rooms, message boards, and self-help material are all available on the internet. It is interesting to note that these new "helplines" appear to be more attractive to men than women. This is in contrast with telephone helplines, which women use more than men.

The Samaritans of Great Britain and Ireland run an international service that uses trained volunteers in existing intervention centers to respond to e-mail messages from suicidal individuals. When an e-mail message is received it can be automatically forwarded for reply to a Befriender volunteer in virtually any part of the world. This system allows for an efficient use of resources, for example, by sending messages to centers that are less busy at different times of the day in different time zones. This system also allows for subsequent correspondence from an individual to be routed to the same, initial center. A basic assumption with this procedure is that little local cultural specificity is needed to provide help. This globalization of help, which is now becoming technically feasible and economically more attractive, means that telephone services need not be provided in the communities where callers live. Information about resources in any specific community can be available from any location in the world, thus allowing helpers in another country to provide callers with local phone numbers for other sources of help, as well as any other information, such as the hours when a community clinic is open.

If the assumption that help is generic is accurate, local telephone helplines and suicide prevention services may become obsolete. In fact, when these services are supported by public funds, some communities may find it to be less expensive to buy suicide prevention telephone help from centers in other areas. This would cost less per call than the cost of supporting a local community agency. However, the assumption that local cultural differences are of little importance in telephone suicide prevention activities has not yet been tested and is worthy of attention. Perhaps cultural factors and first hand local knowledge is an important variable for effective suicide prevention activities.

New technologies also will mean that telephones may be replaced by cheap portable communication devices that provide interactive pictures of callers and helpers. If communication with video becomes the norm, helplines will have to tackle the problem of anonymity (perhaps distortion devices will need to be used to protect the identity of helpers). Furthermore, having a direct image of callers may influence interventions. It is one thing to have a caller say that he has a loaded gun in his hand, but it is quite different to see the caller holding the gun in a video call. These new technologies may lead to questioning the specificity of telephone help, as opposed to face-to-face interventions. Up to now telephone intervention services have been keen on emphasizing the advantages of this form of anonymous contact. The development of video telecommunications may result in some confusion over the perceived differences between talking on the telephone and discussing one's problems face-to-face.

Challenging the Separation of Mental Health and Crisis Intervention Services

Fairly convincing research indicates that people who die by suicide often have long standing mental health problems, particularly affective disorders (Tanney, 1992). Statistics on callers to crisis centers and helplines indicate consistently that a significant proportion (often around 50%) have had previous contact with professional mental health practitioners. Many take psychotropic medication, have been treated in mental health facilities and psychiatric hospitals, or have been treated for depression from a general practitioner. Unfortunately, a lack of communication between mental health professionals and persons involved in telephone helplines is common. Even when the best mutual respect exists, it is rare to find collaborative efforts at simultaneously helping the same clients by different complementary approaches. There are rarely direct communications about client treatment among traditional mental health care providers and those offering the alternative services of telephone interventions and support.

Perhaps this separation of roles is necessary in order to avoid professionalization of lay volunteers and persons working on helplines. Maybe it is best to recognize the needs for specific diagnosis and treatment of mental health problems by mental health professionals and avoid the possibly negative impact of involving helplines with such labels and psychiatric techniques. Nevertheless, there have been interesting pilot programs attempting to integrate volunteer and professional services that warrant further investigation and formal evaluation. For example, volunteer organizations in Quebec have been involved in working with mental health professionals to provide follow-up support after a suicide attempt. In some areas, professionals often contact voluntary organizations to arrange for resources and support for their clients between treatment sessions. The extent to which these collaborative efforts will develop in the future is one of the challenges for the voluntary and professional sectors.

Specific Versus General Approaches to Providing Help

Services covered by this chapter vary greatly from listening services that do little more than offer the presence of a considerate listener to all persons in distress, to highly interventionist services that use systematic procedures to evaluate the risk and urgency of suicidal crises and then offer a specific method of intervention that is then rigorously applied. Some centers focus only upon suicide prevention and refer all other clients elsewhere. Others centers are general helplines that do not systematically ask if clients are suicidal. Over the past decade many United States centers have dropped the word "suicide" from their title and telephone listings in order to attract a much wider range of clientele in distress. The opposite has occurred in Quebec where suicide prevention centers are clearly identified as offering services only for suicidal individuals and their friends and family. The Quebec centers receive over 90% of their calls from individuals who are suicidal, persons who are concerned about suicide in a friend or relative, or those who have experienced a loss by suicide.

There is little empirical basis in research or evaluation studies to indicate if it is better to be specifically focused on suicide prevention or more helpful (and one must be careful how "help" is defined) to have a more varied focus. We need to learn more about the relative advantages and disadvantages of adopting a more interventionist rather than a more open listening approach.

Very often decisions about the specificity of an organization in terms of suicide prevention are based upon financial and political constraints rather than well thought out considerations of what is most beneficial for target populations in distress. An interesting example is the Los Angeles Suicide Prevention Center, which may be the most famous center in the world in terms of developing specific intervention methods in suicide prevention and integrating research on suicidal behavior with models of practice. Over time, for a variety of reasons not directly related to the center's historic roots and its original mandate focusing upon suicide prevention, this center expanded into other areas, such as helping people with drug problems, and curtailed their emphasis on innovative research and practice in suicidology. Although financial and political considerations are often crucial in determining how organizations change and develop, it would be useful to obtain empirical information that could help organizations determine if having a specific focus and specialized practices in suicide prevention and having a more generic approach to providing help are equally effective. It may be useful to conduct more research linking process measures with outcomes (Mishara & Daigle, 1997) in order to better clarify what approaches are most effective with suicidal individuals.

The Theoretical Wasteland

Most activities by helplines and crisis centers are based upon models developed over 20 years ago. The content of training sessions of helpers often differs today very little from training in the 1970s or the 1960s. It may be that this is because centers are on to a good thing, and do not want to make changes just for the sake of being different. Nevertheless there has been a significant increase in our understanding of the etiology and dynamics of suicide over the past 30 years, as well as in the identification of risk factors and high risk groups. However, there has been relatively little systematic integration of these new findings into training and practice. Furthermore, there has been few new theoretical developments in suicidology linking our understanding of suicide with methods of intervention.

We need more research to find out what works, with whom, and why. We need to find out if certain approaches and methods of intervention are more effective than others for certain clients. But we also need to better understand the theoretical basis for our actions.

Suicide prevention organizations rarely formulate *explicit* statements about why they feel their activities should be effective in preventing suicides. However, there are often *implicit* theories of why their activities should be beneficial in preventing suicides. The most simple of these implicit assumptions is the belief that isolated individuals need someone to listen to their problems and that this form of active empathic listening can diffuse crisis situations, make people feel less alone with their problems, and thus generally decrease psychological distress. Reducing psychological distress may be considered as a means of reducing suicide potential.

On the other hand, more interventionist centers base their approach upon the belief that people need help in finding alternative solutions to their problems and support in their struggle to reduce the pain that makes them want to end their lives. Specific aspects of the intervention, such as making a contract to not commit suicide during a specific period of time, agreeing to seek help, calling back the center, and other, similar characteristics of the intervention may be considered of crucial importance to effectively reducing suicide risk and urgency. A focus on these technical aspects of the intervention may be justified theoretically in several ways. For example, if suicide is construed as a way of coping with seemingly unbearable psychic pain, these technical aspects of telephone interventions may be seen as ways of mobilizing alternative coping strategies.

All of the above justifications for practices have little links to theories of suicide and our understanding of the suicide process. Most suicide theories focus upon inherent etiological factors which are rarely the object of telephone interventions. One of our greatest challenges for the future is to develop theoretical models that not only justify the existing practices but also generate hypotheses concerning how practices in the future should evolve and change to better serve the needs of suicidal individuals.

☐ References

American Association of Suicidology. (1989). *Organization certification standards manual* (4th ed.). Denver: Author.

Apsler, R., & Hoople, H. (1976). Evaluation of crisis intervention services with anonymous clients. *American Journal of Community Psychology, 4,* 293–302.

Bagley, C. R. (1968). The evaluation of a suicide prevention scheme by an ecological method. *Social Science and Medicine, 2,* 1–14.

Barraclough, B. M., Jennings, C., & Moss, J. R. (1977). Suicide prevention by the Samaritans. A controlled study of effectiveness. *Lancet, i,* 237–239.

Bridge, T. P., Potkin, S. G., Zung, W. W. K., & Soldo, B. J. (1977). Suicide prevention centers: Ecological study of effectiveness. *Journal of Nervous and Mental Disease, 164,* 18–24.

Crocker, P. J. (1985). *An evaluation of the quality of service at a volunteer-run telephone distress centre.* Unpublished master's thesis, Wilfrid Laurier University, Waterloo, Ontario, Canada.

Daigle, M., & Mishara, B. L. (1995). Intervention styles with suicidal callers at two suicide prevention centers. *Suicide and Life-Threatening Behavior, 25,* 261–275.

D'Augelli, A. R., Handis, M. H., Brumbaugh, L., Illig, V., Searer, R., Turner, D. W., & D'Augelli, J. F. (1978). The verbal helping behavior of experienced and novice telephone counselors. *Journal of Community Psychology, 6,* 222–228.

Day, G. (1974). The Samaritan movement in Great Britain. *Perspectives in Biology and Medicine, 17,* 507–512.

Dew, M. A., Bromet, E. J., Brent, D., & Greenhouse, J. B. (1987). A quantitative literature review of the effectiveness of suicide prevention centers. *Journal of Consulting and Clinical Psychology, 55,* 239–244.

Eastwood, M. R., Brill, L., & Brown, J. H. (1976). Suicide and prevention centres. *Canadian Psychiatric Association Journal, 21,* 571–575.

Echterling, L. G., Hartsough, D. M., & Zarle, T. H. (1980). Testing a model for the process of telephone crisis intervention. *Community Psychology, 8,* 715–725.

Fowler, D. E., & McGee, R. K. (1973). Assessing the performance of telephone crisis workers: The development of a technical effectiveness scale. In D. Lester & G. W. Brockopp (Eds.), *Crisis intervention and counseling by telephone* (pp. 287–297). Springfield, IL: Charles C. Thomas.

France, K. (1982). *Crisis intervention: A handbook of immediate person-to-person help.* Springfield, IL: Charles Thomas.

France, K., & Kalafat, J. (1975, March). Effects of worker training an experience and of caller value orientation on the performance of lay volunteer crisis telephone workers. Paper presented at the Southeastern Psychological Association Convention, Atlanta, Georgia.

Garfield, S. L., & Bergin, A. E. (Eds.). (1986). *Handbook of psychotherapy and behavior change.* New York: John Wiley.

Genthner, R. (1974). Evaluating the functioning of community-based hotlines. *Professional Psychology, 5,* 409–414.

Goodman, G., & Dooley, D. (1976). A framework for help-intended communication. *Psychotherapy: Theory, Research and Practice, 13,* 106–117.

Greaves, G. (1973). An evaluation of a 24-hour crisis intervention clinic. *Canada's Mental Health, 21*(3–4), 13–15.

Greenberg, L. S., & Pinsof, W. M. (1986). *The psychotherapeutic process: A research handbook.* New York: Guilford.

Hill, C. E., & Corbett, M. M. (1993). A perspective on the history of process and outcome research in counseling psychology. *Journal of Counseling Psychology, 40,* 3–24.

Hirsch. (1981). A critique of volunteer-staffed suicide prevention centres. *Canadian Journal of Psychiatry, 26,* 406–410

Kalafat, J., Boroto, D. R., & France, K. (1979). Relationships among experience level and value orientation and the performance of paraprofessional telephone counselors. *American Journal of Community Psychology, 7,* 167–180.

Kiesler, D. J. (1973). *The process of psychotherapy: Empirical foundations and systems of analysis.* Chicago: Aldine.

King, G. D. (1977). An evaluation of the effectiveness of a telephone counseling center. *American Journal of Community Psychology, 5,* 75–83.

Knickerbocker, D. A., & McGee, R. K. (1973). Clinical effectiveness of nonprofessional and professional telephone workers in a crisis intervention center. In D. Lester & G. W. Brockopp (Eds.), *Crisis intervention and counseling by telephone* (pp. 298–309). Springfield, IL: Charles C. Thomas

Kolker, H., & Katz, S. (1971). If you've missed the age you've missed a lot. *Crisis Intervention, 3,* 34-37.

Kreitman, N. (1976). The coal gas story. United Kingdom suicide rates, 1960–71. *British Journal of Preventive and Social Medicine, 30,* 86–93.

Lambert, M. J., Christensen, E. R., & DeJulio, S. S. (1983). *The assessment of psychotherapy outcome.* New York: Wiley.

Lester, D. (1970). Steps toward the evaluation of a suicide prevention center *Crisis Intervention, 2* (Suppl. to 1, 12–21; Suppl. to 2, 42–45; Suppl. to 4, 20–22).

Lester, D. (1972). The myth of suicide prevention. *Comprehensive Psychiatry, 13,* 555–560.

Lester, D. (1974). Effect of suicide prevention centers on suicide rates in the United States. *Health Services Reports, 89,* 37–39.

Lester, D. (1990). Was gas detoxification or establishment of suicide prevention centers responsible for the decline in the British suicide rate? *Psychological Reports, 66,* 286.

Maris, R. W. (1969). The sociology of suicide prevention: Policy implications of differences between suicidal patients and completed suicides. *Social Problems, 17,* 132–149.

McGee, R. (1973). The delivery of suicide and crisis intervention services. In H. L. P. Resnik & B. Hathorne (Eds.), *Suicide prevention in the 1970's* (pp. 81–89). Rockville: National Institute of Mental Health.

McGee, R. K. (1974). *Crisis intervention in the community.* Washington, DC: Union Panamerica.

McGee, R. K., Knickerbocker, D. A., Fowler, D. E., Jennings, B., Ansel, E. L., Zelenka, M. H., & Marcus, S. (1972). Evaluation of crisis intervention programs and personnel: A summary and critique. *Life-Threatening Behavior, 2,* 168–182.

McKenna, J., Nelson, G., Chatterson, J., Koperno, M., & Brown, J. H. (1975). Chronically and acutely suicidal persons one month after contact with a crisis intervention centre. *Canadian Psychiatric Association Journal, 20,* 451–454.

Miller, H. L., Coombs, D. W., Leeper, J. D., & Barton, S. N. (1984). An analysis of the effects of suicide prevention facilities on suicide rates in the United States. *American Journal of Public Health, 74,* 340–343.

Mishara, B. L., & Daigle, M. (1992). The effectiveness of suicide prevention centres. *Santé Mentale au Canada/Canada's Mental Health, 40*(3), 24–29.

Mishara, B. L., & Daigle, M. (1997). Effects of different telephone intervention styles with suicidal callers at two suicide prevention centers: An empirical investigation. *American Journal of Community Psychology, 25,* 861–895.

Morissette, P. (1982). Le Centre de Recherche et de Prévention du Suicide de Québec: Historique, philosophie, fonctionnement et ,valuation d'un programme en sant, mentale communautaire. *Canadian Journal of Community Mental Health, 1,* 37–51.

Motto, J. A. (1971). Evaluation of a suicide prevention center by sampling the population at risk. *Life-Threatening Behavior, 1,* 18–22.

Motto, J. A., Brooks, R. M., Ross, R. M., & Allen, N. H. (1974). *Standards for suicide prevention and crisis centers.* New York: Human Sciences Press.

Murphy, G. E., Wetzel, R. D., Swallow, C. S., & McClure, J. N. (1969). Who calls the suicide prevention center: A study of 55 persons calling on their own behalf. *American Journal of Psychiatry, 126,* 314–324.

Paul, T. W., & Turner, J. (1976). Evaluating the crisis service of a community mental health center. *American Journal of Community Psychology, 4,* 303–308.

Roberge, D. (1982). *Evaluation du Centre de prévention du suicide de Québec.* Québec: Service Evaluation-Sant,, Ministère des Affaires Sociales du Québec.

Rogers, C. R. (1951). *Client-centered therapy.* Boston: Houghton-Mifflin.

Rogers, R. L., & Rogers, C. A. (1978). An analysis of telephone crisis intervention counseling based upon consumer evaluation. *Crisis Intervention, 9,* 102–116.

Ross, C., & Motto, J. (1971). Implementation of standards for suicide prevention centers. *Bulletin of Suicidology, 8,* 18–21.

Rossi, P. H., & Freeman, H. E. (1986). *Evaluation. A systematic approach* (3rd ed.). Beverly Hills, CA: Sage.

Rutz, W., von Knorring, & Walinder, J. (1984). Frequency of suicide on Gotland after systematic postgraduate education of general practitioners. *Acta Psychiatrica Scandinavica, 80,* 151–154.

Sawyer, J. B., Sudak, H. S., & Hall, S. R. (1972). A follow-up study of the 53 suicides known to a suicide prevention centre. *Life-Threatening Behavior, 2,* 227–238.

Slaikeu, K. A. (1984). *Crisis intervention. A handbook for practice and research.* Boston: Allyn & Bacon.

Speer, D. C. (1971). Rate of caller re-use of a telephone crisis service. *Crisis Intervention, 3,* 83–86.

Stein, C. M., & Cotler, S. (1973). Crisis phone services: Evaluation of a hotline program. *American Journal of Community Psychology, 12,* 101–126.

Stein, D. M., & Lambert, M. J. (1984). Telephone counseling and crisis intervention: A review. *American Journal of Community Psychology, 12,* 101–126.

Stengel, E. (1964). *Suicide and attempted suicide.* London: Pelican.

Streiner, D. L., & Adam, K. S. (1987). Evaluation of the effectiveness of suicide prevention programs: A methodological perspective. *Suicide and Life-Threatening Behavior, 17,* 93–106.

Suicide Prevention Center of Los Angeles. (1966). [Brochure]. Los Angeles, CA: Author

Tanney, B. L. (1992). Mental disorders, psychiatric patients and suicide. In R. W. Maris, A. L. Berman, J. T. Maltsberger, & S. R. I. Yufit (Eds.), *Assessment and prediction of suicide* (pp. 277–320). New York: Guilford Press.

Tekavcic-Grad, O., & Zavasnik, A. (1987). Comparison between counselor's and caller's expectations and their realization on the telephone crisis line. *Crisis, 8,* 162–177.

Trowell, I. (1979). Telephone Services. In D. Hankoff & B. Ensidler (Eds.), *Suicide theory and clinical aspects* (pp. 401–409). Littleton, MA: PSG.

Truax, C. B., & Carkhuff, R. R. (1967). *Toward effective counseling and psychotherapy: Training and practice.* Chicago: Aldine.

Walfish, S., Tulkin, S. R., Tapp, J. T., Slaikeu, K. A., & Russell, M. (1976). The development of a contract negotiation scale for crisis counseling. *Crisis Intervention, 7,* 136–148.

Weiner, I. W. (1969). The effectiveness of a suicide prevention program. *Mental Hygiene, 53,* 357–363.

Whittemore, K. (1970). *Ten centers.* Atlanta, GA: Lullwater Press.

Wold, C. I. (1973). A two-year follow-up of suicide prevention center patients. *Life-Threatening Behavior, 3,* 171–183.

10

CHAPTER

Wolfgang Rutz

The Role of Primary Physicians in Preventing Suicide: Possibilities, Short-Comings, and the Challenge in Reaching Male Suicides

In some European countries the mortality rate from suicide is higher than the mortality rate from traffic accidents. Some 20–25% of depressions are insufficiently treated and lead to suicide. Depressed individuals with prior suicidal attempts and depressive periods, as well as indications for disturbed serotonin metabolism, have a one year mortality, exceeding that of many malignant diseases.

Although the majority of those with depression are seen by general practitioners (GPs), only a minority is diagnosed correctly. Research shows that between 50–70% of suicides are not committed in a rational state but rather in a condition of clinical and deep depression in which depressive cognitive distortions can be found and rational judgments are no longer possible. Suicides committed for existential or philosophical reasons are in the minority, even though these motivations can be found to a lesser extent as a background factor in depressed suicides.

There are patterns of increasing morbidity and increasing suicide mortality in depression in some European countries, for example, the Baltic states and some Eastern European countries. Other countries, like Sweden, have witnessed an increasing depression morbidity but a steady or decreasing suicide mortality. Still other countries have witnessed decreasing depression morbidity and suicide mortality. The reasons for these differences are perhaps found in psychosocial background factors relevant to the multifactoral etiology of depression and suicide, but most importantly in factors of accessibility to the adequate diagnosis and treatment of depression (Goldney, 1998; Rihmer, 1996; Rutz, Walinder, von Knorring, Rihmer, & Pihlgren, 1997).

A history of depression is as strong a suicide predictor as earlier suicide attempts. However, postvention for depression and suicidal attempts by means of follow-up is poor both in psychiatry and primary care. Thus, an important strategy for preventing depression-related morbidity and suicide mortality would be to enable GPs to diagnose and treat depression. At the present time, however, the ability for this in general practice is quite poor. Considerable differences in different European countries exists. In Western European countries, where there are good standards of health care, about 70% of people with major depression consult a GP, but only between 30–50% of them are getting medical treatment of some sort. Eighteen percent are getting antidepressants, but often in inadequate dosages. In spite of the fact that between 50–70% of all suicides suffer from depression, a further 20% of them are alcoholics, primarily men, typically using alcohol for self-medication of their depression.

In Sweden a majority of suicides (86%) have not been treated specifically for depression. In Hungary, a high suicide rate in the regions is associated with a low degree of recognized depression; improvements in the diagnosis of depression appear to lower suicidal rates. In Sweden and other countries, it has been shown that only about 15% of all suicides were undergoing specific antidepressive treatment at their time of death, despite the fact that a majority of them probably were depressed.

The increased prevalence of depression and the concomitant dramatic increase of suicide in at least some European countries has led to this question by a well known Swedish epidemiologist: Are we entering an age of melancholy? However, looking around Europe, it is interesting to see that, despite an increasing prevalence of depression and the continuous existence of psychosocial and existential depressogenic factors, some countries show stable or decreasing suicide rates. One of the factors behind this phenomenon could be the increasing and sometimes good access to the detection, treatment, and monitoring of depression in these countries.

The above considerations are leading us to ways to improve the well-established antisuicidal preventive effect of the treatment of depression by using education programs as a way of relieving the world wide burden of depression and suicide (Colleges join together to fight depression, 1992; Isaacsson, Holmgrenn, & Wasserman, 1994; Joukamaa, Lehtinen, & Karlsson, 1995)

☐ The Gotland Study: A Model

During the 1980s an interesting experiment was conducted on the Swedish island of Gotland. Gotland has 58,000 inhabitants and constitutes one psychiatric catchment area with one psychiatric institution. At that time, Gotland society was changing dramatically from an agricultural structure to a more tourist and industrialized structure. It offered an ideal epidemiological laboratory for follow-up interventions in the public health of the island.

An educational project directed at all general practitioners of the island was carried out in 1983 and 1984. At that time the suicide rate was high (one of the highest in Sweden), especially in females, and a high number of suicides appeared to be caused by depression. There was a low prescription rate of antidepressants, but a high prescription rate for nonspecific sedatives and hypnotics. The island's GPs reported an increasing number of apathetic states in their patients, characterized by helplessness and hopelessness in those who committed suicide. This situation existed despite educational programs and professional improvements within the psychiatric services of the island which, however, had not reached the primary health-care system.

The sociological situation of the island at that time was similar to the situation that can be found today in Eastern Europe and some of the countries bordering the European Union. It was characterized by traditional gender-related role expectations, an incapacity and unwillingness to seek for help and to recognize one's own depression and helplessness, and alienation and loss of identity, especially in males. Among the farming population, the need to change jobs or to sell the farm was felt to be humiliating and shameful.

As a result, the general practitioners demanded education and supervision. This led to a decision to offer GPs a structured and long-term educational project staffed with a group of motivated teachers, experienced clinicians, and scientists who were willing to educate this highly motivated group. This educational program was offered over a two-year period to all GPs on the island, with two two-day sessions in a somewhat luxurious hotel atmosphere, with opportunities for social, communicative, interactive and relaxed meetings. The program consisted of a combination of oral and written information, group work, video-taped and written case reports, and sharing of personal experiences, focusing on the multi-dimensional process of becoming depressed and suicidal and recovering from it.

The training was evaluated prior to the educational intervention and finalized five years after the intervention. Some of the evaluation data, however, have been continuously followed up until the present time. Several different and partly interacting results have be found. In semistructured interviews before, during, and after the educational procedures, the general practitioners reported many results: 1) increased knowledge and capacity to detect patients with depressive conditions; 2) increased willingness to abandon reductionistic psychotherapeutic or biological approaches in favor of a more comprehensive approach; 3) integrating both psychotherapeutic supports and medical interventions, 4) improved capacity for risk assessment concerning suicidality; and 5) improved diagnostic, therapeutic, and monitoring ability to detect and follow-up depressions in a comprehensive way. At the time of maximum effect, two years after the educational intervention, referrals to psychiatric services for depressive conditions had decreased by about 50%, and for the most severe melancholic states by 85%. Sick leave on the island for depressive conditions had decreased by 50%, and inpatient care for depressive states at the local psychiatric institution decreased by 75%. The number of police-reported suicides on Gotland was evaluated in order to exclude the possibility that giving responsibility for the treatment of depression to general practitioners would lead to an increase in suicide. Instead, suicides fell dramatically (by 60%) to the lowest suicide rate ever observed on Gotland and in Sweden. However, the prescription of antidepressants at that time increased from 50% of the Swedish average to 80%, accompanied by a decrease in the prescription of nonspecific sedative medication (including benzodiazepines and neuroleptics) by 25% compared to the Swedish average. After three years, lithium prescriptions increased by 30%. Trend analyses showed that these changes were in contrast to earlier trends in Gotland and contemporary trends in Sweden.

However, a fading out of these changes was observed in 1988. Suicide, for example, increased again to numbers just below the baseline values. This fading out could partly be explained by forgetting, competition by other educational programs, and a change of focus to other medical problems. The main reason, however, was the fact that by 1988, 50% of the original group of general practitioners who were present at the time of maximum impact (1986) had left their positions on Gotland.

To summarize, the good news was that, after the educational intervention on Gotland, there was an increase in competency and stringency in treating and preventing depressive disorders. This was associated with a decrease in the use of psychiatric inpatient care, a decrease in sick leave due to depression, a reduction in the number of suicides, at least temporarily, and changes in the prescription of psychopharmacological drugs in a desired direction. Even the fading out effects over time argued in favor of the specificity of the results. In a cost-benefit analysis, it also was shown that the intervention resulted in considerable savings to the society in monetary terms. All these results have been described extensively elsewhere (Rutz, von Knorring, & Walinder, 1992).

A detailed study of all suicides on Gotland during the 1980s illustrated the shortcomings and partial failures of the project. It appears that the main decrease in suicides was in the group of suicidal patients with a diagnosis of major depression and in those in contact with GPs. This was expected, due to the fact that the education program was directed at GPs. Also, the number of violent suicides had decreased, which was also expected because depressed suicides often appear clinically to be the most decisive ones. What we did not expect, however, was that those changes were primarily found in the group of female suicides, and that this group had shown the greatest decrease in suicide. Male (and male violent) suicides were almost unaffected by the educational program, most males being unknown to the medical system. The only group of male suicides that decreased significantly after the educational intervention was the group over 60 years of age, a group of men who we know are often in contact with general practitioners (Rihmer, Rutz, & Pihlgren, 1995).

A further finding was that seasonality in the pattern of suicides had decreased after the educational project and into the 1990s. This may be a consequence of the better recognition, treatment, and monitoring of depressed suicidal patients in contact with GPs, leading to a decrease of depressed suicide. Seasonality in suicidal patterns in a region or a country is probably an indication of the proportion of depressed suicides among all suicides, and so the program may have prevented many of these potential suicides (Rihmer, Rutz, & Pihlgren, 1998).

Thus, the finding was that the decrease in suicides on Gotland was mainly a result of a decrease in suicides by patients who were in contact with general practitioners, who had a diagnosis and history of major depression and a strong suicidal intention, and in suicides linked to seasonality, but mostly (almost exclusively) in females. We found that 80% of the males committing suicide on Gotland during the 1980s were not known to the medical system, whereas only 40% of the female suicides were unknown to a doctor.

Twenty percent of the males, but only 3% of the female suicides, were known to the substance abuse and alcoholism services on the island; fifteen percent of the males and none of the females were known to the police. A significant number of males were known to the local tax authorities.

Taking this into consideration, the researchers critically scrutinized our work and found that the few males who were known to the medical system but later committed suicide belonged to a group not being diagnosed as depressed and suicidal, often due to their aggressive behavior, alcohol abuse, lack of compliance, and incapacity to accept help. Retrospectively, however, significant signs of help-lessness, desperation, and depression could be found, mostly combined with acting-out behavior as well as lack of impulse control. Even the suicidal patients not in contact with the medical system could, by using retrospective psychological autopsy and interview techniques, be found to have been either introverted or aggressively acting-out, again often without the capacity to sense their need for help, to ask for help, or to accept it when offered (Rutz, 1999).

☐ Learnings from the Gotland Study

Educational programs for general practitioners require teamwork and community support. As the Gotland experience indicates, there is a need for motivated, concerned, and interested GPs asking for help, supervision, and education, and a source of motivated and experienced (both clinically and scientifically) teachers to give this education. There is even a need for a motivated psychiatric system in a region that feels responsible for follow-up, supervision, and continuing education.

On Gotland, the educational program was given as two two-day sessions to all GPs on the island and led to a significant decrease in morbidity, mortality, and sick-leave regarding depressive states and a change in medication patterns away from sedative, anxiolytic, and dependence-generating prescriptions to specific antidepressive prescriptions. It appeared that a single focus on depression for general practitioners, without other concurrent educational programs, was important. However, a fading-out effect was found after three years, and a need for continued booster education (perhaps at three-year intervals) was evident.

The program showed the value of an educational package containing lectures, video sessions, case discussions, interactive seminars, and the sharing of both professional and private experiences, combined with slides repeating and deepening the oral messages and the distribution of written material. However, local adaptations are needed due to sometimes unavoidable limitations. Even short, single-lecture interventions may have some effect.

☐ The Timing and the Design of Education

One of the most important presuppositions for the success of an educational project on depression and suicide is a situation in which depression in the region is underdiagnosed and undertreated. This situation may be indicated by a high prevalence of depression, possibly expressing itself by a high degree of sick-leave due to depressive and psychosomatic problems, conditions of helplessness, loss of vitality, and substance abuse. Other important indications are a high rate of suicide, a low prescription rate for antidepressants, a high rate of prescriptions of sedative or anxiolytic medications, and a seasonality in suicide in the region (which might be related to a high prevalence of nonprevented and nontreated depressions). There may also be an interest among GPs for knowledge about depression.

A sociological situation in a region that is conducive to suicide often includes the phenomena of societal transition, lack of autonomy, increased helplessness, loss of identity, alienation, and alexithymic habits, particularly in men (Rutz, von Knorring, Pihlgren, & Walinder, 1995; Varnik, 1996).

Our experience on Gotland shows that an interactive and multimodal program, balancing structured lessons and sessions with free discussions and exchanges of experiences seems to be effective. Lessons, group work, personal sharing of professional and private experiences, video sessions, and written case reports, complemented by the distribution of written educational material seems to be a good basis for this education.

An integrative ideology, describing the processes of becoming depressed and suicidal and recovery, avoiding a dualistic split of body versus mind, psychotherapy versus somatotherapy, and biological versus psychological reference frames, seems to be important. There is a need for introducing process thinking. The use of the stress vulnerability model, exemplifying the interaction between biological, psychosocial, and existential factors concerning pathogenesis and therapy, seems to be an ideal basis for helping GPs understand the complexity of psychiatric diseases and their treatment. This also seems to be the basis for compliance in the patients. Patients faced with a reductionalist, biological, diagnostic attitude and a cool psychopharmacological approach feel misunderstood and do not believe in the efficacy of unempathically-offered drug treatment and, as a result, often do not comply.

To encourage them to be positive about the program, GPs were given an inducement and reward for their participation, either by making their participation a duty, as it was in Gotland, or by making the educational program part of an obligatory postgraduate educational program.

Single lectures are good; including personal and intimate sharing in a somewhat luxurious atmosphere, as we did on Gotland, is better. Furthermore, encouraging the GPs to teach their own teams of health workers and nurses is a good way to deepen the educational effect. Continuous follow-up supervision is also necessary.

Symptom cards and guidelines on depression are useful but should always be preceded by and distributed after oral education. Balint groups are not enough. Experience shows that Balint-educated GPs are worse in diagnosing and treating depression. New ways of educating, perhaps including computerized, multimedia programs consisting of the above-described ingredients, may facilitate self-learning.

For primary care physicians, topics including classification and symptomatology, comorbidity, atypical depressions, management, and practical therapeutical guidelines should be presented. In addition, long-term treatment and prophylaxis, the choice of different pharmacological and psychotherapeutic treatment strategies, and stressing an integrative view on depression are important. Suicidology and especially risk assessment is often neglected, and experiences from Gotland and England show that education about the impact of depression and suicide on family and the society is valuable. An important part of an educational program is also teaching about depression in the elderly, adolescents, and children and a focus on the overlap of anxiety and depression which is found in between 60–90% of all depressed patients in GP settings.

The Gotland educational project failed to affect male depression and suicide. This made it necessary to give our recent, follow-up education projects a focus on gender differences in the clinical picture of depression, describing the masculine depressive and suicidal syndrome and stressing the coexistence and masking effects of substance abuse in male depression. Most important seems to be the avoidance of reductionism and the endogenous/exogenous split in favor of an integrative and holistic view for the GPs. A capacity to meet depressed patients not only as cases of depression but also human beings is also vitally important.

The Gotland program and the program of the World Psychiatric Association launched the International Committee for Prevention and Treatment of Depression. The Gotland program has been a model for this committee and is a good pragmatic and practical example of extensive educational activities, applied in different countries and cultures and in different medical structures.

☐ Teachers and Participants

Different models are under discussion and in use today; psychiatrists educating GPs, GPs with special interests and knowledge on depression educating other GPs, or GPs and health workers together educating other colleagues under the supervision of specialists or experts.

What is important appears to be the initiation and execution of these educational programs under expert professional and psychiatric supervision and with an engagement of postgraduate university or academic institutions. The educational resources of many countries are limited. In the United States, the natural interest of psychopharmaceutical industries in legitimate depression education might be able to provide an adequate organizational and funding basis for common educational activities. However, the psychopharmaceutical industry should not be the sole organizer for more structured educational activities since, in the long run they may not be unpartial. They may bring in a commercialized, reductionistic, psychopharmacological focus. Thus, the involvement of academics in the programs is important.

The Gotland model used an approach in which the local educational authorities and a group of Swedish experts on depression and suicide (the Swedish Committee for Prevention of Depression and Suicide), jointly carried out the educational program, with sponsorship partly from psychopharmaceutical firms. Our model proved to be realistic, nonreductionalist, objective, and well-accepted.

Educational programs on a disease like depression, that is characterized by a high morbidity and mortality, but is easily treatable, should be obligatory. This was possible in Sweden where GPs are employed by the state welfare system and were paid for their participation in the educational program. In other countries with private GPs, this system cannot be used, and strong inducements should be provided to motivate GPs to participate. These inducements should compensate the GPs for the loss of working time and income, and perhaps be part of an obligatory postgraduate educational program for recertification and updating of their therapeutic and medical knowledge.

Local adaptations to the Gotland model can and should be done. It is most important to reach the front-line health care practitioners, and the front-line is different in different countries. In Sweden, GPs are on the front-line; in some parts of Norway, district nurses fill this role. In some countries with a high density of private psychiatrists, as in Germany, psychiatrists should be the focus of education. In developing countries, education should focus on direct health-care workers or social workers (Varnik, 1996).

☐ Positive Outcomes

Based on the Gotland experience, we can expect an increase in competence in treating and preventing depressive disorders in groups of recently educated GPs. This also has been proved by the Defeat Depression Campaign in England, and in Hungarian and Swiss programs. On Gotland, we found a decrease in psychiatric inpatient care due to depression of more than 70%, as well as a 50% decrease in the sick leave frequency due to depressed conditions. Providing the educational program in an epidemiologically closed system like the island of Gotland, resulted in a reduction in the number of suicides which can be directly related to the educational program. In bigger, less isolated regions, confounding factors may be more prominent, and these reductions may be more difficult to demonstrate. However, examining whole nations for the efficacy of educational activities that follow the Gotland model, one finds, for example in Hungary, a 20% reduction in suicides, along with a 200% increase in the number of diagnosed depressed patients. In Sweden also, the diagnosis and treatment of depression has improved, and the prescription of antidepressants has increased threefold during the 1990s, accompanied by a decrease in the suicide rate by more than 15% between 1990–1995.

Another change that can be expected is a change in the prescription patterns of psychopharmacological drugs. On Gotland, a high prescription rate of anxiolytics, sedatives, and hypnotics decreased by 30%, accompanied by an increase in the prescription rate of specific antidepressive medications.

Educational programs provide savings for society, and the individuals, families, and social networks around depressed and suicidal patients. Individual suffering declines, and the suffering, morbidity, and mortality in the families of depressed and suicidal patients are significantly decreased too. Economic savings also result. An investment of over 400,000 Swedish Crowns during the educational program on Gotland was calculated to lead to savings for the society of 150,000,000 Crowns during a three-year period due to reduced morbidity, reduced mortality, reduced inpatient care, and reduced drug costs. Thus, the recognition and management of depression improved in the group of GPs and, in addition, the interest of GPs in psychiatric patients and in psychiatry in general increased.

☐ Problems and Failures

The positive effects which were clearly shown on Gotland were time-related to the educational program and started to fade away after about three years. Thus, booster dosages of maintenance education are required to counteract GPs' forgetting and losing interest and to educate new GPs who replaced the educated colleagues when they took other positions.

Educational programs are hard to evaluate, especially in regions that do not have as favorable epidemiological conditions as the island of Gotland. Our type of evaluation could be replicated in other isolated areas, like islands or remote valleys, where closed medical and sociological systems exist. In these cases a before/after evaluation strategy can be used, taking the circumscribed population in a catchment area as its own control as we did in the evaluation of the Gotland project. However, this might be difficult to carry out. Evidence-based approaches lead increasingly to demands for controlled trials, but even a controlled approach in one region, letting one group of GPs act as controls for the other, noneducated ones, leads to difficulties. In geographically close regions, contacts, and interactions lead to confounding factors. Perhaps, the best evaluations can be made after intensive educational programs are carried out and changes in diagnosing and treating depression and depression-related suicidality, can be measured using the whole nation as its own control (Rutz, 1999).

☐ Male Suicidality

Another problem is to reach depressed and suicidal patients who may be seen by the medical system with somatic complaints, not seen by the medical system, or actively avoiding the medical system. In Gotland the number of female suicides who were depressed, in contact with a GP, and using drastic methods decreased. Male suicides, however, were not affected by the GPs' improved ability to diagnose and treat depression. The difficult-to-reach groups were males, adolescents, abusive patients, aggressive and sociopathic acting-out individuals, and those with alexithymia who are incapable of insight into their own depression and helplessness and are also in need of support and treatment.

Today, considerable scientific information exists about the linkage between serotonin metabolism, aggression, acting-out, and outbursts of anger as associated features of especially male major depression. There is also evidence about the significance of serotonin levels in acute suicidality and in relation to stress related conditions. Furthermore, there is increasing clinical experience with the usefulness of serotonin-active drugs in the treatment of abuse, violence, acting-out, sociopathic behavior, and impulsiveness, as it can be found in these patients. Taking these factors into account, together with investigations about which diagnoses, according to DSM-IV, are considered to be treatable by serotonin-active drugs, a male depressive syndrome can be recognized. It corresponds with a form of temporary personality disorder and seems to confirm that the breakdown of the fight, flight, and coping ability, which to a great extent seems related to serotonergic decompensation and which we call depression, may have a different phenomenology in males and females. Even data from research on antidepressive drugs with animals in provoked learned helplessness situations show a distinction between male and female behavior. Based on these findings, Rutz et al. (1999) postulated a male depression syndrome characterized by temporary lower stress tolerance, acting-out, aggression, low impulse control, indecisiveness, irritability, substance abuse, antisocial features, morning discomfort, depressive thought content, and hereditary factors regarding suicide, depression, and male hereditary alcoholism type II.

On Gotland a scale was constructed with a focus on the male depression syndrome which often is missed by using conventional depression diagnostic criteria. This diagnostic system has been introduced to the GPs of the island and is presently being subjected to scientific validation (Beck et al., 1999; Rutz, Walinder, Walinder, Rihmer, & Pestality, 1999).

☐ Male Depression and Premature Mortality

Studies of the Amish people show that male depression in a society where violence and abuse is strictly banned are as prevalent as female depression. Even the number of depressive patients among suicides is over 90% in this group, suggesting that depression in this kind of society cannot be camouflaged by symptoms of violence and abuse.

In many countries, it is a recognized truth that females are twice as often depressed as males. Paradoxically, however, males commit suicide up to five times more often than females. The explanation for this paradox is probably the lower recognition, underdiagnosis, and undertreatment of depression in males.

Increased knowledge about the male depression and suicidal syndrome, probably linked to a breakdown in the serotonin-mediated ability to cope, fight, and flee, should be the focus of further research. Today, in the societies undergoing sociological and economical transition, especially in the former Soviet Union and other Eastern European countries, a dramatic decrease in life expectancy, especially in males, can be seen. In some parts of the European Region, officials speak of an ongoing depopulation with suicide figures up to 55 per 100,000 in the general population and up to 190 per 100,000 in males. Looking at these countries, an interesting observation can be made: suicide mortality and death due to external causes such as homicide, traffic accidents, and forms of risk-taking behavior, as well as mortality from cardiovascular diseases, has increased dramatically during the 1990s, whereas the corresponding figures were stable in countries of Western Europe.

Male premature mortality is an issue of increased concern these days. In times of stress, social transition, and loss of identity, the male population seems to be the most vulnerable one. This, combined with male alexithymia and their inability to recognize their own depression and need for help, probably leads to one of the striking paradoxes in general health care today: the fact that male mortality is so high, especially in times of transition and stress, despite low male morbidity rates. Female morbidity instead generally tends to be much higher. Despite this, females live longer and are not as sensitive to stress and transitional phenomena as are males.

Suicide rates, similar to those found earlier on Gotland and in other Swedish rural areas, where the female:male ratio was 1:5, are found today in the Baltic countries and in Eastern Europe, and they are a challenge. On the other hand, there are indications for hope. Education on depression is reported to be effective and can double the recognition rate for these problems by general practitioners.

Today, in some developed and developing countries, an increasing psychosocial pressure can be found in the society. Due to the multifactoral pathogenesis of depression and suicidality, better education, increasing accessibility, and increasing quality of medical care leading to better diagnosis and treatment of depression, sometimes has a limited effect. They can only buffer the increasing number of depression states, and only as long as the psychosocial pressure is not increasing too dramatically and getting too strong, thereby overwhelming and overloading the medical resources.

Therefore, it is both interesting and exciting to notice the decrease in suicidality in Hungary and Sweden in spite of a probably increasing prevalence of depression due to psychosocial and existential problems in these societies.

However, we have to keep in mind that an educational intervention focusing on the better diagnosis and treatment of depression, thereby counteracting depression morbidity and depression-related suicide mortality, is clearly a medical intervention, directed to components of the medical system. It should always, therefore, be accompanied by other social or network approaches directed to the multifactoral background factors behind the process of becoming depressed and suicidal, such as problems of unemployment, helplessness, transition, existential emptiness, alienation, loss of identity and dignity, and economic problems.

☐ Challenges

Educational programs should be adapted to local conditions regarding the possibilities of reinforcement for the GPs and also should be focused on the medical staff on the front-lines. Programs could last several days as on Gotland, or occur regularly during evening hours, depending on local circumstances. Education should be given continuously. Fading-out effects are expected after three years and should be counteracted by repeated educational programs, rehearing earlier information, and reviewing new diagnostic and treatment advancements.

A special focus should be on males and adolescents who today are not reached by prevention efforts due to diagnostic problems or problems of nonattendance in the medical system. These groups are often underdiagnosed and undertreated today in regard to their depression and suicidality, and commit suicide at high rates as a consequence. Experience from Gotland shows that depressed and suicidal persons in these groups are often known to school services, the local police, the social welfare system, the alcoholic treatment organization, or the local tax authorities. Thus, educational efforts concerning the recognition of these patients should be given to professionals in these organizations. Moreover, public relations efforts given in different formats, and repeatedly, are importance for sensitivity to, recognition of, and destigmatization of depression and suicide. Stressing the multifactoral background and the high depression related-morbidity and mortality, not only in depression but also in somatic conditions, both in patients and their families, and the treatability of the depressive condition, especially with modern treatment methods today, is a fundamental journalistic task and of crucial importance to public health.

The diagnostic concept of depression and suicide should be widened with a focus on the serotonin-related adolescent and masculine depression and suicidal syndromes and should become integrated into public information efforts and the educational programs directed at GPs. Modern research proves the existence of an aggressive, suicidal, and serotonin-related syndrome, masked by self-medication and alcoholism especially in males, and the efficacy of modern serotonin drugs. Finding the patients, getting working alliances and compliances with them, and making them aware of their need for help are the problems.

Occasional interventions directed at GPs need to be complemented and coordinated with efforts of postvention, such as the follow-up of previously-treated depressed patients, the follow-up of suicide attempters, and longitudinal secondary prevention and prophylaxis using psychotherapeutic support and medications. A cognitive psychotherapy approach and lithium treatment, which has been shown to have a serotonin-mediated antisuicidal effect on its own, are of great importance here.

Moreover, complementary interactive and supporting network activities directed to families, friends, work places, clubs, and religious communities should be given.

Alcohol services, police, the social welfare system, and tax authorities need knowledge and education, and public information by the mass media should be complemented by sociological and political approaches. On Gotland as well as in other countries the involvement of politicians, journalists, and other public personalities with their own experiences of depression and suicidality has been shown to be very helpful. Consumer, survivor, or patient organizations like the English and Irish depression-aware campaign can have a strong impact on societies. Where these organizations do not exist, their foundation should be facilitated and implemented with help from professional psychiatry. In spite of all these possibilities, we have to keep in mind that our medical system can only help people who are identified correctly by it and if there are not dramatic increases in psychosocial and existential problems in the society.

In Hungary, the recognition of depression from 1986–1992 has increased by 200% and suicide rates have decreased by 20%. In Sweden, the number of suicides and probable suicides has decreased by 25% during the 1990s, whereas the prescription of antidepressants has increased by 200%. On Gotland, the decrease in suicides of 50% percent and the increase in antidepressant prescriptions by 300% during the same period, was probably related to continuous and comprehensive education focusing on the detection and monitoring of depressions. Since 1995, these programs have focused specifically on the male depressive syndrome, leading now to a steady decrease also in male suicidality. The number of male suicides during the last three years on Gotland was 8 per 100,000 per year, compared to 13 per 100,000 during the previous six years.

The challenge is now to continue to fight depression and depression-related suicides by educating the front-line providers of health care, in most countries the GPs, and to give them continuing education to avoid fading-out and loss of effect. A special challenge is the development of strategies to reach male depression and suicidality by widening the diagnostic concept of depression by means of a focus on the masculine depression, suicidal, and stress-related syndrome. Consideration should be given to the linkage to other stress-related conditions such as serotonin-mediated risk-provoking and risk-taking behaviors and lifestyles, as well as to stress-related cardiovascular diseases.

Presently, cholesterol levels are today to be one of the significant biochemical predictors of suicidality, a knowledge that can facilitate our understanding of depression, helplessness, abuse, and aggression as well as cardiovascular consequences of stress.

Male depressives today seem to be a population that is underdiagnosed, undertreated and overly-suicidal. Also, more and more females are showing a masculine-type of stress-related behavior, with a consequent increase in cardiovascular disease, substance abuse, and suicide. Considering the fact that the costs for stress-related conditions amount to nearly half of all the health care expenditure in European countries, one of most important challenges for health promotion is the prevention of stress related mental and physical disability and related mortality.

However, we have to keep in mind that educational interventions, such as focusing on the causal connection between depression and suicide, must include efforts to take into account the complex psychosocial and existential etiology of the depressive diseases. Sociological interventions to counteract psychological, social, and existential background factors of depression must be combined with the previously-described approaches in order to increase the recognition and monitoring of depressive disease in order to prevent depressogenic suicides (Isaacsson, Holmgren, & Wasserman, 1994).

☐ An International Perspective

Educational models in line with the Gotland study are today used as significant parts of complex depression and suicide prevention programs in an increasing number of regions and countries. Such examples might be the British Defeat Depression Campaign or the Depression Awareness Campaign in the USA that uses the Gotland experience as one of its models. Also, the World Health Organization is using structured education on depression and suicide for family doctors and health workers in a public health perspective in regional and national programs. Recently the World Psychiatric Association and the International Committee for Prevention and Treatment of Depression launched a world-wide program, structured in didactic modules to be used in educational activities all over the world. National activities based on educational programs for GPs are today ongoing in the Baltic countries, Hungary, Canada, and Norway and other Scandinavian countries. These activities can be found on a national level and also as regional and local activities in a multitude of variations. The World Health Organization has given the area of depression and suicide highest visibility and importance by making it a Cabinet project. WHO's European Program on Mental Health has a focus on depression and suicide as one of its highest priorities to fight premature mortality due to stress, helplessness, risk-taking behavior, and lifestyles in the East European countries in transition.

Globally, principles of defeating depression and depression related suicide by educational programs directed toward medical workers in the front-line are hardly questioned any more. However, they should be complemented by activities of public education in cooperation with consumer organizations and political forces. Consequently, the first goals in treating the increase of depressions, suicide, and premature mortality in Europe are:

- to increase the access to decent management of depression in all European countries;
- to educate people in health care;
- to inform the different sectors of the society;
- to empower the individual; and
- to encourage governments and decision-makers to decrease the psychosocial and existential stress generated in the society by all means in multisectoral and multiprofessional societal action (Sartorius, 1996; World Health Organization, 1998).

☐ References

Bech, P., Raaback. L., Rasmussen, N. A., Solin, E., Rutz, W., & Zierau, I. (1999). Male depression. *Proceedings of the International Meeting on "Depression—Social and Economic Time Bomb."* London.

Colleges join together to fight depression. (1992). *British Medical Journal, 304,* 334.

Goldney, R. D. (1998). Suicide prevention is possible. *Archives of Suicide Research, 4,* 329–339.

Isaacsson, G., Holmgren, P., & Wasserman, D. (1994). Use of antidepressants among people committing suicide in Sweden. *British Medical Journal, 308,* 506–509.

Joukamaa, M., Lehtinen, V., & Karlsson, H. (1995). The ability of general practitioners to detect mental disorder in primary health care. *Acta Psychiatrica Scandinavica, 91,* 52–56.

Lester, D. (1993). The effectiveness of suicide prevention centers. *Suicide & Life-Threatening Behavior, 23,* 263–267.

Rihmer, Z. (1966). Strategies on suicide prevention. *Journal of Affective Disorders, 39,* 83–91.

Rihmer, Z., Rutz, W., & Pihlgren, H. (1995). Depression and suicide in Gotland. *Journal of Affective Disorders, 35,* 147–152.

Rihmer, Z., Rutz, W., & Pihlgren, H. (1998). Decreasing tendency of seasonality in suicide may indicate lowering rate of depressive suicides in the population. *Psychiatry Research, 16,* 223–240.

Rutz, W. (1992). *Evaluation of an education program on depressive disorders given to general practitioners on Gotland.* Unpublished doctoral dissertation, Number 356, Linkoping University.

Rutz, W. (1999). Improvement of care for people suffering from depression. *International Clinical Psychopharmacology, 14*(Suppl. 3), 27–33.

Rutz, W., von Knorring, L., Pihlgren, H., & Walinder, J. (1995). Prevention of male suicides. *Lancet, 345,* 524.

Rutz, W., von Knorring, L., & Walinder, J. (1992). Long-term effects of an educational program for general practitioners given by the Swedish Committee for Prevention and Treatment of Depression. *Acta Psychiatrica Scandinavica, 84,* 545–549.

Rutz, W., Walinder, J., Rihmer, Z., & Pestality, P. (1999). Stress-triggered cortisol-induced serotonin related depression. *Swedish Medical Journal.*

Rutz, W., Walinder, J., von Knorring, L., Rihmer, Z., & Pihlgren, H. (1997). Prevention of suicide and depression by education and medication. *International Journal of Psychiatry & Clinical Practice, 1,* 39–46.

Sartorius, N. (1996). The WPA-PTD educational program on depression. World Congress of Psychiatry, Madrid, Spain.

Varnik, A. (1996). Suicide in the former USSR and in the Baltic countries. 6th European Symposium on Suicide, Lund, Sweden.

World Health Organization. (1998). *Health 21.* Copenhagen: Author.

Norman L. Farberow

Helping Suicide Survivors

Grief, mourning, and bereavement follow the death of a loved one. The loss by suicide is distinguished by the fact that the deceased voluntarily chooses to die, adding an element to the bereavement that for some survivors profoundly affects the individual and familial recovery from the loss. It is only relatively recently that the extent and degree of problems experienced by the survivor of a suicide of a loved one have been recognized and addressed by the mental health profession.

☐ Feelings of Survivors After the Death of a Loved One

All survivors of the death of a loved one are faced with the task of mourning their loss. This means accepting the reality of their loss, experiencing the pain of the loss, and adapting to a life in which the deceased is now missing. During this period the person experiences grief, characterized by feelings, in varying frequency and intensity, of severe emotional distress, deep sorrow and sadness, frequent thoughts and memories of the deceased, and a painful recognition of what has been lost. Generally, the bereavement state does not require medical attention or treatment. Personal, social, and environmental support, along with the natural resources of the person and the passage of time, will enable the survivor to recover. However, when the reactions in the bereavement state are crippling, persistent, and disruptive to the bereaved, the bereavement is recognized as maladaptive. Our society tends to be uncomfortable with the fact of death and the process of dying. Peretz (1990) has pointed out that our current society provides little support for the bereaved. Expressions of grief are generally seen as less than desirable, and admiration is shown toward those who appear strong and do not express much emotion. Socially, the expectation is that the bereaved individual will return to his work and family responsibilities as soon as possible and be rather quiet about his grief.

Freud (1917/1957) describes mourning as a necessary process after the death of a loved one because there is a task to be performed by the survivor, that is, to detach the hopes the survivor has had of the loved one and to develop a new and different relationship with the memories previously held about their loved one. This is necessary so that they can move on with their lives. Mourning is hindered when the past memories are held so tightly that new attachments and bonds cannot be formed. Worden (1991) identifies the tasks of mourning as 1) to accept the reality of the loss, 2) to work through the pain of grief, 3) to adjust to an environment in which the deceased is now missing, and 4) to relocate the deceased emotionally and to move on with life. Survivors of all kinds of death run the gamut of reactions after the loss of a loved one. These have included disbelief, denial, shock, numbness, crying, sadness, anxiety, mental pain, anguish, sleeplessness, loneliness, helplessness, hopelessness, yearning, despair, dejection, depression, confusion, guilt, shame, relief, emptiness, lack of feeling, fatigue, agitation, sleep and appetite disturbances, apathy, withdrawal, nervousness. illusions, and hallucinations (Burnell & Burnell, 1989; Peretz, 1990; Worden, 1991). While all survivors experience the same kinds of emotions and feelings of grief (Cleiren, Diekstra, Kerkhof, & Van der Wal, 1994; McIntosh & Kelley, 1992; Van der Wal & Diekstra, 1987;), the reactions have been felt by some to be different for suicide survivors. (Bailley, Kral, & Dunham, 1996; Barrett & Scott, 1990; Chance, 1988; Colt, 1991; Rando, 1984; Van Dongen, 1990).

☐ Feelings of Survivors of Suicide

Clinical opinion strongly suggests that the survivors of suicide find the experience different in the pattern and in the intensity of the feelings (Dunne, 1987). The impact on the family is generally disruptive and frequently destructive.[1] "Suicide is the one violent death, except for intrafamily murder, where the intense suffering is caused by a family member. Family members have few culturally accepted avenues for externalizing and validating their grief" (Moritz, 1986, p. 134). A suicidal death in our society is a stigmatized death, one that is frequently accompanied by secrecy, silence, and even distortion (Calhoun, Selby, & Abernathy, 1984). The survivor is disenfranchised (Doka, 1989) because the loss is of someone who is in some way socially sanctioned. As a result, the death often cannot be publicly mourned or openly acknowledged, and there is an expectation of social disapproval and a withdrawal of social support. Cain's early review of the literature (1972) reports that practically all the investigators of the reactions of the survivors of suicide found qualitative and quantitative features that ranged significantly beyond those typical of bereavement in other deaths, with greater severity of psychopathology and intrinsic vulnerability. In addition to the feelings usually reported in bereavement, there were feelings of rejection, scapegoating by other members of the family, fear of hereditary influences, anger at the medical and

---

[1]See McIntosh's (1987) exhaustive review of the research into survivor family relationships up to 1987.

mental health professions, troublesome involvement of the police and insurance investigators, and possible intrusions by press and other media. Cain (1972) summarizes the reactions of survivors as: reality distortion; massive use of denial and confusion of memory; fantasy and misconceptions; tortured object-relations; distrust of human relationships and closeness; guilt; a feeling that the suicide could or should have been prevented; a pervasive sense of complicity; disturbed self-concept; feelings of shame, worthlessness, and being unlovable; impotent rage; a sense of rejection and desertion; intense frustration of ongoing needs; identification with the suicide, masked or overt, with sometimes bodily sensation of the suicidal act; depression and self-destructiveness; hollow emptiness; apathy; withdrawal; fantasies; sometimes suicidal impulses; searches for meaning and the answer to "why," often colored with guilt and despair; and incomplete mourning, because of denial, concealment, and mutual withdrawal of family and social support. On top of all these negative feelings there were the persistent recurring questions of whether they had any actual or possible role in precipitating the suicidal act or whether they could have prevented it (Cain, 1972).

Depression is the most common emotion encountered in bereavement. It is normal to be saddened and unhappy and to experience the pain of the loss. The grief-stricken person generally will begin to shift from the grief state to a more normal one in which the sadness lessens in both intensity and frequency. Depression, however, becomes more evidently pathological when the survivor remains persistently less able to function in his usual routine, continues to express feelings of despair and hopelessness, and remains unresponsive to help or support. The depressed person feels totally empty, apathetic, has trouble concentrating, and is unable to think clearly. Many times there are physical complaints that are related to old ailments or are new hypochondriacal manifestations. It is important to distinguish between the sadness of normal grief and the depression that has reached psychiatric syndrome status. A helpful distinction between the emotional states is that the depressed person is more likely to be preoccupied with himself than with the loss of the deceased loved one (Peretz, 1990). The self-preoccupation appears in a negative, self-reproachful, self-deprecating way. Guilt and shame may appear often but are more likely to be related to the negative feelings of self than to the personal relationship with the deceased.

The two negative feelings that most differentiate the bereavement of a suicide from that of other kinds of deaths are shame and guilt. These derive from the taboo that has branded the act since ancient times, stigmatizing not only the actor but also the family. Often, the feelings of guilt and shame are not recognized as such for they may take many forms and be expressed in different terms, such as self-blame, humiliation, failure, and embarrassment. The literature identifies both shame and guilt as highly important in both the individual and social development of a person's sense of self and his or her relations to others. Society makes certain there is a clear knowledge of what is criminal and immoral, as well as what desirable personal characteristics, traits, and social behaviors are (Farberow, 1998). In some views, guilt has been considered a subset of feelings emerging from shame; in other views it has been seen as an independent affect with its own set of characteristics. Miller (1985) sees shame and guilt as having many elements in common, with shifts occurring between them so rapidly that it is difficult to maintain their conceptual boundaries. Differentiation between them is facilitated by noting the direction of the attention. In shame the attention is on some defect exposed in the self-image; guilt implies the presence or absence of a criminal or immoral act. Some survivors find the aftermath of suicide so confusing and disruptive that they assume blame as a way of explaining the suicide and thus regaining control of their shattered world. By regaining control they are also lessening the shame (Leonhardi, Maria, & Callahan, 1988).

Anger is one of the most common feelings after a suicide, but it is mentioned less frequently because it is troublesome and difficult to deal with for many people. It has become complicated by society and by some religions that make anger un-desirable or unacceptable, even when it occurs only in the form of thoughts. Much of the process of growing up is one of learning how, when, and where anger is acceptable. Anger in suicide survivors may be directed at the deceased, the self, or at others, but generally is a mixture of all three. Some of the reasons for the ap-pearance of anger at the deceased may be: choosing to die when other alternatives were possible; rejecting the help that was available; depriving the survivor of the opportunity to intervene; abandoning the survivor and deserting family and chil-dren; violating the survivor's trust; depriving the survivor of a shared future; forc-ing the discarding of cherished dreams; being put into a position where others can blame the survivor; being required to handle new problems formerly handled by the deceased, such as financial and legal problems; and being forced to rebuild a whole new lifestyle.

Anger at one's self may arise from: not having seen the now-obvious clues that suicide was impending; not having prevented the death even though the signs were there; failing to make the relationship valuable enough to prevent the suicide; and being so worthless that even your loved one could not love you enough to continue.

Anger at others may be directed at: family and friends for blaming the survivor unjustly; friends for "dropping away" because they felt awkward about the sui-cidal death; professionals who failed to prevent the suicide; society that condemns suicide so unjustly and saddles the survivor with so much shame and guilt; and a bureaucracy that demands insensitively for the sake of its official records and of-fers little compassion and understanding. "In many ways, official agencies in the community serve to remind the bereaved that the death was not a natural one and to create unpleasant experiences that the bereaved are ill-equipped to handle" (Lester, 1990, p. 54). Anger may even be directed at one's religion—that not only does not provide comfort but condemns the action by refusing typical burial ser-vices and burial in the church—and even at God for letting the suicide happen.

☐ Treatment

Individual and/or Family Treatment

Most survivors of a suicide of a loved one do not seek the help of a mental health professional and many do not need it. The social support they receive from their family and network of relatives and friends is sufficient to help the bereaved survivors endure the loss, work through the grief and reestablish their lives again. Peace is made with the realization that, while the pain subsides to a bearable level, the grief never disappears completely but remains as memories and fantasies. The time that is required for such grief to be integrated and life to be resumed varies for individuals, some requiring as short a time as a few weeks while others will mourn for as long as several years.

Unfortunately, when a survivor does feel the need and does turn to mental health professionals for help, he is not likely to find a therapist who is either familiar with the survivor's special needs or has received formal training on effective ways to help them (Dunne, 1992). Suicide survivors present a unique constellation of symptoms, conditions, and defenses that pose challenges for therapists. Untrained and inexperienced therapists often have to overcome personal and professional biases before the survivor can be helped. These include awareness of their own attitude toward suicide which, if unaccepting, might lead to judgmental blaming or scapegoating, negative countertransference, and inability to distinguish normal mourning from pathological grief (Dunne, 1987).

Within the last two decades the number of reports on treatment of survivors has begun to increase. Early reports consisted of treatment accounts of children who were survivors of a family member's suicide. Such accounts used play therapy with a four-year-old child (Lindemann et al., 1972) and art therapy with a 12-year-old child (Jakab & Howard, 1969). Individual treatments of adults were reported by Augenbraun and Neuringer (1972) who counseled a daughter and a widow in short-term supportive therapy; and by Wallerstein (1972) who reported on the psychoanalytic treatment of a woman who lost her father by suicide when she was very young. Dunne (1992) summarizes the experiences of working with more than 20 individuals and 12 families who sought therapy after the death of a family member by suicide. The themes he encountered are familiar: "An obsessive search for the 'why' of the suicide, guilt, a sense of stigmatization, an incomplete or unusual grieving pattern, an invasion of conscious thought by the idea of suicide as an acceptable solution, a sense of helplessness, low self-esteem, reduction in the size and complexity of their social contacts, and, most troubling for the therapist, an erosion of basic trust" (p. 37). There were also conflicts over such things as who should be blamed, how to mourn, and what to write on the inscription on the deceased's tombstone

Dunne (1992) recommends a psychoeducational approach for the therapy of the individual survivor. He assumes first of all that the distressed survivor needs help because of the difficulty in dealing with the death as a suicide rather than that there is an underlying morbid pathological process. The approach includes the presentation of current information on suicide, a description of the grief process, normalization of the usual reactions, and a discussion of frequent social reactions that may be disappointing or irritating. He avoids suggesting stages that all survivors must experience, and points out the need to be alert for any evidence of suicidal thoughts and actions by the survivor or anyone in the family. He determines the impact of the suicide on the survivor's social network and other sources of support. Other issues the therapist will frequently encounter include: an exaggerated sense of responsibility, interrupted family life, marital discord, a sense of helplessness associated with the feeling of a stigmatized identity, and feelings of anger, despair, and guilt. Dunne ends by identifying a number of elements that will generally affect the outcome: the method of the suicide; its social context; the age of the decedent and the age of the survivor; witnessing the suicide; discovering the body; psychiatric illness of the decedent; degree of stigma; and the support network.

Bereavement for Children

Death of a parent for school-age children is generally recognized as a very stressful event, regardless of the mode of death, impacting most aspects of a child's life. To evaluate the full impact it is important to know the context, that is, how the loss is seen by the survivor, the availability of personal and social resources, and how these resources are used. Silverman and Worden (1993), in a review of the Harvard Child Bereavement study, a normative prospective study of children between the ages of 6 and 17 who lost a parent to death, found stress in most children, but it did not seem to overwhelm most of them. In the first few months after the death, only 22% showed any dysfunctional behavior, such as sadness, confusion, sleep disturbance, and restlessness. Although they were obviously grieving, the traditional prolonged crying, aggression, or withdrawal behavior did not appear for the large majority. Most continued going to school and maintained relationships with family and friends. Interesting findings included a need to maintain a connection to the deceased; that many children had very few tools to talk about death; that conversations about the dead parent were an important part of grief work; and that there were clear gender differences in the coping of the remaining parent with the new situation. Most of the time mothers dealt with the affective life of the family and provided stability in the daily routines. Fathers were, for the most part, not as comfortable with the nurturing role, although their comfort did increase with time.

The question has been raised whether children mourn, and if so when the capacity to do so appears. To some degree the controversy has risen around the definition of mourning which has been used in different ways by researchers. Most theorists agree that the ability to grieve in childhood develops as the child grows able to comprehend the finality of death. Some have found it present in young infants (Furman, 1974; Bowlby, 1960), while others have concluded it actually does not appear until adolescence (Wolfenstein, 1966). Webb (1993) has defined this development in terms of broad age groups, corresponding to Piaget's classification of overlapping developmental stages. The preoperational stage, generally years 2–7, is characterized by magical thinking and distortion of reality, in which the child does not recognize the irreversibility of death and does not differentiate death from sleeping. The concrete, operational stage, years 7–11, finds cognitive abilities developing, but death is visualized in external forms like ghosts that can be avoided if seen in time. The prepubertal child, years 9–12, shows thinking that becomes increasingly logical, is able to deal with abstractions and hypotheses, and which recognizes death as final and irreversible. Nagy's (1959a, 1959b) three stages are very similar, with death seen in the first stage, between ages 3–5, only as a departure but with the deceased still existing elsewhere; as personified and avoidable in stage 2, ages 5–9; and finally as inevitable and affecting everyone in stage 3, ages 9–11. Webb (1993) feels that while very young children can experience sadness, rage, longing, detachment, and protest, it can not be considered mourning until the child is able to understand the finality of the loss and its significance. This comes only when the child has developed reality testing and object constancy, which develops gradually into adolescence.

The literature on the topic of children as survivors of a suicide death is small. Dunne-Maxim, Dunne, and Hauser (1987) found that conceptualizing the impact of the loss as post-traumatic stress disorder (PTSD) was most helpful in understanding the reactions of the child who has been become a suicide survivor. The major symptoms are those characterizing PTSD, that is, cognitive-perceptual difficulties (with cognitive and perceptual distortions and overgeneralizations), a foreshortened sense of the future (with premonitions of their own early death or the end of the world), collapse of developmental accomplishments (especially around the child's sense of basic trust and excessive clinging and immaturity), and compulsive repetition. Children react to suicide deaths with similar feelings as adults but with very different behavior. There is the initial shock and disbelief, but then some become model children or try to be parents to their remaining parent. Some devote themselves to school, while other show deteriorating performance in school. Some withdraw completely, isolating themselves, while others slip into truancy and substance abuse. First efforts in treating the child should be by the remaining parent with the advice of the therapist. If the remaining parent is too consumed with his or her own grief and psychologically unavailable to the child, it will be necessary to focus first on helping the parent to recover and then coaching the parent in meeting the needs of the child.

Children, even very young ones, should from the beginning be told that the death is a suicide. Attempts to keep the truth from the child almost invariably fail; sooner or later the guilty secret will come out and ultimately serves only to increase the child's confusion and anger. Children easily mix facts and fantasy and need the truth in order to avoid forming disturbing fantasies about death. Some children may develop the fear that they are responsible for the death of their loved one and need careful reassurance to alleviate these unwarranted feelings of guilt. The parents need to understand the normal feelings that arise from a suicide, such as anger, shame, guilt, and anxiety, so that they can reassure their children when these feelings emerge. Both older and younger children should be encouraged to resume their activities with their friends and peers to combat the sense of differentness and avoid withdrawal. When marked change in behavior, such as poor school performance, substance abuse, truancy, and fighting appear, these should be interpreted as continued exaggerated expressions of grief which, if unabated, may merit the intervention of a trained psychotherapist who is also trained in suicide prevention (Dunne-Maxim et al., 1987).

Family Treatment of Survivors

Accounts of family treatment that often included children can be seen in a report by Whitis (1968) after the suicide of a 13-year-old child; by Schuyler (1973) after the suicide of a 16-year-old child; by Hajal (1977) in the treatment of a woman and her children following the suicide of her husband; and by Rogers et al (1982) who sent trained nonprofessional volunteer therapists to a family home to discuss a suicide with the remaining members of the family. These visits continued for eight two-hour sessions after which the family then attended biweekly group sessions with other survivor families. Doyle (1975) started a program in 1972 that consisted of providing counseling services both by telephone and by visits to the home in the months immediately following a suicide to help the individual survivor or the family with social support and assistance. The contacts were most frequent during the first three to four months of intense mourning, and decreased until the anniversary interview one year after the suicide. Lynd (1975) arranged to have a professional member of her staff accompany the coroner's deputy to all scenes of sudden death so that support could be offered to the survivors during the initial shock phase of their grief. A follow-up visit occurred several days later to provide any needed help with both practical and emotional problems. Further contacts occurred with individuals or entire families for about a half year, and then on request by the survivor. A final contact was made on the anniversary date.

A slightly different model was the program conducted by Weber-Slepicka (1985). It also was greatly facilitated by a close relationship with the County Coroner's Office who notified her when there was a suicide in the community and who distributed brochures to the families when appropriate. Weber-Slepicka would contact two outreach helpers who would visit the home to evaluate the most useful approach—to visit again, to recommend therapy (individual or group) or to judge no further contact was needed. Rosenfeld's (1987) S.A.F.E.R (Suicide Attempt Follow Up Education Research) program offers a several stage process to survivors. Both individual and family members first meet in an all-day workshop designed to help mourners share feelings and reactions. This is followed by breaking into small groups where they tell their stories in order to get to their feelings. After the lunch break, small groups again meet to discuss what they think the deceased's feelings must have been; and then they meet in the large group again to discuss what their experience has been and to set the date for the next group. Individual counseling or an ongoing therapy group are available in the interim and a follow-up survivor group is held in the next few weeks. In their training of counselors for the workshop, the author stresses what has become a crucial point in working with survivors—that the caregiver is not treating an illness but rather is enabling a healthy process to take place (Rosenfeld, 1987).

Group Treatment of Adult Survivors

Probably the most common method for treating adult survivors of the suicide of a loved one has been in groups. However, it is a process that has emerged more out of the ranks of the survivors themselves rather than out of a recognition of and response to their needs by the mental health profession. Ross (1997), for example, writes of her difficulties in finding help for her loss after her husband killed himself in 1975. She found little help in her search for relevant reading material, returned to school looking for answers, and attended widows' group meetings, but found them all unsatisfactory. After meeting several other suicide survivors she arranged a meeting herself and was overwhelmed by the positive response of the other survivors. Further meetings led to the start of a national organization, Ray of Hope, in 1980, with headquarters in Iowa.

At the same time, increasing attendance of survivors at the annual meetings of the American Association of Suicidology (AAS) brought the problems and needs of survivors to eventual professional attention. In the mid-1980s, AAS began to set aside specific program time for papers and presentations in their annual meetings and more and more survivors attended the conferences. In 1993, survivors were recognized as an aspect of suicide prevention of equal concern for AAS, and the Division of Survivors was established alongside the Divisions of Research, Clinical Services, Crisis Services, and Prevention Programs. In April 1994 the AAS was influential in the designation of May 1 as annual National Recognition Day of Survivors of Suicide

☐ International Activities In Survivor Groups

The growth of interest in clinical services for survivors has not spread evenly throughout the world, however. In an effort to gain a more comprehensive picture of the extent and kind of services for survivors available in different countries of the world, a survey was undertaken of the 52 countries in the International Association of Suicide Prevention (IASP) (Farberow, 1997). Seventeen of the 31 countries, most of them in eastern Europe (Russia, Lithuania, Romania, Bulgaria, Greece, Yugoslavia) or in the eastern part of the world (Iran, India, South Korea, Japan, China) responding had no formal programs. The reasons given for the absence of this service were that the countries' suicide prevention programs were just getting started and that it was not yet possible to extend the program to survivors, or that suicide itself was considered too great a religious sin or was such culturally unacceptable behavior that care could not be considered a professional obligation.

The countries that reported having the greatest number of suicide programs in place were primarily the English speaking countries (England (16+), Ireland (5), Australia (6+), Canada (50), and the United States (363) and the Scandinavian countries (Sweden (10), Denmark (5), and Norway (3). Some countries had already established bereavement organizations with specialized branches for suicide survivors, such as CRUSE in England, Compassionate Friends in several countries, SPES (HOPE) in Sweden and "Verwaiste Eltern" (Abandoned Parents) in Germany. In some of the countries, the survivors programs were affiliated with IASP, but in most countries the programs were offered by individual suicide prevention centers. The United States has seen a spurt in the growth of the number of survivor programs over the last three decades. In 1984, the AAS felt the need to study the burgeoning number of groups, 70 at that time, many of which had turned to AAS for affiliation, guidance, and an opportunity to share experiences (Heilig,

1985). Of the 41 questionnaires returned, half of the groups had been started by survivors while the other half were affiliated with suicide prevention or mental health programs. In 1992–1993 a list of survivor groups published by the AAS numbered 258 groups, and in 1997, the list published by the American Foundation for Suicide Prevention contained the names of 363 groups. In the United States, most of the groups (135) are led by a professional with a peer (survivor) facilitator, while an almost similar number are run by survivors alone. Most of the programs (85%) do not charge a fee, while the rest depend on fees based on sliding scales and on donations. Many publish newsletters that are distributed to present and past participants in the program. The names adopted by the programs are of interest. Survivors Of Suicide is used most often, undoubtedly because it also makes for a very appropriate acronym, SOS. In Los Angeles there was a deliberate effort to distinguish between those persons who had attempted suicide and survived and those persons who had experienced the suicide of a loved one. The result was Survivors After Suicide. Many names identified the purpose, such as Suicide Survivors Bereavement Support, and Healing After Suicide. Others offered encouragement (Take Heart, Ray Of Hope) or support (Safe Place, The Caring Network).

☐ Basic Assumptions of Survivor Groups

The basic assumptions of the group approach are well defined by Moritz (1986). The group provides a compassionate forum for . . . a free discussion of the suicide, the impact of the suicide on the survivors lives, expression of emotions unique to suicide grief, negative affect, discussions of the grief process, observance of models of coping, and provision of mutual comfort and support" (p 133). Moritz also describes the curative factors in the group: installation of hope through observation of other stages of grief, universality of the unique feelings, imparting of information by the leader, altruism toward other members and persons in the environment, and imitative behavior, particularly in acceptance and resolution. Appel and Wrobleski (1987) list additional reasons why self-help groups help: They provide members with the opportunity for personal interaction based on a common identification or shared status, to learn more about their common problem, to receive help freely given, to experience feeling cared about and supported; to develop interdependence with group members based upon shared similar problems; to gain a sense of community; to normalize their experience by discovering that others have similar reactions; to learn more fundamental coping strategies based on realistic expectations; to serve as role models for each other; to obtain reinforcement of positive change; to engage in advocacy and social change; to become a resource for the education of professionals and the public; to find continuing support and socialization; and to become a "helper."

The group approach as a method for treating survivors has developed over two major tracks as a survivor-initiated, self-help activity and as a mental health professional activity. Eventually it became most commonly a combination of the two.

Research on bereavement groups has been relatively sparse, possibly because so many of the groups started as self-help groups. Models have developed with differing formats and methodology that most often have depended on who was leading the group. A number of variables have been recognized as influencing the results but for the most part their individual and combined effects have remained unresearched, such as the role of kinship, age of the suicide, age of the survivor, family and nonfamily relationships, time elapsed since the death, leadership of the groups (professional, survivor, or mixed) open versus closed membership, limited or unlimited number of sessions, and others. Although evaluation of effectiveness has been subjected to comparatively few methodologically sound explorations, the clinical activities have continued to grow, mostly on the basis of survivor enthusiasm (Farberow, 1993).

Examples of Early Peer-Led Groups

The Suicide Survivors Grief Group (Wrobleski, 1983), an example of an early self-help group, was established in 1978 in the Minneapolis–St. Paul area. The open-ended, two-hour, twice a month meetings are led by a survivor, typically without a specific agenda, in different locations, and attended as needed by the participants. Groups are confidential but not anonymous, and offer unconditional support, catharsis, sharing of experiences, and coping techniques, as well as help in reframing the suicidal death. The number of members ranges from 8 to 14, and most attend only once or twice. The group publishes a newsletter and provides other written materials on request. Another early self-help group is HEARTBEAT (Archibald, Farberow, Koenig, & Rubey, 1990) that was started in 1981 in Colorado Springs, Colorado, as peer support for suicide survivors, under the sponsorship of The Pikes Peak Health Association. Most of the chapters are facilitated by survivors, some of whom are also mental health professionals. Funding is through memorials and donations. Meetings are opened with a statement of identity and a disclaimer that the group is not a therapy group, but an open-ended meeting of survivors "transforming their loss and grief into healing by extending understanding and encouragement to other survivors" (p. 82). The last hour of each meeting is spent in interaction with similar kinship survivors and in promoting a buddy system of an advanced griever with a new griever for between-meeting support. Reading material is available for education and support.

A completely different model of a survivor-initiated and conducted program is Friends for Survival in Sacramento, California by Marilyn Koenig (Archibald, Farberow, Koenig, & Rubey, 1990). The program was formed by two survivors' families who met through Compassionate Friends, felt their community needed a suicide survivor group, and published a notice of their first meeting in Compassionate Friends' newsletter. Incorporation papers were filed when a Board of Directors was formed. A brochure was prepared that described their purpose and identified the services and the persons to contact. An education/support meeting, featuring a community professional as speaker, is held monthly. Six home support meetings are scheduled each month in which peer support and education, not therapy, is offered. A lending library, speakers bureau and a monthly newsletter is mailed to over 1,000 known survivors. The program is financed by donations.

Examples of Professional and Professional/Peer Survivor Groups

One of the earliest reports of group treatment was by Johnson (1973) in which he offered psychological services to the nearest of kin of persons who had died recently by suicide. Later the group was opened up to survivors of any kind of sudden or violent death. The monthly meetings were led by a clinical psychologist, with the most frequent attendees being wives and parents of suicides. Hatton and Valente (1981), psychiatric nurses, met for 8 weeks in 1½ hour sessions with two married couples, one widow and one mother (the husband did not attend). The deaths had occurred from 3 weeks to 6 months before this meeting, and the ages of the suicides at death ranged from 15–30 years. The major themes discussed were the difficulties in mourning (as a result of society's attitudes), disruption of usual coping devices, isolation from friends and family, and crises in parental identity and personal control. The results were reported to be quite positive.

The Survivors of Suicide Project, functioning under the aegis of the University of Medicine and Dentistry of New Jersey Community Mental Health Center, was started by three clinicians who were themselves survivors who combined the elements of a self-help group and multiple family therapy (Appel & Wrobleski, 1987). In addition to the objective of enabling survivors to deal with their grief, the clinicians tested whether being survivors themselves would have any beneficial effect. The group is open-ended, ongoing, and meets monthly for 2½ hours. The clinicians share their own grief experiences as survivors, helping to normalize the experiences of the members. However, it was found that newcomers were helped most by acknowledging the suicide and telling their story, and that they looked to each other most often for mutual support. The fact that the clinicians were also survivors became less important, although it did help to establish their initial credibility. They were relied on more for information regarding suicide, and for their skill in facilitating the group.

Battle's (1987) experience with group treatment of survivors is noteworthy because he was one of the early group leaders who recognized the need to evaluate the effectiveness of his model. He determined the emotional status of the survivors, pre- and postsessions, by questionnaires and compared the results with two control groups, survivors who did not attend a group, and a group of individual psychotherapy patients. Battle found the predominant problem to be guilt about the loved one's death, so much so that 50% of the survivors had considered suicide for themselves subsequent to the death of their loved ones. (Three members later did attempt suicide.) The primary concerns discussed in the group meetings dealt with helplessness, accusations, alienation, rejection, guilt, and self-blame.

The Crisis Line of the Fox Valley A.I.D. in Aurora, Illinois reported a monthly self-help Survivors of Suicide support group (Weber-Slepicka et al., 1986). The group meetings are led by a professional and last for two hours. Included are certain rites and rituals such as formalizing the beginning of the meeting with a reflection to set the tone, then a "go-around" in which each person introduces themselves with their own name, the name, age, and relationship of the person who died, and the method used in the death. A discussion topic may be brought up by anyone, or may be introduced by the leader. The meeting is then ended with a formal reading, but people are encouraged to linger after. Although there is no time limit, people tend to stay with the group for a year, then return around the anniversary of the death or the birthday of the deceased.

Moritz (1986) describes a survivors group program that has been meeting since 1982 in a community health center in Allegheny County in Western Pennsylvania. The meetings are held for ten consecutive weeks and are then followed up by a once-a-month group, open to all group members. Kinship is heterogeneous, ages are 18 and older, with referrals from other professionals and referral agencies. The group is led by a professional who considers the role as one of providing education, reality testing, gatekeeping, and a safe atmosphere. The discussion is focused on the grief process with the use of a three stage grief model. Within the ten weeks, a former member attends one of the sessions to provide a model of resolution and coping; and another former group member discloses her own suicide attempt, thus helping the other group members to understand better their own deceased family member.

Another model of a survivors group is L.O.S.S. (Loving Outreach to Survivors of Suicide), developed in Chicago, Illinois (Knudson, 1987; Archibald, Farberow, Koenig, & Rubey, 1990), an individual program of the Catholic Charities of Archdiocese of Chicago, that was founded in 1979. The groups are led by a mental health professional and by trained survivors. Eight consecutive weekly group sessions, two hours in length, are held for newly grieving people. These are generally small groups with 8–12 participants and relatively structured with a set agenda for each session. In addition, monthly groups are held that are divided by kinship, that is, parents, spouses, adult siblings, and adult children of suicide, based on the reasoning that the grief experience is somewhat tempered by the specific relationships. As other issues surface within a family or individual, the mental health professional can also draw on other services of the Catholic Charities. The process is seen as stages of group psychological development: Parallel, Inclusion, Mutuality and Termination. There are structured activities called rounds. In the first round, participants briefly describe their previous week; in the second round the group decides what issue they wish to talk about; in the third round those topics are discussed; and in the final round any unfinished business is conducted. The group process of Parallel finds most interaction channeled through the leaders; the Inclusion stage focuses on member-to-member interaction; in the Mutual stage the process is balanced among members and leaders, with content reflecting genuine care and insight; and the Termination stage finds the members decathecting.

Survivors After Suicide (SAS) is a program of the Los Angeles Suicide Prevention Center which is now part of the Didi Hirsch Community Health Center in Los Angeles, California (Farberow, 1992). Started in 1981, the program is based on the concept that the survivors (all adults) are essentially normal people who have been subjected to severe emotional stress and need help in working through their grief.

The format is limited to eight sessions, once a week, conducted by two leaders, one a mental health professional and the other a survivor who has gone through the program and then has received additional training. Kinship losses are mixed as are sex and age. Time between death and entry into the program ranges from one month to many years, with the average being four to six months. Following the eight weekly meetings, the members are invited to attend monthly meetings as often as they wish. At each of the group sessions reading material from various books and articles is distributed, along with suggested topics for discussion. The program is supported by fees, but no one is excluded because of lack of funds. A newsletter is published quarterly. An evaluation used pre- and postratings of status of relevant feelings and of effectiveness and compared the members with a control group made up of survivors who enlisted in the program but either did not attend or else did not return after the first meeting. Of interest is that the three feelings, grief, shame, and guilt, that had been rated by the members as significantly higher than the controls before the program began, were no longer different from the controls in the postprogram ratings. Two other feelings (depression and puzzlement), however, were rated higher by the members that had not been different before. It was felt that this was because the intensive confrontation and working through of the feelings around the death had temporarily rearoused the pain and questioning of the loss.

Children Suicide Survivor Bereavement Groups

Treating young children suicide survivors in a group has generally not been recommended, mostly because verbal facility in the ages below adolescence are not developed enough to facilitate the kind of expression of feelings, sharing, listening, and understanding that are a vital part of the group's usefulness for adults. Also for most young children, the preferred method of assisting them is through helping the parent(s) to provide the therapy. However, for a number of years the Baton Rouge Crisis Intervention Center in Louisiana has been conducting a nine-week bereavement program for children ages 6–12 with reports of marked success (Campbell & Goldstein, 1990). Activities are introduced into each session with specific aims. In the first two sessions the focus is on established group rapport and trust. Breaking the ice get acquainted games, charades, animal puppets, and singing are used. The story of Bambi is introduced so that the effect of the death of the mother deer on the little deer can be discussed. The third session focuses on losses with the use of puppets to help the children talk about their specific losses. Sessions four and five focus on gaining the understanding that all feelings are acceptable, and to help the children identify and share feelings. Drawing and flash cards and the Dealing with Feelings card game are used. The sixth session looks at grief feelings using examples from other groups and encouraging the children to share their own feelings and experiences. The leader answers questions to dispel guilt and fear of the members. The seventh session focuses on family grief with role-play activities designed to give the children practice in asking to have their needs met. They are helped to identify safe people to talk to and a safe place to go when they are feeling bad. The eighth session is the last meeting with children only and the time is spent helping each child list the feelings, thoughts, and concerns they would like to share with their parents the following week. Activities designed to enhance self-esteem are included: making full length body silhouettes, drawings of friends, and filling a treasure box of phone numbers and mementos of the group. The final session is with both children and parents in which the child is helped to talk about his list of concerns with his parent. At the end the children participate in goodbye activities with each other while the parents are given suggestions for home activities to encourage further sharing of feelings and to help their children grieve. The activities performed in each meeting change depending on the composition of the group. The number of sessions may change also, varying up to 12 when felt necessary.

Helping Professional Caregivers

Although most significant survivor relationships stem from family kinship or intense friendship/love relationships, there is also a significant relationship that appears between professional caregivers and their patients. Apparently, this is not an infrequent experience. Reports of the number of therapists who have experienced the suicide of a patient while in a psychotherapeutic relationship vary, ranging from 14%, or one out of every seven therapists, to 51%, or about one out of every two therapists; and are reported for therapists in all kinds of venues and disciplines, such as therapists in training, office practice, hospital and clinic, and psychiatrists, psychologists and psychiatric social workers (Brown, 1987a, 1987b; Chemtob, Hamada, Bauer, Kinney, & Torigoe, 1988; Chemtob, Hamada, Bauer, Torigoe, & Kinney, 1988; Feldman, 1987; Holden, 1978; Kahne, 1968; Kleespies et al., 1993; Lapp, 1986; Moritz, Van Ness & Brower, 1989)

The feelings aroused in the therapist after a suicide of a patient are strikingly similar to those reported in the survivors of a loved one (Goldstein & Buongiorno, 1984; Gorkin, 1985; Jones, 1987; Kolodny, Binder, Bronstein, & Friend, 1979; Litman, 1965). These are, at first, shock, disbelief, confusion, and denial (Brown, 1987a; Cotton, Drake, Whitaker, & Potter, 1983; Hamel-Bissell, 1985), followed closely by grief, guilt, shame, anger, depression, rejection, and anxiety (Cotton et al., 1983; Feldman, 1987; Kleespies, Smith, & Becker, 1990; Sacks, Kibel, Cohen, Keats, & Turnquist, 1987). However, these reactions are also mixed with feelings directly related to professional status, such as feelings of failure, responsibility, loss of self-esteem, fear of being blamed for the suicide, feelings of professional incompetence, and self-doubt regarding one's therapy skills and clinical judgment (Cotton et al., 1983; Feldman, 1987; Kleespies et al., 1990). There may also be fantasies of silent accusations and criticisms by colleagues and supervisors, depressive ruminations while searching for the "fatal mistake" (Sacks et al., 1987); fear of the relatives' reactions; fear of legal liability; and intrusive thoughts and dreams related to the client suicide (Chemtob et al., 1988a; Jones, 1987; Sacks et al., 1987). Thoughts and concerns about malpractice and legal issues are not infrequent (Chemtob et al., 1988b; Sanders, 1984). Cognitive dissonance from compet-

ing thoughts about the realization of one's own limitations in working with suicidal patients, and the thought that the suicide could be related to a failure in
empathy may occur (Bartels, 1987). Changes in professional practice may occur in
the form of much greater conservatism in handling of patients and record-keeping, hospitalizing even low risk outpatients, accepting patients only if there is no
indication of suicidal threats or tendencies, avoiding undertaking treatment of
severely depressed patients, putting more inpatients on suicide precautions, and
canceling inpatient passes.

In general, research among therapists has shown that, among psychiatrists, the
older the therapist and the more years of practice, the less the guilt, the less the
negative intensity, and the more likely a minimal loss of self-esteem. For psychologists there was no relationship between age or years of practice in intensity of
reaction (Chemtob, Hamada, Bauer, Kinney, & Torigoe, 1988a). Trainees, however, experience greater emotional stress from a patient's suicide than do the more
experienced therapists in either discipline (Brown, 1987b; Cotton, Drake, Whitaker,
& Potter, 1983; Kleespies, Smith, & Becker, 1990). In addition to their relative
immaturity as professionals additional feelings of stress may stem from the frequently competitive forces in a residency or intern program that make for a feeling of being in a fish bowl and that result in a strong need to win the approval of
the faculty (Brown, 1987; Kleespies et al., 1993; Sacks, Kibel, Cohen, Keats, &
Turnquist, 1987). The impact is not always completely negative. For instance, Brown
(1987) reported that some of the psychiatrists in residency training seemed to gain
a sense of their own aspirations and their limitations and to develop an appreciation for how little real control they actually have over another individual's life.
Strong recommendations were made for better preparation for traumatic events
within the training programs by providing immediate professional and personal
support, assisting the trainee with working through the resulting feelings, and
resolving issues of failure and blame as quickly as possible (Brown, 1987b). The
help suggested has included such procedures as consultation, formal reviews, support through networking, and individual or group meetings. A support group would
function to help the therapists manage their grief and integrate their experience
in redefining their personal and professional roles (Goldstein & Buongiorno, 1984;
Jones, 1987; Valente, 1994). Use of the psychological autopsy procedure has been
reported to be helpful, especially in such places as training hospitals, clinics, and
group practices. The supervisor plays an important role in actively encouraging
and supporting the trainee in working through the feelings regarding the suicide
(Feldman, 1987; Horn, 1994). Feldman sees the process as reparative in nature,
enabling the student or trainee to integrate the experience at a higher level of
performance. As the issues are clarified, the student increases awareness of the
effects of countertransference and is helped to a more realistic limitation on therapeutic ambition.

☐ Initiating and Conducting a Suicide Survivors Group

For many mental health professionals and suicide survivors, the possibility of participating in, much less that of forming, initiating, and leading, a survivors group

is daunting. Recognizing this, there have been efforts to provide guidance with the preparation of guidelines, books, and manuals by experienced professionals and accomplished survivors that have proven helpful with instructions, directions, suggestions, and comments. Groups work because they provide among other things support, information, and reassurance, sometimes directly and other times indirectly.

With the aim of providing readers who may be interested in the details and specifics of initiating and operating survivors groups, this section presents a condensation of the Survivor Support Group Guidelines published by the AAS in 1992. The Guidelines contains 14 chapters, 11 of them written by Ed Dunne, and one each by Jay Callahan, Craig Fisher, and John Bolton, that are specifically aimed at helping the leader start and run a group effectively. In the first chapter, entitled How to Start Your Own Support Group, Dunne focuses on the concerns and anxieties in initiating a support group to recognize personal limits in the amount and degree of investment made. In Chapter 2, Getting Grounded—What Makes Support Groups Work, Dunne specifies three functions which he describes as the backbone of good survivor support groups: providing support, offering specialized information about the recovery from a loss of suicide, and offering reassurance they are on the road to recovery. Chapter 3 (Dunne), Getting Going: The First Steps, calls attention to the great many logistics involved in the arrangements that the leaders or their delegates have to attend to, like location, advertising, and meeting format, to mention only a few.

Craig Fisher, in Chapter 4, Putting Rituals to Work In Your Survivors Support Group, describes the use of rituals aimed at presenting new understanding to life's experiences through symbolism. He describes a ritual followed in the Christmas/Hanukah season in which the candles are lit, the room darkened, and the members stand in a circle and are invited to make a statement, silently or out loud. Sometimes the message is to the person who died; sometimes it is a statement of new knowledge or confidence. When finished they blow out their candles, and the lights are turned on again. The ceremony has different meanings to each person, with some saying it made the holiday season more bearable and others saying they found new strength. The idea is to look at the rituals that emerge in the group and to support the meanings that will help the group.

In the next four chapters, Dunne continues with specific instructions for conducting the groups. Chapter 5, Defining the Role and Task of the Leader, describes the group skills that need to be developed. The leader takes care of most of the mechanics, like announcing the schedule and starting and ending on time, but also has to make sure the process keeps flowing and that the vulnerable are protected. Dunne (p. 16) has compiled a list of guidelines for the participants which he has found useful to hand out as they enter the group. For example, the cardinal rule is that adults learn best by hearing the experiences of other adults. Advice, persuasion, and exhortation do not work as well, if at all; Do not be critical or judgmental and respect the opinions and experience of others; Share your experiences, even your mistakes, for they might be helpful for someone else to avoid repeating; Respect others grief; Don't interrupt; Don't monopolize the group's time; The information shared is confidential.

In Chapter 6, Examining the "Go-Round" Phase, Dunne describes the phases through which he feels the meetings go, starting with premeeting socializing, followed by the formal opening, go-round and discussion phases, and then the summary/closing phase. Postgroup socializing is encouraged. Coffee is fine before or after, but not during. Use circular seating to enhance participation. Adhering to the announced schedule signals that time is limited and everyone needs to get a chance to speak. Dunne feels the group operates best with a moderate structure, a sort of middle ground between assigned topics and free-form that allows the group to go wherever the topic leads it.

Chapter 7, The Discussion Phase of an S.O.S. Meeting, opens with a discussion of the role of the effective leader is as a shepherd, able to flow with the group as it goes from topic to topic, but keeping the group moving in more or less the same direction, while alert to any actions that might be harmful to the participants. Dunne identifies some problem situations such as monopolizers, and help-rejecting complainers and indicates they are best understood as individuals with mistaken expectations of the group. These arise from their not knowing what things the group does and does not do, an expectation that advice will help to resolve their difficulties, or an expectation that the group is there to take care of them in some way. Chapter 8, Maintaining Your Focus, identifies further problems from people who are rude and insensitive, hurting other group members in the process, or who express such strong feelings of anger, depression and guilt that they produce overwhelming feelings of powerlessness in the other members of the group. Perhaps the most serious and difficult of the problems encountered arises when a group member threatens suicide during the course of the group. This cannot be ignored but it should not be allowed to trap the members of the group into becoming the life-line for the person. Group members should be cautioned to contact the leader if the problem comes up between meetings whether in oneself or in another member, and all members should be informed about the professional resources available in the community so that aid can be enlisted as quickly as possible.

Jay Callahan's Chapter 9, Survivor Groups: Open-Ended vs. 8-week Series, relates his experiences in running an open-ended group and an eight-week, time-limited group in Ann Arbor, Michigan. He found that the open-ended group gave him difficulties, specifically sporadic attendance beyond the first session, poor response to announcements of their availability, and a lack of trust which he attributed to the constantly changing membership that never allowed the discussions to be more than superficial and basic. When Callahan changed to a coleader survivor-facilitator format that met for 8 weeks, he found that attendance flourished and became regular which, in turn, promoted trust and group-building. In addition, the members were able to discuss topics, such as guilt, shame, grief, and anger that never came up in the open-ended sessions. Later, a monthly open-ended group was added, and it, too, flourished, a result that speculatively was attributed to the slow payoff of seven years of conducting groups and the gradual increase in public knowledge that word of mouth provides.

In Chapters 10 and 11, Group Leader Burn-Out, Part One and Battling Burn-Out, Part Two, Dunne discusses the problem of burn-out as it applies to leaders of survivor groups, giving indications of how to recognize it, what are the warning signs, and where the usual sources of stress for the leader are found (as the initial contact person, as the ongoing contact person and as the meeting organizer). Burn-out is much easier to prevent than it is to treat or cure.

In Chapter 12, Identifying Support Group "Cultures," Dunne muses about the support group culture as a collection of shared attitudes, beliefs, and behaviors that appears whenever the group is together. Most of a group's culture is relatively benign and serves to establish the way each group functions. Some negative be-haviors, such as always starting late, can become characteristic of that group and control its functioning for a long time. One way to understand how the group is going is to arrange for ongoing supervision with a professional or, alternatively, seek occasional consultation with a professional.

In Chapter 13, Themes and Variations, Dunne describes some procedures de-veloped by a group meeting in New Brunswick, NJ, a result of having too many survivors coming to the first meeting and having to subdivide into smaller sub-groups. The dividing has been based on kinship and often has been operated without a designated leader when none has been available. The advantages and disadvantages to both situations, similar kinship and leaderless goups, are dis-cussed in detail. A third activity, Booster Groups, has been the self-arranging of additional group meetings for those who wished to contine to meet after their original group has ended. Again, there may be pros and cons for such activities, as discussed in this chapter.

Finally, John Bolton, noting how often men avoided coming to survivor group meetings, or, when they did come, participated very little and offered comments that they knew were more acceptable to their wife or companion, recommends in Chapter 14, "Get the Men!" that sessions be scheduled exclusively for men. He has found that many of his male members of a mixed group find it too painful and threatening to share their own grief. He postulates that men have difficulty shar-ing their intimate feelings in the presence of women because it is contrary to their societal training to be strong. This experience has been contrary to that of the present writer.

Group experiences will vary for reasons as far ranging as geography, culture, attitudes, format, personalities and skills. This unpredictability lends much to the attraction and challenge of the work.

☐ The Outlook for the Next Century

A major difficulty confronts the area of bereavement counseling and helping sur-vivors in the coming millennium: the continuing resistance found in the entrenched taboos, cultural denials, and religious condemnation toward suicide itself still found in many countries throughout the world, a resistance that must be overcome, or at least diminished, before it will be possible to develop services for those left behind after suicide—the survivors. Reports from the Middle East, most Asian countries, and Central and South America describe a struggle to initiate suicide prevention and treatment services for suicidal people. Isolated individuals and a few nongov-ernmental agencies emerge as the lone protagonists struggling against the institu-tionalized denial (Farberow, 1997). They report that bereavement counseling, much less survivor services, cannot be offered when the survivors feel that they must conceal the suicide of a family member and can never admit to friends, neighbors, and the community the mode of death. Nevertheless, there is slow progress with scattered activities reported in some countries, such as survivor groups and research programs in Slovenia, clinical services emerging in Mexico, Argentina, and Venezuela, and the formation of suicide prevention associations in the Baltic countries (Estonia, Latvia, and Lithuania) and in Japan. The International Association for Suicide Prevention should do all it can to support the struggling national associations, agencies, and individuals with encouragement, advice, and information. It would also be helpful if the experiences and suggestions of persons who have been able to overcome the taboos and cultural-religious hurdles in their own countries could be provided.

Interest in the field of bereavement in suicide has grown with the passing of time. Evidence is seen in the fact that, according to information from the Suicide Information and Education Center in Calgary, Canada, the 1970s saw only approximately 100 articles about survivors after suicide, whereas this number increased fourfold in 1980 to 400 articles. Over 400 articles have already appeared in the first seven years of the 1990s. It seems that interest will continue to grow as the number of suicidologists increases and they become aware of the need for informed help, and as the general public learns that treatment is available during this painful period.

Many publications over the past several decades have described the characteristics of survivor groups and the problems encountered in their establishment and operation. Others have reported in depth on the feelings experienced during the bereavement of a suicide and the similarities and differences from the feelings aroused in the survivors of other kinds of death. But there are still great gaps in our knowledge which point to the need for greatly increased activity in research and a heightened emphasis on training for those who will be offering the help. In research, for example, the basic question of the effectiveness for each of the various models and formats for survivor groups persists. Almost all groups, regardless of the great variety in model and format, report positive results. But how is effectiveness measured—by participant reports, leaders' observations, the use of standardized instruments (and, if so, what instruments), third party reports, behavioral changes, feeling changes (or both), or social and environmental changes? Some changes require time to appear. When should measurement take place—during, immediately after, or months and years later? Not everyone profits from the group experience. Who can profit and who will not? And why?

Other significant questions continue to be unanswered. For example, what kinds of groups work best—those whose memberships are homogeneous in kinship loss (all parents, all children, all siblings) or those mixed in terms of kinship loss? What is the effect of differences in age, sex, and socioeconomic status? Is there an optimal time that should pass between loss and entry into the group? What is the most effective leadership arrangement—survivor-facilitator, professional, or both? Does the time-limited group serve the needs of the survivor better than the group with no time limit? If the group is to be time-limited, is there an optimal number of sessions? Should the process be structured in content or nonstructured? Methodologically, what are the most appropriate control or comparison groups—grief groups with membership from any other kind of death or from deaths similar in suddenness (such as accidental deaths)?

Particular attention needs to be paid to the training and education of mental health professionals in the skill and art of bereavement counseling and the intricacies of conducting survivor groups. While courses on suicide have been introduced into the curricula of medical schools and into the graduate programs for mental health professionals, such as psychologists and social workers, there has been relatively little attention paid to the specific problems of the treatment of bereavement grief and mourning. As Dunne (1987) has outlined, therapists working with the bereaved, especially the suicidally bereaved, face formidable tasks. They need to learn about their own feelings toward suicide, avoid judgmental reactions, determine the existence of scapegoating, and distinguish normal from pathological grief. They may be faced with, and may have to know how to handle, inconsolable grief, intense guilt and self-blame, and unrecognized anger. They will have to counter the sense of stigma and tendencies toward withdrawal, isolation, and depression, especially that which comes with an exaggerated sense of responsibility, and possibly thoughts of and impulses toward suicide in the survivors. There may be specific feelings of trauma that will need to be addressed if the survivors witnessed the suicide or discovered the body. There also may be problems that related to gender differences or kinship differences (for example, between a child survivor of a parent suicide and the surviving spouse). National and international associations will have to accept the responsibility for encouraging the inclusion of such information in the curricula of the universities and colleges in their countries.

Survivors after a suicide can experience intense, enduring, and disruptive pain that is made especially difficult because of the nature of the death. There is a need for help, and that need *must* be met.

☐ References

American Association of Suicidology. (1992). *Survivors of suicide: Support group guidelines.* Washington, DC: Author

Appel, Y. H., & Wrobleski, A. (1987). Self-help and support groups. In E. J. Dunne, J. L. McIntosh, & K. Dunne-Maxim (Eds.), *Suicide and its aftermath* (pp. 215–233). New York: Norton.

Archibald, L., Farberow, N. L., Koenig, M., & Rubey, C, (1990). Starting and maintaining a strong support group. In D. Lester (Ed.), *Suicide' 90* (pp. 82–84). Denver, CO: AAS.

Augenbraun, B., & Neuringer, C. (1972). Helping survivors with the impact of a suicide. In A. C. Cain (Ed.), *Survivors of suicide* (pp. 178–185). Springfield, IL: Charles C. Thomas.

Bailley, S. E., Kral, M. J., & Dunham, L. (1996). Survivors of suicide do grieve differently. In J. L. McIntosh (Ed.), *Suicide '96* (pp. 59–60). Washington, DC: AAS.

Barrett, T. W., & Scott, T. B. (1990). Suicide bereavement and recovery patterns compared with non-suicide bereavement patterns. *Suicide and Life-Threatening Behavior, 20,* 1–15.

Bartels, S. J. (1987). The aftermath of suicide on the psychiatric inpatient unit. *General Hospital Psychiatry, 9,* 189–197.

Battle, A. (1987). Group therapy for survivors. *Crisis, 5,* 48–58.

Bowlby, J. (1960). Grief and mourning in infancy and early childhood. *Psychoanalytic Study of the Child, 15,* 9–52.

Brown, H. N. (1987a). The impact of suicide on therapists in training. *Comprehensive Psychiatry, 28,* 101–112.

Brown, H. N. (1987b). Patient suicide during residency training. *Journal of Psychiatric Education, 11,* 201–216.

Burnell, G. H., & Burnell, A. L. (1989). *Clinical management of bereavement.* New York: Human Sciences Press.

Cain, A. C. (Ed.). (1972). *Survivors of suicide.* Springfield, IL: Charles C. Thomas.

Calhoun, L. G., Selby, J. W., & Abernethy, C. B. (1984). Suicidal death. *Journal of Psychology, 116,* 255–261.

Campbell, F. R., & Goldstein, M. (1990). Survivor group services. In D. Lester (Ed.), *Suicide '90* (pp. 102–104). Denver, CO: AAS.

Chance, S. (1988). Surviving suicide. *Bulletin of the Menninger Clinic, 52,* 30–39.

Chemtob, C. M., Hamada, R. S., Bauer, E., Kinney, B., & Torigoe, R. T. (1988). Patients suicides. *American Journal of Psychiatry, 145,* 224–228.

Chemtob, C. M., Hamada, R. S., Bauer, G., Torigoe, R. Y., & Kinney, B. (1988b). *Patient suicide. Professional Psychology, 19,* 416–420.

Cleiren, M. P. H. D., Diekstra, R. F. W., Kerkhof, A. J. F. M., & van der Wal, L. (1994). Mode of death and kinship in bereavement. *Crisis, 15,* 22–36.

Colt, G. H. (1991). *The enigma of suicide.* New York: Summit Books.

Cotton, P. G., Drake, R. E., Whitaker, A., & Potter, J. (1983). Dealing with suicide on a psychiatric inpatient unit. *Hospital and Community Psychiatry, 34,* 55–58.

Doka, K. (1989). *Disenfranchised grief.* New York: Free Press.

Doyle, P. (1975). The anniversary interview in grief counseling for the survivors of suicide. *Proceedings of the 8th Annual Meeting of the American Association of Suicidology,* Denver, CO: AAS.

Dunne, E. J. (1987). Special needs of suicide survivors in therapy. In E. J. Dunne, J. L. McIntosh, & K. Dunne-Maxim (Eds.), *The aftermath of suicide.* New York: Norton.

Dunne, E. J. (1992). Psychoeducational intervention strategies for survivors of suicide. *Crisis, 13,* 35–40.

Dunne, E. J., McIntosh, J. L., & Dunne-Maxim, K. (1987). *The aftermath of suicide* (pp. 234–244). New York: Norton.

Dunne-Maxim, K., Dunne, E. J., & Hauser, M. (1987. When children are suicide survivors. In E. J. Dunne, J. L. McIntosh & K. Dunne-Maxim (Eds.), *The aftermath of suicide.* New York: Norton.

Farberow, N. L. (1992). The Los Angeles Survivors-After-Suicide Program. *Crisis, 13,* 23–34.

Farberow, N. L. (1993). Bereavement after suicide. In A. A. Leenaars (Ed.), *Essays in honor of Edwin Shneidman* (pp. 337–345). Northvale, NJ: Jason Aronson.

Farberow, N. L. (1997). Suicide survivors programs in IASP countries. In R. J. Kosky, H. S. Eshkavari, R. D. Goldney & R. Hassan (Eds.), *Suicide Prevention* (pp. 293–297). New York: Plenum Press.

Farberow, N. L. (1998). Shame and guilt in suicide and survivors. In D. De Leo, A. Schmidtke, & R. F. W. Diekstra (Eds.), *Suicide prevention* (pp. 153–162). Dordrecht, The Netherlands: Kluwer.

Feldman, D. (1987) A social work student's reaction to client suicide. *Social Casework, 68,* 184–187.

Freud, S. (1957). Mourning and melancholia. *Complete psychological works.* (standard ed., Vol. 14) (James Strachey, trans.). London, Hogarth Press. (Original work published 1917)

Furman, E. (1974). *A child's parent dies.* New York: Yale University Press.

Goldstein, L. S., & Buongiorno, P. (1984). Psychotherapists as suicide survivors. *American Journal of Psychotherapy, 38*, 392–398.

Gorkin, M. (1985). On the suicide of one's patient. *Bulletin of the Menninger Clinic, 49*, 1–9.

Hajal, F. (1977). Post-suicide grief work in family therapy. *Journal of Marriage and Family Counseling, 3*(2), 35–42.

Hamel-Bissell, B. P. (1985). Suicidal casework. *Journal of Psychosocial Nursing, 23*(10), 20–23

Hatton, C. L., & Valente, S. M. (1981). Bereavement group for parents who suffered a suicidal loss of a child. *Suicide and Life-Threatening Behavior, 11*, 141–150.

Heilig, S. M. (1985). Survey of 41 survivor groups. In R. Cohen-Sandler (Ed.), *Proceedings of the 19th Annual Meeting of the American Association of Suicidology* (pp. 110–113). Denver, CO: AAS.

Holden, L. D. (1978). Therapist response to patient suicide. *Journal of Continuing Education in Psychiatry, 39*(5), 23–32.

Horn, P. J. (1994). Therapists' psychological adaptation to client suicide. *Psychotherapy, 31*, 190–195.

Jakab, I., & Howard, M. C. (1969). Art therapy with a 12 year old girl who witnessed suicide and developed school phobia. *Psychotherapy and Psychosomatics, 17*, 309–324.

Johnson, B. M. (1973). Psychological services for relatives of suicide victims. In N. Speyer, R. F. W. K. Diekstra, & K. van de Loo (Eds.), *Proceedings of the 7th International Conference for Suicide Prevention* (pp. 372–375). Amsterdam: Swets & Zeitlinger.

Jones, F. A. (1987). Therapists as survivors of client suicide. In E. J. Dunne, J. L. McIntosh, & K. Dunne-Maxim (Eds.), *The aftermath of suicide* (pp. 126–141). New York: Norton.

Kahne, M. J. (1968). Suicide among patients in mental hospitals. *Psychiatry, 31*, 32–49.

Kleespies, P. M., Penk, W. E., & Forsyth, J. P. (1993). The stress of patient suicidal behavior during clinical training. *Professional Psychology, 24*, 293–303.

Kleespies, P. M., Smith, M. R., & Becker, B. R. (1990). Psychology interns as patient suicide survivors. *Professional Psychology, 21*, 257–263.

Knudson, G. (1987). L.O.S.S. In R. I. Yufit (Ed.), *Proceedings of the 20th Annual Conference of the American Association of Suicidology* (pp. 224–225). Denver, CO: AAS.

Kolodny, S., Binder, R. L., Bronstein, A. A., & Friend, R. L. (1979). The working through of patients' suicide by four therapists. *Suicide and Life-Threatening Behavior, 9*, 33–46.

Lapp, G. E. (1986). Therapists' response to client suicide. *Dissertation Abstracts International, 47*, 2622B.

Leonhardi, M., Maria, V., & Callahan, J. (1988). Guilt and anger after suicide. In D. Lester (Ed.), *Suicide '88* (pp. 99–100). Denver, CO: AAS.

Lester, D. (1990). Surviving a suicide. In A. Kutscher, S. Bess, S. G. Klagsbrun, M. E. Siegel, D. J. Cherico, L. G. Kutscher, D. Peretz, & F. Selder (Eds.), *For the bereaved* (pp. 52–55). Philadelphia: Charles Press.

Lindemann E., Vaughan, W. T., & McGinnis, M. (1972). Preventive intervention in a four-year-old child whose father committed suicide. In G. Caplan (Ed.), *Emotional problems of early childhood* (pp. 5–30). New York: Basic Books.

Litman, R. E. (1965). When patients commit suicide. *American Journal of Psychotherapy, 19*, 570–576

Lynd, J. G. (1975). Helping survivors with the impact of suicide through grief counseling. In B. S. Comstock & R. Maris (Eds.), *Proceedings of the 8th Annual Meeting of the American Association of Suicidology* (pp. 33–35). Denver, CO: AAS.

McIntosh, J. L. (1987). Survivor family relationships. In E. J. Dunne, J. L. McIntosh, & K. Dunne-Maxim (Eds.), *Suicide and its aftermath* (pp. 73–84). New York: Norton.

McIntosh, J. L., & Kelley, L. D. (1992). Survivors' reactions. *Crisis, 13*, 82–93.

Miller, S. (1985). *The shame experience.* Hillsdale, NJ: Lawrence Erlbaum.

Moritz, G. (1986). Bereaved family members of suicide victims. In R. Cohen-Sandler (Ed.), *Pro-*

ceedings of the 19th Annual Meeting of the American Association of Suicidology (pp. 133–135). Denver, CO: AAS.

Moritz, B., Van Ness, H. & Brouwer, W. (1989). The professional helper as a concerned party in suicide cases. In R. F. W. Diekstra, R. Maris, S. Platt, A. Schmidtke, & G. Sonneck (Eds.), *Suicide and its prevention* (pp. 211–226). Leiden: Brill.

Nagy, M. H. (1959a). The child's theories concerning death. *Journal of Genetic Psychology, 73,* 3–27.

Nagy, M. H. (1959b). The child's view of death. In H. Feifel (Ed.), *The meaning of death* (pp. 79–88). New York: McGraw Hill.

Peretz, D. (1990). Understanding your mourning: A psychiatrist's view. In A. Kutscher, S. Bess, S. G. Klagsbrun, M. E. Siegel, D. J. Cherico, L. G. Kutscher, D. Peretz, & F. Selden (Eds.), *For the bereaved* (pp. 24–36). Philadelphia: Charles Press.

Rando, T. A. (1984). Grief after suicide. In T. A. Rando (Ed.), *Grief, dying, and death* (pp. 149–153). Champaign, IL: Research Press.

Rogers, J., Sheldon, A., Barwick, C., Letofsky, K., & Lancee, W. (1982). Help for families of suicide: Survivors support program. *Canadian Journal of Psychiatry, 27,* 444–449.

Rosenfeld, L. (1987). Left to live: Mourning in a group. In R. I. Yufit (Ed.), *Proceedings of the 20th Annual Conference of the American Association of Suicidology* (pp. 226–228). Denver, CO: AAS.

Ross, E. (1997). *Life after suicide.* New York: Plenum.

Sacks, M. H., Kibel, H. D., Cohen, A. M., Keats, M., & Turnquist, K. N. (1987). Resident response to patient suicide. *Journal of Psychiatric Education, 11,* 217–226.

Sanders, C. M. (1984). Therapists, too, need to grieve. *Death Education, 8,* 27–35.

Schuyler, D. (1973). Counseling suicide survivors. *Omega, 4,* 313–321.

Silverman, P. R., & Worden, J. W.(1993). Children's reactions to the death of a parent. In M. S. Stroebe, W. Stroebe, & R. O. Hamson (Eds.), *Handbook of bereavement* (pp. 300–316). Cambridge, MA: Press Syndicate of the University of Cambridge.

Valente, S. M. (1994). Psychotherapist reactions to the suicide of a patient. *American Journal of Orthopsychiatry, 24,* 614–621.

Van der Wal, J., & Diekstra, R. F. W. (1987). Grief reactions of survivors of suicide: Results of a sample survey. In R. I. Yufit (Ed.), *Proceedings of the 20th Annual Conference of the American Association of Suicidology* (pp. 222–223). Denver, CO: AAS.

Van Dongen, C. J. (1990). Agonizing questioning. *Nursing Research, 39,* 224–229.

Wallerstein, R. S. (1972). Reconstruction and mastery in the transference of psychosis. In. A. C. Cain (Ed.), *Survivors of suicide* (pp. 242–255). Springfield, IL: Charles C. Thomas.

Webb, N. (1993). *Helping bereaved children.* New York: Guilford.

Weber-Slepicka C. (1985). Survivors of suicide more than just a monthly meeting. In R. Cohen-Sandler (Ed.), *Proceedings of the 18th Annual Meeting of the American Association of Suicide* (pp. 117–119). Toronto, Canada: AAS.

Whitis, P. R., (1968). The legacy of a child's suicide. *Family Process, 7,* 159–169.

Wolfenstein, M. (1966). How is mourning possible? Psychoanalytic Study of the *Child, 21,* 93–123.

Worden, J. W. (1991). *Grief counseling and grief therapy* (2nd ed.). New York: Springer.

Wrobleski, A. (1983). Suicide survivors grief group. In C. Vorkoper & K. Smith (Eds.), *Proceedings of the 16th Annual Meeting of the American Association of Suicidology* (pp. 67–68). Denver, CO: AAS.

CHAPTER

Antoon A. Leenaars

Suicide Prevention in Schools: Resources for the Millennium

Childhood and adolescent problems in adjustment have been an increasing concern in this century. In 1910, Sigmund Freud and his colleagues identified numerous adjustment problems in youth. By the 1960s, up to 30% of youth were identified as displaying some maladjustment (Glidewell & Swallow, 1969), with current rates being even higher, and about 1–3% being serious (Durlak, 1995). Schools are natural environments to address these problems through prevention programs.

Youth, in most parts of the world, attend school. Schools are institutions designed to aid in the child's development and to address the problems of children and youth. There are numerous programs to address these problems, e.g., health, sex and AIDS education, suicide prevention, drinking and driving, substance abuse, and violence programs. There are also programs to address academic needs and to promote personal and social growth. There are numerous reasons for these efforts, primarily because our health care systems alone cannot meet all the needs (Durlak, 1995). Kazdin (1990) estimates that only 10–30% of youth currently receive needed mental health care—and that is only in the developed world. It is likely that this lack in services will not disappear, requiring schools and their communities to respond even more in this next millennium.

Suicide is a major mental health and public health problem worldwide (Diekstra, 1996). Adolescents and even children commit suicide (Pfeffer, 1986). An even greater number of youth attempt or seriously think about suicide as the solution to their life's difficulties (Berman & Jobes, 1991). As was stated at the turn of this century (Friedman, 1910/1967), schools and communities must respond (Leenaars & Wenckstern, 1990b). The current mental health systems are so strained—and in some areas, nonexistent—that schools and communities must assist now, and even more so in the future.

Our intent here is to provide an overview of the suicide problem and the needs for the future, to provide an outline for a comprehensive model to address the

213

problems for the millennium, and finally to isolate some issues and pitfalls in what is being done in the present. Hopefully, in the future, we will not continue to commit the same errors as in the past. Yet, before we give a current and future perspective, let us go back in history some 90 years.

☐ A Historical Perspective

[A school] should give them [students] a desire to live and should offer them support and backing at a time of life at which the conditions of their development compel them to relax their ties with their parental home and their family. It seems to me indisputable that schools fail in this, and in many respects fall short of their duty of providing a substitute for the family and of arousing interest in life from the world outside. (S. Freud, Vienna, June 26, 1910) (Friedman, 1910/1967, p. 61)

These observations were some of Sigmund Freud's suggestions for suicide prevention in schools at the monumental symposium on suicide almost 90 years ago (Friedman, 1967). The comment is as relevant for us today and in the future, as it was then. It is within this context that we reflect on the meeting in 1910 that took place in Freud's home in Vienna. It was, in fact, the first formal statement on suicide prevention in schools. At that meeting, David Ernest Oppenheim represented the field of education and believed that:

If, since it [suicide] is the negation of the strongest of all human instincts, that of self-preservation, suicide is always anomalous; it is even more so when the suicide takes place in childhood, since we believe that youth combines an undiminished life force with an indestructible will to live (Friedman, 1967, p. 34).

In part, Oppenheim was reflecting on the tragic increase in suicide in 1910 in Vienna (Friedman, 1910/1967). Suicide in youth at that time was even sometimes called "student suicide," a situation that repeats itself today in much of the developed world. Oppenheim wondered whether "the school will be burdened with the blame for this sad event?" He quickly showed, even then, that suicide is a multidimensional malaise. He stated that "our schools are not the only force that drives young people to suicide." Rather, he looked at what schools can do to help. He said "If a teacher is given the necessary clues, he may be able to do a great deal to protect an overstimulated boy from a desperate act" (Friedman, 1910/1967, p. 51).

As an example of such education, he suggested that teachers should be informed about clusters. He promoted education about contagion saying, "every suicide, no matter how it is carried out, lures others to precise imitations." Indeed, he leads one to conclude that postvention in schools is necessary to address such a phenomenon and he even proposes something echoed today, that "newspapers confine(d) themselves to brief reports."

He proposed that fruitful cooperation be established between the school, home, and community to assist youth. Prophylactic measures should be avoided; rather, sound measures are needed. For example, he said "much could be gained if we tried to make suicide more difficult for the potential candidate." Oppenheim proposed that schools support the restriction of the availability of weapons (such as handguns) to prevent suicide. Oppenheim, in the end of his presentation, also looked to Freud, Stekel, Adler, and others to assist (intervene) with suicidal young people. Oppenheim, thus, advocated a multidimensional approach for prevention in schools; yet, little was done until the 1980s.

What do we need to do—more than 90 years later—about suicide and schools? What resources for the millennium are needed in our schools and communities?

☐ Suicide Prevention Is an Art

Suicide prevention is an art, not a technology. All too frequently, however, individuals respond to the suicidal malaise in our schools without an adequate understanding of this mental and public health problem and without a prearranged comprehensive plan of action (Leenaars & Wenckstern, 1990b; Satcher, 1998). In such a case, it may be better that nothing is done, that childhood and adolescent problems be left alone, and that schools do nothing. Schools, in such situations, may actually impede youth development and even promote suicide (Center for Disease Control, 1988). However, if one accepts the complexity of suicide and adjustment in general, only then, as was already documented at the turn of the 20th Century (Friedman, 1910/1967), schools should actively play a role in the prevention of suicide.

The rationale for beginning such a comprehensive suicide prevention program in schools includes the following:

1. The sheer number of suicides and suicidal behaviors in youth worldwide.
2. The large number of unhappy—many depressed—youth. Depression is common in young suicidal people. Dissembling is a problem. Kazdin (1990) reported that only 10–30% of youth needing clinical help, receive that care. It can, therefore, be asked: How many depressed and suicidal youth are not identified?
3. Schools are asking for assistance. Therefore, it would be appropriate that those most knowledgeable (psychiatrists, psychologists, crisis workers, educators, etc.) assist.
4. The survivors (significant others) of suicide are often in distress. All too many youth in our schools are traumatized by the suicide of their peers, something I first noted in a clinical case in 1980 (Leenaars, 1985).

There is a rationale for suicide prevention. The important question is not that we do it, but how we do it.

It was these and other facts that led to the establishment of a response in schools in the 1980s. Charlotte Ross (1985) is often credited with the first systemic efforts in these prevention endeavors. The first book was *Suicide Prevention in Schools*, edited by myself and Susanne Wenckstern (1990). This edited volume is still the only comprehensive text in the field. It brought together, in the 1980s, experts in school suicide prevention—a sort of recapitulation of the 1910 discussion on the topic in Freud's home. The 1990 volume, however, needs an update for the future if it is to assist in the schools in 2000 and beyond.

☐ Prevention/Intervention/Postvention

The classical approach to the prevention of mental health and public health problems is that of Caplan (1964), who differentiated primary, secondary, and tertiary prevention. The more commonly used concepts for these three modes of prevention are prevention, intervention, and postvention, respectively. Oppenheim, in fact, had argued for such diversity 90 years ago and the book, *Suicide Prevention in Schools*, is based on this model (Friedman, 1910/1967). All three modes of response have a place in helping the suicidal child and adolescent in a reasonably prudent fashion in the present and in the future. Caplan's view still provides the best model for addressing suicide in schools for this century.

Prevention relates to the principle of good mental hygiene in general. It consists of strategies to ameliorate the conditions that lead to suicide—to do something before the event occurs. Preventing suicide is best accomplished through primary prevention. Prevention is education. Young people (and their gatekeepers) must be educated about suicide. Such education—given that suicide is a multidimensional malaise—is enormously complicated, almost tantamount to preventing human misery.

In *Suicide Prevention in Schools*, chapters by Ronald Dyck, Cathie Stivers, Linda Sattem, Roger Tierney, Diane Ryerson, and James Overholser presented the state of the art in the 1980s. Topics included system entry issues, promotion of self-esteem, programs for elementary schools, the need for comprehensive programs, issues of modification for special populations, and observations about sex differences in the response to programs.

Intervention relates to the treatment and care of a suicidal crisis or suicidal problem. Secondary prevention is doing something during the event. Suicide is an event with biological (including biochemical), neuropsychological, sociocultural, interpersonal, psychological, and philosophical and existential aspects. Obviously, suicide is not solely a medical problem, and many people can serve as lifesaving agents. Nonetheless, professionally trained people, psychologists, psychiatrists, social workers, psychiatric nurses, crisis workers, and so on continue to play the primary roles in intervention. Although equally true for postvention, intervention in schools will call for the development of community linkages, a hallmark of a public health response.

In *Suicide Prevention in Schools*, chapters by Lee Ann Hoff, Kim Smith, James Eyman and Joseph Richman presented the state of the art in intervention. Topics included a model for crisis intervention, therapeutic care of students, transference and countertransference issues, and an outline for family therapy with young people and their families.

Postvention, a term introduced by Shneidman (1973), refers to those things done after the event has occurred. Postvention deals with the traumatic afteref-fects in the survivors of a person who has committed suicide (or in those close to someone who has attempted suicide). It involves offering mental health and pub-lic health services to the bereaved survivors. It includes working with all survivors who are in need—children, parents, teachers, and so forth.. School systems, as we stated initially, are an especially critical force in these endeavors.

Chapters in *Suicide Prevention in Schools* by Antoon Leenaars, Susanne Wenckstern, Bonnie Frank Carter, and Karen Dunne-Maxim included a posttrau-matic stress model, illustrations of postvention in schools, an outline for clinical opportunities, and common issues facing postvention in schools and communi-ties.

The book, however, went beyond presenting the current state of the art and provided an array of critical reflections on the topic by John Kalafat, Alan Berman, and Antoon Leenaars. These authors called for critical reflection and research, things that are still urgently needed for the future.

Next, we outline in some detail some myths, issues, and pitfalls in each preven-tion endeavor. Hopefully, it will stimulate ongoing discussion on the issues for the future.

Prevention

Prevention relates to the principle of good mental hygiene in general. In schools, this means education. This is in keeping with the general aims of schools, namely to educate our youth.

A current popular formulation regarding suicide is that suicide is simply due to an external event or stress such as a rejection by a friend or the influence of a popular singer. Although there is always a situational factor in each suicide, there is much more. We are here reminded of a clinical example. A 16-year old was found dead in a car, having died of carbon monoxide poisoning. People were per-plexed. Why did this young person, from an upper middle class family, kill him-self? The parents found out that his girlfriend rejected him the day of his suicide. That was the reason—when a young person gets rejected and is so in love, he may kill himself. A few friends and his teachers knew that he had been having prob-lems in school, and that was the reason. A few others knew that his father was an alcoholic and abusive. That, too, was the reason. His physician knew that he had been adopted and had been recently upset about that. So she knew the real rea-son. And so on.

The youth himself or herself is equally often blinded by a single event. Here we are speaking about lethal suicidal people. The teenager who is about to put a bul-let through his head with his father's gun or the teenager who is about to take her mother's prescription pills, at the moment of decision, may be the least aware of the essence of the reasons for doing so. The adolescent's conscious perception is a critical aspect. Yet, to simply accept that perspective is not only simplistic, but may well be suicidogenic (iatrogenic, destructive). The pain simply makes it impossible for the young person to give a complete and accurate recitation of the event. Suicide is complex, more complicated than the child's or adolescent's conscious mind is aware.

Regrettably all too often, adults—including parents, teachers, medical doctors, psychologists—are willing to share in the misconception. Misconceptions are, in fact, rife. This has gone as far as some stating that "suicide is normal." Suicide is *not* normal. It is an indication of major pathology (King, 1997). To have stated otherwise—as occurred in the late 1970s and 1980s—was not only a pitfall but also a disservice to prevention efforts. We must continue to address the complexity of suicide in youth in the future.

Here are a few more current misconceptions and our response to each of them:

Suicide prevention has no place in schools. Suicide prevention is a system entry issue, a common concern, highlighting the need to begin the entry and development of such programs with administration, followed by school staff and other individuals involved. Dyck (1990) has noted the following:

> Some Departments of Education, school boards, and even individual school administrations have resisted the introduction of these programs in schools for a variety of reasons, some based more on myth than fact, and others that are legitimate and should be given serious and careful consideration (p. 48).

Strategies for school entry include: mandatory prevention programs through government legislation, introduction through particular school boards, and, although least effective, entry through a local school. It is, however, the clinicians and professionals who wish to gain entry, who must develop our skill before gaining access. Such skills include credibility, suicide prevention training, participation in education, conferences, research, and so forth. Regrettably, there are many individuals with limited training and skills who are attempting to gain entry into schools, some of whom have been suicidogenic themselves.

Talking about suicide will cause suicide. This is a myth. Of course, sensationalism will cause sensationalism. The issue is not *that* we talk about suicide, but *how* we talk about suicide. Sound discussion will facilitate openness of a suicidal person, leading to intervention. Talking about suicide and all problems can lead to improving many mental health and community skills, raising self-esteem, reducing school failure, increasing self-control, and reducing depression, for all youth.

Programs are not cost effective. We believe that programs are cost effective, provided one has a clear and distinct understanding of the purpose. Prevention is intended to educate—about clues, available resources, and other factors.. They are not intended to be intervention. Furthermore, such programs can generate mental health strategies, even in low risk people.

Schools can be sued if they have a program. On the contrary, the staff at schools must act in a prudent and competent fashion. We believe not having a program actually opens the schools to liability concerns.

In America, for example, the Secretary's Task Force on Youth Suicide (U.S. Department of Health and Human Services, 1989) noted that schools offer an excellent opportunity for reaching a large number of young people. The Task Force concluded that schools have an important role in addressing problems of youth. Indeed, we would go further and state that staff in schools must act as "reasonably prudent persons" (Leenaars & Wenckstern, 1996). The decision of the U.S. Ninth Circuit Court of Appeals in Kelson versus the City of Springfield, 1985, supports this view, a decision that continues to be applicable for the future. In that case, the parents of a 14-year-old boy sued the school for negligence, complaining that the school had a duty to provide training in suicide prevention and that the school had failed to do so. The case was deemed to be admissible in court because the court (although settlement was finally made out of court) held that a person may bring action against a school for nonprudent behavior. This is equally true around the world. We have consulted in a case where school administrators allowed a special "Nerd Day"—an American/Canadian euphemism for a socially awkward individual—that resulted in significant abuse of a few individuals and, we believe, significant stress in one individual, within the context of that person's life, to contribute to his suicidal solution. That boy attempted to kill himself at the school that day, only surviving because of quick medical response. Is allowing Nerd Day prudent behavior by the school?

A last myth is that programs *lead to contagion*. The issue of contagions arises because, since Goethe (1774/1951) in the 1700s published *The Sorrows of Young Werther*, there have been reports that talking about suicide causes suicide. Oppenheim made note of it. Phillips (1974) was one of the first in this century to document the impact of media reporting on suicide rates—but that finding was limited to sensational media stories only. It is now a well established fact that reports about celebrities in print and electronic media that are multimodal, repeated, explicit and front page, and that glorify the suicide lead to an increase of suicide (Martin, 1998). Yet, reports in the media are not equivalent to prevention programs. Indeed, with regard to prevention programs, there is no sound data to show that a Werther (contagion) effect was caused by an education program.

We write "sound" above because unsound research, for example, by Shaffer and his colleagues (Shaffer, Garland, Viland, Rojas, Underwood, & Busner, 1990) left the following message in the press worldwide: School suicide prevention programs may be dangerous. The message "massaged" the world (McLuhan & Fiore, 1967)—including many school jurisdictions and politicians around the world. Programs were banned in the 1990s. This is unfortunate because Shaffer did not show that suicide prevention programs are dangerous. All that he showed was that a few males who had previously attempted suicide thought that their friends would not like the program. This is to be expected, because as Clark (1991) noted, "psychologically impaired persons don't like to be confronted with their shortcomings in public" (p. 1).

Shaffer's study had numerous shortcomings (see, for example, Tierney & Lang, 1995), including the following:

1. Shaffer et al. studied only two programs. Is this representative? (A third program was deleted. Why?)

2. Measurement was problematic. Kappa coefficients of .22 to .51 are reported, indicating low reliability.
3. The instruments were self-reports, open to doubts about the validity of the measures. (Should suicidal youth be the basis for evaluating their own risk?)
4. Shaffer et al. based their conclusion on two observations: attitudes were not changed positively and negative views were recorded by a small number of attempters. What about students in general? Are attitudes the best measure? Is suicidal behavior a better measure?
5. Pre- and posttesting resulted in different data. (What does this say?)

Shaffer et al. concluded, however, that there were negative reactions to school programs and reports circulated that suicide prevention in schools did not help suicidal people. Of course, (primary) prevention was never intended to address intervention. Shaffer (1991) was confronted about the shortcomings of his research and the media message at the conference of the American Association of Suicidology in Boston in April of 1991. Shaffer confirmed that his research was problematic and not conclusive on programs in schools. He also stated that he did not support the behavior of the press when it reported his study. But the sensational press stories had already had a significant impact in the slowing of school programs in America, Australia, and elsewhere. The Werther effect was "proved," now about suicide prevention.

Sound research (e.g., Eggert, Thompson, Herting, & Nicholas, 1995; Kalafat & Elias, 1994) has, in fact shown that prevention helps. However, further study is needed in this century.

Intervention

Intervention relates to the treatment and care of a suicidal crisis or a suicidal problem. Many people, including those in schools, can serve as life-saving agents. Nonetheless, professionally-trained people, often outside the schools, continue to play the primary roles in intervention.

Misconceptions are rife today, not only about suicide, but also about treatment of suicidal people. Often there are overly simplistic solutions. In part, this is an outcome of the myth that suicide is due only to stress. Even in youth, the common consistency in suicide and suicidal behavior is not the precipitating event but rather life-long coping patterns (Shneidman, 1985). Suicidal youth are unable to cope with the demands of life. Their pain is unbearable, and suicide becomes a solution. The ego has been weakened, and so forth. Therefore, the mere focus on suicide as a result of stress grossly underestimates the pathology that these young people face (King, 1997) and is actually instrumental in the subsequent lack of help that they receive. The truth is that these young people need long-term help, often of a multifaceted nature, not short-term counseling and other simplistic solutions. We must avoid such reductionistic misconceptions.

Some of the current simplicity in the intervention in schools has, in fact, been absurd. Here are a few samples of actual guidelines in a school that are not only absurd, but iatrogenic: Remove the student from the group or activity until he or she can demonstrate appropriate behavior and self-control, and avoid discussion or prevent stimuli in the environment that remind the student of unpleasant experiences or sensations (e.g., divorce, death, unemployment, alcoholism).

Although professionals (e.g., psychiatrists, psychologists) have a central role in the treatment of suicidal youth, others have an equally valuable role. Parents, in fact, have and will continue to have a critical contribution (if on the side of life) (Richman, 1990). Not only should parents be included in our interventions, but also siblings, friends, teachers, priests, elders, doctors—anyone who serves, directly or indirectly, to nullify the pain.

It is worth noting that the search for a singular universal simplistic response to suicide in youth is a chimera, an imaginary and nonexistent conceptual fabrication. Only prescribing medication as a cure-all is, for example, such a chimera. The search for a simplistic response is a foolish and unrealistic fancy. There is no cookbook!

To illustrate, here are three examples of such current 'cookbook' fabrications and a response

Suicide and suicidal behavior is easy to predict. Response: The statistical rarity of suicide and the imperfection of the prediction instruments lead to an enormously large number of false positives, so many in fact that prediction instruments are of limited use to clinicians. The National Institute of Mental Health (NIMH) in the United States evaluated the area of suicide prediction and assessment (Lewinsohn, Garrison, Langhinrichsen, & Marsteller, 1989) and they concluded that few, if any of the tests, are useful.

"No Suicide" contracts are the best tool for prevention. The use of "No Suicide" contracts has come under increasing scrutiny. Often, these are simplistic written contracts. There is an over-reliance on them, especially in schools with little, if any, evidence for contracts' utility. Frequently, they are used more to reduce the therapist's own anxiety than for their clinical value. Suicide contracts cannot be an alternative to sound treatment. In a court of law, there are no substitutes for sound and prudent behavior. Gutheil, a forensic lawyer (Brown, Berman, Gutheil, Leenaars, & Moore, 1989) notes that legally, contracts are meaningless. (Of course, we do not mean that verbal contracting, such as "If you are suicidal, will you call me?" has no utility, only the simplistic use of them, which is not what Drye, Goulding, & Goulding [1973] intended when they introduced the concept years ago.)

Peer counseling, especially because teens prefer to talk to teens, is the best mode of treatment. This is a deadly error now and for the future. We are not suggesting that peer groups have no utility, only that they do not address the need of truly suicidal young people (King, 1997; Leenaars, 1990). Peer counseling is not treatment or psychotherapy. There is no research to suggest that peer counselors can provide the therapeutic care that suicidal youths need. On the other hand, a peer, teacher, guidance counselor, or minister, among others, may assist in the identification of a suicidal individual and provide support. However, they must refer the adolescent to a professional for care. The fact that teenagers prefer to talk to teenagers is no justification to follow their wishes, often defensive ones. The defense is an expression of the magnitude of the pain and the inability to cope with it.

Treatment of suicidal children and adolescents is complex and must be multi-faceted (Leenaars, Maltsberger, & Neimeyer, 1994). Treatment obviously embraces many people beyond school staff and may include, but is not limited to the following: assessment, crisis intervention, psychotherapy, family therapy, psychopharmacotherapy and hospitalization. There is no simple tactic for the future.

By definition, intervention efforts with suicidal youth involve the evaluation and management of a crisis situation. Many mental health and public health professionals must be called on to serve as life-saving agents. Suicide risk assessment is one of the most challenging tasks they face (Leenaars, 1995; Maltsberger, 1986; Maris, Berman, Maltsberger, & Yufit, 1992). Intervention rests on sound assessment. Crisis intervention, whether performed by crisis-line staff or by mental health professionals, should provide an immediate and informed response to a suicidal child or teen through the use of a systematic process of crisis definition and problem resolution (Hoff, 1984, 1990; Leenaars, 1994; Leenaars & Wenckstern, 1994; Shneidman, 1981a).

Once a youth is no longer in an acute suicidal crisis, a diversity of psychotherapeutic approaches can be used, depending on the child's or adolescent's unique requirements (Berman & Jobes, 1991, 1994; Eyman, 1990; Pfeffer, 1986; Smith, 1990; Zimmerman, Grosz, & Asnis, 1995). It is a truism that the suicidal person is in deep pain. Therefore, as a rule, suicidal youth need psychotherapy to make their unbearable pain more bearable and to prompt them toward long-term solutions to life's demands. In choosing among the range of specialized treatment formats and approaches now available, the clinician must give special consideration to an array of patient factors: developmental age, sex, health status, cultural issues, and more (Leenaars, Maris, & Takahashi, 1997).

Although suicidal pain in youth is often readily amenable to psychotherapeutic influences, medication and hospitalization should not be eschewed in the future by any competent mental health professional in our schools with high-risk youth. Today we know that suicide is multidetermined. Many factors, including biogenetic factors, may contribute to elevated risk. Medication (Slaby, 1994) may be essential in some cases, as is hospitalization during periods of acute perturbation or heightened lethality (Goldblatt, 1994; Sederer, 1994). Yet, both medication and hospitalization can add complications to the treatment of suicidal youth. Although the safety needs of a suicidal patient are of utmost importance, the decision to admit a suicidal child or teen to hospital is often difficult and vexing, especially in this era of decreased resources.

Regardless of the treatment model or format used, certain clinical, legal, and ethical issues confront the person working with the suicidal patient, some unique to youth in our schools (Bongar, 1991; Bongar & Greany, 1994). There is a need for clear guidelines for assessment and intervention in schools. Legally and ethically, the professional must act in a reasonable and prudent fashion. However, clinically, calculated risk with young people must be taken (Maltsberger, 1994). For example, discharge of a teen from an inpatient setting to a school is therapeutically desirable for some suicidal youth, while for others it is not. At times, the return to a home or school can be problematic. Nonetheless, economic factors are now making prolonged care almost impossible for most people, even in developed countries. These economic factors will likely continue to impact on our response to suicide. Regardless, school and mental health professionals must not compromise the standards of care that they provide.

Here are a few further considerations that were derived from discussions with Edwin Shneidman (personal communication, June 29–30, 1991; for details, see Shneidman, 1981a, 1985).

1. *Monitoring*. A continuous, preferably daily, monitoring of the child's or adolescent's lethality should occur.
2. *Consultation*. There is almost no instance in a therapist's professional life when consultation with a peer is as important as when he or she is dealing with a highly suicidal youth. The items to be discussed might include the therapist's treatment of the case; his or her own feelings of frustration, helplessness, or even anger; his or her countertransference reactions generally; the advisability of hospitalization for the child or adolescent, and so forth.
3. *Hospitalization*. Hospitalization is always a complicating event in the treatment of a suicidal adolescent but it should not, on those grounds, be eschewed. Obviously, the quality of care—from doctors, nurses, and others—is crucial.
4. *Transference*. As in almost no other therapeutic situation and at almost no other time in therapy, the successful treatment of a highly suicidal person depends heavily on the transference. The therapist can be active, show his or her personal concern, increase the frequency of the sessions, invoke the "magic" of the unique therapist-adolescent relationship, be less of a tabula rasa and give "transfusions" of (realistic) hope and succorance.
5. *Confidentiality*. Careful modification of the usual canons of confidentiality may have to happen. Admittedly, this is a touchy and complicated point, but the therapist should not ally himself or herself with death. Statements given during the therapy session relating to the youth's overt suicidal (or homicidal) plans obviously cannot be treated as a secret between two collusive partners.

Research on intervention in general is sparse (Leenaars et al., 1997; McLeavey, Daly, Ludgate, & Murray, 1994) and nonexistent in youth. This state of affairs in suicidology resulted in Leenaars et al. (1997) stating: "The future of research will have to include careful intervention studies, treatment research and controlled psychotherapeutic and psychopharmacological trials" (p. 148). Studies of intervention are urgently needed in the future to not only lend credibility to the field, but also to determine cost-effective responses.

Despite the lack of research, there is one empirically supported tactic that has been shown to be useful, especially in youth (Brent, Perper, Allmen, Moritz, Wartella, & Zelenah, 1991; Leenaars & Lester, 1997). These studies show that restricting the availability of lethal means, for example, gun control, is effective at preventing suicides.

The highly suicidal youth wants to egress, to escape, to be gone. It follows that, when possible, the means of exit should be blocked. A practical application of this view is to "get the gun" in a suicidal situation when it is known that the individual intends to shoot him- or herself and has a weapon. The explosive situation of an at-risk youth needs to be defused until that person no longer has the need for a suicidal weapon. The same principle applies to any method, e.g., medications. Maltsberger's words on consultation (Berman, 1990) apply to this situation too. "I would consult as much to avoid charges of negligence as to deal with my own anxiety. I think that any time I get into a difficult case, where I am concerned that somebody is imminently suicidal . . . I would want to be careful. It is enormously helpful to ask a colleague to help to monitor one's own judgment when in a tense, anxiety-provoking situation" (cited in Berman, 1990, p. 118). The same approach can be used for method restriction, media control, and so forth. (Leenaars, Deleo, Goldney, Gulbinat, & Wallace, 1998). However, research (Wisler, Grossman, Kreusi, Fendrick, Franke, & Ignatowicz, 1998) shows that few clinicians use such efforts in their crisis response to teens at risk. Greater emphasis, as a practical suggestion, on educating parents, teachers, and others with regards to means restriction, in emergency wards, guidance offices, and doctors' offices is needed for the millennium.

Postvention

Postvention refers to those things done after a suicide or any trauma has occurred (Shneidman, 1981b). Postvention deals with the traumatic aftereffects in the survivors. School systems, within the context of their communities, are an especially critical force in such endeavors with our children and teens (Center for Disease Control, 1988).

Leenaars (1985, see also Leenaars & Wenckstern, 1990b, 1998) provided one of the first conceptual models for postvention in schools in the literature in this century, namely one of an acute stress and posttraumatic stress perspective. Suicide is a trauma for the survivors (Leenaars & Wenckstern, 1990a), a view supported by research (Gleser, Green, & Wignet, 1981; Horowitz, 1979; Wilson, Smith, & Johnson, 1985). Freud, (1917/1974), already noted that loss of a significant other (related primarily to attachment) results in a traumatic response with special symptoms of depression. Indeed, from his clinical records, Freud had noted that the greater the degree of trauma, the greater the stress. This is especially true for suicide since there is almost no other death in our society for which there is a higher social (and often personal dynamic) stigma for the survivors. Thus, it is heuristic to view the event from the acute stress and posttraumatic stress framework.

There are victims of many and diverse traumatic events (Janoff-Bulman, 1985), including suicide (Leenaars, 1985), although there are common psychological experiences in trauma. Recognition of the commonalities had been furthered, over a decade ago, by the American Psychiatric Association's (APA's) DSM-III (APA, 1980). In that diagnostic manual, there was a new classification—Post-traumatic Stress Disorder (PTSD)—that spells out characteristic symptoms that may follow "a psychologically traumatic event that is generally outside the range of usual human experience." PTSD was first associated in 1900s with the trauma of military combat, particularly the victims of the Vietnam War (Figley, 1978, p. xix). However, as Janoff-Bulman (1985) points out, PTSD can be equally associated with other traumatic events such as serious crimes, homicide, accidents, and disasters. Suicide is clearly outside the usual human experience and, indeed, evokes "significant symptoms of distress in most people" (Leenaars, 1988; Shneidman, 1985). It is not simply a grief reaction; rather, it is a grief reaction and much more.

Traumatic stress response refers to those natural behaviors and emotions that occur during a catastrophe. Figley (1985) defined a posttraumatic stress response "as a set of conscious and unconscious behaviors and emotions associated with dealing with the memories of the stressors of the catastrophe and immediately afterwards." These are common aftershocks, and by no means do all or even most survivors exhibit the necessary characteristics of such a reaction to be labeled a disorder, i.e., PTSD (Figley, 1985). We intend here, rather, to use PTSD as a heuristic label since it best approximates the reaction in survivors of suicide and trauma in our schools and communities. In addition to the existence of a recognized stressor, symptoms of the aftershocks may include the following: reexperiencing of the trauma (e.g., recurrent recollection, recurrent dreams, associations that the event is recurring); numbing of responsiveness to a reduced involvement with external world (e.g., diminished interest, detachment, constricted affect); depression, grief, hyperalertness, sleep disturbance, survivor guilt, problems in memory or concentration, avoidance of events that evoke recall, and intensification of symptoms by events that symbolize events just to name a few of the various possible symptoms.

This is not meant to suggest that the realization of a posttraumatic reaction is new. In 1917, Freud (1917/1974) described what he called a psychical trauma; he saw this as a process started by a threatening situation that is acute and overwhelming. He described this as a developmental sequence to trauma. In 1985, Janoff-Bulman made the important observation that "much of the psychological trauma produced by victimizing events derives from the shattering of very basic assumptions that victims have held about the operation of the world." We all have constructs, a theory of the world, for example: "Johnny, the ten-year-old, doesn't kill himself." With a suicide, our view of the world may be shattered, resulting in possible PTSD. We have to cope with "Johnny killed himself."

Adjusting to a suicide and any trauma is remarkably difficult. Freud (1926/1974; 1939/1974) distinguished between positive and negative effects of trauma. He saw remembering, repeating, and reexperiencing as positive, which is opposite of the more typical denial approach. Forgetting, avoidance, phobia, and inhibition were described by Freud as negative. These are, however, common responses in many victims after a suicide (and other traumas), even in adults who are to guide our youngsters, such as principals and psychologists. A common response in the past and present is to deny it: "Don't talk about it; after all, talking about suicide causes suicide." We firmly believe, as has been so well-documented with Vietnam veterans, that this approach only exacerbates the trauma. However, as Wilson, Smith and Johnson (1985) have pointed out, it is important for us to see that the victims of a suicide may be caught in a no-win cycle of events. They note the following:

> To talk about the powerful and overwhelming trauma means risking further stigmatization; the failure to discuss the traumatic episode increases the need for defensive avoidance and thus increases the probability of depression alternating with cycles of intensive imagery and other symptoms of PTSD (p. 169).

We need to help survivors work the trauma through. We need to foster positive adjustive strategies in the future.

It should be noted that PTSD was initially intended for adults (APA, 1980). However, Eth and Pynoos (1985) have presented convincing arguments for applying PTSD to children and adolescents. They note that children of trauma have exhibited such symptoms as "deleterious effects on cognition (including memory, school performance, and learning), affect, interpersonal relations, impulse control, aggressive behavior, vegetative function, and the formulation of symptoms" (p. 41). Terr (1979) as well as Lifton and Olson (1976) have observed in classical studies of abducted children and in children surviving a disaster (e.g., Hiroshima) that there is a posttraumatic reaction. Indeed, there are amazing commonalities in how children respond to various unusual trauma (Leenaars & Wenckstern, 1990a). Bowlby (1977) has made a number of observations about traumatic reactions to loss. Most important, he notes, is anxious attachment behavior. Often children do not appear to be exhibiting a reaction dissembling (e.g., there are few recognizable overt verbalizations), but this may well be a negative reaction that could be fostered by an adult who also wants to deny the trauma. Years ago, Anna Freud (1966) noted that children often rely on various forms of denial, evident in fantasy, action, and affect, all to ease (numb) the pain. Alcohol and drug use are obvious examples in teens. In respect to such observations, the APA (1987) has clarified its definition to include children and teens.

Our outline above on reactions after a suicide has been more extensive than previous discussions in this chapter because, all too often in the field today, responders seem to minimize the psychological nature of acute stress and posttraumatic stress in young people. This is as true about their reaction to suicide, as it is about death and other traumas. This has been and continues to be a significant error. Indeed, the error is as pervasive as the normalizing of suicidal behavior in youth in prevention efforts. Equally, the response to suicide and trauma in schools must be complex, more complex than a simplistic one to three hours of group discussion. Postvention is multifaceted and takes a while—from several months to the end of life, but certainly more than three hours or six sessions.

PTSD work is multifaceted and we can offer here only a few highlights of such efforts. More comprehensive discussion of the strategies for postvention is presented elsewhere (Leenaars, 1985; Leenaars & Wenckstern, 1990a, 1996, 1998; Wenckstern & Leenaars, 1990, 1993). Here is a brief summary of essential aspects for the next decades:

Consultation

Discussion, coordination and planning are undertaken at every phase, beginning with school administration and then followed by school staff, and by other involved individuals, such as students and parents, under the direction of the postvention coordinator, that is, a mental health expert who takes charge and provides structure. Community personnel may need to be included during every sequence of the process, depending on the evaluation of the mild–moderate–severe level of the traumatic event (Goodstein, 1978). Concurrent peer consultation and review among professional staff who are involved in the postvention program (postvention team) are undertaken to review the plans that were implemented and to plan or coordinate further action. For example, a flexible contingency plan must be preplanned to allow for alternative actions, if needed. Territorial problems between school and community (and their own internal politics) need to be addressed since often these are the very elements that raise the traumatic levels of the event.

Crisis Intervention

Emergency or crisis response is provided, using basic problem solving strategies. We believe that students and staff of the local school(s) are likely to need support in response to a suicide trauma. It is crucial not to underestimate the closeness of relationships or the intensity of reactions of individuals who might be experiencing posttraumatic reactions (Caplan, 1964; Farberow, 1967; Hoff, 1984, 1990; Leenaars, 1994; Leenaars, Maltsberger, & Neimeyer, 1994; Leenaars & Wenckstern, 1990b; Shneidman, 1981a & b).

Community Linkage

Since it is imperative that survivors of suicide be provided with the appropriate support, we must assist these individuals to obtain such services. Educational systems need to develop a linkage system or network to aid in making referrals to the appropriate community services and to exchange information and coordinate services as needed. Such a network is central to responding to a trauma and should be predefined. No individual or system can address all the needs, a problem that is especially evident in contracted service. Being familiar with and updating local community resources before a traumatic event such as suicide occurs, e.g., knowing which agency or service to contact (e.g., police, ambulance, hospital emergency) and preferably the name of the contact person, is highly recommended. In the case of culturally different students, having a directory on hand listing local cultural centers and names of translators, with pre–established communications, may be not only very helpful but also a necessity.

Assessment and Counseling

Evaluation and therapy are provided as needed or requested by the postventionists or the school administrator, for example, the principal or his or her designate.

Assessment, as we already noted, is complex but can be approximated (Leenaars, 1995; Maris, Berman, Maltsberger, & Yufit, 1992). Psychotherapy is equally complicated and, contrary to current efforts, often must be long term and, in some cases, will call for medication and even hospitalization. Adolescents at risk are often suffering long-term pain that has undermined their ego. We strongly believe that once students are identified, the treatment should be individual, not in groups. Groups may serve the initial task of response to a shared trauma, but the student in need should be referred to a therapist for scheduled appointments as soon as possible. One needs to defuse the aftershock, not add to the hysteria (Callahan, 1996; Goldney & Berman, 1996). An outline for psychotherapy has been presented elsewhere (Leenaars, 1994; Leenaars, Maltsberger, & Neimeyer, 1994;).

Education

Information about suicide and its prevention (e.g., clues, myths, causes, what to do, where to go for help, etc.) are provided through discussion, seminars, workshops, and small assemblies or classes (30–50 people) at the school and within the community (Leenaars & Wenckstern, 1990b). This aspect of the program, based on the current literature, is oriented toward prevention. As a final note, educational programs should be undertaken after the aftershocks are normalized, not as part of the early crisis intervention.

Liaison with the Media

Information about suicide in the form of publicity, especially that which tends to sensationalize or glamorize the suicide, should be avoided. It is not and should not be the school's responsibility to provide information about the details of the suicide, or any trauma, to the media. This falls within the jurisdiction of the police department, coroner's office, or other authorities. However, our experience has shown us that (1) a media spokesperson for the school must be appointed at the outset of the crisis, and (2) this role should be filled by the postvention coordinator and not by a school administrator (e.g., the principal). Not only does this ensure the accuracy and consistency of information being given out but, most importantly, it ensures that this information is being provided by someone who understands the postvention procedures and positive impact of the program. It is the procedures and their impact that should be emphasized to the media, not the trauma itself.

Follow-up

Periodic follow-ups are undertaken with the school administrators, school staff, and mental health professionals. A formal final consultation and evaluation is provided several months after the suicide to facilitate a formal closure to the program. Our experience has shown that such consultations and reviews should be supportive in character (e.g., "What did we do?"; "What helped/didn't help?"; "What other things might we have considered?"). Aggressive and overly critical reviews (e.g., "Did you do_____?", "Why did/didn't you do_____?", etc.) are of little help. A supportive approach from the first contact to follow-up is most helpful, although we should not eschew constructive feedback. Every attempt is made to let all concerned know that the postventionists are available on request for follow-up if the need arises. Obviously, postvention is not only one aspect of these strategies (such a view is too limited), nor is it scientifically sound to evaluate the impact of suicide by, for example, a paper and pencil follow-up of one group (such as students) of such endeavors.

It is, thus, obvious that work in postvention lasts more than six sessions. To limit it to one session is absurd.

Misconceptions are as rife in postvention, as they are in prevention and intervention. Pollyannish optimism or banal platitudes, however, should be avoided. Let us begin with the most common misconceptions, and a response.

Postvention doesn't work. To illustrate that this is a myth, let us cite an example from the professional literature (Hazell & Lewin, 1993). Hazell and Lewin sought to evaluate postvention by examining suicide cases in two schools, albeit with limitations. They equated postvention with group counseling. Yet, postvention does not simply equal group counseling. Group counseling can be one strategy of postvention, although we strongly believe that individual work is a more appropriate primary mode of treatment for individuals at risk for PTSD, depression, and so forth. Hazell and Lewin evaluated only increases in suicidal risk, but contagion is only one possible aftershock. They developed a risk index for suicide, which itself is of questionable validity according to a review by the National Institute of Mental Health (Garrison, Lewinsohn, Marsteller, Langhinrichsen & Lann, 1991; Lewinsohn, Garrison, Langhinrichsen, & Marsteller, 1989), to measure the aftershocks. Group counseling, in the situations examined by Hazell and Lewin, also presents problems because it consisted of seeing 20–30 children in a group for 90 minutes. Not only is this not postvention, it is not group therapy (Yalom, 1975). Hazell and Lewin concluded that postvention does not work and schools should not implement such programs. However, all they showed is that a few hours of group sessions, often called debriefing, should not be equated with postvention, an important finding given confusion about this issue among practitioners (e.g., Paul, 1995). This is the real value of the work of Hazell and Lewin, namely that a few hours of debriefing may not only be unhelpful, but also counterproductive. Regrettably, some people have now argued that postvention is useless.

Postvention must be based on sound research in the future. The same issue, as we saw, has arisen in the field of prevention (i.e., education) in the schools about suicide and death. Conclusions are drawn from methodologically unsound studies. The present author (Leenaars, 1985) has, in fact, encouraged sound research in the field since the early 1980s, echoing a call made 90 years ago (Friedman, 1967).

Postvention is grief counseling. Here, we believe, persons holding this view have gone awry. Postvention may include grief counseling; but, they are not equivalent. A response to a trauma must be more than mere counseling, whether focused on grief or other behavior.

Other misconceptions include: Postvention is debriefing; Don't talk about the trauma, it will go away; Don't worry—we will save you; All people respond the same—we will tell you how they will react; and Postvention is the same as prevention.

Are postvention efforts effective? There is a need for more data to support the practice of postvention. Yet, until then, should we do nothing, for example, after the homicide-suicide in Carrolton, Georgia? At Central High in Caroltton on January 8, 1999, Jeff Miller shot his girlfriend, Andrea Garrett and then himself, in what authorities called a suicide pact. A panic occurred subsequently at the school. Should we not assist the students at Central High? Should we, as another example, do nothing after the homicides-suicide in Dunblane, Scotland?

There are some studies in the current literature that show that postvention has value (Dyregrov & Mitchell, 1992). Robinson and Mitchell (1993), for example, report that people found a postvention after a trauma to be helpful, and they felt less stressed. Yet, there is a lack of systematic research (Raphael, Meldrum, & McFarlane, 1995). The question is: Do programs prevent PTSD? Raphael, et al. (1995) offer a very pessimistic response to this question. They cite, for example, a study by Deahl, Gillham, Thomas, Searl, & Srinivasan (1995). Deahl and his coinvestigators examined the effect of a debriefing effort on troops returning from the Gulf War. It is a systematic study that concludes that that program had no effect. Of course, it does not study suicide, or youth, or schools. Even more important methodologically, all postvention programs are not alike. Deahl et al. (1995) examined only debriefing, a procedure that by itself is questionable for schools. There are, however, many simplistic programs. It is, thus, difficult to conclude from the study of program A that program B is ineffective. There are even differences in populations, e.g., differences between war victims and suicidal victims. Be that as it may, Goldney and Berman (1996) echo Raphael et al. (1995), asking why we should do postvention in schools and communities. Studies like the one by Hazell and Lewin (1993) discussed above, do not assist in addressing these questions. There is great diversity in traumas and our responses, as well as individual differences and cultural issues, and most programs are too simplistic to address the diversity. Postvention, we believe is more complex than many postventionists realize.

Callahan (1996), for example, presents a recent case study, raising questions about some postvention strategies. He outlines a case of debriefing, when the strategies themselves may have increased suicidal behavior. Of course, Wenckstern and Leenaars (1991) have elsewhere presented a case when, because no program was allowed by a principal, aftershocks occurred. The principal simply denied the event stating, "We don't want to put ideas in their heads." A number of serious attempts occurred subsequently in that school. This event led to Wenckstern and Leenaars' conclusion, and this is critical, that "a principal or school administrator simply should not be allowed to make that decision" (1991, pp. 193–194). This is equally true about any individual who simply wants to deny the event, whether psychiatrist, psychologist, or principal. Once more, this conclusion echoes Oppenheim. The past, in fact, should continue to be a guide for the new millennium.

Prologue

It may seem odd to call our concluding remarks a Prologue. A prologue means an event serving as an introduction. Yet, in a subject as complex as suicide prevention—prevention, intervention, and postvention—in schools/communities, it seems most appropriate to call our reflections here a prologue for the future. Like Oppenheim's statements, ours are only that, a prologue to future endeavors—not a cookbook.

We end, here with a few summations (and hopefully not misconceptions):

Despite unacceptable high rates, suicide continues to be anomalous, even more so in youth.

Suicide is a multidimensional malaise, not merely a stress response.

Suicide in youth is an issue for students, and thus, schools and their communities.

Schools need to help. Suicide clusters, for example, continue to illustrate why suicide prevention is needed.

Fruitful cooperation is needed between schools, home and the community—especially the professional community (e.g., psychiatrists, psychologists, researchers).

Sound prevention is needed.

A multidimensional approach, i.e., prevention, intervention, postvention, is needed.

Research is needed to evaluate and develop our approach for the future.

Schools should provide youth with prevention, intervention and postvention. This is as true for suicide as it is for other trauma. Hopefully, a comprehensive approach will assist our youth in a desire to live. We, at the turn of this new millennium must ask: Do schools and communities still fail in prevention? Has suicide prevention developed at all since 1910? Will it develop by 2010?

References

American Psychiatric Association. (1980). *Diagnostic and statistical manual of mental disorders,* 3rd ed. Washington, DC: Author.

American Psychiatric Association. (1987). *Diagnostic and statistical manual of mental disorders,* 3rd ed., rev. Washington, DC: Author.

Berman, A. (Ed.) (1990). *Suicide prevention: Case consultations.* New York: Springer.

Berman, A., & Jobes, D. (1991). *Adolescent suicide: Assessment and intervention.* Washington, DC: American Psychological Press.

Berman, A., & Jobes, D. (1994). Treatment of the suicidal adolescent. In A. Leenaars, J. Maltsberger, & R. Neimeyer (Eds.), *Treatment of suicidal people* (pp. 89–100). New York: Taylor & Francis.

Bongar, B. (1991). *The suicidal patient: Clinical and legal statements of care.* Washington, DC: American Psychological Press.

Bongar, B., & Greany, S. (1994). Essential clinical and legal issues when working with the suicidal patient. In A. Leenaars, J. Maltsberger, & R. Neimeyer (Eds.), *Treatment of suicidal people* (pp. 179–193). New York: Taylor & Francis.

Bowlby, J. (1977). The making and breaking of affectionate bonds. *British Journal of Psychiatry, 130,* 201–208, 421–431.

Brent, D., Perper, J., Allmen, C., Moritz, G., Wartella, M., & Zelenah, J. (1991). The presence and accessibility of firearms in the homes of adolescent suicides. A case control study. *Journal of the American Medical Association, 266,* 2989–2995.

Brown, R., Berman, A., Gutheil, T., Leenaars, A., & Moore, J. (1989, Oct.). Forensic Issues in Suicide. Panel presented at the conference of the American Academy of Psychiatry and the Law, Washington, DC.

Callahan, J. (1996). Negative effects of a school suicide postvention program. A case example. *Crisis, 17,* 108–115.

Caplan, G. (1964). *Principles of preventive psychiatry.* New York: Basic Books.

Center for Disease Control (1988). Recommendations for a community plan for the prevention and containment of suicide clusters. *MMWR, 37*(Suppl.), S6.

Clark, D. (1991). School-based suicide prevention programs. *Suicide Research Digest, 5,* 1.

Deahl, M., Gillham, A., Thomas, J., Searle, M., & Srinivasan, M. (1995). Psychological sequelae following the Gulf war: Factors associated with subsequent morbidity and the effectiveness of psychological debriefing. *British Journal of Psychiatry, 265,* 60–65.

Diekstra, R. (1996). The epidemiology of suicide and parasuicide. *Archives of Suicide Research, 2,* 1–29.

Drye, R., Goulding, R., & Goulding, M. (1973). No suicide decisions: Patient monitoring of suicide risk. *American Journal of Psychiatry, 130,* 171–174.

Durlak, J. (1995). *School-based prevention programs for children and adolescents.* Thousand Oaks, CA: Sage.

Dyck, R. (1990). System-entry issues in school suicide prevention education programs. In A. Leenaars & S. Wenckstern (Eds.), *Suicide prevention in schools* (pp. 41–49). New York: Hemisphere.

Dyregrov, A., & Mitchell, J. (1992). Work with traumatized children. Psychological effects and coping strategies. *Journal of Traumatic Stress, 5,* 5–17.

Eggert, L., Thompson, E., Herting, J., & Nicholas, L. (1995). Reducing suicide prevention among high-risk youth: Tests of a school-based prevention program. *Suicide and Life-Threatening Behavior, 25,* 276–298.

Eth, G., & Pynoos, R. (1985). *Post-traumatic stress disorder in children.* Washington, DC: American Psychiatric Press.

Eyman, J. (1990). Countertransference when counseling suicidal school-aged youth. In A. Leenaars & S. Wenckstern (Eds.), *Suicide prevention in schools* (pp. 147–157). Washington, DC: Hemisphere.

Farberow, N. (1967). Crisis, disaster, and suicide: Theory and therapy. In E. Shneidman (Ed.), *Essays in self-destruction* (pp. 373–398). New York: Science House.

Figley, C. (Ed.). (1978). *Stress disorders among Vietnam veterans.* New York: Brunner/Mazel.

Figley, C. (1985). Introduction. In C. Figley (Ed.), *Trauma and its wake* (pp. xvii–xxvi). New York: Brunner/Mazel.

Friedman, P. (Ed.). (1910/1967). *On suicide.* New York: International Universities Press. (Original work published 1910)

Freud, A. (1966). *Ego and mechanisms of defense.* New York: International Universities Press.

Freud, S. (1974). Introductory lectures in psychoanalysis, In J. Strachey (Trans. & Ed.). *The standard edition of the complete psychological works of Sigmund Freud,* Vol. XVI. London: Hogarth. (Original work published 1917)

Freud, S. (1910/1974). Inhibitions, symptoms and anxiety. In J. Strachey (Ed. & Trans.). *The standard edition of the complete psychological works of Sigmund Freud,* Vol. XX. London: Hogarth. (Original work published 1926)

Freud, S. (1974). Moses and monotheism. In J. Strachey (Ed. & Trans.). *The standard edition of the complete psychological works of Sigmund Freud,* Vol. XXIII. London: Hogarth. (Original work published 1939)

Garrison, C., Lewinsohn, P., Marsteller, F., Langhinrichsen, J., & Lann, I. (1991). The assessment of suicidal behavior in adolescents. *Suicide and Life-Threatening Behavior, 21,* 217–230.

Gleser, G., Green, B., & Wignet, C. (1981). *Buffalo Creek revisited: Prolonged psychosocial effects of disaster.* New York: Simon & Schuster.

Glidewell, J., & Swallow, C. (1969). *The prevalence of maladjustment in elementary schools.* Chicago: University of Chicago Press.

Goethe, J. (1951). *Die Leiden Des Jungen Werther* (The Sorrow of Young Werther), Goethe's Werke, Vol. 6. Hamburg: Chistian Wegnen Verlay (Original work published 1774).

Goldblatt, M. (1994). Hospitalization of the suicidal patient. In A. Leenaars, J. Maltsberger, & R. Neimeyer (Eds.), *Treatment of suicidal people* (pp. 153–165). New York: Taylor & Francis.

Goldney, R., & Berman, A. (1996). Postvention in schools: Affective or effective? *Crisis, 17,* 98–99.

Goodstein, L. (1978). *Consulting with human service systems.* Menlo Park, CA: Addison-Wesley.

Hazell, P., & Lewin, T. (1993). Postvention following adolescent suicide. *Suicide and Life-Threatening Behavior, 23,* 101–109.

Hoff, L. (1984). *People in crisis,* 2nd ed. Menlo Park, CA: Addison-Wesley.

Hoff, L. (1990). Crisis intervention in schools. In A. Leenaars & S. Wenckstern (Eds.), *Suicide prevention in schools* (pp. 123–134). Washington, DC: Hemisphere.

Horowitz, M. (1979). Psychological response to serious life events. In V. Hamilton & D. Warburton (Eds.), *Human stress and cognition* (pp. 542–545). New York: Wiley.

Janoff-Bulman, R. (1985). The aftermath of victimization: Rebuilding shattered assumptions. In C. Figley (Ed.), *Trauma and its wake* (pp. 15–35). New York: Brunner/Mazel.

Kalafat, J., & Elias, M. (1994). An evaluation of a school-based suicide awareness intervention. *Suicide and Life-Threatening Behavior, 24,* 224–233.

Kazdin, A. (1990). Psychotherapy for children and adolescents. *Annual Review of Psychology, 41,* 21–54.

King, C. (1997). Suicidal behavior in adolescence. In R. Maris, M. Silverman, & S. Canetto (Eds.), *Review of suicidology, 1997* (pp. 61–95). New York: Guilford.

Leenaars, A. (1985). Suicide postvention in a school system. *Canada's Mental Health, 33*(4).

Leenaars, A. (1990). Suicidology in schools. In A. Leenaars & S. Wenckstern (Eds.), *Suicide prevention in schools* (pp. 257–264). Washington, DC: Hemisphere.

Leenaars, A. (1994). Crisis intervention with highly lethal suicidal people. *Death Studies, 18,* 341–360.

Leenaars, A. (1995). Clinical evaluation of suicide risk. *Japanese Journal of Psychiatry and Neurology, 49* (Suppl. 1), 561–568.

Leenaars, A., DeLeo, D., Diekstra, R., Goldney, R., Kelleher, M., Lester, D., & Nordstrom, P. (1997). Consultation for research in suicidology. *Archives of Suicide Research, 3,* 139–151.

Leenaars, A., DeLeo, D., Goldney, R., Guilbinat, W., & Wallace, D. (Eds.). (1998). The prevention of suicide: Controlling the environment. *Archives of Suicide Research, 4,* 1–107.

Leenaars, A., & Lester, D. (1997). The impact of gun control on suicide: Studies from Canada. *Archives of Suicide Research, 4,* 25–40.

Leenaars, A., Maltsberger, J., & Neimeyer, R. (Eds.). (1994). *Treatment of suicidal people.* Washington, DC: Taylor & Francis.

Leenaars, A., Maris, R., & Takahashi, Y. (Eds.). (1997). *Suicide: Individual, cultural, international perspectives.* New York: Guilford.

Leenaars, A., & Wenckstern, S. (1990a). Post-traumatic stress disorder: A conceptual model for postvention. In A. Leenaars & S. Wenckstern, (Eds.), *Suicide prevention in schools* (pp. 173–180). Washington, DC: Hemisphere.

Leenaars, A., & Wenckstern, S. (Eds.). (1990b). *Suicide prevention in schools.* Washington, DC: Hemisphere.

Leenaars, A., & Wenckstern, S. (1994). Helping lethal suicidal adolescents. In D. Adams & E. Deveau (Eds.), *Threat to life, dying, death and bereavement: The child's perspective* (pp. 131–150). Amityville, NY: Baywood.

Leenaars, A., & Wenckstern, S. (1996). Postvention with elementary school children. In C. Corr & D. Corr (Eds.), *Handbook of childhood death and bereavement* (pp. 265–283). New York: Springer.

Leenaars, A., & Wenckstern, S. (1998). Principles of postvention: Application to suicide and trauma in schools. *Death Studies, 22,* 357–391.

Lewinsohn, P., Garrison, C., Langhinrichsen, J., & Marsteller, F. (1989). *The assessment of suicidal behavior in adolescents: A review of scales suitable for epidemiological clinical research.* Rockville, MD: National Institute of Mental Health.

Lifton, R., & Olson, E. (1976). The human meaning of total disaster: The Buffalo Creek experience. *Psychiatry, 133,* 306–312.

Maltsberger, J. (1986). *Suicide risk.* New York: New York University Press.

Maltsberger, J. (1994). Calculated risk taking. In A. Leenaars, J. Maltsberger & R. Neimeyer (Eds.), *Treatment of suicidal people* (pp. 195–205). Washington, DC: Taylor & Francis.

Maris, R., Berman, A., Maltsberger, J., & Yufit, R. (Eds.). (1992). *Assessment and prediction of suicide.* New York: Guilford.

Martin, G. (1998). Media influence to suicide: The search for solutions. *Archives of Suicide Research, 4,* 51–66.

McLeavy, B., Daly, R., Ludgate, J., & Murray, C. (1994). Interpersonal solving skills training in the treatment of self-poisoning patients. *Suicide and Life-Threatening Behavior, 24,* 382–394.

McLuhan, M., & Fiore, Q. (1967). *The medium is the message.* New York: Bantom.

Paul, K. (1995, Oct.). Toward developing outcome measures for school critical incident stress debriefing as a postvention method. Paper presented at the conference of the Canadian Association for Suicide Prevention, Banff, AB.

Pfeffer, C. (1986). *The suicidal child.* New York: Guilford.

Philips, D. (1974). The influence of suggestion on suicide: Substantive and theoretical implications of the Werther effect. *American Sociological Review, 39,* 240–233.

Raphael, B., Meldrum, L., & McFarlane, A. (1995). Does debriefing after psychological trauma work? *British Medical Journal, 310,* 1479–1480.

Richman, J. (1990). Family therapy with suicidal children. In A. Leenaars & S. Wenckstern (Eds.), *Suicide prevention in schools* (pp. 159–170). Washington, DC: Hemisphere.

Robinson, R., & Mitchell, J. (1993). Evaluation of psychological debriefing. *Journal of Traumatic Stress, 6,* 367–382.

Ross, C. (1985). Teaching children the facts of life and death: Suicide prevention in the schools. In M. Peck, N. Farberow, & R. Litman (Eds.), *Youth suicide* (pp. 147–169). New York: Springer.

Satcher, D. (1998). Bringing the public health approach to the problem of suicide. *Suicide and Life-Threatening Behavior, 28,* 325–327.

Sederer, L. (1994). Managing suicidal inpatients. In A. Leenaars, J. Maltsberger & R. Neimeyer (Eds.), *Treatment of suicidal people* (pp. 167–176). New York: Taylor & Francis.

Shaffer, D. (1991, April). School board curriculum. Paper presented at conference of the American Association of Suicidology, Boston, MA.

Shaffer, D., Garland, A., Viland, V., Rojas, Underwood, M., & Busner, C. (1990). Adolescent suicide attempters: Response to suicide prevention programs. *Journal of the American Medical Association, 264,* 3151–3155.

Shneidman, E. (1973). Suicide. *Encyclopedia Britannica,* Vol. 21 (pp. 383–385). Chicago: William Benton.

Shneidman, E. (1981a). Psychotherapy with suicidal patients. *Suicide and Life-Threatening Behavior, 11,* 341–348.

Shneidman, E. (1981b). Postvention: The care for the bereaved. In E. Shneidman (Ed.), *Suicide thoughts and reflections* (pp. 157–167). New York: Human Sciences Press.

Shneidman, E. (1985). *Definition of suicide.* New York: Wiley.

Slaby, A. (1994). Psychopharmacotherapy of suicide. In A. Leenaars, J. Maltsberger, & R. Neimeyer (Eds.), *Treatment of suicidal people* (pp. 141–149). New York: Taylor & Francis.

Smith, K. (1990). Therapeutic care of the suicidal student. In A. Leenaars & S. Wenckstern (Eds.), *Suicide prevention in schools* (pp. 135–146). Washington, DC: Hemisphere.

Terr, L. (1979). Children of Chonchilla: Study of psychic trauma. *Psychoanalytic Study of the Child, 34,* 547–623.

Tierney, R., & Lang, W. (1995). Cutting suicide prevention programs in schools. In S. Wenckstern, A. Leenaars, & R. Tierney (Eds.), *Suicide prevention in Canadian Schools: A resource* (pp. 73–74). Calgary, Canada: Canadian Association for Suicide Prevention.

U.S. Department of Health and Human Services. (1989). *Report of the Secretary's Task Force on Youth Suicide.* Washington, DC: U.S. Government Printing Office.

Wenckstern, S., & Leenaars, A. (1990). Suicide postvention in a secondary school. In A. Leenaars & S. Wenckstern, (Eds.), *Suicide prevention in schools* (pp. 181–195). Washington, DC: Hemisphere.

Wenckstern, S., & Leenaars, A. (1993). Trauma and suicide in schools. *Death Studies, 17,* 253–266.

Wilson, J., Smith, W., & Johnson, S. (1985). A comparative analysis of PTSD among various survivor groups. In C. Figley (Ed.), *Trauma and its wake* (pp. 142–173). New York: Brunner/Mazel.

Wislar, J., Grossman, J., Kreusi, M., Fendrick, M., Franke, C., & Ingnatowicz, N. (1998). Youth suicide-related visits in an emergency department serving rural counties: Implication for means restriction. *Archives of Suicide Research, 4,* 75–87.

Yalom, I. (1975). *The theory and practice of group psychotherapy.* New York: Basic Books.

Zimmerman, D., Grosz, D., & Asnis, G. (Eds.). (1995). *Treatment approaches with suicidal adolescents.* New York: Wiley.

III

THE ORGANIZATIONS

M. David Wallace

The Origin of Suicide Prevention in the United States

In 1968, a World Health Organization report indicated that more than one thousand persons commit suicide each day. At that time, more than half a million suicides were being registered each year, and this number is a *serious* underestimate due to inadequacies and variations in the registration process across countries (Small & Opler, 1971). Moreover, the suicide rate for many age groups increased over the next two decades (Bongar, 1991). In effect, it is quite possible that more individuals have committed suicide in this century than have died in both World War I and World War II combined.

Suicide is currently the ninth leading cause of death in the United States, with an average of one person committing suicide every 17.1 minutes (Peters, Kochanek, & Murphy, 1998). In fact, more people die by their own hands than by the hands of others (Bongar, 1991) yet, given the focus of our media it is difficult for many to believe that suicide kills more than homicide. Despite the severity of the problem of suicide, suicide prevention centers are of very recent origin in the United States, and it was not until the 1960s that suicide prevention centers became more numerous, coinciding with the large steps being taken by what is now known as the field of suicidology. The question becomes: What happened in the 1960s, and how did social forces affect the evolution of the field of suicidology?

This chapter is divided into two parts. The first section outlines some of the relevant sociocultural, political, and economic influences during the decade that resulted in the growth of the suicide prevention movement. The second section outlines the significant changes that took place in the 1960s in what became known in 1968 as the field of suicidology and discusses the ways in which the sociocultural, political, and economic trends affected the growth of suicide prevention centers in the United States. The assumption behind this chapter is that understanding the historical influences on suicidology is relevant to better understanding the current context and future directions of the field: To know where you're going, it helps to know where you've been. In effect, it will be argued that it was because of the combination of these social forces and the influence of Edwin Shneidman, the father of suicidology, that the growth in the suicide prevention movement occurred at that particular time.

☐ Political and Economic Forces in the 1960s

The United States presidential election of 1960 set the stage for a decade that began with a strong liberal influence. With the largest voter turnout in half a century, John F. Kennedy was elected to office. Matusow (1984) describes this time as one influenced by the changes in the moods of the intellectual elites during the postwar years. Changed were ideals of utopianism and the romantic delusions where common folk were idealized to a view where "the world now seemed grim, intractable, menaced on all sides by the forces of unreason. As the appeal of Marxism waned, Sigmund Freud's pessimistic speculations on the human condition became the indispensable text" (Matusow, 1984, p. 4).

In the 1950s, intellectuals had largely stopped worrying about economic inequalities. It was not until the late 1950s and primarily the 1960s that this attitude changed. It was not a view that poverty did not exist, but rather a move was taking place away from the quantitative liberalism (e.g., the New Deal) towards what Schlesinger (1956) has called a qualitative liberalism. In effect, Schlesinger was noting that "while private wealth heaps up in our shops and homes, we refuse to undertake adequate programs to improve our schools, our hospitals, . . . our public domain" (p. 8).

John Kenneth Galbraith (1958) made a similar call for the American people to change their preeminent social goal from one of increasing production (of consumer goods) for private use to one of increasing taxation to divert wealth from private consumption into schools, hospitals, slum improvement, and scientific research. In sum, there were calls raised in the late 1950s, to be taken up in the 1960s, to move away from the materialistic individualism towards an increased attention to public welfare.

These calls did not go ignored in the 1950s. However, the various welfare measures that were advanced by Democrats in Congress were unsuccessful (Matusow, 1984). The election of Kennedy increased the potential for these recommended social changes to come to fruition. In short fashion, he launched his five "must" bills (housing, aid to depressed areas, assistance to public schools, hospital assistance, and an increase in the minimum wage) to fight the War on Poverty

In 1961, the Joint Commission on Mental Illness and Health released its final report. In it were recommendations that provided the impetus for the community mental health movement. It suggested that the objective of treatment should be to enable patients to maintain themselves in the community and thus avoid the debilitating effects of hospitalization (Perry, 1976). In addition, the report recommended that the federal government assume much of the costs of developing such programs.

But it was not until February of 1963 that Kennedy took the message to Congress by arguing for the establishment of a strong federal commitment to community health centers (Perry, 1976). Later that year, the Community Mental Health Centers Act (CMHCA) was passed by Congress. This act provided the funding for community mental health centers, as long as they met five essential services (e.g., 24-hour emergency service, consultation and education programs, outpatient service, etc.). The 24-hour emergency service requirement, though originally included to increase the availability of service, in part gave rise to the crisis intervention movement (Heller, Price, Reinharz, Riger, & Wandersman, 1984; McGee, 1974).

After easily winning the election of 1964, Lyndon B. Johnson carried on the torch of the war on poverty. In addition to continuing with the five "must" bills with an added emphasis on health-care, Johnson passed the Economic Opportunity Act, which included the Community Action Program (CAP). Although not directly sponsoring suicide prevention centers, the CAP is an example of the increasing focus of a community level attack on social problems. In this case, the CAP focused on fighting poverty at the level of the community. In effect, the increased focus on health-care and fighting poverty took place in a larger movement that involved a refocusing of the attention of the American people towards the problems in their own country.

Economic change was also in the air. The post-World War II prosperity of the late 1940s and 1950s paved the way for the political and social reforms that were taking place in the 1960s. Collier, Minton, and Reynolds (1991) state that the "affluence during this period brought expectations that the benefits of prosperity and democracy would be extended to everyone . . . [and] this belief formed the basis for a new liberal consensus" (p. 238). These expectations were reflected in the policies of both Kennedy and Johnson.

The strong economic times coupled with a trend towards liberalism resulted in most of the 1960s being a period of social reform, where "Americans as a whole were inspired by both individual and communal values, and they created a social and political coalition that sought to maximize individual rights and liberties while extending them to less fortunate minorities" (Collier et al., 1991, pp. 238–239).

It is difficult to give a single summary of the political, economic, and related social influences in the 1960s, as this decade cannot be viewed as one consistent period of social reform. The continuation of the Vietnam War in the late 1960s not only became an increasing drain on the federal budget (and thus drawing monies from other areas), but also united a diversity of groups, including elements of the counterculture and many civil rights activists, who were opposed to the war (Collier, Minton, & Reynolds, 1991). Instead of the war drawing the nation together under the flag and thus focusing Americans' attention outward (i.e., away from the nation's internal problems), as almost all wars do (see, for example, Clausewitz [1818/1984]), the Vietnam War in many ways left the country discouraged and divided. In short, the lack of public support for the war and the continued pleas for addressing social concerns in the United States benefited community efforts in fighting poverty (e.g., Johnson's CAP) and the community mental health movement. The full force of the drawn-out loss in Vietnam would not be felt until the late 1960s and early 1970s (especially following Watergate), whereby citizens became increasingly suspicious of government intervention (Heller, Price, Reinharz, Riger, & Wandersman, 1984).

In sum, Levine and Levine (1970) have pointed out that during periods of political or social reform, mental theories emphasize environmental determinants, while during periods of political and social conservatism intrapsychic theories are more prevalent. As emphasized in the following section, the 1960s were in many ways a period of social reform.

☐ Social Forces in the 1960s

The Growth of Community Psychology

Although Zax and Specter (1974) date the birth of community psychology as May 1965, when a group of psychologists met in Boston to consider community mental health, these authors argue that the seeds were sown earlier. In 1958, Sanford called for the field of psychology to move from its exclusive focus on clinical (i.e., psychiatric) problems towards a greater focus on less obvious (i.e., more social) problems. Similarly, just a few years later, Jones and Levine (1963) argued for the rejection of the medical (disease) model in favor of an approach that promotes healthy living in general. In effect, during the late 1950s and early 1960s there were related calls being issued for: 1) a renunciation of the exclusive emphasis on the mentally ill, 2) mental health professionals to concern themselves more with healthy adaptation of larger groups of people, and 3) greater appreciation for the role of environmental forces (and their relation to what became increasingly viewed as behavioral disorders).

Community psychology arose partially out of a conceptual change in the field of abnormal psychology. The role played by the environment became viewed as integral, both as being a cause of behavioral problems, and as a primary source of intervention. In essence, mental health professionals would have to take a more active role in the community. Zax and Specter (1974) assess the impact of this conceptual change by noting that "the recognition of behavior of greater and greater subtlety as deriving from emotional and psychological causes has extended the sphere of psychology into areas formerly considered relevant to other fields such as law, the church, and education" (pp. 23–24).

Government funding also played a role in the growth of the community psychology movement. After World War II, the Veterans Administration, "faced as it was with the overwhelming task of building facilities and professions at the same time that it had to care for thousands upon thousands of individuals—had appropriated to it [the psychology movement] large sums of money" (Sarason, Levine, Goldenberg, Cherlin, & Bennett, 1966, p. 9) from the federal government. Much of the money went into university training programs. The field of psychology in general was becoming increasingly responsive to social needs, due in part to receiving this governmental support for doing so. But, in light of the need for psychiatric care for veterans, combined with the Boulder Conference in 1949 which officially established the scientist-practitioner model, why did community psychology not develop until the 1960s?

Community involvement for psychologists became even more prominent in the 1960s in light of the social forces occurring at this time. There was a major conceptual reorientation taking place in mental health disciplines in general, including clinical psychology. Many treatment facilities had a long-standing problem of being both overcrowded and understaffed (Albee, 1959), and the accidental discovery of chlorpromazine as a treatment for schizophrenia in the mid-1950s kickstarted a deinstitutionalization trend. This trend was in turn accelerated when the Community Mental Health Centers Act was passed in 1963. Aftercare facilities then became necessary, and these took the form of mental health centers.

The use of mental health centers for the aftercare of people with severe mental disorders was quickly expanded to include centers to focus on social problems (e.g., rape counselling, child abuse problems, and the underserved populations more generally) (Heller, Price, Reinharz, Riger, & Wandersman, 1984). While clinical psychology as a field began to orient itself partially in response to the influence of the veterans, it increasingly moved in the early 1960s in the direction of training mental health professionals who could work in the community to address these social problems.

There was also a growing dissatisfaction with the traditional psychotherapeutic approaches. The blind faith that had been placed in the effectiveness of psychotherapy was called into question by Eysenck's (1952) study. Not only did Eysenck find that psychotherapy did not improve on his calculated spontaneous recovery rate of two-thirds for neurotic patients, but his figures also indicated an inverse correlation between the length of psychotherapy and the recovery rate. Heller, Price, Reinharz, Riger, & Wandersman (1984) noted that while there were attempts to refute Eysenck's study (e.g., Luborsky, 1954; Rosenzweig, 1954), these arguments never received much publicity, and consequently Eysenck's claim became "part of the accepted lore of the field" (Heller et al., 1984, p. 13). In sum, there was a strong trend in the mental health field away from psychotherapy due to an increased doubt that psychotherapy was effective. Moreover, many in the field began to doubt whether psychotherapy was a practical answer to the large scale health problems in the United States even if it was effective (Zax & Specter, 1974).

Overlooked by most of the literature in community psychology is that these social trends took place within a larger context that involved a general looking inward, whereby the important problems that were seen as confronting the United States were ones inside their own nation. But the increased inward attention also included a change in focus regard to what to study:

> Faced with the realities of urban riots, racial conflicts, student protests and the poor, problems such as neuroses and schizophrenia that have long commanded the undivided and full energies of the mental health professions now pale by comparison (Iscoe & Spielberger, 1970, p. 3).

In sum, two clear trends can be seen. One is a trend away from the psychology that was largely academic prior to World War II and toward a psychology that also included a practical (i.e., applied) side. Whereas most psychologists had worked in university settings where their main responsibilities were teaching and research, after the war there was a need for clinical psychology training programs (with an emphasis on intervention and not assessment) to respond to the thousands of military psychiatric casualties. Yet such changes could not be implemented without political and financial support. Initially, the financial backing for the development of such programs was provided largely by the Veterans Administration (Iscoe & Spielberger, 1970).

Second, psychologists and other mental health professionals were starting to focus more on what were perceived as social problems of American society, including suicide, and less on the more traditional topics, such as psychopathology. As presidents Kennedy and Johnson took up more *interest* in these social problems in the 1960s, it was another federal agency, the National Institute of Mental Health (NIMH), that later took up the *funding* for these programs.

Finally, it should be noted that psychology was one of many disciplines involved in this change in focus toward the community. Psychiatry, social work, and other mental health disciplines were all involved in the community mental health movement during the 1960s and had no less important a role to play in its growth. It is only because of the scope of this chapter that I have simply selected one example.

The Volunteer Movement

In the 1960s, it was argued by some that "a central problem—if not the central problem—of mental health services is manpower" (Zusman & Davidson, 1971, p. 33). It would be the volunteer movement that would help to fill this gap in manpower in the United States.

The volunteer movement in North America was highly influenced by the Samaritans. The Samaritans were established as an organization in London, England, by Chad Varah in 1953. With only one paid staff member, the agency consisted at the time of about 150 volunteers who worked with psychiatric and social work consultants (Farberow & Shneidman, 1961). Initially, clients were self-referred; however, with time the Samaritans established strong community support with the police and many physicians who started sending them referrals.

This agency is significant not only for being one of the first community efforts to deal with psychological problems, but also as a model for the use of volunteers in dealing with clients with a variety of problems (i.e., loneliness, depression, suicidality, sexual perversions, etc.) (Varah, 1965). Given the incredibly small amount of money that an agency had for operations at this time, whether in England, the United States, or most other nations, the use of volunteers was essential.

Yet, such a solution was not so easy to come to, given that many were unsure as to what degree of success volunteers would have dealing with such problems that were normally the work of professionals. Kelly (1980), however, echoed the views of Varah by arguing that "the Samaritan does not need to be versed in psychiatry, psychology or the social services . . . " (p. 180). Moreover, there were research data (e.g., Fox, 1973; Varah, 1980) that demonstrated a drop in the suicide rate over the course of 20 years in the areas of the United Kingdom that had Samaritan services. This research supported the organization, and thus the use of volunteers in front-line work. Interestingly, the role of volunteers would become of significant importance when the CMHCA was passed by Congress in 1963. The act, while authorizing funds for the construction of mental health centers, omitted funds for staffing (Levine, 1981). In effect, this omission forced community mental health centers to find alternate routes to solve the problem of insufficient manpower.

Increasing Emphasis on Prevention and Crisis Intervention

Highly related to the growth in the community mental health movement was the trend towards emphasizing the prevention, as opposed to the amelioration, of mental illness. Perhaps the most influential treatise on the subject continues to be Gerald Caplan's (1964) *Principles of Preventative Psychiatry*. Caplan's argument, reflective of the social psychiatry movement, was for effecting change in a whole population rather than in an individual. Thus, the main process is the use of interventions that ameliorate harmful environmental conditions.

Caplan (1964) outlined three types of prevention: primary, secondary, and tertiary. Primary prevention involves lowering the rate of new cases in a population by counteracting harmful circumstances before they have a chance to cause the problem. Secondary prevention attempts to lower the prevalence of a problem through early diagnosis and treatment. Finally, tertiary prevention aims at large scale rehabilitation of those with the problem, largely by attempting to reincorporate them into the community.

This model is significant in that it is based on a community approach that is concerned with prevention as much as it is with treatment. Also fundamental is its avoidance of "hospitalism" by launching transitional institutions in the community, that enable the individual to maintain communication within his or her social network, while also helping to counteract the alienation due to prejudice (of being suicidal, having a mental disorder, etc.) (Caplan, 1964).

Crisis intervention would also provide an important influence. Lindemann (1944), considered by many to be the founder of crisis intervention, outlined three main ingredients for crisis work: emotional catharsis, cognitive appraisal, and the development of alternative behaviors. Although Lindemann originally described these ingredients for grief work, Heller, Price, Reinharz, Riger, & Wandersman (1984) note that starting in the 1960s they have been applied for use in a wide range of areas, from dealing with trauma after natural disasters to that experienced during a divorce.

Crisis intervention developed out of a recognition that individuals who are going through extreme but acute stress could benefit from intervention. Theoretically, this development was consistent with the change in emphasis of mental health professionals away from the medical model. And practically, it reflected the desire of mental health centers to receive federal funding under the CMHCA's requirement of around-the-clock emergency service. Perhaps it is because these influences did not occur until the 1960s that the influence of Lindemann (1944), a senior colleague of Caplan's at Harvard, was minimal during the 1940s. Until the emphasis changed in community mental health (i.e., social influences) and the CMHCA's funding requirement began in 1963 (i.e., political and economic influences), Lindemann's ideas were not widely applied.

The step towards crisis intervention involved a major change for many professionals away from traditional psychotherapy. Much of psychotherapy in the 1960s was generally long-term with respect to treatment, had a lofty goal such as "personality change" or "personal growth," and often focussed on past events in the person's life. In contrast, crisis intervention has a short-term focus with the almost singular aim of getting the person through the crisis, and tends to be ahistorical in focus.

☐ The Impact on Suicidology in the 1960s

The Los Angeles Suicide Prevention Center (LASPC) was opened in 1958. Although predated by such organizations as the National Save-a-Life League, founded by a Baptist minister in New York in 1906 (Farberow & Shneidman, 1961), the LASPC was distinctive for its emphasis on: 1) combining research and prevention, 2) not being religion based, and 3) having a strong multidisciplinary nature (Shneidman, Farberow, & Litman, 1961). It was not until the 1960s, however, that suicide prevention caught on nationwide. In looking back at the birth of the LASPC, Shneidman (1971) notes that there were such pervasive taboos about suicide that the major question of the NIMH was whether suicide prevention would be laughed at or pushed out of existence by the police, press, and general citizenry. But by the end of the 1960s, there were "more than one hundred suicide prevention programs, an American Association of Suicidology, a *Bulletin of Suicidology* and a major unit" (Shneidman, 1971, p. 21) at NIMH. But why was there such a significant growth in suicide prevention?

Early in the 1960s many significant changes took place in the field. First, there was an acknowledgment that suicide was a serious problem and second, there was a growing realization that something could be done about it. In addition to giving credit to Gerald Caplan and Erich Lindemann for their influencing the preventive and crisis intervention aspects of suicide prevention, Shneidman (1971) gave four reasons to justify suicide prevention. First, the individual calling for help is ambivalent. Second, individuals bent on self-destruction are that way only acutely. Third, the suicidal act is inherently an interpersonal act in a social context. And fourth, postvention was stressed as a method to mollify the after-effects of a suicide attempt so as to prevent a future attempt or completion. In effect, suicide was beginning to be seen as an acute state of mind of an ambivalent individual in a larger social context, rather than as a symptom of a mental disorder.

This thinking is very much in line with the conceptualizations of community psychology in the 1960s. It is therefore not surprising that the growth in the number of suicide prevention centers took place in a larger context of a growing community mental health movement. In the 1960s, the alleviation of social problems, including suicide, was beginning to receive more emphasis than was the treatment of psychopathology.

Suicide prevention centers would not be feasible if they were confined to using only professionals (e.g., psychologists, psychiatrists, and social workers). In effect, the only way to expand the mental health services provided was to increase the number of programs offered or to incorporate nonprofessionals. Suicide prevention centers made use of the latter approach. McGee (1971) noted that "there is a shortage of professional manpower . . . and . . . this situation demands the utilization of specially trained, nonprofessional people who have access to professional consultation" (p. 60).

It is quite possible that the development and growth of the suicide prevention center would not have taken place without the influence of the volunteer movement. At the first meeting of the American Association of Suicidology (AAS) in 1968, Louis Dublin noted that "the lay volunteer was probably the most important single discovery in the 50-year history of suicide prevention. Little progress was made until he came into the picture, for he alone apparently was qualified to make the live and fruitful contacts with the person in distress" (cited in Shneidman, 1988, p. 11).

It is interesting to note that the Samaritan movement, beginning in England, was influenced by religion; in contrast, the suicide prevention centers that developed in the United States were much more influenced by the growth in community mental health. In turn, both developed very differently and with emphases in treatment that reflected their respective ties to these influences. Dublin noted that in contrast to the American volunteer, the Samaritan is not satisfied with simple contact, and becomes a "befriender" in what is often a long-lasting relationship (Shneidman, 1973a). The American volunteer is more likely to deal on a crisis-to-crisis basis with many individuals, thus reflecting the larger social influence of the crisis intervention movement. This contrast points to the importance of social factors in determining the nature of suicide prevention.

The political influences on the growth in the suicide prevention movement are more indirect. Both President Kennedy, through his five "must" bills and his support of the CMHCA, and President Johnson, through his continued efforts and refinements of Kennedy's direction, had a clear interest in addressing some of the harsh environmental conditions at a community level. These factors had a more direct influence on the growth of the community mental health movement, which in turn helped shape the direction that the suicide prevention movement would take.

The growth in community mental health helped to provide a model with which a suicide prevention program could be established. Attacking the problem at the community level, rather than in hospitals, demonstrated a greater appreciation for the social and cultural forces that were operating. In arguing in favor of the feasibility of the LASPC, Shneidman and Farberow (1970) even referred to suicide as a "community mental health problem" (p. 99). Small and Opler (1971) stated the importance of understanding "the relationship between man and his environment and how each affects the other within the family structure, within the community, and within the culture" (p. 12) in order to more effectively intervene at these levels with suicidal individuals. Such an approach to intervention at the community level suggests the strong influence that the community mental health movement had on suicide prevention.

The goals of the suicide prevention centers, including various aspects of prevention, were outlined prior to Caplan's (1964) work on prevention (e.g., Shneidman, 1961). It is likely that Caplan's work, however, had an influential impact on the way that many mental health professionals came to look at problems. In effect, the social climate was perhaps not ready when Shneidman first outlined the various preventive aspects that the suicide prevention center would have. Caplan's arguments were influential both among mental health professionals and funding agencies such as NIMH, and would help refine the goals of suicide prevention (e.g., see Farberow, 1967). Moreover, Caplan's (1964) discussion of community-based institutions provided a method to help counteract both the alienation and prejudice of being suicidal, taken up later by others who furthered the suicide prevention movement, such as Shneidman and Farberow (1970) who discuss the importance of removing the taboo from the topic of suicide.

Farberow (1967) has noted the importance of crisis intervention, especially while in the early stages in developing suicide prevention centers. He pointed out that when the LASPC was opened that its caseload was made up almost entirely of suicide attempters. Over time, as it developed stronger ties with the community and became better known, the focus of intervention shifted to persons with suicide threats, thoughts, and ruminations. In other words, the focus of "intervention gradually moved to an earlier point on the continuum of the development of the suicidal crisis . . . " (Farberow, 1967, p. 394). Farberow seems to imply that suicide prevention programs can aim for both secondary prevention and tertiary prevention. Whereas tertiary intervention would involve the continuation of crisis intervention techniques with suicidal attempters, secondary intervention strategies would aim at intervening with individuals who are ruminating about suicide. In the latter case, centers would "attempt to anticipate a potential crisis and apply intervention procedures as prevention rather than as remediation" (Farberow, 1967, p. 394). The influence of both Caplan's (1964) and Lindemann's (1944) ideas on prevention are clear.

The American Association of Suicidology (AAS) was born in 1968. At last the field of suicidology was officially founded, a long 58 years after the psychoanalytic meetings were held in Vienna on suicide (Shneidman, 1973b). In part, the birth of AAS reflected the culmination of the advances in the field in the 1960s coupled with the tremendous growth in the preventive aspects.

The combination of research and practice are fundamental to the AAS, and they are two components of suicide prevention. The argument can be made that true suicide prevention requires research—research into early identification of target groups, education, and many other topics. Further, education programs in schools are an example of a primary intervention strategy aimed at building peer support and encouraging help-seeking behavior in times of crisis, and thus lowering the suicide rate. In short, Shneidman and Farberow (1970) argued that "a comprehensive program of suicide prevention must include not only the saving of lives today but the investigation of why individuals take their lives—so that lives can be saved more expeditiously tomorrow" (p. 100), and they later referred to research as the raison d'être of the LASPC.

The first NIMH grant for work in suicide went to Shneidman in 1955 for research (Shneidman & Farberow, 1970). Yet it would require: 1) great efforts on his part to demonstrate the feasibility of a suicide prevention center, 2) local funding from private sources and hospital settings (A. Leenaars, personal communication, December 3, 1994), and 3) the passing of the CMHCA in 1963, to allow for the vast expansion of suicide prevention centers that occurred in the mid-1960s across the United States. It is interesting that Shneidman (1988) later noted that, when comparing the nine administrations from Roosevelt to Reagan,

> . . . more liberal federal leaderships tend in general to tolerate and support a variety of approaches, including sociological and psychological approaches, to what we call our social problems, including suicide; conversely, more conservative federal leadership—on a generally reduced overall level, specifically in the case of suicide—tends to emphasize biological and medical solutions, with the implied locus of blame in the person rather than in the social structure . . . (p. 9)

Given that suicidology exists within a larger social setting, it is worthy of note that while social factors impacted on suicidology, suicidology has in turn influenced its social environment. As previously mentioned, one effort of the field has been to more readily identify those at greatest risk for suicide. It has been argued by Zimmermann (1988) that the more identifiable the risk, the more closely will the public and legislative target the response. It remains to be seen, however, as to the validity of this statement with respect to suicide prevention. Given the lack of legislation and government funding to address some of the high-risk groups, one can speculate that this is because of who the high-risk groups are for suicide completion. For differing reasons, social issues that have greater impact on high risk groups such as males, Native Americans, the elderly, homosexuals, and alcohol and drug users have arguably been of less *political* interest since the 1960s. But even more importantly, the topic of suicide continues to be invisible to many government agencies, with proportionately less money going to support suicide research than to many other causes of death.

There have, in contrast, been numerous influences of the suicide prevention movement in the 1960s on psychology and the community mental health movement. The suicide prevention movement provided an example in North America of how volunteers could be used in the front lines, how prevention and crisis intervention goals could be combined, and how both individual and social factors need to be addressed in looking at many of the problems of society. Moreover, the feasibility of suicide prevention was demonstrated through the early efforts of the LASPC staff (Farberow, 1992).

In addition, the LASPC popularized the approach of using the telephone to intervene and triage clients in crisis, which was largely an unexplored option for dealing with individuals in crisis. Another early contribution of the LASPC was in the form of research. Early work on 1) epidemiology, 2) characteristics of suicidal persons, 3) descriptions of the center and its staff, and 4) psychological assessments was conducted by LASPC staff (Farberow, 1993).

Further, the impact of the LASPC is notable for not only the development and refinement of prevention and intervention procedures but also the public sharing of these procedures to help others learn to intervene with suicidal individuals and to set up similar programs. Thus, for example, when the LASPC continued the tradition of a 24-hour telephone answering service first established by the National Save-A-Life League, it became "the focus of thoughtful analysis, careful evaluation, and extensive description" (McGee, 1974, p. 6). Further, the running of training institutes as well as the training of psychology and social work interns, psychiatry residents, and research fellows would facilitate the establishment and improvement of programs elsewhere. And while the educational thrust of the LASPC laid the groundwork for the growth in suicide prevention and crisis centers across the United States, the importance of evaluating and refining such agencies was not overlooked (see, for example, Motto, Brooks, Ross, & Allen, 1974).

Great Man or Zeitgeist?

It is difficult to distinguish the degree to which the growth in suicide prevention was a function of, on the one hand, social, political, and economic factors, and on the other, of several special individuals. Indeed, individuals such as Edwin Shneidman, Robert Litman, Ronald Maris, and Norman Farberow had to fight against many forces operating against them. And even earlier, Louis Dublin, the "pioneer of suicidology" (McGee, 1974), published *To Be Or Not To Be* in 1933. Dublin, although attempting to draw national attention to suicide, was seen by McGee (1974) as having been "frustrated in his attempts" and to have had only "a relatively minor impact" (p. 4) until the 1960s. Was it the Zeitgeist in the late 1950s and 1960s that finally wore away the apathy of public health professionals? Or, was it largely the influence of Shneidman that was of fundamental importance in the growth of suicide prevention movement? The "Great Man" view of history, in contrast to Zeitgeist history, proposes that it is through the thinking and research of an individual that great discoveries, events, and ideas occur (see, for example, Leahy, 1992).

The influence of Shneidman cannot be overstated in the founding and development of the LASPC. Shneidman's work, along with that of Farberow, was pivotal in landing a five-year grant from NIMH in 1958 that would allow for the launching of the LASPC, and a seven-year grant to support the LASPC through 1969. And although it was the fortuitous circumstance of Shneidman and Farberow's finding a gold mine of several hundred suicide notes from the Los Angeles Country Medical Examiner-Coroner that originated the idea of a suicide prevention center, it was the suicide of Marilyn Monroe that led to a greater demand for suicide prevention services. Shneidman and Farberow, who performed a psychological autopsy investigation following Monroe's suicide, have described being flooded with calls as the media spread word of the LASPC (Farberow, 1993). This increase in demand for services in turn required the incorporation of a telephone services staffed by volunteers, that in turn allowed for higher numbers of suicidal individuals and individuals in crisis to receive intervention. This larger clientele would ultimately assist in the development of "concepts, procedures, and empirical data which formed the technology of suicide prevention," and "this technology, which was unknown prior to the LASPC, has been the basis upon which all of the new programs which have followed have been built" (McGee, 1974, p. 5). In short, McGee (1974) cites the LASPC as central not only in the origin of suicide prevention, but also in crisis intervention.

Yet Shneidman did far more than simply coin the term "suicidology" and help found the LASPC. As chief of the Center for Studies in Suicide Prevention at NIMH from 1966 to 1969, Shneidman had "national visibility and an established communication apparatus which reaches into every community in the United States" (Zusman & Davidson, 1971, p. 7). This national visibility helped Shneidman to continue drawing attention to the issue of suicide. Moreover, Shneidman had access to a large but limited source of funding, with which he was able to stimulate local individuals and groups who would provide the main source of funding needed to operate community suicide prevention centers.

It was also Shneidman (1971) who set up the main goals for effective suicide prevention: 1) removing the stigma, and thus making it easier for those in crisis to seek help; 2) providing easier access to services; and 3) encouraging research to understand and treat the causes of suicide, so that new information can inform our treatment and prevention services (see also Zusman & Davidson, 1971).

Shneidman was also at the center of things when AAS was founded in 1968. This organization and its yearly conferences would help to both attract new members and solidify the new specialized profession of suicidology. In short, not only did Shneidman draw international attention to the importance of suicide, but he also was largely responsible for the beginnings of the suicide prevention movement in the United States. He, along with Farberow, set up a model of suicide prevention that was feasible and ultimately successful. Maris (1988) commented that "Dr. Shneidman's enduring gifts to us all are those of a suicidological Linnaeus or Plato" (p. viii). Shneidman and Farberow (1970), in thinking back to their accomplishments, commented that "we have reflected as to whether we just happened to 'come along at the right time' or whether we had played some active role in creating a more permissive Zeitgeist in relation to suicide study" (p. 105). Perhaps it was both.

Counter-Forces

Although social forces contributed to the advances in the field, there were also social forces operating against such changes. First, the establishment and growth of suicide prevention centers was dependent upon changing many time-worn and inadequate conceptions of death and suicide. Moreover, these battles were fought when the whole topic was taboo, a battle which has been referred to as running up hill (Shneidman, Farberow, & Litman, 1961). Suicidology today, however, is much further up the hill than it was 30 years ago, thanks in large part to the efforts of Shneidman. Many of these conceptions changed during the 1960s, when a "new permissiveness to discuss and study suicide and death" (Shneidman, 1988, p. 2) developed.

In addition, a second counter-force was the opposition of the American Medical Association (AMA) to any plans to change the mental health system throughout the early 1960s. The AMA viewed the effort to change towards a more community-based approach as an effort from the federal government to involve itself in health care delivery and thus as an attempt to undermine the traditional private practice model of medicine (Heller, Price, Reinharz, Riger, & Wandersman, 1984). The growth in community mental health had already come too far, however, and the opposition from the AMA did little to slow the hundreds of community mental health centers from opening following the passing of the CMHCA.

☐ Conclusions

While there was one well-organized suicide prevention center in the United States in 1958 (the LASPC), there were still only 11 by 1964. It was after 1964 that the number of suicide prevention centers began to soar. By 1968, there were more than 100 (McGee, 1971). One might conclude that the social trends that took place in the 1960s occurred in the context of more liberal policy from Kennedy and Johnson. These trends, when combined the leadership of Edwin Shneidman, were enough to outweigh the counter-forces, and led to the establishment of a large suicide prevention center network across the United States. As Heller, Price, Reinharz, Riger, & Wandersman (1984) have noted:

> Social, political, and economic factors always will affect the fate of social innovations, regardless of their effectiveness. However, without taking seriously the need for analysis, evaluation, and the subsequent accumulation of verified knowledge, it is not likely that innovative ideas will survive the vicissitudes of history (p. 47).

It is in part because of the scientific study of suicide that over 40 years after the opening of the LASPC, the suicide prevention movement shows no signs of slowing.

Why did this occur in the 1960s? Dublin (1973) has argued that there are four aspects of suicide prevention that are necessary for suicide prevention centers: 1) an interest in suicide prevention, 2) the discovery of the possibilities of prevention, 3) the use of volunteers, and 4) a firm base of financial support. Before the 1960s, none of these aspects were present in any strength. But the turning of people's attention to internal (i.e., social) problems in the United States in the 1960s both affected and was affected by more liberal federal policy as well as the growth in community mental health, with the increasing emphases on both prevention and crisis intervention. The possibility of suicide prevention, as seen in the Samaritan movement in the United Kingdom, and as further advocated by Shneidman, sparked an already growing interest in suicide prevention. But, it was the use of nonprofessional volunteers and the growth in financial support from both the community and federal agencies that allowed these possibilities for prevention to be put into practice. By the latter part of the 1960s, all four of these factors were strongly present in America for the first time.

☐ References

Albee, G. (1959). *Mental health manpower trends: A report to the staff director, Jack. R. Ewalt.* New York: Basic Books.

Bongar, B. (1991). *The suicidal patient: Clinical and legal standards of care.* Washington, DC: American Psychological Association.

Caplan, G. (1964). *Principles of preventive psychiatry.* New York: Basic Books.

Clausewitz, Carl von. (1984). On War. In M. Howard, & P. Paret (Eds. and Trans.). *On War.* Princeton: Princeton University Press. (Original work published 1818).

Collier, G., Minton, H., & Reynolds, G. (1991). *Currents of thought in American social psychology.* Toronto, Canada: Oxford University Press.

Dublin, L. (1973). Suicide prevention. In E. S. Shneidman (Ed.), *On the nature of suicide* (pp. 43–47). San Francisco: Jossey-Bass.

Eysenck, H. (1952). The effects of psychotherapy: An evaluation. *Journal of Consulting Psychology, 16,* 319-324.

Farberow, N. L. (1967). Crisis, disaster, and suicide: Theory and therapy. In E. S. Shneidman (Ed.), *Essays in Self-Destruction* (pp. 373–398). New York: Science House.

Farberow, N. L. (1993, April). From the Los Angeles Suicide Prevention Center to the crisis center movement: Past, present, and future challenges. Annual conference of the American Association of Suicidology, San Francisco.

Farberow, N. L., & Shneidman, E. S. (1961). A survey of agencies for the prevention of suicide. In N. L. Farberow, & E. S. Shneidman (Eds.), *The cry for help* (pp. 136–149). Toronto, Canada: McGraw-Hill.

Fox, R. (1973). The Samaritan contribution to suicide prevention. In C. Varah (Ed.), *The Samaritans in the '70s* (pp. 136–145). London: Constable.

Galbraith, J. K. (1958). *The affluent society.* Boston: Houghton-Mifflin.

Heller, K., Price, R., Reinharz, S., Riger, S., & Wandersman, A. (1984). *Psychology and community change: Challenges of the future.* Homewood, IL: Dorsey.

Iscoe, I., & Spielberger, C. (1970). The emerging field of community psychology. In I. Iscoe & C. Spielberger (Eds.), *Community psychology: Perspectives in training and research* (pp. 3–16). New York: Appleton-Century-Crofts.

Kelly, N. (1980). On being a volunteer. In C. Varah (Ed.), *The Samaritans in the '80s* (pp. 180–182). London: Constable.

Leahy, T. (1992). *A history of psychology: Main currents in psychological thought.* Englewood Cliffs, NJ: Prentice-Hall.

Levine, M. (1981). *The history and politics of community mental health.* New York: Oxford University Press.

Levine, M., & Levine, A. (1970). *A social history of helping services: Clinic, court, school and community.* New York: Appleton-Century-Crofts.

Lindemann, E. (1944). Symptomatology and management of acute grief. *American Journal of Psychiatry, 101,* 141–148.

Luborsky, L. (1954). A note on Eysenck's article "The effects of psychotherapy: An evaluation." *British Journal of Psychology, 45,* 129–131.

Maris, R. (1988). Preface. In R. Maris (Ed.), *Understanding and preventing suicide* (pp. vii–xxiii). New York: Guilford.

Matusow, A. (1984). *The unraveling of America: A history of Liberalism in the 1960s.* Philadelphia: Harper & Row.

McGee, R. (1971). Selection and training of nonprofessionals and volunteers. In J. Zusman & D. Davidson (Eds.), *Organizing the community to prevent suicide* (pp. 37–42). Springfield, IL: Charles C. Thomas.

McGee, R. (1974). *Crisis intervention in the community.* Baltimore: University Park Press.

Motto, J., Brooks, R., Ross, C., & Allen, N. (1974). *Standards for suicide prevention and crisis centers.* New York: Behavioral Publications.

Perry, J. (1976). Four twentieth-century themes in community mental health programs. In B. Kaplan, R. Wilson, & A. Leighton (Eds.), *Further explorations in social psychiatry* (pp. 46–73). New York: Basic.

Peters, K., Kochanek, K., & Murphy, S. (1998). Deaths: Final data for 1996. *National Vital Statistics Report, 47,* Number 9. Hyattsville, MD: National Center for Health Statistics. DHHS Publication No. (PHS) 99-1120.

Rosenzweig, S. (1954). A transvaluation of psychotherapy: A reply to Hans Eysenck. *Journal of Abnormal and Social Psychology, 49,* 298–304.

Sarason, S., Levine, M., Goldenberg, I., Cherlin, D., & Bennett, E. (1966). *Psychology in community settings: Clinical, educational, vocational, social aspects.* New York: Wiley.

Shneidman, E. S. (1971). The national suicide prevention program. In J. Zusman & D. Davidson (Eds.), *Organizing the community to prevent suicide* (pp. 19–29). Springfield, IL: Charles C. Thomas.

Shneidman, E. S. (1973a). Discussion: A question of research. In E. S. Shneidman (Ed.), *On the nature of suicide* (pp. 87–99). San Francisco: Jossey-Bass.

Shneidman, E. S. (1973b). Fifty-eight years. In E. S. Shneidman (Ed.), *On the nature of suicide* (pp. 1–30). San Francisco: Jossey-Bass.

Shneidman, E. S. (1988). Some reflections of a founder. In R. Maris (Ed.), *Understanding and preventing suicide* (pp. 1–12). New York: Guilford.

Shneidman, E. S., & Farberow, N. L. (1970). Feasibilities of the Los Angeles Suicide Prevention Center. In E. S. Shneidman, N. L. Farberow, & R. Litman (Eds.), *The psychology of suicide* (pp. 97–107). New York: Random House.

Shneidman, E. S., Farberow, N. L., & Litman, R. (1961). The suicide prevention center. In N. L. Farberow & E. S. Shneidman (Eds.), *The cry for help* (pp. 6–18). Toronto, Canada: McGraw-Hill.

Small, S., & Opler, M. (1971). Suicide: Epidemiologic and sociologic considerations. In J. Zusman & D. Davidson (Eds.), *Organizing the community to prevent suicide* (pp. 9–18). Springfield, IL: Charles C. Thomas.

Stengel, E. (1965). Lay organizations and suicide prevention. In C. Varah (Ed.), *The Samaritans* (pp. 107–114). New York: Macmillan.

Varah, C. (1965). Introduction. In C. Varah (Ed.), *The Samaritans* (pp. 9–87). New York: Macmillan.

Varah, C. (1973). Introduction. In C. Varah (Ed.), *The Samaritans in the '70s* (pp. 13–75). London: Constable.

Varah, C. (1980). Introduction. In C. Varah (Ed.), *The Samaritans in the '80s* (pp. 17–76). London: Constable.

World Health Organization. (1968). Prevention of suicide. Geneva: *Public Health Papers,* Number 35.

Zax, M., & Specter, G. (1974). *An introduction to community psychology.* Toronto, Canada: Wiley.

Zusman, J. (1971). Suicide prevention, crisis intervention, and community mental health services. In J. Zusman & D. Davidson (Eds.), *Organizing the community to prevent suicide* (pp. 85–93). Springfield, IL: Charles C. Thomas.

CHAPTER 14

Alan Berman
Virginia Lindahl

The American Association of Suicidology: Past, Present, and Future

☐ Past

With apologies to Durkheim, contemporary American suicidology can be said to have begun with the 1933 publication of Louis Dublin's *To Be or Not To Be*, an epidemiological study of suicide in the United States. Dublin was a vice-president of the Metropolitan Life Insurance Company and a statistician. His chapter, How May We Prevent Suicide? was the first contribution to a new field—the study of suicide prevention. Dublin's effort to spur research in and public awareness of the problem failed to catch the eye of the scientific or public policy communities, however, and it was not until the 1950s that local and subsequent national attention began to be paid to suicide prevention.

To this point, the seminal event in the development of American suicidology, and the genesis of the American Association of Suicidology (AAS), was the founding of the Los Angeles Suicide Prevention Center (LASPC). The LASPC was funded by a grant from the National Institute of Mental Health (NIMH) to two Los Angeles area psychologists, Drs. Edwin Shneidman and Norman Farberow. Shneidman and Farberow built the LASPC with the aims of providing clinical services and public health programming to the community and conducting research into suicide. Within their first few years of operation, they also discovered the potential of using trained volunteers to handle calls from suicidal people, thus initiating a golden age of volunteerism on telephone hotline services.

Within the next decade, growing interest from the NIMH in suicide prevention research energized Louis Dublin to become an impassioned and outspoken leader in the field. With Dublin's help, the NIMH founded the Center for Studies in Suicide Prevention (CSSP) in 1966, with the goal of supporting research, education, and clinical programs in this area. Not surprisingly, the first director of the CSSP was Dr. Edwin Shneidman, recruited by the NIMH from the LASPC.

Under Shneidman's leadership, the CSSP organized the First National Conference on Suicidology to follow the meetings of the American Orthopsychiatry Association in Chicago in March, 1968. This meeting featured a full afternoon Symposium on Suicide with an interdisciplinary panel of luminaries including, in addition to Dublin, philosopher Jacques Choron, psychoanalyst Paul Friedman, professor of education Robert Havighurst, and psychiatrists Lawrence Kubie, Erich Lindemann, Karl Menninger, and Erwin Stengel. Immediately following this symposium, Shneidman chaired a business meeting at which he presented an agenda (and a prewritten Constitution) for the establishment of the AAS.

Shneidman's vision for the organization was far-reaching. Its main missions would be education, prevention, and research. Mirroring the aforementioned Symposium on Suicide, he had in mind a broad-based, multidisciplinary association of individuals who shared a common mission. The AAS would focus on public outreach, including the provision of referrals, crisis intervention, and volunteer training. Recognizing the burgeoning importance of volunteer crisis workers throughout the country, Shneidman wanted to harness the power of these centers for use in research. In exchange, the AAS would serve as a resource for the crisis intervention community, providing support, certification, education, and networking opportunities. Again, it was no surprise that Shneidman was elected the first president of AAS, the first national nonprofit organization dedicated to suicide prevention. The organization's by-laws were adopted and Articles of Incorporation were filed with the State of California in April, 1972.

Annual Conferences

In accordance with Dr. Shneidman's vision, professional conferences followed this meeting on an annual basis. These annual conferences brought together researchers, academics, students, and community activists and facilitated the sharing of research and clinical and community advances in suicidology. Over the years, the conference has expanded in scope and breadth and has become a multidisciplinary forum for debate, discussion, and education. Conferences grew to include full-day preconference training workshops, think tanks which challenged attendees to debate and interact on a controversial issue or the implications of a research finding, and numerous opportunities for the sharing of information and networking.

Agenda Setting: Shaping the Federal, State, and Local Debate

Historically, the annual conferences have served a crucial role in setting the agenda for the year to come. While these goals are sometimes specific to the AAS, over time the organization has increasingly led the national public health debate over suicide prevention. Over the years, AAS has issued position papers and press releases targeted at increasing public awareness and community activism in suicide prevention. For example, in 1975, (Newslink, 1975) the AAS drafted a position paper on suicide prevention that was subsequently adopted by the American

Public Health Association. The paper laid out a framework for better public education about suicide and the risk of suicide, increased access to mental health care for those in crisis, and dissemination of general information about suicide.

At the Annual Conference business meetings, AAS members have debated a number of significant resolutions affecting national policy. In 1976, AAS resolved that a suicide prevention barrier on the Golden Gate Bridge in San Francisco was a priority, beginning more than 20 years of advocacy efforts for this project. In 1979, the AAS passed a resolution in support of effective handgun control, adopting a position that 20 years later has put the organization at the heart of the gun violence prevention movement in the United States. Similar resolutions have been adopted over subsequent years to encourage research regarding the higher risk for suicide in gays and lesbians and in support of nuclear disarmament.

AAS has also played an important part in advocating national suicide prevention programs. May 19–25, 1974, marked the first National Suicide Prevention Week, a major triumph in drawing much-needed attention to suicide prevention. Through the efforts of then president Nancy Allen and public service announcements featuring celebrities such as Charlton Heston, Kirk Douglas, and Deborah Kerr, crisis centers received an impressive packet of information from AAS for use during the week, including posters, copies of radio and TV spots, press releases, and ideas for community involvement in prevention activities. In the 25 years that have followed, annual Suicide Prevention Week programs have fueled an increasing amount of public and media attention and community interest.

In 1986, with the support of both private foundations and the National Education Association, AAS organized an working group of interested parties to a Frank Lloyd Wright designed conference center (Wingspread) in Racine, Wisconsin, to review and evaluate school-based suicide prevention programs and to recommend model programs. In the same year, through the advocacy and leadership of the Association's Legislative Committee, the first Youth Suicide Prevention Act was introduced and received support in the United States Congress. Other examples of AAS's role in influencing the national agenda include that of forging a collaborative working alliance with the Centers for Disease Control (CDC) to improve the quality of surveillance by better defining our nomenclature and (in 1996) holding a multidisciplinary work group meeting to develop a Consensus Statement of Youth Suicide by Firearms, a document now cosigned by some 40 national organizations.

Over the years, AAS's role in the national legislative debate has increased as the organization became increasingly known for its expertise. It is no longer unusual that AAS members are asked to consult with federal, state, and local lawmakers regarding pending legislation. In 1990s, for example, AAS members have testified before Congress on the subject of elderly suicide and have advocated increased federal appropriations for suicide prevention.

Crisis Worker and Crisis Center Certification

The merging of community activism and research allowed AAS to begin certifying individual crisis counselors and centers. AAS began certifying centers in 1986 using what developed into a stringent set of evaluation criteria (American Institute of Suicidology, 1995). Centers were (and are still) evaluated on the basis of seven areas: 1) administration and organizational structure; 2) training program; 3) general service delivery system; 4) services in life-threatening crises; 5) ethical standards and practices; 6) community integration; and 7) program evaluation. Centers also agree to a site examination, during which the examiner collects data on, among other things, client satisfaction with the center. To date, almost 90 centers have met these criteria and are certified.

In 1989, AAS expanded its certification to individual crisis workers, requiring that examinees demonstrate knowledge of both the theory and the application of the principles of crisis intervention. Certified individuals must have at least two years or 500 hours of clinical experience, undergo an evaluation of their crisis skills, and pass a written examination. This comprehensive exam covers three general areas: knowledge, skills, and attitudes. Required knowledge includes such crucial topics as crisis theory and management, principles of suicidology, ethical and legal issues, hospitalization criteria, and use of community resources. Skills such as active listening, efficient mobilization of community resources, and accurate record-keeping are evaluated, and certified individuals are expected to demonstrate a nonjudgmental attitude, a realistic view of death, dying, and suicide, and a balanced understanding of the role of a crisis worker. To date more than 300 crisis workers in the United States and Canada have been certified.

Targeting Youth Suicide

AAS has been influential in shaping the national debate on suicide prevention in several specific populations. During the 1980s, the public became increasingly concerned with youth suicide, particularly with the problem of suicide in the schools. AAS sponsored and participated in a variety of programs in this area, including organizing a National Conference on Adolescent Mental Health, held in October, 1988 in coordination with the American Medical Association. The program called on the resources and expertise of professionals including psychologists, physicians, educators, and juvenile justice workers to address crucial issues such as youth suicide.

In 1986, for example, AAS members were influential in working with the federal government's Department of Health, Education, and Welfare's Task Force on Youth Suicide Prevention. The majority of chapters published in the subsequent four-volume (1989) report were authored by AAS members (Alcohol, 1989).

Perhaps AAS's most far-reaching effort in the area of youth suicide occurred with the publication of *Suicide Postvention Guidelines: Suggestions for Dealing with the Aftermath of Suicide in the Schools*. Distributed to schools throughout the country, this manual was designed to help schools put postvention systems in place before a suicide. In the unfortunate event that a suicide should occur within the school, administrators would then be able to respond quickly and effectively.

Reacting to the very real fear of suicide contagion in this population, the *Suicide Postvention Guidelines*, now in its second edition, suggests three main goals in the development of an effective postvention plan: to prevent future suicides; to help students, faculty, staff, and administrators cope with their grief; and to assist in the school's return to normal functioning.

Drawing on the expertise of its members, AAS's guidelines explained the current gold-standard of youth postvention programs. Such programs effectively establish a trained and prepared crisis team, which is also expected to draw on community resources. *Suicide Postvention Guidelines* suggests best practices for providing individual and group counseling to those affected by the death, holding memorial services, facilitating visits to the family, addressing the concerns of parents, and responding to the media. Additionally, the manual suggests effective ways of disseminating information about the suicide immediately after it occurs, and includes sample fact sheets, letters to parents, and a memo to faculty that can be modified to fit the needs of the school. Lastly, the manual includes a bibliography to which school districts can refer for future resources.

Education and Training

In cooperation with Merck, Sharp, and Dohme's Health Information Services, AAS developed and widely disseminated *Suicide Prevention Training Manual* in 1977 (AAS, 1977). This document was the first in a long line of efforts by the association to impact the quality of training of both professional mental health clinicians and front-line gatekeepers.

In 1990, AAS presented the first of five successive week-long Summer Institutes for professional continuing education. These training experiences brought professionals from all disciplines together for programs ranging from the Assessment and Treatment of Suicidal Adolescents to Forensic Suicidology and The Suicidal Borderline. Using an eminent faculty and teaching in the relaxed atmosphere of a resort community, these programs were extraordinarily well-received and unique in their intensive focus on a single topic and the development of both knowledge and skills in these areas.

Servicing Survivors of Suicide

As community involvement in AAS grew, so did its role as a resource for survivors of suicide. Accordingly, in 1991, AAS inaugurated a second, concurrent conference designed specifically for survivors. The conference, which draws hundreds of participants yearly, focuses on issues specific to bereavement following suicide, and serves an educational, networking, and support function to participants. AAS's position as a bridge between community activists, researchers, clinicians, and survivors allows for a unique interaction between these groups, with the annual conferences encouraging multidisciplinary dialogue, learning, and debate.

AAS has embraced survivors of suicide as integral to accomplishing its mission. *A Directory of Survivor Support Groups* throughout the United States is published and updated annually by AAS. In addition, through a restricted account, funding is provided annually to support scholarships for survivors otherwise unable to attend the annual conference.

Awards

Central to AAS's mission is the recognition and public acknowledgment owed those that tirelessly work to better understand suicide through research and to prevent suicide through service. To this end, AAS annually makes awards to individuals who have made lifetime contributions to suicidology, early career professionals who have made outstanding contributions to research in suicidology, research in schizophrenia and suicide, student research, and service.

☐ Present

Organization and Membership

AAS now consists of approximately 800 individual members and 200 organizations (agencies, crisis centers, suicide prevention centers, etc.). Membership comes from every state (and the District of Columbia) and transcends the borders of the United States to include more than 50 members of the international community. Consistent with Dr. Shneidman's initial vision, members represent a wide-variety of professions and disciplines, including psychology, psychiatry, public health, and social work, and includes clinicians, researchers, academics, community activists, school district personnel, students, and survivors of suicide. Accordingly, the association is now comprised of five Divisions representing the primary interest areas of its membership: 1) Research, 2) Clinical, 3) Prevention Programs, 4) Survivors, and 5) Crisis Centers.

Recently, an Advisory Board was established, in an effort to increase the organization's visibility and to aid in fundraising. This Board currently includes a number of survivors who have been public about their experiences including: Senator Harry Reid of Nevada, a survivor of his father's suicide, actress Mariette Hartley (father's suicide), radio/television personality Art Linkletter (daughter's suicide), novelist Danielle Steel (son's suicide), and social worker Jo Pesaresi (husband's suicide). Also serving on the Advisory Board is physician/novelist/screenwriter Michael Palmer, who specializes in treating physicians with physical and mental illness.

Beginning in 1997, AAS began lobbying Advisory Board member Senator Harry Reid to promote legislation to establish the first Suicide Research Prevention Center (SPRC) through increased funding to CDC. In 1998 the SPRC was established and granted to the University of Nevada School of Medicine to focus primarily on the problem of suicide in the 8-state intermountain region which has for years led this country in rates of suicide. AAS has a working collaboration with the Medical School in this grant and is providing consultants and expertise in the eight objectives currently established to both better understand and prevent suicide in this region and in developing models of prevention that will have applicability beyond this region.

Currently, the SPRC is developing a tracking and surveillance system to compile a database of completed suicides in these states, developing intervention and prevention programs to be tested in communities in the region, and drafting a plan to influence professional training programs in the region. Committees are developing targeted plans to address suicide in specific populations, including youth, Native Americans, and the elderly.

The role of AAS in the development of the SPRC is considerable. In addition to consulting with Nevada's Medical School on various aspects of the grant, AAS is developing a modified psychological autopsy protocol for use in the targeted states. Integrating public health, epidemiological, and psychological perspectives, the study will collect data on various psychological variables from the next-of-kin of completed suicides. AAS will also coordinate the elderly and youth suicide plans, and will facilitate consensus on nomenclature and the development of data-driven intervention strategies.

In 1999, AAS continued its work with Senator Reid, helping Congressional passage of a bill to designate a National Survivors for Prevention of Suicide Day. In the past two years AAS also lent its support to a case before the California State Supreme Court and to the State of Massachusetts' efforts to hold handgun manufacturers to consumer product safety standards.

An Information Clearinghouse

Presently, AAS sees its most crucial role as educational, providing resources to the public, community activists, survivors of suicide, researchers, students, and clinicians. AAS maintains an extensive and up-to-date referral directory, including over 600 crisis centers and over 300 survivor support groups. AAS's Central Office fields thousands of calls yearly requesting referrals and information and hundreds more from the media. In response to these requests, fact sheets and brochures on specific issues in suicide and suicide prevention are complied and updated regularly. AAS also publishes abstracts of each annual conference as Proceedings, and two quarterly newsletters. *Newslink* provides information on suicide and suicide prevention drawn from sources around the country, a summary of current publications in the field, and news about AAS activities and future plans. *Surviving Suicide* is edited by and for survivors and those who work with them. *Surviving Suicide* includes news articles, personal stories, commentary, and resource information.

Professional Development and Training for Caregivers

While AAS's newsletters are targeted at its membership as a whole, the organization has edited and published since 1971 a professional, peer-reviewed journal, *Suicide and Life-Threatening Behavior* (SLTB). This highly respected quarterly journal presents original research, case studies, editorials, and book reviews. In coordination with SLTB's publishing company Guilford Press, AAS also collaborates on a number of books of interest to the suicidology community.

AAS increasingly has been sought out to help others educate their communities about suicide and to develop effective suicide prevention programs. In 1999, AAS developed an "All Hands" film and facilitator's training manual (AAS, 1999) for the United States Navy and a *Suicide Prevention Manual* (AAS, 2000) for the United States Army. Tailored specifically to the needs of each branch, the materials will be used by line officers and others on military commands worldwide. They are designed to provide best practices, resources, and practical interventions to be easily adapted to situations that might arise in different military environments.

AAS has entered the age of the Internet having established a web page (www.suicidology.org) to provide information about the association, suicide, resources, and to provide support to all who visit.

The Right to Die Debate

AAS has also become involved in the growing debate over the issue of physician-assisted suicide, prompted by the increasingly public question regarding the right to die and the actions of Dr. Jack Kevorkian. Although debate continues, AAS actively works to educate the public about the issue, particularly as it must understand the transient and ambivalent nature of suicidal ideation. A report of the committee on Physician-Assisted Suicide and Euthanasia has been published as a supplement to SLTB (Volume 26, 1996). This report raises and discusses the myriad of research issues yet to be addressed and calls forth the need for this research to better inform public policy. Moreover, it was at the forefront in calling for improved palliative care for the terminally ill. Thus, AAS, again, conceives its role as educational, that is, informing the public debate about a very difficult societal issue.

The Debate over Gun Control

Similarly, AAS has become increasingly involved in the issue of firearms and suicide, taking the position that making firearms less accessible and available in our homes will save lives. AAS has argued persuasively that gun violence prevention advocates need to understand the pervasive use of guns to complete suicide by those of all ages in American society. This has come into sharper focus following a number of highly publicized school shootings in which the youthful perpetrators have been shown in great proportion to have murder-suicide motives. Although AAS's position on the problem of easy access to firearms has remained steady for many years, its role in supporting legislation in this area has increased in the wake of increased random violence involving firearms. AAS has provided testimony and expertise to legislators throughout the country, advocating that prevention efforts must focus in part on the issue of gun control and the easy access of firearms, particularly to youth.

☐ Future

At the dawn of the millennium it appears that AAS's role in informing the public, training professionals, and preventing suicide will be even more significant. In July, 1999 Surgeon General Satcher issued his *Call to Action to Prevent Suicide* (USPHS, 1999). This document placed suicide on the national agenda and in the national consciousness. It accepted suicide prevention as a public health priority and laid out 15 recommended strategies to increase **A**wareness (A) and **I**nterventions (I), and to improve **M**ethodologies (M). This template, AIM, will guide the next decade's efforts and, with increased federal support, allow greater collaboration between and among public and private efforts toward suicide prevention.

Concurrent with suicide being embraced as a public health problem, the changing climate of mental health care in this country is severely testing the viability of our traditional ways of treating suicidal patients. With the rise of managed care, no longer can a suicidal patient be hospitalized for long periods of time. Rather, mental health clinicians find it increasingly difficult to get suicidal patients admitted to inpatient units at all; when they are admitted, they are rarely kept for more than a few days. Similarly, managed care constraints are making it increasingly difficult for chronically suicidal patients to manage financially continued outpatient care. Thus, new best practices in treating suicidal patients must be developed and tested. This is where organizations, like AAS, can play a major role. The collective expertise of the organization and its members must be harnessed and involved in the training of mental health caregivers in effective treatment modalities, those that are at-once efficient, efficacious, and cost-effective means of treating these patients.

AAS's vision is to expand its educational and training functions to meet this need. Similarly, the organization will increase its efforts to train and certify crisis workers and centers to assure that best practices are utilized, and to urge school systems to train guidance counselors in suicide assessment. Other front-line care givers with whom suicidal individuals come in contact must be further trained, including care givers in the justice system, military, social services, and so on.

Upgrading standards of training for professionals who assess and treat suicidal individuals is a major goal of AAS. Currently, only a very small percentage of medical schools, graduate psychology programs, school counseling programs, or nursing schools require specific training in suicide assessment and treatment. AAS will continue to push for required knowledge of the theory, practice, and application of suicidology for these professionals. Practically, training programs, licensing boards, and continuing education programs should be targeted. At the highest level, AAS must also spearhead an effort to establish a professional certification for suicidologists, one of Dr. Shneidman's original visions for the organization.

AAS intends to take the lead in seeking collaboration with government resources such as NIMH and CDC to forge alliances toward the study of a number of issues and setting standards for others. We have interests that range from those of standardizing our nomenclature to validating our research and forensic tools such as the psychological autopsy. We hope to influence hospital standards for defining suicide watch protocols and increasing ease of access to supportive services for survivors struggling to cope with the tragic loss of a loved one.

One of AAS's greatest strengths—its integration of research, clinical practice, and academics, and the all-embracing nature of the organization—is unique to suicide prevention organizations. However, AAS does not envision itself as competing with other similar organizations in the future. Rather, more cooperation between AAS and organizations such as the American Foundation for Suicide Prevention (AFSP) and the Suicide Prevention Advocacy Network (SPAN) must be fostered. This suicide prevention consortium would encourage a sharing of resources and greater support for each organization's individual goals and agenda. Perhaps most important, such an alliance would allow each organization to better flesh out its strengths in suicide prevention, and more efficiently allocate energy, resources, and expertise. The common goal of preventing suicide can (and will) be better reached in that manner.

☐ References

Alcohol, Drug Abuse, and Mental Health Administrcltion. (1989). *Report of the Secretory's Task Force on Youth Suicide.* Volumes 1–4. Washington, DC: Supt. Of Docs., U.S. Govt. Print. Off.

American Association of Suicidology. (undated.). *Suicide postvention guidelines; Suggestions for dealing with the aftermath of suicide in the schools.* Washington, DC; American Association of Suicidology.

American Association of Suicidology. (1977). *Suicide prevention training manual.* West Point, PA: Merc Sharp & Dohme.

American Association of Suicidology. (1995). *Organizational certification standards manual.* Washington, DC: American Association of Suicidology.

American Association of Suicidology. (1999). *Suicide prevention facilitator's training manual.* Final report to the Department of the Navy. Washington, DC: American Association of Suicidology.

American Association of Suicidology. (2000a). *Suicide prevention: A resource manual for fhe United States Army.* Washington, DC: American Association of Suicidology.

American Association of Suicidology. (2000b). *Directory of survivors of suicide support groups.* Washington, DC: American Association of Suicidology.

Dublin. L. I., & Bunel, B. (1933). *To be or not to be.* New York.

Newslink. (1975). 2 (2). Washington, DC: American Association of Suicidology.

The Committee on Physician-Assisted Death of the American Association of Suicidology (1996). Report of the committee on physician-assisted suicide and euthanasia. *Suicide and Life-Treatening Behavior, 26* (Suppl.).

Youth Suicide by Firearms Task Force (1998). Consensus statement on youth suicide by firearms. *Archives of Suicide Research, 4,* 89–94.

U.S. Public Health Service. (1999). The Surgeon General's call to action to prevent suicide. Washington, DC.

CHAPTER

15

Crisis Services

☐ Befrienders International: Volunteer Action in Preventing Suicide
Vanda Scott

Befrienders International had its origin in The Samaritans, which was founded almost 50 years ago in the United Kingdom by Dr. Chad Varah. Befrienders International serves as an umbrella association for more than 40,000 trained volunteers who provide emotional support for the despairing and suicidal in 40 countries. Its aim is to encourage the establishment and development of community-based and community-resourced befriending services. The service the volunteers provide complements the work of other professional, statutory, and voluntary agencies. By building on local action by local people, and using trained volunteers rather than paid staff, Befrienders International provides cost-effective services that are available when they are needed by anybody in crisis. Contact with the befriending services can be made by telephone, visit, letter, or e-mail.

In the past decade Befrienders International has delivered over 200 training events, ranging from five-day international conferences to two-day workshops in more than 30 countries. The training includes the development of the core skills required for starting and expanding befriending services and the promotion and exchange of learning and good practice by means of publications, workshops, and twinning programs through which befriending centers can help each other.

Befrienders International plays a unique role in the field of suicide prevention. Its volunteers have a level of commitment and motivation far in excess of that normally found among employees in a workforce. Each year the volunteers worldwide provide over five million hours of care, which, if paid for at the United States minimum wage, would represent an annual bill of over 30 million US dollars.

Background

Befrienders International grew out of a need first identified by Chad Varah in London in the early 1950s. He inaugurated a small drop-in center to which emotionally isolated and distressed people could go to talk of their despair and suicidal feelings. Initially he envisaged that this facility would provide a conventional counseling service. However, within a few months, five crucial factors were identified:

1. A significant number of people who were in crisis and suicidal in the Greater London area had nowhere or no one to go to for emotional and psychological support.
2. The number of people who sought help was far greater than had been anticipated and was beyond the level to which Dr. Varah and his few colleagues could respond with the necessary immediacy.
3. Rejection and isolation are often key factors for those in distress.
4. The majority of the distressed wanted someone to talk to who would give them time and space, and to whom they could express their deepest, most anguished thoughts, someone who would be prepared to listen, in confidence with acceptance and compassion.
5. All the requirements could be met by lay volunteers who were not necessarily professionally qualified but who had the human attributes of care and compassion and were willing to listen constructively, nonjudgmentally and with acceptance.

In the light of these factors, Varah recognized the therapeutic value of listening, and he inaugurated the first befriending center, which became known as The Samaritans. Befriending entails active listening. The volunteers steer toward the caller's pain. While they listen to the caller's stories, their prime concern is to help the callers talk about their sense of despair and their suicidal feelings. Thus, the callers are encouraged to ventilate their anger and to talk about their distress and frustration. In this way the volunteers offer emotional support to those for whom life may be getting too much to bear and who may be in danger of suicide.

Today, befriending is an established component of the multifaceted approach to suicide prevention. It is an immediate response to emotional crises. The lay volunteers who provide it are given professional support by appointed medical and psychiatric consultants. An important aspect of the service is that those who use it are in control—the decision when to make contact is theirs, as is the freedom to end it. Thus, contacts may last a few seconds or two or three hours. Although callers are encouraged to talk, they may remain silent if they so wish.

Since the first Samaritan center opened, a great deal has been learned, and a number of useful concepts and models of practice have evolved. For all the changes that have taken place, however, the central concept of befriending (active listening) has remained constant. It is nondiagnostic and nonjudgmental, and it does not require callers to have any philosophical or religious affiliations. It enables distressed people to articulate their innermost fears and anxieties, thereby gently relieving the pressure these have caused. By offering total confidentiality and undivided attention, volunteers encourage callers to explore both positive and negative feelings in order to help them to reach their own decisions. Volunteers respond to the callers on equal terms, with warmth, unconditional acceptance, and respect.

Twenty years after starting the first center in London, Varah founded the international organization, calling it Befrienders International, since he recognized that the name given to the volunteers in the United Kingdom and Ireland, The Samaritans, would not be readily understood everywhere. Now, as we enter this millennium, the worldwide movement has grown to such an extent that it reaches corners of the world as far afield as Australia, Argentina, Armenia, and China. As it responds to the urgent needs of distressed people in communities around the world, the organization has a unique role in developing volunteer-resourced suicide prevention services based on Varah's original simple model.

Aims

Befrienders International seeks to develop volunteer action to reduce the incidence of suicide. In part this is achieved by increasing general awareness of suicide as a social problem and by promoting relevant research. The main approach, however, is to enable the establishment of centers run by volunteers for the benefit of those who are in crisis and may be in danger of taking their own lives. Thus the aims of the organization are:

- to promote worldwide awareness of suicide and its means of prevention particularly through the efforts of volunteers,
- to promote life-coping skills that will reduce the risk of suicide,
- to develop suicide prevention work through the deployment of volunteers in areas of need where no service exists,
- to stimulate the development of networks in the field of suicide prevention, and
- to develop and support existing suicide prevention services.

Core Values

The core values of Befrienders International are encompassed by an eight-point Charter, which is adopted by all member centers (Befrienders International, 1981). It is a statement of what the centers offer and how they operate. Its purpose is to present to the public at large the essential features of the service provided by the centers. Moreover, by indicating what the centers do, it lays a foundation for cooperation with other services, both lay and professional. The eight-point Charter is as follows:

1. The primary purpose of the centers is to give emotional support to people when they are suicidal.

2. The volunteers who serve the centers also seek to alleviate misery, loneliness, despair, and depression by listening to those who feel they cannot turn to anyone else who would understand and accept them.
3. Contact with a center does not limit individual freedom, which is further protected by the right to remain anonymous.
4. The fact that someone has been in contact with a center (whether by telephone, letter, visit, or any other means) is confidential, as is everything revealed by or about the person.
5. The centers are nonpolitical and nonsectarian, and the volunteers do not seek to impose their own convictions on anyone.
6. Volunteers are selected, trained, guided, and supported by other experienced volunteers.
7. Centers may on certain occasions request advice from professional consultants.
8. In appropriate circumstances individuals may be invited to consider seeking professional help in addition to the support offered by a center.

The Volunteers

Volunteers are carefully selected, trained, monitored, supervised, and thoroughly prepared to respond to callers' emotional crises. As the work is both vital and demanding, volunteers do not operate in isolation but have the structured support of colleagues, supervisors, a network of experienced practitioners and professional consultants, and national associations. Volunteers come from all walks of life and, while they can be health professionals, the vast majority have no medical or mental health qualifications. The criteria for selection centers upon the ability to listen actively and supportively. They also encompass the capacity to:

- communicate warmth,
- focus on people, not problems,
- care about feelings not facts, and
- be enablers rather than doers.

Thus, volunteers are chosen for their qualities rather than for their qualifications—for their tolerance, humility, patience, and willingness to stand alongside someone who is on the verge of suicide. The ability to remain a volunteer despite the harrowing and emotionally draining nature of befriending comes from the strong and secure support structure. The selection process never stops. A volunteer can be asked to leave at any time if the quality of his or her befriending in any way diminishes.

Most of the centers in the Befrienders International network have between 50–200 volunteers.

Appropriate Service Delivery

One of the roles of Befrienders International is to assist in identifying particular groups in which the risk of suicide appears to be high. By focusing on a specific community within a given social context, for example the tea pickers in a rural community in Sri Lanka, it is hoped that a clear understanding will be found for the causes of suicide within the group. Then information and education initiatives can be effectively targeted, and the provision of care can be developed along socially appropriate and culturally sensitive lines.

Accessibility is a key consideration in developing befriending services. People who are distressed, despairing, and suicidal require immediate support, available at any hour of the day or night. In a life-or-death situation, time is critical. The befriending service has to be available at times best suited to the particular community. In an urban environment, or one in which the telephone is the normal means of contact, the aim is to provide a 24-hour service, seven days a week.

In many countries, however, telephones are not readily available, and callers have to visit the befriending center. Often only a daytime befriending service is acceptable, since public transport closes down at night, cutting off access for both volunteers and callers. Moreover, in some cultures it is not acceptable for female callers or volunteers to be out of doors after sunset. Thus adaptability is essential to the provision of viable suicide prevention services in the wide range of social and geographical environments in which Befrienders International operates. When it is appropriate to do so, befriending is offered away from the centers and taken into the community. In India and Sri Lanka drop-in centers have been established to meet the needs of those seeking help, and it is not unusual for callers to walk many miles to talk to a volunteer about their distress and suicidal feelings.

Once a community identifies for itself a need and the way in which volunteer-based services might satisfy that need, Befrienders International can enable the development of a service that the community itself will support.

Examples Of Befriending Initiatives

Hong Kong

After considerable consultation with the government, nongovernmental agencies, potential sources of funding, and mental health professionals in Hong Kong, Befrienders International commissioned research. This revealed that there was a need for a second, Chinese-speaking befriending center. The requirement was specifically (Scott, 1992):

1. to establish more telephone lines to be available 24 hours a day,
2. to promote suicide awareness programs for all age groups,
3. in partnership with social services, to identify any elderly person who was at risk and to arrange a visit by a volunteer,

4. to mobilize teams of volunteers to go out into the community for educational purposes in schools, factories, and emergency services, and
5. to establish satellite befriending facilities for those who are unable to use the phone service.

South Africa

In high-density towns and also in remote rural areas where there are few private telephone facilities, direct contact with volunteers is the most appropriate working model. Befrienders International, in partnership with Befrienders South Africa (the national member organization), embarked on a major project with the aim of developing appropriate volunteer-based befriending services in communities where suicide is a major issue. A dual research study in two townships focused on attitudes to volunteering and to suicide and suicide prevention (Heslop, 1998). The findings were the key to developing a model of befriending appropriate to townships.

Sri Lanka

In the rural areas of Sri Lanka, the suicide rate is extremely high (110 per 100,000). Geographical and psychological isolation is prevalent, psychiatric support is minimal, and agricultural pesticides and other poisonous substances are readily available in the home. Remote villages seldom have access to social services that could offer support in time of crisis, and codes of honor preclude revealing personal problems to outsiders. Research into suicidal behavior in Sri Lanka has, in the main, focused on gathering factual information about suicide rather than investigating the causes. There are, however, many theories about the effects of alcohol, poverty and deprivation, and the war in the northern region of the country on suicide.

Recognizing the lack of basic health facilities, the prevalent fatalistic attitude, and a readiness to accept death and dying through suicide, volunteers from Sri Lanka Sumithrayo (the national member organization) devised a research study (Ratnayeke & Marecck, 1998). The study took place in a remote village where the incidents of both attempted and completed suicide are the highest in the world. By introducing befriending into village life over a period of 12 months, the volunteers were able to compare data with those from a neighboring village which has had no access to befriending activities. It was shown that access to carefully trained volunteers could have a favorable impact on the suicide rate. The Sumithrayo volunteers have now opened a volunteer training center (with accommodation facilities) located in this remote area.

Canada

When a high-risk group was identified in prisons in Canada (and in the United Kingdom), a listeners' scheme was developed in which prisoners volunteer to give emotional support to their fellow inmates. Volunteers from the local befriending center provide the initial training and, slowly, as the listeners become more confident and competent they, too, can train new recruits within the prison walls. Supervision is provided by the more experienced listeners and through a weekly visit from a member of the local befriending center (Befrienders International, 1994).

Disaster Response

Following a major disaster, psychological care for survivors and rescue workers is essential, and on many such occasions, Befrienders International member centers have made available their resources and expertise. After the 1988 Lockerbie air crash in Scotland, volunteers from a number of neighboring centers were mobilized and a temporary service point was established in the village providing emotional support for the rescue teams, the relatives of the victims, and the villagers.

In India, volunteers from Befrienders India (the national member organization) were asked by the government to organize and provide emotional support to the victims of the 1993 earthquake in Latur. In a similar set of circumstances in Japan, volunteers from the Osaka suicide prevention center, in collaboration with three other voluntary agencies, provided a support system for the victims of the 1995 Great Hanshin Earthquake and to the teams of rescuers.

Reaching The Young

Reaching Young Europe is a preprevention program, being piloted in Denmark. It is based on the idea that providing children with well-developed coping skills will make them less likely to mature into adults with suicidal behavior. The project equips children with an array of coping mechanisms that will not only help them but will enable them to help others facing difficult situations.

E-Mail

Befrienders International has responded to new electronic communication technology by establishing the use of e-mail as a means of communication with individuals in need. This approach is aimed at reaching people, mainly isolated young males, who are at greatest risk of suicide—a group who are often reluctant to talk about feelings either by telephone or face-to-face. Research shows that a high proportion of the people who have made contact through the e-mail befriending scheme have revealed suicidal feelings.

A Case Study

To ensure the confidentiality of the caller, some of the details of this case have been altered. However, the caller did give the author permission ot present her case in order to extend awareness of seeking emotional support from volunteers and the concept of befriending as a therapeutic model for suicide prevention.

Susan was 16 years old when she first contacted her local befriending center. It was the year of her exams. She was popular at school. Life, it seemed, was good to her, though there was some doubt about her health, for she kept visiting the family doctor with minor ailments, until one day the doctor visited her—in the hospital. On the previous evening she had had a dreadful headache and had taken some of her mother's sleeping pills. This was the first attempt Susan made on her life. A few weeks later she made a further attempt; fortunately it too was unsuccessful.

Susan's life had become unbearable. Her mother was drunk by lunchtime every day; her father was trying to keep his job, but his life was falling apart. Studying for exams was becoming impossible. Each day when Susan returned from school the house would be a wreck, and her mother would be unconscious.

The doctor suggested to Susan that she phone the local Befrienders' center, and with her permission he contacted the director to advise him of Susan's vulnerable state. The volunteers were alerted, but she did not make contact. Or, did she?

It was a number of weeks later when the volunteers realized that silent calls were occurring more frequently between 11:00 p.m. and 3:00 a.m. The calls varied in length: often a few minutes, then on one occasion, 18 minutes, and finally, 47 minutes. It was thought that these calls were being made by one caller; the sound of the silence was the same.

Susan recounts her experience: "To dial the number—I can still remember it, 327000—and hear a voice was all I needed. I was locked into my mind, my thoughts, my whole body. Words would not come. I felt strangled, voiceless, yet the noise and pain in my world were excruciatingly loud and painful.

"For weeks I phoned the center, and always someone answered—oh, the comfort of listening to a person! Once or twice I felt the volunteer was frustrated with me and I put the phone down. Many times I felt guilty. I couldn't say anything and would only want to hear the volunteer say "hello" before I put the phone down, fast. Then I would cry and cry, almost uncontrollably, until I was exhausted and could sleep.

"I was sorry to be a nuisance, but I needed someone to care for me, to worry about me, to listen to me. And then after getting through on the phone I could not talk. It was all very confusing, yet I knew it stopped me hurting myself—well, I mean, killing myself.

"I made these calls late at night. Always after my parents had finished fighting and screaming and killing each other. The noise was tremendous, yet they loved each other. I don't think they loved me—I was never noticed. Early one morning after a long period of silence I suddenly found my voice and said something. I remember it sounded stupid—but I started to talk. Only a few words, but it was a start. I kept telling myself 'I am speaking to a stranger; they can't hurt me.' And I talked.

"I have wondered over the years whether the talking helped more than being silent for all those weeks. And I don't know the answer. All I do know is the enormous relief I felt every time I dialled that number and found a real person was there for me, waiting for me."

In Conclusion

Edwin Shneidman brought his book *Definition of Suicide* to an end with words: "In the last analysis, the prevention of suicide is everybody's business" (Shneidman, 1985). If we agree with Shneidman, we must surely endorse the view that those in despair should have immediate access to emotional support. This is the primary purpose of Befrienders International's member centers.

Promoting suicide prevention initiatives and working alongside health professionals, academics, and other professional support groups are also important functions of the organization. Befrienders International plays an important part in helping communities formulate comprehensive health policies. This is particularly so because negative public attitudes towards psychiatric problems and their treatment can inhibit people from seeking help. Education to increase public awareness of suicide and other mental health issues should be part of the overall strategy for both health professionals and the voluntary sector. Their roles are complementary, and there is a need for a multidisciplinary and collaborative approach when suicide prevention strategies are being devised. Fortunately there is in many communities and countries a close working relationship between volunteers and professionals. Moreover, on several occasions Befrienders International has responded positively to requests from governments, the European Commission, and the World Health Organization by participating in strategic planning for service provision in the mental health arena.

Throughout the past decade collaboration between agencies has demonstrably been a major component in the development of effective suicide prevention strategies. Befrienders International intends to continue:

- to collaborate with other agencies,
- to participate in the international debate on suicidal behavior,
- to influence and keep in touch with current developments in suicide prevention, and
- to focus on projects that will result in self-sustaining suicide-prevention services in areas of need.

Two specific themes have emerged to provide a focus of attention for the organization: 1) devising ways of enhancing coping strategies in young people, and 2) addressing the needs of geographically, socially, and emotionally isolated people.

Experience in the 40 countries in which Befrienders International operates has validated Varah's original concept that the suicidal can benefit from emotional support given by trained volunteers. The organization has come a long way since its formation in 1974. The way ahead will be long too, but the vision is clear: a world in which every human being in emotional distress has immediate access to emotional support.

☐ The International Federation of Telephonic Emergency Services
Eliane Bezençon

Graham Bell's invention of the telephone in 1874 opened a way for seeking help or for reaching somebody in a moment of crisis. M. Warren who was working in New York in overpopulated areas was continually confronted with the problem of suicide. In 1896, with the help of volunteers, he created the Save-A-Life League in order to bring help to people in despair. He was apparently the first one to formulate the ideas which later on would be considered as fundamental in the prevention of suicide:

- Most suicidal people are not mentally ill.
- The secret for the prevention of suicide resides in the fact that people can regain confidence in themselves once they realize that they are worthy of the attention of others.
- To doubt the meaning of life is not pathological, even if it leads to suicide. By creating a personal relationship, one can enable the other person to discover other solutions than death and to find new hope and an opening towards life.

There were other isolated attempts to bring relief and to offer help to people in distress. But it was not until some years after the end of the Second World War that a way using modern methods was found that caught on. In 1953, an Anglican priest in London, Chad Varah, advertised a telephone number for people in despair who were often suicidal. He received so many calls that he had to set up a kind of consultation service, and he needed the help of volunteers to serve tea to those who were waiting to meet him. He soon discovered that the attention that the volunteers were giving to these people was far more efficient than what he himself could have achieved with them. From there originated the idea of training volunteers to listen to people in distress and so was born the association of the Samaritans.

By 1956, two services offering this kind of help had started in Germany, the first of them in West Berlin, a city that had one of the highest suicide rates in the Western World. These services then developed in most other European countries.

In 1959, shortly after a Protestant minister, Raynald Martin, had founded the first French speaking Telephone Emergency Service (TES), La Main Tendue, in Geneva, Switzerland, he received a phone call from a Frenchman, Georges Lillaz, unknown to him, who told him, "I have just read in the Journal de Genève an article on the opening of your service. I want to meet you as soon as possible so that you can explain your work." Three hours of discussion brought Lillaz to the decision that a service of this kind had to be founded in France. Soon the first center of SOS Amitié France was born.

Lillaz encouraged Martin, providing the necessary financial assistance for him to travel throughout Europe in order to visit the existing TES posts in various countries which were typically called at that time Telephone Services of Moral Support. All of these had to face the same difficulties, but each one had a rich individual experience. Martin was convinced that it was imperative to hold an international conference in order to enable the people in charge of these telephone services to exchange experiences. He wrote to all his colleagues and friends inviting them to meet.

The first international meeting took place in Switzerland, more precisely in the Ecumenical Centre of Bossey near Geneva. More that 80 persons, from all confessions (most of them priests and ministers), accepted his invitation. For two days they compared their experiences. Eleven countries were represented: Austria, Belgium, Denmark, Finland, France, Germany, Great Britain, the Netherlands, Norway, Sweden, and Switzerland.

The meeting could take place thanks to the generosity of Lillaz, owner of the well-known Bazar de l'Hôtel de Ville in Paris, who paid all the expenses. The newspaper *British Weekly*[1], reported this event in an article called "Telephone Samaritans spread abroad."

At the end of this meeting, the first International Information and Documentation Center was opened in Geneva, which later became the International Federation of Telephonic Emergency Services (IFOTES). At present the Secretariat is situated in Switzerland.[2] Two other international meetings took place before the official founding of IFOTES, one in Bad Boll in 1962 and the other in Oxford in 1964.

In 1967 in Brussels, IFOTES came officially into being. The Statutes and the International Norms were conceived and accepted by all members. These were reformulated in 1973 and readjusted in 1994, and they are still in force.

Aims and methods of work were laid down and, most important, the principles of the Federation. These deal with matters such as:

- the 24-hour availability of the services to people in distress who may be suicidal,
- confidentiality,
- the possibility for the caller to remain anonymous (whether he or she calls on the telephone or in person),
- the selection and the training of the volunteers, and
- the refusal to exercise pressure of any kind, whether religious, political, or ideological, on either callers or volunteers

As an international umbrella organization, IFOTES promotes the exchange of ideas and information among its members and creates opportunities for contacts by organizing international Congresses and Seminars. The most important task is to support members' activities and training. In particular, IFOTES tries to support all efforts to create TES centers and national associations in countries where these do not exist. In addition, IFOTES maintains contacts with similar international organizations.

[1] *British Weekly,* September 22, 1960.
[2] Chemin du Verney, 1112 Echichens, Switzerland. Telephone and fax: 0041 21 802 33 77.

Organization

According to its Statutes,[3] IFOTES holds a General Assembly every three years, during the Congress. A President is elected and members appointed to the International Committee according to proposals made by member countries. All appointments are for a period of three years and can be renewed indefinitely.

The International Committee meets at least twice a year. It consists of representatives of member countries where a number of telephonic emergency services have joined in a national organization. The Committee deals with all questions relating to the Federation, such as general policy, administrative matters, and the organization of International Congresses. It takes the initiative in developing new methods of help and counseling, tries to take up new ideas coming from members and their volunteers, and attempts to provide places of meeting and to promote possibilities for research.

Four persons chosen from and by the members of the International Committee, together with the president of IFOTES, form the Executive Committee. These are two vice-presidents, a treasurer, and an additional member. The general secretary attends the meeting of the executive committee as an advisor. The executive committee prepares the work of the International Committee.

Volunteers

The most distinctive feature of the work of IFOTES is the lay character of its volunteers—voluntary and unpaid and very carefully chosen and trained during periods varying from 3–12 months. Each member country has, apart from the principles of the International Norms, developed its own type of training for volunteers and its particular way of working. There are countries where the entire service is provided by telephone. Recently some branches have opened an e-mail service. In other countries, clients are encouraged to come to the center for counseling or befriending which may extend over weeks, months, and even years. In some centers, therapy is offered by psychologists and social workers or by therapeutic groups of various kinds. All services are free of charge. Further training and supervision for volunteers has become more and more important in the course of the years.

Members of IFOTES

See Table 1 for a list of IFOTES members. IFOTES groups two kinds of members: 1) National Associations where they exist, and 2) independent services where there is no National Aassociation.

Full members are National Associations or Federations that have set themselves the goal of living up to the standards set by the Statutes, the Ethical Charter, and

[3] IFOTES STATUTES approved July 14, 1994. Available at the secretariate, ch. du Verney, 1112 Echichens. Switzerland.

the International Norms, consider these to be binding, and pay the membership fee in due time. Full members have the right to vote.

Associated members can be:

1. National Associations or Federations which have set themselves the goal of living to the standards set by the Statutes, Ethical Charter, and International Norms, but cannot yet do so,

TABLE 1. Present members of IFOTES

Country	(Group Name)	No. of branches
Full members		
Austria	(Telefonseelsorge)	9
Belgium	(Tele-Accueil,Tele-Onthaaldiensten, Telefonhilfe)	11
Estonia	(Usaldus Telefon)	17
Finland	(Palveleva Puhelin)	26
France	(SOS Amitié, France)	49
Germany	(Telefonseelsorge)	93
Hungary	(Ass. of Hung. Tel. Em. Ser.)	19
Indesui Dominican Republic	(Telefono della Esperanza)	1
Israel	(Eran)	8
Italy	(Telefono Amico)	33
Netherlands	(Telephonische Hulpdienst)	25
Norway	(Kirkens SOS)	13
Poland	(Telefon Zaufania)	21
Portugal:		1
Singapore	(Samaritans)	1
Slovenia	(Slovene Nat. Ass. of Tel. Em. Services):	12
Spain	(El Telefono de la Esperanza)	15
Sweden	(Jourhavande Medmeniska)	19
Switzerland	(Die DargeboteneHand—German) (La Main Tendue—French) (Telefono Amico—Italian)	13
Associated members		
Bulgarian Red Cross	(Bulgarian Hotline)	1
Croatia	(Telephone for psychological help)	1
Ecuador	(Telefono Amigo)	1
Italy	(Voce Amica)	1
Lithuania	(LATES)	1
Luxembourg		1
Romania	(Green Telephone)	1
Russia	(RATES)	200
Slovenia	(POT)	1
Ukraine	(UNATEC)	20

2. Telephonic Emergency Services which are specialized in offering services to particularly defined groups,
3. Federations or organizations working in close collaboration with IFOTES and having similar aims, and
4. National associations or federations that live up to the standards set by the Statutes, Ethical Charter, and International Norms, but cannot pay their membership fee.

Associate members do not have the right to vote.

There are some important differences between the TES branches in the various countries members of IFOTES. Some services were set up by churches and considered originally as (and some still remain) a Christian commitment. Manned at the beginning mostly by priests and ministers, they opened their doors, as time went on, to lay volunteers, even though priests are responsible for running the services in some cases. Nowhere is there any kind of discrimination between callers, and the same help is offered to all callers, whatever the structure of the service. Close links between telephone services and churches exist in countries like Austria, Germany, the Scandinavian countries and Spain. These services may differ in the way they are financially supported. Some are well subsidized by churches, while others rely mainly on donations and fundraising.

Another group of services, mainly those in East European countries, are closely connected with psychiatric hospitals. They were originally set up by psychiatrists who usually run the services. They use, however, volunteers to answer the phone, although many of the psychiatrists also take up this activity on a voluntary basis.

In other countries, such as France and the French part of Switzerland and Italy, services are totally independent and have no link with any institution. It is felt that a totally neutral image from a religious point of view may attract more easily some kinds of callers.

There are also some differences in the way services are financed. Besides those which are fully supported by churches, others rely on subsidies from various sources, including state sources, donations, and fundraising campaigns. Others are mainly financed by their own volunteers who provide contributions to give their local service the necessary financial stability.

International Congresses

One of the most important activities of IFOTES is the International Congress, which now takes place every three years. It is organized in and by one of the member countries and is conducted in the five languages of IFOTES: English, French, German, Italian, and since 1994, Spanish. They are working congresses, mainly for the volunteers of the services who welcome this opportunity for meeting and working with volunteers from other countries and for exchanging ideas, thereby being stimulated in their own work.

To take part in an IFOTES congress is an unforgettable experience. It usually involves 600–800 people getting together. (In Lindau there were more than 1,000 persons from all over Europe.) It gives a feeling of belonging to a great community of people working in the same direction with the same ideal.

Each congress entails two aspects: 1) the possibility of meeting and exchanging with participants in the various workshops in an informal way, and 2) seminars and research presentations to enlarge the horizon of the participants. There are also plenary sessions which present material to be discussed in the various workshops.

During the first two congresses, in Bossey in 1961 and Bad Boll in 1962, practical issues were discussed such as: giving advice, and facing specific problems. Great importance was focused on knowing how to listen to the caller. The main themes of the first two congresses were the tasks of the matrimonial counselor, becoming close to the person who calls, and solitude and the possibility of relating to others.

In Oxford in 1964, apart from two important themes (the liberating dialogue and the selection and the training of volunteers), a vigorous debate about the religious aspects of the services took place. Eventually almost everyone could come round to the fact that every human being has a potentiality of love and that TES should try to activate this potential without asking the caller what his or her ideology or convictions are.

In Brussels in 1967, IFOTES was officially set up. Statutes and Norms were discussed and accepted. They allowed every member country to keep its own way of working, but they prohibited all tendencies to influence the caller. In essence:

> The Telephonic Emergency Services are not a new social service but a particular attitude that cannot be found in talking to a minister, a doctor, or a social worker.

The first President was elected, Remy Mens from Belgium also in 1967.

The congress in Stockholm in 1970 focused on the theme The Liberating Dialogue. Participants discussed the three principles of Carl Rogers' Person-Centered Counseling: empathy, congruence, and nondirectivity. For the first time, delegates from Canada, New Zealand, and Singapore took part.

In Geneva in 1973, a new turn was taken—an invitation to the other international organizations that work in the same field. IFOTES had for the first time financial problems. At first, it had received substantial help from the Rejoindre Foundation, but now it had to survive on its own resources. The membership fees of the various members had to be increased. Remy Mens, the president, handed over the reins to the new elected president, Bruno Burger from Italy.

In Berlin in 1976, the theme was the possibilities and limits of interventions in case of a crisis. A German president was elected: Ellen Balaszeskul. In Reims in 1979, the theme was Solitude and Suicide, and the congress had more than 800 participants. In York in 1982, the theme was People in Crisis: Challenge and Response. Shortly after the York Congress, the Samaritans decided to leave IFOTES in order to join Befrienders International, an organization that was founded in 1974 and has its headquarters in Great Britain.

In Rome in 1985, the theme was the Possibilities of TES in Today's Society. A new President was elected, Peter Stern from Sweden. The theme in Helsinki in

1988 was The TES: for Whom, for What and How? Peter Stern agreed to carry on as president until it became possible to reach a consensus on a new election.

In Noordwijkerhout (the Netherlands) in 1991, the theme was The Encounter: Encounters with Myself, with the Caller, with the Volunteers, and with my Partner. A new president was elected: Theo van Eupen. The decision was taken to develop a professional secretariat in Geneva. In 1979, it had seemed a good idea to move the secretariat to the vicinity of the president. However, by working with a professional secretariat, IFOTES hoped to become more efficient. Thirty eight persons from the eastern countries were invited to come to the congress. Members of IFOTES and the Dutch Federation provided the necessary funds to enable them to participate.

The theme in Jerusalem in 1994 was Help and Hope. Thanks to the assistance of various countries and colleagues from ERAN (an IFOTES member) who opened their homes. 36 people from Eastern countries were able to attend.

In Lindau in 1997, the theme was Living Borders—Moving Borders. It attracted more than 1,000 persons. Again, thanks to the generosity of various countries, a number of people from Eastern countries were present. A new president was elected, Anne Ormond from Switzerland.

The next congress will take place in Sevilla (Spain) in 2000, organized by the Spanish Federation. The theme will be Reasons to Live, Reasons to Hope in the Year 2000 and the Coming Millennium.

IFOTES is a member of IASP (the International Association for Suicide Prevention) and WFMH (the World Federation for Mental Health, a section of WHO).

IFOTES has no desire to extend its action and establish itself where other associations are already at work. Its policy from the beginning has been, however, to establish contact with such associations in order to exchange ideas and publications and make sure that the rich experiences gathered around the world are made full use of. New ideas always spring up from discussions with others. IFOTES has regular contacts with the two other international organizations: Befrienders International and Life Line. They have recently concluded a Memorandum of Understanding[4] between the three organizations in order to improve our collaboration.

A representative of the other international organizations is always invited to the IFOTES Congress and vice-versa. Delegates from the Japanese organization Inochi No Denwa and from Contact in the States have been also invited to take part. The TES, in spite of their differences, form a large family. They all share the same ideal: to be present, to listen to the person living a crisis, and to respect his or her freedom.

IFOTES does not insist on the prevention of suicide as much as other organizations do, even if it is at the center of our preoccupations. They feel that, in insisting on the importance of listening, they are carrying out a kind of primary prevention of suicide. Suicide is still very much a taboo in some countries, and there is a

---

[4] Memorandum of understanding. Available at the secretarial of notes. ch. du Verney. 1112 Echicheas. Switzerland.

fear of discouraging people from calling if IFOTES associates itself too closely with suicide.

IFOTES has to remain modest in its activities. Its only financial resources are its membership fees. It is difficult to find money at the international level. IFOTES does not belong to any country, and everyone is already battling at home to find the necessary funds for its own TES. Apart from the general secretary who works half-time at a minimal salary, there are no paid staff. All the rest of the work is done by the president and the various delegates from the member countries. The new president has recently been able to visit a number of member countries. Her visits have been greatly appreciated and are a very important part of the role of president.

Plans for the Coming Years

The priority now, of course, is preparation for the Congress which will take place in Seville in 2000. Other goals are:

1. to improve various publications: the Newsletter could contain elements that could be useful to members (new ways of training, fundraising, how to improve public relations, etc). A pamphlet[5] is about to be distributed widely to make IFOTES better known,
2. to work on establishing general statistics that could be used by all member countries in order to present to organizations like WHO a kind of barometer of the society,
3. to encourage solidarity and encourage branches to twin with branches in another country if they wish to do so,
4. through the Spanish Federation, to support the creation of TES centers in South America,
5. to improve communication and information exchange between members about conferences and seminars held in various countries, and
6. to keep members informed about books and documents available at the secretariat.

Other issues for the future include:

- establishing a strategy for IFOTES 2000
- preparing a statement of intent
- exploring what members expect from IFOTES—is IFOTES offering enough?
- developing a corporate identity
- deciding whether to branch out into other fields of social help
- considering change or continuing to carry on the traditional way of listening

---

[5] IFOTES—available at the IFOTES secretariat. ch. du Verney. 1112 Echichens. Switzerland.

International Norms

These norms were reformulated in 1993 and voted at the General Assembly in Jerusalem in 1994. In order to gather as much input from all member countries, they were discussed with delegates, together with the Ethical Charter, in France, Germany, Norway, and Russia.

1. Telephone Emergency Services are available at any time, to any person wishing to make contact, regardless of his or her age, sex, religion, or nationality.
2. Any caller has the right to be listened to and to be respected, regardless of his or her beliefs, convictions and personal choices.
3. Listening is offered with a welcoming and open attitude, and the listener's golden rule is to never impose any obligation on the caller.
4. The contents of a call are highly confidential within the branches, especially with regard to any information pertaining to private life.
5. During a telephone conversation, the listener should remain strictly anonymous, and the caller has the right to remain anonymous.
6. Branches work on a voluntary basis, and listeners are selected, trained, and supervised in order to improve their listening ability.
7. Telephonic Emergency Services are entirely free of charge to the caller.

☐ Lifeline International and Suicide
Clyde Dominish

> Historically speaking the initial focus for Life Line was upon suicide prevention, and this still is a very important focus for the movement. Suicide is the one ultimate irreversible act in personal experience. The Life Line movement seeks to relieve all people from the impositions of such un-freedom. The insights of preventative community psychiatry have confirmed that the suicidal act is but the cumulative response to a series of unresolved crises, consequently Life Line is a ministry to people in crisis, whatever the perceived intensity of that crisis may be. (Becoming Whole, Report of the Life Line International's Study Commission, 1980)

Life Line began in Sydney, Australia in 1964 as a response to a suicidal call taken by the Reverend Alan Walker of the Central Methodist Mission in the middle of the night. This experience prompted him to recognize the importance of being available 24 hours a day, seven days a week.

From these simple beginnings, Life Line has spread to many places around the world. It now encompasses a wide community of people in ten countries who embrace a diversity of faiths, cultures, and experiences and who agree to work with the accreditation standards, beliefs, and values of the international movement. Life Line counselors, who are usually trained volunteers, respond to people from all walks of life. They respect personal differences, provide support, listen as callers tell their stories, and help them to make life-affirming choices that are meaningful to them.

Because Life Line is an international movement, a great deal of responsibility for the day-to-day supervision of centers falls to the National Committees. Cultural differences are a major factor in determining appropriate responses to indications of suicidal behavior. Life Line centers also develop a range of ancillary services in response to needs that are evident from their callers. These responses are often the basis for community groups to develop services.

During the last few years Life Line International has become aware from its statistics of the growth in calls from people at risk and now recognizes that in some national communities suicide has become one of the major causes of death in some age groups. It is now a major topic of discussion and action when national and international gatherings are held.

Life Line has a long history of dealing with suicidal behavior and has developed a listening ear for indicators of suicide risk. Protocols have been developed that ensure informed assessment and effective action. Every effort is made to safeguard callers' privacy unless there is an overriding need to place safety first due to imminent threats to a caller's life or safety. Collectively, these protocols help ensure that every possible step is taken to preserve life.

Life Line has worked with academic and professional groups to develop a broad understanding of suicidal behavior and recognizes that there are many self-inflicted behaviors that will not result in death but do require effective therapies.

Coming as Life Line did out of a life-affirming faith situation, there is a strong commitment on the part of every counselor to take action to save life. Life Line training ensures that this is done with compassion and sensitivity. This training involves them in a process of self-understanding, listening, and caring skills and at the same time enables them to recognize and assess the risk of suicide and respond in ways that promote safety. This means that volunteers are able to develop new skills and affirm existing skills and personal qualities relevant to their role. Because suicide intervention training has been a strong feature of Life Line's work, it has been able to offer this not only to its own counselors but also to the wider community.

An important part of a Life Line center support system is the availability of a well-maintained data base of available community services and referral options. By those means, the counselor is able to offer callers a wide variety of possibilities that they may be able to access to enable them to work creatively through the crisis. Some centers are able to offer face-to-face counseling services.

Life Line centers work on developing strong links between themselves and other community organizations and professional services. These services provide the center with valuable information that enables the counselor to put the client in touch with the appropriate service.

Because of Life Line's experience, it is also able to offer to the general community, and many organizations within that community, skills in sensing when people are vulnerable, and help putting them in touch with organizations working in the field of suicide prevention.

Some Life Line centers build a strong relationship with the caller and encourage them to continue their story, reporting goals achieved, progress made, and difficulties encountered.

All Life Line counselors receive training appropriate to their role. They are volunteers, motivated by a deep concern for people. They staff a service that is available any hour of the day or night to listen to callers irrespective of the age, race, creed, or culture. Centers operate under guidelines set down by the international association. The center must have an adequate referral base of services and, after initial basic training, a counselor must be involved in constant and regular supervision and provide professional support and adequate resources.

In the past decade, there has been an increasing emphasis within Life Line on establishing agreed standards of good practice. In some countries, Life Lines have been funded to fulfill a particular role within national suicide prevention strategies. In meeting this challenge, many Life Line centers have also sought to articulate more clearly the role that telephone counseling fulfills in responding to people at risk and how that role complements that met by other service providers.

References

Befrienders International. (1994). An internal document on service postion. London. (unpublished).

Befrienders International (1984). Memorandum and articles of Association, the Schedule (Special Resolution 1990). London. Legal Document, vi.

Heslop, A. P. (1998). Models of volunteering in black townships: Attitudes to suicide and prevention. London: Befrienders International, 12–18.

Ratnayek, L., & Marecek, J. (1988). Suicide prevention initiative in the rural community. Columbo. Sri Lanka Sumithrayo paper (unpublished).

Shneidman, E. (1985). Definition of suicide. New York: Jason Aronson, 238.

Scott, V. (1992). Strategy document on developing services in Hong Kong and China. London: Befrienders International, (unpublished).

CHAPTER

Right-To-Die Organizations

☐ The Hemlock Society
Faye Girsh

Founded in Los Angeles in 1980 by Derek Humphry, the Hemlock Society's mission is to maximize the options for a good death, including legal physical aid in dying for mentally-competent, terminally-ill adults who request it, with careful safeguards.

The impetus for starting the organization was the death of Humphry's first wife, Jean. Dying painfully of metastasized breast cancer, having exhausted all the treatments and the limits of palliative care, she asked Humphry, then a journalist in England, if he would help her die when the time came. This is probably one of the most difficult questions one person can ask another. Humphry agreed to help and was able to get the necessary medication from a cooperative doctor. When Jean was ready he mixed the pills in tea, they said their goodbyes, and she drank the tea and died. Humphry stayed inconspicuously in the garden when the police investigated and was never prosecuted although he later wrote a book about their relationship and her death.

Humphry and his second wife, Ann Wickett, moved to Los Angeles and, with the proceeds of *Jean's Way* (Humphry & Wickett, 1978), started the Hemlock Society in their garage with a small, dedicated board of directors. Encouraged by the world wide, positive response to the first book, Humphry realized that people were hungry for information on planning for a peaceful death and wrote the first, somewhat indirect manual for self-deliverance, *Let Me Die Before I Wake* (Humphry, 1984). Realizing that the law had to be changed to permit this practice to become a legal option, Hemlock became involved with legislative change for the first time in 1988 when a bill was introduced in the New Hampshire legislature by a Hemlock member and, in California, Hemlock supported the Humane and Dignified Death Act (Risley, 1989) as a ballot initiative. Both proposals provided a carefully safeguarded procedure by which a mentally-competent and terminally-ill adult could request and receive help from a doctor to hasten death after a waiting period and examination by two doctors.

Hemlock was not the first organization advocating medical assistance to achieve a good death. There were Euthanasia Societies both in the United States and England in the 1940s and 1950s. The American group evolved into Concern for Dying, which later took a stance against euthanasia. The English group became the Exit Society and is now the Voluntary Euthanasia Society. This is also the name of organizations in Australia and in Scotland. In the United States, an assisted dying bill was introduced into the Ohio legislature in 1906 but was defeated in Committee by a vote of 78 to 22. (For an excellent history of the movement through the late 1980s see Humphry & Wickett [1986].)

Also in 1980, Dying with Dignity of Canada was formed by Marilynne Seguin. As a nurse, she spent the next 18 years traveling around Canada helping people achieve a gentle death, which she chronicled in a book of the same name (Seguin & Smith, 1994). A serious illness stopped her work, but the organization goes on as an advocacy group for physician assistance in dying, as do three other Canadian right-to-die groups.

In the 1980s several other organizations developed internationally. D.M.D. (Fundacion Pro Derecho a Morir Dignamente) was started in Colombia by Beatriz Gomez, a well-educated woman who raised her children in New York and worked with Planned Parenthood and then with the Society for the Right to Die (which was merged with Concern for Dying and is now called Choice in Dying). Both D.M.D. and Choice in Dying are devoted to living wills and mechanisms to ensure that patients have some say in their end-of-life treatment—quite a challenge in a Catholic country. In 1997 the Colombian Constitutional Court, in a surprise ruling, declared that mercy killing of terminally ill patients by doctors at the patients' request, was not a crime. D.M.D. supported that change, although it meant the resignation from their board of a priest who had been a loyal member and his replacement by a more tolerant priest.

In 1980, the World Federation of Right to Die Societies was formed. This is an organization to promote international understanding of choices in dying. It is now composed of 33 member groups from 20 countries including Japan, India, Zimbabwe, Israel, Colombia, Canada, and most European countries. For many of the groups, the goal is to legalize living wills and health care proxies, which are still quite controversial, even in the United Kingdom. In other organizations, physician aid in dying is the major objective.

The goal of permitting a hastened death with medical assistance has been achieved in several places all over the world over the past 25 years. The first country to allow this choice was The Netherlands, spurred by a court case in 1973 concerning a physician who helped her cancer-ridden mother to die with a lethal injection of medication. The courts there ruled that, although she had broken the law, there was a *force majeur* or a competing higher law, that justified her actions. Over the years the courts have issued guidelines which, if followed, almost guarantee that a doctor will not be prosecuted although no law has ever been passed permitting the practice. (See Thomasma, Kimbrough-Kushner, Kimsman, & Ciesielski-Carlucci [1998] for details of the Dutch debate.)

In Switzerland, since 1937, it has been legal for a physician to prescribe lethal medication for self-administration by a terminally-ill person as long as the intention is benign and not for personal gain. Approximately 120 persons die each year under that provision through the auspices of the Swiss-German Exit Society (Schar, 1997).

In 1995 the parliament of the Northern Territory of Australia ruled that, under strict guidelines including a mandatory examination by a psychiatrist, a terminally ill person could die with the help of a doctor. The law went into effect the following year and lasted five months during which one doctor, Philip Nitschke, helped four people with cancer die peacefully. In March 1997, the law was rescinded by the federal parliament. (See Humphry & Clement [1998] for the history of the Australian debate.)

In 1997 the Constitutional Court in Colombia ruled that mercy killing of a terminally ill person by a physician would no longer be considered a crime. Colombia is a Catholic country; the shocked church appealed the decision, which was again upheld. Regulations must be drafted by the parliament which, not surprisingly, is dragging its feet, so it is not clear what the present status of the law is in that country.

In Oregon in 1994, the people voted for the Death with Dignity law but it did not go into effect as it was tied up in the courts, challenged by the National Right to Life Committee. The Supreme Court refused to review the case in 1997. It was turned back to the people by the legislature and was voted in again in 1997 by a wide margin. The law currently is working in an orderly way. By the end of 1999 43 people have used the law since according to two published studies (Chin, Hedberg, Higginson, & Fleming, 1999; Sullivan, Hedberg, & Fleming, 2000).

This brief contextual background is necessary to put the activities of the Hemlock Society in perspective. This is a book about suicide. The Hemlock Society and other organizations in the so-called right-to-die movement do not encourage suicide in the traditional sense in any way. The goal is to make more choices available so that people whose irreversible physical diseases cause suffering and irreversible deterioration in their quality of life can have the option of hastening their death with medical assistance. The choice of a peaceful and dignified death, in the presence of loved ones, in the face of an incurable disease is significantly different from the irrational, impulsive, desperate choice of a person who ends his or her life in the face of a temporary emotional problem, alone, usually violently, and to the eternal sadness and guilt of those who loved her because she could have had more life to lead.

Unfortunately, the term "physician-assisted suicide" is often used when the goals of the right-to-die movement are referred to, especially by its opponents. It is shocking, even to those who know what the term is supposed to mean, to think that a doctor would help an emotionally distraught person end his or her life. The term "physician-assisted dying" is more accurate since it is the hastening of the dying process, rather than the interruption of life. Kent Woodman, a Hemlock chapter leader who died from Amyotropic Lateral Sclerosis (ALS), said,

I abhor suicide. Suicide is when one takes a life when there are alternatives, as in when one loses a job or a wife or a marriage, or a business. Snap out of it, man! In my case, however, it's a death and it's been creeping up on me for over 10 years, and most recently it's been pretty violent. Each day I go to sleep certain that the day I just spent is the best one I will ever see again, that the next one will be weaker, more painful and worse. (Anchroage Daily News, 1998)

The Hemlock Society and the Hemlock Foundation focus on two activities as a way of achieving the goal of maximizing the options for a good death: 1) education on end of life issues, including information and support for planning for a peaceful death, and 2) changing the law so that physician-assisted dying can become a legal option in the continuum of care at the end of life.

Education, through speaking and writing, is done through Hemlock's publications, speeches, debates, articles, and interviews with its president, medical director, board members, and chapter leaders. Professional members of the Hemlock Medical Advisory Board and Mental Health Advisory Committee have written books, chapters, and articles educating other professionals and the public about end of life issues (e.g., Burnell, 1993; Greenberg, 1997; McKhann, 1999). Derek Humphry, a prolific writer, authored several books during his tenure as head of the organization until 1992. The sale of these financed the chapter activities. In 1991 he published *Final Exit: The Practicalities of Self-Deliverance and Assisted Suicide for the Dying* (Humphry, 1991), which was on the New York Times best seller list for 14 weeks and has been translated into 12 languages. "It is the best insurance policy I ever bought," one enthusiastic Hemlock member told me. Hemlock continues to distribute books, pamphlets, video and audio tapes, and advance directives, all having to do with rights and choices at the end of life, including methods of self-deliverance. Some of these are only available to members. The Board has always agreed that Hemlock must continue to be the source for accurate information so that people who do choose to end their lives do not cause further trauma to themselves and their loved ones by dying violently, by failing in the attempt and ending up worse than they were, or by jeopardizing compassionate helpers in legal entanglements.

Planning for a peaceful death is facilitated through Hemlock's publications and through phone counseling which is available through the Denver office and through its chapters. Two services available to Hemlock members only are the Patient Advocacy Program and the Caring Friends Program. A Patient Advocate keeps copies of members' advance directives on file. If a member or a loved one tells us that the member's advance directive is being ignored Hemlock will intervene. Members carry the authorization for the Patient Advocate on their wallet membership card, which also contains information on their medical wishes. The Patient Advocate will also step in if a member is dying and his or her pain is not being treated. Lawsuits are one way to deal with these problems if less drastic ways are not effective.

The Caring Friends Program is for terminally-ill and hopelessly ill members who are considering a hastened death. Trained volunteers, backed up by a professional support team, work personally within legal parameters with these members and their families. The three goals are to make sure the member has explored all alternatives, that if they choose a hastened death they will not fail in the attempt, and that they do not die alone.

The Hemlock Society USA, now through our political arm, the Patient's Rights Organization, or PRO-USA, is the only organization that has provided support to every statewide initiative effort since the first attempt in 1988 in California with the Humane and Dignified Death Act, which did get not enough signatures to qualify for the ballot. In 1991 Hemlock supported the first initiative that did get on the ballot, Proposition 119, the Washington Death with Dignity Act, which received 46% of the vote. A year later with Hemlock's help both financially and in manpower, Proposition 161 qualified for the California ballot. It garnered four and a half million votes, but not a majority. In 1994 Hemlock supported the Oregon Death with Dignity Act, which won with 51% of the vote but was held up in the courts for three years by a challenge from the National Right to Life Committee. With that case dismissed, the law went into effect in October 1997. By that time the Oregon legislature had decided to send it back for a repeal vote. PRO-USA contributed to a new campaign; the law was upheld by 60% of the voters, thus making Oregon the first state to permit assistance in dying. The following year Proposal B in Michigan was defeated by 71% of the voters, thanks to a six million dollar campaign run primarily by the Catholic church and Michigan Right to Life. PRO-USA is also supporting the Maine Death with Dignity Act, which will be on the Maine ballot in November 2000. It will be the sixth citizens' initiative. In every case, money for the opposition has come primarily from Catholic sources and the religious right.

Since 1988, Hemlock chapters have worked with more than 20 legislatures to initiate physician aid in dying legislation. None of these bills have been successful but more are being seriously introduced and supported.

The Hemlock Society is proud that, in 20 years of pointing out that the dying process is often slow and agonizing, the message has been heard. Millions of dollars are now spent to improve end-of-life care. The American Medical Association has begun its Education for Physicians on End of Life Care (EPIC) sponsored by the Robert Wood Johnson Foundation. That same foundation has given large grants to improve access to hospice care in several states, coincidentally where assisted dying legislation has been introduced. The Robert Wood Johnson Foundation spent 28 million dollars on the SUPPORT (Study to Understand Prognosis and Preferences for Outcomes and Risks in Treatment) study that found that, even in the best American teaching hospitals, patients die in pain, in anguish, being treated when they do not want to be, with many families ending up in bankruptcy. It is the threat and popularity of the concept of assisted dying that has focused attention on care of the dying.

Hemlock applauds all of these efforts and hopes that dying will be made sufficiently comfortable in this country so that no one will ever ask for an assisted death. We know, however, that this will not happen. No matter how much better pain treatment gets—and it has a long way to go—and no matter how compassionate hospice care is, there will still be people who value their dignity and autonomy and who do not want to live through the last humiliating throes of their disease.

Those people, if they are lucky enough to be hooked up to treatment, can ask to have the treatment stopped, as James Michener and Richard Nixon did. But, what about those who cannot ask for help because they are not influential or don't have access to a compassionate doctor? When Jacqueline Kennedy Onassis died, surrounded by the people who were important to her, her son John announced that she had done it "her way," probably with the help of a caring physician.

Hemlock is a national nonprofit organization. It is now set up in two parts: the Hemlock Foundation is the 501(c)(3) organization that funds its educational and charitable work; all contributions to it are tax deductible. The Hemlock Society USA, is a membership organization and is a 501(c)(4) organization so that contributions are not tax deductible. A subpart of the Hemlock Society is PRO-USA, which directly funds ballot initiatives and lobbying activity.

These 20 years of Hemlock activities have been responsible, in part, for the increase in public agreement (from 45% in 1980 to 70% in 1998) that physician aid in dying should be a legal option for competent dying adults who request it. Since 1987 several other right-to-die groups have developed, under excellent leadership, that have helped to call attention to this issue. Hemlock, however, remains the only organization that:

- has members (25,000)
- provides membership benefits (*TimeLines,* our quarterly publication, access to the Patient Advocacy and Caring Friends programs, chapter membership, discounts on publications, discount on registration to national conferences)
- has national conferences (the 11th will be in September 2000)
- has 50 chapters
- provides information on self-deliverance and all end of life options, and
- has participated in every campaign to change the law in this country by ballot initiative.

Since 1990 Dr. Jack Kevorkian has boldly and persistently taken a more direct approach to the problem of suffering people by providing direct assistance to more than 130 terminally and chronically ill people. Starting with his "mercitron," where the patient was hooked to an IV drip and triggered the flow of lethal medications (Kevorkian, 1991), he graduated in November 1998 to euthanasia, in which Thomas Youk, a terminally ill man with ALS died with a direct lethal injection. For that act he was convicted of a second degree murder and sentenced to 10–25 years in prison despite the gratitude of the Youk family. His appeal is pending. Jack Kevorkian is not part of Hemlock or any other organization, but is working to focus attention on the actuality that suffering people who want to die and who have exhausted all alternatives can receive the help of a caring and compassionate physician to achieve a gentle, quick, and certain death. He not only advocates it, but he does it and publicizes who his patients are and why he helped them. We know from repeated surveys that somewhere between 6% and 53% of doctors provide help in dying to their patients. Dr. Kevorkian was the only one who was public about it. He has not been the only force for change in the last nine years, for there have been many events that have focused attention on this issue with different approaches including:

- the publication of *Final Exit* in 1991 (Humphry, 1991)
- the Oregon victories in 1994 and 1997, and
- the Supreme Court decision in 1997.

These have all been serious efforts to change the law, but Kevorkian remains the one name associated with the right to die internationally.

As more people are living longer, there will be an increased demand for more choices at life's end. People do not want to suffer needlessly. They want to maintain their dignity and know they can get compassionate help from a doctor if they choose to hasten an agonizing dying process. Although there are certainly arguments from other viewpoints, the main objection comes from religious sources who are imposing their views on those who find a hastened death compatible with their own values. To quote Justice Stephen Reinhardt, in an opinion later overturned by the United States Supreme Court in 1997:

> Those who believe strongly that death must come without physician assistance are free to follow that creed, be they doctors or patients. They are not free, however, to force their views, their religious conditions, or their philosophies on all the other members of a democratic society, and to compel those whose values differ from theirs to die painful, protracted and agonizing deaths. (from the opinion of the 9th circuit court of Appeals, March 6, 1996)

☐ The Power of Hope and the Freedom to Choose Assisted-Dying: Compassion in Dying Michael Bonacci[1]

Wednesday evening after Christmas, around 8 p.m., Sheila and Susan met at the bottom of the steps leading to Mary Ann's home. They embraced, took a deep breath, and as they climbed each thought to herself, "May this all go well." Even though this was not the first hastened death at which they would both be present, there's a qualm in the stomach, an uneasiness, each time a patient finally chooses the moment of death.

Mary Ann's decision to choose aid-in-dying came after prolonged and futile therapies and treatments to check the spread of cancer throughout her body. She decided that before her ability to make her own choices was compromised by physical and possibly mental deterioration, and rather than being sedated with pain medications into a stupor, she would choose both the time and the way her life would end.

Mary Ann herself met Susan and Sheila at the door, hugged them both, and led them to the Christmas tree. Her two daughters and their husbands were gathered there, and a certain calm seemed to have taken hold of everyone present.

---

[1]Additional contributions were made to this section by Barbara Coombs Lee, JD, PA, FNP, Executive Director, Compassion in Dying Federation of America, and Susan J. Dunshee, past president, Compassion in Dying of Washington.

Mary Ann had chosen a special nightgown and robe and her daughters helped her get ready. Everyone gathered around her bed. All the details had been seen to; even a tumbler of mouthwash was at the side of her bed to help in ridding the bitter aftertaste of the medications.

As part of the protocol, Susan and Sheila reminded Mary Ann again that she could postpone or cancel the night's event if she had any desire to. "Oh no," she instantly replied. "My family and I have had a lovely day together, and a perfect goodbye dinner. I am absolutely ready to proceed." With that, she reached up to each of her daughters and their husbands and gave them a last hug and kiss, telling them how much she loved and appreciated each of them.

Since she had already eaten a light meal and taken her antinausea tablets, Mary Ann was ready to proceed with the mixture of medications and yogurt that she had already prepared. As she ate each spoonful, she commented on the bitter taste, but finished every last bite nonetheless. After a quick shot of whiskey, and some lighthearted joking, she followed with the mouthwash. Then Mary Ann reached out for each of her daughters' hand, and they talked quietly of simple, inconsequential matters, as though she were merely preparing for another night's sleep.

Mary Ann represents the typical person who requests Compassion in Dying's services. Even though they receive over 5,000 requests for information each year, only about 300 to 400 of those who contact this organization wish to pursue the subject of hastening death for themselves. Callers or visitors—students, hospice nurses, physicians, media—to our web site indicate a steadily increasing interest in death and dying in America.

Those who request more information and consultation about their end-of-life options express relief and gratitude for the opportunity to discuss openly and honestly how they feel about dying. All too often they are silenced or shamed by health care providers or family members if they mention the possibility of stopping medical treatment or requesting a prescription to hasten their death. Compassion staff and case management volunteers listen to the needs of the dying individual, and then offer as much information and emotional support as the person requests.

Susan and Sheila are two founding members and volunteer case managers of Compassion in Dying of Washington, and they, along with eight other volunteers provide information, consultation, and emotional support to terminally ill, mentally competent adults who are considering how their lives should end. They also consult with members of Compassion's Medical Advisory Team, a group made up of a hospice nurse, cardiologist, palliative care specialist, and pharmacist.

Compassion in Dying challenged the Washington and New York prohibitions against assisting in a suicide, and in 1996 the U.S. Ninth and Second Circuit Courts of Appeal declared that mentally competent, terminally ill patients have a constitutional right to request medications with which they can end their suffering. These decisions were appealed to the United States Supreme Court, and in 1997 the Justices declined to find laws against assisted suicide unconstitutional. The majority opinion, however, encouraged the debate to continue at the state level.

Compassion in Dying developed a national organization during 1997, Compassion in Dying Federation of America, that advocates for legal change to recognize an individual's right for aid-in-dying. The Federation coordinates the development of Compassion affiliates throughout the country, modeled on the flagship organization in Washington. It is headquartered in Portland, Oregon. Besides the Washington affiliate, there are new organizations in Northern California, New York, Connecticut, Orego, Alaska, and Southern California.

There are several other right-to-die organizations throughout the United States and the world. Compassion works in cooperation with these and other organizations to achieve its dual goals of improving care for the dying and expanding choices at the end of life. These goals are accomplished by providing information, consultation, and emotional support to individuals and their loved ones about end-of-life choices. Volunteers and staff help terminally ill individuals talk to their health care providers about accessing intensive pain management and comfort or hospice care.

Compassion's direct services program is grounded in relational care; one way of ensuring patients' empowerment and autonomy is counseling them about ways of talking with their physicians about choosing the time and manner of their death, and the most safe, effective methods for hastening death. Case managers and Compassion's medical advisors are willing to provide collegial support to health care providers who want to consider ethical and effective means to help their patients achieve a peaceful death.

Compassion's message is one of hope and personal choice. The option of aid-in-dying allows individuals to find peace of mind and cease their anxieties about the circumstances of their death. Inadequate treatment for pain, however, should not be the primary reason for considering a hastened death. In addition to exploring this issue at the personal level, the Federation is working with the legal system to promote effective pain treatment in the following ways: 1) working with medical licensing boards to decrease physicians' risk of discipline for prescribing adequate narcotics for pain at the end of life; 2) seeking prompt disciplinary action in specific cases where physicians undertreat pain and cause unnecessary suffering; and 3) challenging state laws that deter doctors from providing good pain management.

The Board of Directors and members of Case Management Teams at each Compassion affiliate follow extensive Guidelines and Safeguards that outline the eligibility requirements to receive consultation about hastening death. A summary follows:

Supportive Counseling And Information

Consultation and emotional support are available to everyone, especially adults diagnosed by their physician with either a terminal illness or an incurable, progressive illness that will lead to a death. Case managers help patients to understand their condition, prognosis, and the range of treatment, pain management, and comfort options. Patients are encouraged to explore hospice and palliative care, symptom management, and all end of life care. Ongoing spiritual support and ethical guidance is available upon request.

The Option Of Hastening Death

Compassion may provide additional consultation about obtaining the means for a hastened death, if all other options fail, only if a patient meets the guidelines listed below:

- Only adult, mentally competent, terminally ill patients are eligible. Alternatives to hastening death must have been adequately considered.
- Patients must request assistance for aid-in-dying three times in writing, with established waiting periods between each request.
- Advance directives, durable power of attorney, or requests by anyone other than the patient are not accepted.
- Requests cannot result from inadequate care or pain management, lack of health coverage, or other economic concerns.
- A consulting physician must verify the terminal diagnosis. If indicated, a mental health evaluation is requested. Any sign of mental instability or patient indecision cancels the request.
- The means of hastening death must be obtained and self-administered by the patient.
- If the patient requests a personal presence, two Compassion case managers will attend the hastened death.
- After a hastened death, ongoing emotional and spiritual support is available to the patient's loved ones. In jurisdictions like Oregon, where aid-in-dying is legal under certain circumstances, Compassion ensures that all requirements are rigorously met.

These guidelines may seem very stringent, but the organization's founders felt it was absolutely necessary to set parameters around the people they could help and the services they would provide. In the state of Washington, and many others, "assisting with a suicide" is illegal. Compassion's work challenges a broad interpretation of such laws, and takes issue with the use of the word "suicide" to refer to terminally ill, mentally competent adults who are choosing the least worst kind of death. Compassion believes that dying individuals have the right to obtain information about hastening their own death, and they have the right to choose the manner and time of their death according to their personal values and beliefs.

Death resulting from a terminally ill adult's choice to withhold or withdraw treatment, refuse food and water, or to obtain and self-administer life-ending medications should not be classified as "suicide" in the traditional or clinical use of the term. Unlike healthy individuals for whom the choice to live is an option, these people are in the process of dying; their only options are how and in what manner they will die. This should not be considered taking one's life, but rather, ceasing to resist one's death.

Always at the forefront of this discussion should be the question, "How can we soothe the individual's prolonged and agonizing dying process?" Frequently, grieving family members want their loved one to hold on until the family members are ready to say goodbye; or health care providers, unwilling to admit defeat, convince the dying individual to try another medication or treatment that is probably futile as well as burdensome. The question family members and care providers should keep before them is, "What is the most compassionate response I can make to this person's request to end his or her suffering?"

Compassion's vision is to live in a society in which all people have freedom of choice in making end-of-life decisions. The current danger is that health care providers and institutions, the government, and several faith communities seek to substitute their judgment for the individual's right to decide how and when to die. Religious leaders affirm that life is a gift from God and that only God can end a life. All too often, God's gift of free will is lost in that argument. Human reason and the exercise of free will have led to the development of technologies and medicines that keep the physical body alive far beyond its biological life span. Why should personal choice be negated as human life draws to a close?

Compassion affirms that dying individuals should be permitted to make their own end-of-life decisions, and terminally ill individuals who request a hastened death should be offered assistance to avoid a process of dying marked by physical suffering or emotional anguish. Compassion, therefore, encourages health care providers to make available support, empathy, and medications that will assure completion of the dying process in a humane and dignified manner.

Founding members of Compassion in Dying created the organization so that no one would have to die alone because they feared prosecution of their loved ones or health care providers. That is why Compassion's volunteer case managers will be present at the time of death if requested. Competent adults should be free to make their own decisions about the quality of life, and the time and manner of death, according to their personal values and beliefs. One of our patients wrote these words in his letter of request for a hastened death:

> I want to die at home, if possible, free of pain, and to die when I feel ready to go. But it has been difficult to prepare for my desired end. This right should be easier to attain and should be within easy reach of reasonable persons who know what they are doing. I hope I can contribute in some way, writing of my difficulties, to make it easier for others. An efficient prescription should be readily available to those who can prove their sincerity. It should be easier to obtain the necessary medication. Archaic laws must be changed.

Mary Ann's decision to take life-ending medications, at a time of her own choosing, offered her the greatest amount of hope and personal dignity. She was able to decide when the time was right, before her physical condition deteriorated to an unacceptable degree of dependence, and while she could gather her children around her and say goodbye before her disease process robbed her of consciousness, clarity, and the ability to make her own decisions.

A few moments after she had finished taking the medications, she told Sheila and Susan that she didn't feel sleepy, and wondered if the pills were going to work. The two women assured her that they were already working, and as they told her this, Mary Ann laid her head back, closed her eyes, and became still.

The waiting began. For some people, death occurs in as little as twenty minutes to an hour. Others may take several hours to die, but in all the situations in which Compassion volunteers have been present, and where Compassion's medical protocol was precisely followed, no vomiting, seizures, or other complications occurred. For Mary Ann, the wait was brief. In less than an hour she had died.

During that hour, her daughters and their husbands talked quietly to their mother and to each other; they held her hands and continually stroked her hair or arms, none of them leaving her side. After the death, and after they were sure the family members no longer needed their presence, Sheila and Susan left. Mary Ann's daughters contacted them the next day to assure them that all went well. Sheila and Susan shared Mary Ann's story with the other members of the case management team at the following monthly meeting.

Mary Ann was fortunate that her personal physician honored her open and honest request for a prescription with which to hasten her death. All too often an individual's request is met with denial, shock, or anger, or perhaps worse, the uncertain promise that "everything will be taken care of." This is the current situation dying individuals find themselves in, and if they do not want to surrender all control to their health care providers or a hospice or medical institution, then they must seek information and guidance about options for dying on their own terms.

Physicians are under no obligation to provide a prescription or assist with an individual's request to hasten death, but they should at least consider referring their patient to another physician's care. Likewise, the individual has no inherent right to demand assisted-dying from his or her physician or health care provider. But the current system usually places the overwhelmingly dominant decision-making authority with the physician or institution rather than the dying individual. Compassion seeks a more balanced, relational model for making these choices at the end of life.

The present unspoken, covert situation is open to abuse and coercion of many kinds. If an individual has not completed an advance directive, explicitly stating which interventions may and may not be used, and more important, *communicated* this information, health care providers are often uncertain as to how they should respond to a dying person's request to hasten death.

The choice about how and when to die should reside with the dying individual if he or she is mentally competent to make this decision. Alternatives should be examined in consultation with the individual's personal physician, family members, and spiritual advisors if appropriate. But a decisive, persistent request to hasten the dying process should be listened to and explored to its fullest extent.

Many individuals who request a hastened death have not considered all their options, and many of their health care providers may be unclear as to the options the dying individual may be interested in. Together they should talk about advance directives, available therapies and treatments, and the consequences of taking action or refusing treatment. Withdrawing or withholding treatment is often thought only to apply to someone in a permanently unconscious state, but this option is available to any individual as part of their right to make decisions about their body.

Voluntarily stopping eating and drinking is another choice that can hasten the process of dying. It is also a decision that sometimes causes less pain and discomfort for the person in the process of dying.

Increasing doses of pain medications to the point of complete sedation is another legal and ethical option for those individuals who do not want to experience physical or emotional suffering as they are dying. This is often easier for loved ones, too, since signs of suffering are greatly reduced if not altogether absent.

Compassion exists to advocate for these choices as a continuum of end-of-life care. The decision to consciously and honestly hasten one's death is a right that should no longer be denied to competent adults. Choices at the end of life should provide hope to the dying individual, so that suffering and indignities as defined by each individual can be reduced.

To have the knowledge that one can die with loved ones gathered, and avoid a debilitating and exhausting process of physical and perhaps mental deterioration—this should not be interpreted as suicidal ideation or indirect self-destructive behavior. Assisted-dying is not "killing the patient" as right-to-life groups argue. Choosing how and when to die represents the hope and the power that should be the right of dying individuals within our society.

Talking with someone, openly and honestly, about all options at the end of life is perhaps the most compassionate gift any one of us can give to a dying person. Compassion in Dying's unique service is this belief in developing relationships with terminally ill individuals and their loved ones and health care providers. Beliefs about suffering and quality of life are intensely personal. Recognizing this, Compassion in Dying promotes, in all its activities, a respect for life that upholds autonomy and self-determination.

☐ References

Burnell, G. (1993). *Final choices: To live or to die in an age of medical technology.* New York: Plenum Press.

Chin, A., Hedberg, K., Higginson, G. T., & Fleming, D. W. (1999). Legalized physician-assisted suicide in Oregon: The first year's experience. *New England Journal of Medicine, 340,* 577–583.

Greenberg, S. (1997). *Euthanasia and assisted suicide: Psychosocial issues.* Springfield, IL: Charles C. Thomas

Humphry, D., & Wickett, A. (1978). *Jean's way.* New York: Fontana.

Humphry, D. (1984). *Let me die before I wake.* Los Angeles: Hemlock Society.

Humphry, D. (1991). *Final exit: The practicalities of self-deliverance and assisted suicide for the dying.* New York: Dell.

Humphry, D., & Clement, M. (1998). *Freedom to die: People, politics and the right-to-die movement.* New York: St. Martin's Press.

Humphry, D., & Wickett, A. (1986). *The right to die.* Understanding euthanasia. New York: HarperRow.

Kevorkian, J. (1991). *Prescription medicide: The goodness of planned death.* Buffalo: Prometheus Books.

McKhann, C. (1999). *A time to die: The place for physician assistance.* New Haven: Yale University Press.

Reinhardt, S. (1996). Compassion in dying. V. State of Washington. 96 Daily Journal D.A.R. 2639, p. 2660.

Risley, R. (1989). *Death with dignity: A new law permitting physician aid-in-dying.* Eugene, OR: Hemlock Society.

Schar, M. (1997). Assisted suicide in Switzerland: When is it permitted? *Hawaii Medical Journal, 56*(3), 63–68.

Seguin, M., & Smith, C. (1994). *A gentle death.* Toronto: Key Porter Books.

Sullivan, A. D., Hedberg, K.., & Fleming, D. W. Legalized physician-assisted suicide in Oregon—the seond year. *New England Journal of Medicine, 342,* 598–603.

Thomasma, D. C., Kimbrough-Kushner, T., Kimsma, G. K., & Ciesielski-Carlucci, C. (Eds.). (1998). *Asking to die: Inside the Dutch debate on euthanasia.* Boston: Kluwer.

Woodman, K. L. (1998). Parting thoughts from Ken Lee Woodman. Anchorage Daily News, October 6, 1998. F-1, F-4.

CHAPTER

International Organizations

☐ **The International Association for Suicide Prevention**
Robert D. Goldney, Norman L. Farberow,
Nils Retterstol

The International Association for Suicide Prevention (IASP) grew out of a meeting convened by Erwin Ringel in Vienna, Austria in September, 1960. In 1955, Ringel had founded a suicide prevention center in Vienna in cooperation with the Catholic Church and the Catholic welfare organization, Caritas. A team of psychiatrists, doctors, social workers, psychotherapists, psychologists, lawyers, and pastoral workers was established and the center was given the name Lebensmüdenfursorge or The Center for Care of those Tired of Living. It was arranged that those who had attempted suicide would be admitted to the detoxification ward of the University Psychiatric Clinic, and that aftercare would be provided by Lebensmüdenfursorge.

The cooperative work in the Center and the study by Professor Ringel that produced his seminal contribution, *The Pre-Suicidal Syndrome*, provided the initiative for that first meeting in Vienna and was the basis for the foundation of IASP. The initial meeting was attended primarily by mental health professionals from Europe and was the first conference devoted entirely to the subject of etiology and prevention suicide. The IASP became world wide with its second conference in Copenhagen, Denmark in 1963, when clinicians from North America and the Far East participated. Since then biannual conferences have been held regularly in varying parts of the world, bringing the magnitude of the problem of suicide to the attention of the world's scientific, clinical, volunteer, community, and government organizations.

It is a reflection of the nascent state of the study of suicide and its prevention that IASP is one of the few organizations that was first formed on an international basis. Membership of IASP comes from all continents in the world and 52 countries, with a national representative identified in each. Since then a number of these countries, urged by their IASP members, have developed their own national suicide prevention associations.

The original constitution was written by Professors Erwin Ringel and Norman Farberow in 1962, while the latter was on a sabbatical year in Vienna. They were assisted in the formulation of the constitution by frequent consultations with Professor Walther Poeldinger, and with Dr. Vera Aigner, a Vienna government attorney. Another early stalwart of IASP was Professor Erwin Stengel, whose liaison with the Samaritans in England was particularly influential. The Association was officially registered in Vienna, and the Secretariat was maintained in Vienna until 1995 when it moved to Chicago in the United States of America.

The main objectives of IASP are:

1. to provide a common platform for all persons from mental health, public health, social and behavioral sciences, international and national government, and community agencies, survivors, and volunteers who are engaged in the field of suicide prevention and crisis intervention;
2. to provide a forum for the exchange of acquired information, knowledge, and experience from research and clinical activity into suicide and its prevention;
3. to promote the establishment of national and regional organizations for suicide prevention and crisis intervention;
4. to facilitate the dissemination of the results of research into the etiology, assessment, and treatment of suicide in appropriate professional journals and selected public media;
5. to arrange for specialized training of selected persons in the area of suicide prevention in selected training centers, where desired;
6. to facilitate effective international research in suicide that can be pursued only through joint cooperation, such as the comparative contributions of national cultures, philosophies and religions; and
7. to reduce the stigma of suicide by encouraging the development of programs for survivors of the suicide of a loved one.

These objectives have been addressed in part by establishing a Newsletter, *Vita*, in 1965, which was the forerunner to the Association's journal, *Crisis: The Journal of Suicide and Crisis Studies*, which has been published since 1980, with coeditors in Amsterdam and Chicago. Some national branches of IASP have also published their own journals, including *Suicide and Life-Threatening Behavior* in America since 1969; *Suizidprophylaxe: Theorie und Praxis* in Germany since 1974; *Bulletin de Groupement d'Etudes et de Prevention du Suicide* in France since 1982; *Giornale Italiano di Suicidologia* in Italy since 1991; and *Nytt i Suicidologi* in Norway since 1995.

The international nature of IASP is attested to by the diversity of office holders and the widespread geographical locations of its conferences. Presidents have included Erwin Ringel of Austria, Erwin Stengel of the United Kingdom, Norman Farberow of the United States, Walter Poeldinger of Switzerland, Kalle Acht, of Finland, Nils Retterstol of Norway, David Lester of the United States, Jean-Pierre Soubrier of France, and Robert Goldney of Australia.

Venues for the 19 international congresses have been Vienna, Copenhagen, Basel, Los Angeles, London, Mexico City, Amsterdam, Jerusalem, Helsinki, Ottawa, Paris, Caracas, Vienna, San Francisco, Brussels, Hamburg, Montreal, Venice, and Adelaide, with the 20th congress held in Athens in November, 1999. As of this writing, the next meeting is planned for Chennai (Madras) in India in 2001, by which time all continents but Africa will have hosted a conference.

IASP is a unique multidisciplinary organization with its membership coming primarily from the mental health professions, but with additional members from such disciplines as sociology, social work, anthropology, medicine, public health, education, corrections, probation, coroners/medical examiners, pathology, philosophy and others. In addition, members come from volunteer organizations such as the Samaritans, Lifeline, Befrienders International, and survivor groups such as the Suicide Prevention Advocacy Network (SPAN). Close relations also are maintained with organizations such as the International Federation of Telephonic Emergency Services (IFOTES).

IASP also has promoted scientific enquiry by establishing three prestigious Awards: the Stengel Research Award for significant research contributions to the understanding and prevention of suicidal behavior; the Ringel Service Award for outstanding contributions in the provision of suicide prevention services; and the Farberow Award for outstanding contributions in the field of caring for survivors who have been bereaved through suicide, a group whose distress has often been overlooked.

As noted before, IASP has been the forerunner of a number of national associations for suicide prevention. These groups are affiliated with the International Association and provide members with the opportunity to work at the national level on aspects of suicide relevant to their own country, while retaining their international links. A more specialized research group, the International Academy for Suicide Research, has also evolved from the membership of IASP; it retains close links in terms of cooperation on scientific projects and conferences.

IASP has official status as a Nongovernment Organization with the World Health Organization (WHO) of the United Nations, and a number of its members have held office in the World Federation for Mental Health. This has resulted in a number of scientific and educational collaborations with many nations, particularly in providing advice in the interpretation of suicide data, the dissemination of suicide prevention information, and the basic principles in the provision of suicide prevention services. Recently there has been collaboration with the international pharmaceutical industry in providing educational material in regard to the recognition and management of depression, the condition most commonly associated with suicidal behavior.

International research cooperation has emphasized the fact that suicide is a complex phenomenon and that theories of causation and programs of treatment in one country may not be applicable to others. Thus, the sophisticated programs for early identification, assessment and treatment initiated successfully in highly developed countries such as Finland and Norway would not be applicable for less developed countries in which the public health concerns are mostly about physical health and environment control. For example, focusing on the most common methods of suicide would result in programs on firearm control in the United States, while countries such as Sri Lanka, Malaysia, Western Samoa, and Central America would place the highest priority on the restriction and control of organophosphate pesticides. It is only by the fostering of an exchange of views that such differences can be noted and common ground can be reached.

The International Association for Suicide Prevention is in a unique position to provide an umbrella organization in which views from all nations and all individuals directly involved or affected can be shared and coordinated. To this end, during and after the 19th Congress of the IASP in Adelaide in 1997, a broad statement which has become known as "The Adelaide Declaration on Suicide Prevention" (Goldney, 1998) was formulated. This was a daunting task, not only because of the diversity of views noted above, but also because it required admitting that, in this era of evidence-based outcome research, we still do not have convincing controlled intervention studies to demonstrate a direct relationship between programs of intervention and treatment and a reduction in the rate of suicide. It may well be that the objective of evidence-based outcome research in the treatment of suicidal behavior needs to be reconsidered in the evaluation of such highly complex biopsychosocial phenomena as suicide, especially because of the low base rate of suicide. What appears to be needed is an approach that takes into consideration the humanitarian and interpersonal factors of the relief of suffering and distress, while at the same time applying specific measures that appear to be most effective.

Bearing in mind these constraints, representatives of the 39 different countries who attended the IASP congress in Adelaide produced a statement which was then formally ratified by the Executive Board of IASP. The statement is not designed to be of practical use in individual circumstances. Rather, it is designed to embody the broad principles of suicide prevention that have been ratified by the WHO, with specific emphasis on the role of IASP in urging governments and other agencies worldwide not only to acknowledge the magnitude of the problem of suicide in all countries, but also to provide adequate resources to address this major public health issue.

The Adelaide Declaration on Suicide Prevention is presented as an appendix to this chapter.

In retrospect, it seems that the first three major objectives of IASP have been met, at least in part: to provide a common platform; allow interchange of acquired experience in various countries; and promote the establishment of national organizations for suicide prevention. However, much remains to be done in achieving the other objectives. For example, as an international organization, IASP is in an optimal position for the promotion of research activities comparing critical contributions of culture to the etiology of suicide in the respective nations. Anthropologists can be enlisted to join mental health researchers in examining the cultural differences and similarities in family relationships, social values, critical taboos, and so forth. Separately and jointly the domains of early family experiences, physical conditions and medical illness, neurobiological status, psychiatric disorders, personality traits, and others, could be compared by representatives of the various disciplines for significant similarities and differences.

Furthermore, there is a need to be more active in the provision of education and training. Centers known for their clinical effectiveness and innovative services would be designated as training centers and developed to receive selected representatives of other centers who would learn the procedures and take them back to their own centers, modified as needed for the purposes of their community and nation. Other centers may be designated to provide workshops at regular times in the year that could be attended by representatives of other centers interested in adding to their programs and increasing their skills. A Visiting Scholar Scheme could be established, whereby IASP would sponsor experts in various aspects of suicidal behavior who would visit world areas with specific needs. Already under planning is the provision of an Internet site with links to other international and national organizations and research centers. Brochures, abstracts, fact sheets, and other information about suicidal behavior and its prevention that can be readily modified to suit local, national, and regional needs, have been distributed.

Increased coordination of efforts to prevent suicide worldwide are clearly needed. It must be noted, however, that there are significant challenges in the implementation of such efforts. Recognition of the extent of suicide as a serious public health problem, with its ranking within the first ten causes of death in many countries, has not been accompanied by the funding needed to achieve the desired objectives as quickly as possible. Implementation of efforts to reduce the suffering caused by suicide has been accomplished mainly by the ingenuity and creativity of clinic center directors, research professionals, and dedicated volunteers and survivors utilizing foundation grants and appealing to philanthropists. IASP has been supported by individual membership fees and by institutions with whom individual executive board members have been associated. There is an urgent need for IASP to become financially independent, with a permanent executive officer and staff to coordinate its world wide operations.

When IASP was founded almost 40 years ago, there was little government recognition of the magnitude of the problem of suicide world wide, and official statistics, when available, were not reliable. It is now estimated by the World Health Organization that in 2000 there will be 997,000 suicides. This represents an enormous challenge that IASP is poised to meet by providing leadership in reducing this human tragedy.

☐ Appendix

The Adelaide Declaration on Suicide Prevention

Suicide is a significant health problem in every country in the world, being among the ten leading causes of death.

The World Health Organization has six basic steps for the prevention of suicide. These are: 1) treatment of mental disorders; 2) control of the possession of guns; 3) detoxification of domestic gas; 4) detoxification of car emissions; 5) control of toxic substance availability; and 6) toning down reports in the media. These measures should result in a significant reduction in suicide in the world.

The International Association for Suicide Prevention calls on government health organizations, nongovernment health and welfare groups and volunteer organizations to share with the general public the responsibility for the prevention of suicide and to work towards:

the allocation of sufficient funds and human resources for research and suicide prevention strategies;

the establishment of appropriate government agencies to provide leadership, coordination, and resources to prevent suicide;

the establishment of national and local networks of support and partnership for suicide prevention; and

the provision of resources to groups who may have special needs.

The International Association for Suicide Prevention accepts its responsibility to:

place suicide prevention near the top of the agenda of the World Health Organization;

institute networks across the world to bring together professionals and non-professionals in the pursuit of suicide prevention;

urge all countries to secure a budget allocation for suicide prevention;

ensure that international, national, and regional groups are coordinated and have access to the latest information about suicide prevention;

encourage and promote research into the efficacy, effectiveness, and feasibility of suicide prevention programs;

ensure the availability of reliable information about suicide prevention; and

ensure that adequate care is available to those affected by suicide.

Ratified by the Executive Board of the International Association for Suicide Prevention following the 19th congress of the International Association for Suicide Prevention held in Adelaide, Australia, March, 1997 23–27, 1997.

☐ The International Academy for Suicide Research
Diego De Leo and Armin Schmidtke

The International Academy for Suicide Research (IASR) is a nonprofit scientific association that unites many of the most eminent researchers from the field of suicidology throughout the world. Membership is multidisciplinary and includes psychiatrists, psychologists, sociologists, epidemiologists, and philosophers of science. Access to Academy ranks is entrusted to a selection committee. The Academy's activities are oriented around fostering high-level scientific debate through annual meetings, production of a scientific journal, and promotion and patronage of research programs.

History

Design

The decision to establish IASR was made on December 9, 1989 in Hamburg, by the Executive Board (president Nils Retterstol, vice-presidents David Lester and René Diekstra, treasurer Hans Wedler, and secretary Gernot Sonneck) of the International Association for Suicide Prevention and Crisis Intervention (IASP). The official promoters of the enterprise were David Lester and René Diekstra. Both Lester and Diego De Leo had the task of scrutinizing a list of possible members to whom to send a letter requesting support for the proposal. Letters were addressed to 52 of the most eminent scholars from the international community, and 37 of them immediately accepted. At the outset, the Academy was a specialist section of the IASP, devoted exclusively to suicide research. The President of the IASP was to be an ex-officio member of the IASR Executive Board, together with the IASR president, president elect, past president and secretary/treasurer.

Foundation

The IASR was formally established in conjunction with the 3rd European Symposium on Suicide Research, held in Bologna in September 1990. The presence of 15 of the members of the Academy permitted the Institute of Psychiatry of Padua University to organize the inauguration of the Academy, which took place on September 29, 1990, in the ceremonial headquarters of the University of Padua in the presence of academics and a large public audience. In addition to a presentation by De Leo and an address by the Director of the Department of Psychiatry of the University of Padua, contributions were made by the President of IASP, the two vice-presidents, and Walter Gulbinat, who represented the World Health Organization (WHO). During the ceremony the first members of the Board of Directors of the Academy were nominated: Nils Retterstol, in his capacity as president of the IASP, held a position on the Board by right, Ren, Diekstra was appointed first president, Diego De Leo was named secretary/treasurer and David Lester, editor-in-chief of the Academy's evolving journal, the *Archives of Suicide Research*. (Antoon Leenaars took over the position of editor-in-chief after a year.)

Objectives And Statutes

In his inaugural speech, Nils Retterstol clearly outlined the significance of creating the Academy.

> The reason for being here is an important one, not only for Padua, not only for Europe, but for the whole world. We are here to create an organization, The International Academy for Suicide Research. The Executive Committee of our organization, the International Association for Suicide Prevention, decided at our meeting in Hamburg, December 9, 1989, to establish this Academy. The reasons for establishing this Academy are many. IASP was founded exactly 30 years ago by Professor Ringel. The task for IASP has been to promote suicide prevention all over the world. It is actually one of the few organi-

zations which has, since its origin, been based on an international level, rather than a national one. (Many national organizations have been created in recent years.) Now, in spite of the efforts of IASP, suicide rates have increased all over the world, especially in countries with low suicide rates. . . . [Thus] we need to promote high standards of research and scholarship in the field of suicidal behavior by fostering communication and cooperation among scholars engaged in suicide research. This is the background to our being here today in Padua and why we feel it is such an important day for the world's society. We are not alone in feeling this importance. Among the leading researchers in the world within the field of suicidology who have accepted membership in the Academy, many expressed the feeling that this initiative should have been taken a long time ago. One of the first tasks for the Academy will be to provide international criteria on the definition and classification of suicide, attempted suicide and parasuicide for the use of medical examiners officially involved in certification of causes of death. Promising research in the biology of suicide is going on. New national programs for suicide prevention are being established in many countries. What effects have these programs had and which are more effective? We think that suicide, to a great extent, can be prevented. How it can be prevented will very much depend on the results emerging from research work, and in this way the task of our association, namely prevention of suicide, will be promoted. Therefore, we are convinced that the establishment of the International Academy for Suicide Research is important. We think the establishment will be a great step forward for suicide prevention in the years to come. (Dettezotol: Inaugural Ceremony Speech, Padua, September 29, 1990)

The Statutes, presented and read in full in the same venue as the meeting on 29 September 1990, therefore report the main aim of the Academy as " . . . the promotion of high standards of research and scholarship in the field of suicidal behavior by fostering communication and cooperation among scholars engaged in such research." The statute was then signed (in the original order) by Ren, Diekstra, David Lester, Diego De Leo, Walter Gulbinat, George Murphy, Nils Retterstol, Gernot Sonneck, Hans Wedler, Peter Nordstrom, Otmar Buyne, Ferenc Moksony, Jan Beskow, and Michael Kelleher.

The Statutes have since received several important modifications. The first change was prompted during the meeting in St. Louis (April, 1996) and ratified during the gathering in Adelaide (March, 1997) concerning the position of the President of IASP, no longer an ex-officio member of the Board of Directors but simply an ex-officio member of the Academy with the same legal standing as an associate member, without the right to vote (Bylaws, Chapter I, section 7). The second important change, passed during the Gent meeting (September, 1998), concerned the term for elective offices and the possibility of reappointment: two years for the various positions in the Board, without reelection. The only exception is the position of secretary/treasurer who, to guarantee continuity, can be re-elected once (thus the maximum length of service is four years) (Bylaws, chapter II, section 3).

Meetings

Considering the Academy's membership (it is composed of a limited number of scholars), it was decided from the very outset to arrange its meetings (an administrative and a scientific session, the latter being open to the public) in conjunction with larger gatherings organized by bigger associations. Hence some meetings have been held in association with the European Symposia (Padua, Odense, Gent), some with IASP congresses (Hamburg, Montreal, Venice, Adelaide) and some with conferences of the American Association of Suicidology (St. Louis). Table 1 provides a chronological summary of the venues and dates of these meetings.

Forthcoming meetings are planned for November 1999 in Athens in conjunction with the IASP Congress, and for September 2000 in Bled in association with the European Symposium. To date, the scientific part of the meetings have been organized in two main directions: definition and classification of suicidal behaviors, and, methodological problems in terms of both procedures for attribution of causes of death and problems inherent to intervention studies.

Membership

The Academy has two categories of membership: ordinary and associate members. Ordinary or full members are individuals who established a stable reputation as outstanding scholars in the field of suicidology and are currently engaged in scholarly research in that field.

An associate member is an individual who is currently actively engaged in scholarly research in the area of suicidal behavior but has not yet attained the enduring reputation required of the full member.

Ordinary and associate members have the same rights and privileges except that ordinary members only are entitled to vote in any election or in any issue or business matter pertaining to the Academy. As mentioned above, there is a Membership Committee, of multidisciplinary constituency, appointed by the president with the approval of the Board of Directors, that scrutinizes new candidates. It is composed of five members and is chaired, in accordance with the Statutes, by the secretary of the Academy. Presently, it is composed of Armin Schmidtke (chairman), Isaac Sakinofsky, Antoon Leenaars, and Lil Traskman-Bendz (The fifth member was Michael Kelleher who unfortunately passed away July 1988.).

Candidates for ordinary or associate membership may be nominated by any Academy member and must be seconded by another member. Nominations are

TABLE 1. Academy Meetings

Padua, Italy	September 1990	President: R. F. W. Diekstra
Hamburg, Germany	September 1991	President: R. F. W. Diekstra
Odense, Denmark	June 1992	President: R. F. W. Diekstra
Montreal, Canada	June 1993	President: R. F. W. Diekstra
Wassenaar, The Netherlands	November 1993	President: R. F. W. Diekstra
Venice, Italy	June 1995	President: D. De Leo
St. Louis, USA	April 1996	President: D. De Leo
Adelaide, Australia	March 1997	President: D. De Leo
Gent, Belgium	September 1998	President: D. De Leo

directed to the chairman of the Membership Committee. In the case of a full membership candidate, a positive vote is required of the majority of members of the Committee.

At present, there are 44 full or ordinary members. Their names are listed in Table 2, which also notes their nationality.

The Academy has thus far been rather closed. Since its objectives do not include proselytism, with preference being given to controlling the quality of candidates, the limited number of members is a representation of the international scientific panorama of suicidology. Some of the more promising scientists, whose names have already gained international repute, are nonetheless present as associate members (currently 25 in total).

Committees

There are two formal committees within the Academy: one for selecting candidates, mentioned above, and one for assigning the Academy Career Award. The latter committee is presided by the past-president of the Academy and is composed of four other members, who are at present, Marie Asberg, George Murphy, Robert Goldney, and Charles Rich. The prize, conceived to represent the seal on a professional life spent in suicidological research, has not yet been awarded. The Lundbeck International Foundation is the sponsor.

The Archives Of Suicide Research

The Archives of Suicide Research (ASR) is the official organ of the Academy. Published at present by Kluwer, it is now in its fifth year, with four editions per year. Antoon Leenaars is the editor-in-chief of this journal, whose scientific importance has been established in a very short period of time, thanks to its contributors and the dynamic direction by Antoon Leenaars. ASR, now listed in *Current Contents*, has become an impressive international forum and is AMONG the most important scientific journal in the suicidological field. Its associate editors are Robert Goldney, Lil Traskman-Bendz, Armin Schmidtke, and Steven Stack.

During the Gent meeting, Antoon Leenaars' appointment as editor-in-chief of ASR was renewed for five years. His office will therefore expire in 2003.

Ongoing Projects

The Academy has formally four task forces in operation that have been assigned research projects in the following areas:

1. Study of the legal basis of death ascertainment procedures (worldwide). This project, coordinated by Isaac Sakinofsky, has already yielded important findings and is in the process of being written.

TABLE 2. Full members of the Academy (as of April 1, 1999)

Country	Member
Australia	Robert Goldney
Austria	Gernot Sonneck
Canada	Ron Dyck
	Antoon Leenaars
	Isaac Sakinofsky
Denmark	Unni Bille-Brahe
Finland	Jouko Lonnqvist
Germany	Thomas Bronisch
	Walter Felber
	Hans-Jurgen Moller
	Armin Schmidtke
	Manfred Wolfersdorf
Greece	Alexander Botsis
Hungary	Ferenc Moksony
Israel	Israel Orbach
Italy	Diego De Leo
Japan	Yoshitomo Takahashi
Netherlands	Otmar Buyne
	Herman Van Praag
Norway	Nils Retterstol
Sweden	Marie Asberg
	Jan Beskow
	Peter Nordstrom
	Lil Traskman-Bendz
	Danuta Wasserman
UK	Keith Hawton
USA	Margaret Battin
	Alan Berman
	David Clark
	Yeates Conwell
	Norman Farberow
	David Lester
	John Maltsberger
	John Mann
	Ronald Maris
	Jerome Motto
	George Murphy
	Cynthia Pfeffer
	Charles Rich
	Alec Roy
	David Shaffer
	Edwin Shneidman
	Steven Stack

2. Assessment of the effectiveness of preventive strategies (head: Keith Hawton). This project has also produced interesting results which were presented in their preliminary form at the scientific session of the Gent meeting.
3. Validation of the official statistics concerning suicide mortality data (coordinator: Armin Schmidtke). A paper has very recently been published on this subject in the *Archives of Suicide Research*.
4. Preparation of a research protocol at international level (The Five Continents Study/Worldwide Initiative on Parasuicide). Coordinated by Diego De Leo, this project involves the World Health Organization, its Collaborating Centers, and the International Association for Suicide Prevention. The study is now ready to commence in pilot form (in late 1999), while the official inauguration is scheduled for January 2000.

The Academy has built, under the leadership of the Secretary (Armin Schmidtke) its own website (http://www.uni-wuerzburg.de/IASR) that is linked to the major search engines (such as Yahoo). The website provides information about the Academy, a list of members and their addresses, and information about the latest available suicide and attempted suicide rates in the world. The webpage will be developed further in the future.

IASR-IASP Interaction

Although rather modest in number, the suicidology fraternity is rather quarrelsome and has tendencies towards schism. The very history of the Academy is a case in point, but there are several more recent aggregations such as the European Network for Suicidology and le Group Latin pour la Prevention du Suicide.

Born from a rib of the IASP, the Academy subsequently sought autonomy, in an endeavor to promote good neighborly relations with IASP and the other major associations. The modifications applied to the Statutes after formal approval of the general assembly of members are testimony to this. However, its present endeavour is to promote good neighbotly relations with IASP and other major associations.

The authors of this manuscript firmly believe in the underlying idea of the Academy, namely the establishment of an association of exclusively scientific leaning, along the lines of similar groups in other disciplines, a frequent occurrence within the field of medicine. They likewise strongly believe in cooperation, especially coordinated distribution of efforts, both in research and preventive terms, in the broadest sense of the word. They also are convinced that far greater cooperation between the various existing agencies is warranted, with a view both to more effective interactions and less waste due to duplication in research (or any other) projects in competition.

Coordination essentially implies optimization of the (limited) resources existing within the suicidological world and making best advantage of any synergies that may emerge. Benefits from improved interaction would not be gained solely for the scientific or suicidological community, but also and above all, for human society, which is the primary objective of our actions.

☐ References

Goldney, R. D. (1998). The I.A.S.P. Adelaid Declaration on suicide prevention. Crisis, 19, 50–51.
Sonneck, G. (1986). On the phenomenology of the pre-suicidal syndrome. Crisis, 7, 111–117.

INDEX

Index note: page references in italics indicate a figure or table